C++ GUI Programming
with Qt 4

C++ GUI Programming with Qt 4

Jasmin Blanchette

Mark Summerfield

In association with Trolltech Press

Upper Saddle River, NJ · Boston · Indianapolis · San Francisco
New York · Toronto · Montreal · London · Munich · Paris · Madrid
Capetown · Sydney · Tokyo · Singapore · Mexico City

Many of the designations used by manufacturers and sellers to distinguish their products are claimed as trademarks. Where those designations appear in this book, and the publisher was aware of a trademark claim, the designations have been printed with initial capital letters or in all capitals.

The authors and publisher have taken care in the preparation of this book, but make no expressed or implied warranty of any kind and assume no responsibility for errors or omissions. No liability is assumed for incidental or consequential damages in connection with or arising out of the use of the information or programs contained herein.

The publisher offers excellent discounts on this book when ordered in quantity for bulk purchases or special sales, which may include electronic versions and/or custom covers and content particular to your business, training goals, marketing focus, and branding interests. For more information, please contact:

U.S. Corporate and Government Sales
(800) 382-3419
corpsales@pearsontechgroup.com

For sales outside the United States, please contact:

International Sales
international@pearsoned.com

Visit us on the Web: www.prenhallprofessional.com

Library of Congress Cataloging-in-Publication Data

Blanchette, Jasmin.
  C++ GUI programming with Qt 4 / Jasmin Blanchette, Mark Summerfield.
    p. cm.
  Includes bibliographical references and index.
  ISBN 0-13-187249-4 (pbk.: alk. paper)
  1. Graphical user interfaces (Computer systems) 2. C++ (Computer program language)
    I. Summerfield, Mark. II. Title.

  QA76.9.U83B532 2006
  005.4'37—dc22

2006013376

Text printed in the United States on recycled paper at Courier in Stoughton, Massachusetts.

First printing, June 2006

Contents

Part III: Advanced Qt

Appendices

Foreword

Why Qt? Why do programmers like us choose Qt? Sure, there are the obvious answers: Qt's single-source compatibility, its feature richness, its C++ performance, the availability of the source code, its documentation, the high-quality technical support, and all the other items mentioned in Trolltech's glossy marketing materials. This is all very well, but it misses the most important point: Qt is successful because programmers *like* it.

How come programmers like one technology, but dislike another? Personally I believe software engineers enjoy technology that feels right, but dislike everything that doesn't. "Feels right" means many things. In the Qt 3 edition of the book, I mentioned Trolltech's phone system as a particularly good example of some particularly bad technology. The phone system didn't feel right, because it forced us to do apparently random things depending on some equally random context. Randomness doesn't feel right. Another thing that doesn't feel right is repetitiveness and redundancy. Good programmers are lazy. What we love about computers compared to, say, gardening is that we don't have to do the same things over and over.

Let me emphasize this point with a real-world example: travel reimbursement forms. Typically those forms come as fancy spreadsheets; you fill them out, and you get real money. Simple technology, one should think, and given the monetary incentive this should be a simple task for a grown-up engineer.

Reality looks different, though. While nobody else in the company seems to have any problems whatsoever dealing with those forms, the engineers do. And having talked to people in other companies, this seems to be a common pattern. We defer reimbursement until the very last moment, and sometimes we might even forget about it. Why is that? Looking at our form, it's a straightforward, standard procedure. One has to collect receipts, number them, and put those numbers into the proper fields with the date, the location, a description, and the amount. The numbering and copying is designed to ease someone's work, but strictly speaking it is redundant, given that the date, location, description, and amount unambiguously identify a receipt. A tiny bit of extra work to get your money back, one would think.

A small annoyance is the per-diem rate, though, which depends on the travel location. There's some separate document somewhere that lists the standardized rates for all the different travel locations. You can't just select "Chicago"; instead you have to look up the rate for Chicago yourself. There's a similar annoyance with the exchange rate field. One has to find the current exchange rate somewhere—perhaps with Google's help—and then enter the rate in every single field. Well, strictly speaking, you should wait for your credit card company to issue a statement to you with the actual exchange rate that they used. While this is not hard to do, looking up different pieces of information from different sources, and then copying the relevant items to several places in the form feels needlessly awkward.

Programming can be a lot like filling in travel reimbursement forms, only worse. And this is where Qt comes to the rescue. Qt is different. For one thing, Qt makes sense. And for another, Qt is fun. Qt lets you concentrate on your tasks. When Qt's original architects faced a problem, they didn't just look for a good solution, or the simplest solution. They looked for the *right* solution, and then they documented it. Granted they made mistakes, and granted some of their design decisions didn't pass the test of time, but they still got a lot of things right, and what wasn't right could and can be corrected. You can see this by the fact that a system originally designed to bridge Windows 95 and Unix/Motif now unifies modern desktop systems as diverse as Windows XP, Mac OS X, and GNU/Linux, and provides the foundation for the Qtopia application platform for embedded Linux.

Long before Qt became so popular and so widely used, the dedication of Qt's developers to finding the right solutions made Qt special. That dedication is just as strong today and affects everyone who develops and maintains Qt. For us, working on Qt is a responsibility and a privilege. We are proud of helping to make your professional and open source lives easier and more enjoyable.

Matthias Ettrich
Oslo, Norway
June 2006

Preface

Qt is a comprehensive C++ framework for developing cross-platform GUI applications using a "write once, compile anywhere" approach. Qt lets programmers use a single source tree for applications that will run on Windows 98 to XP, Mac OS X, Linux, Solaris, HP-UX, and many other versions of Unix with X11. The Qt libraries and tools are also part of Qtopia Core, a product that provides its own window system on top of embedded Linux.

The purpose of this book is to teach you how to write GUI programs using Qt 4. The book starts with "Hello Qt" and quickly progresses to more advanced topics, such as creating custom widgets and providing drag and drop. The text is complemented by a CD that contains the source code of the example programs. The CD also includes the open source edition of Qt 4.1.1 for all supported platforms, as well as MinGW, a set of freely available development tools that can be used to build Qt applications on Windows. Appendix A explains how to install the software.

The book is divided into three parts. Part I covers all the concepts and practices necessary for programming GUI applications using Qt. Knowledge of this part alone is sufficient to write useful GUI applications. Part II covers central Qt topics in greater depth, and Part III provides more specialized and advanced material. The chapters of Parts II and III can be read in any order, but they assume familiarity with the contents of Part I.

Readers of the Qt 3 edition of this book will find this new edition familiar in both content and style. This edition has been updated to take advantage of Qt 4's new features (including some that were introduced with Qt 4.1) and to present code that shows good idiomatic Qt 4 programming techniques. In many cases, we have used examples similar to the ones used in the Qt 3 edition. This will not affect new readers, but will help those who read the previous edition orient themselves to Qt 4's cleaner, clearer, and more expressive style.

This edition includes new chapters covering Qt 4's model/view architecture, the new plugin framework, and embedded programming with Qtopia, as well a new appendix. And just like the Qt 3 book, the emphasis is on explaining Qt programming rather than simply rehashing or summarizing Qt's extensive online documentation.

We have written the book with the assumption that you have a basic knowledge of C++, Java, or C#. The code examples use a subset of C++, avoiding many C++ features that are rarely needed when programming Qt. In the few places where a more advanced C++ construct is unavoidable, it is explained where it is used.

If you already know Java or C# but have little or no experience with C++, we recommend that you begin by reading Appendix B, which provides sufficient introduction to C++ to be able to use this book. For a more thorough introduction to object-oriented programming in C++, we recommend C++ *How to Program* by Harvey Deitel and Paul Deitel, and the C++ *Primer* by Stanley B. Lippman, Josée Lajoie, and Barbara E. Moo.

Qt made its reputation as a cross-platform framework, but because of its intuitive and powerful API, many organizations use Qt for single-platform development. Adobe Photoshop Album is just one example of a mass-market Windows application written in Qt. Many sophisticated software systems in vertical markets, such as 3D animation tools, digital film processing, electronic design automation (for chip design), oil and gas exploration, financial services, and medical imaging, are built with Qt. If you are making a living with a successful Windows product written in Qt, you can easily create new markets in the Mac OS X and Linux worlds simply by recompiling.

Qt is available under various licenses. If you want to build commercial applications, you must buy a commercial Qt license; if you want to build open source programs, you can use the open source (GPL) edition. Qt is the foundation on which the K Desktop Environment (KDE) and the many open source applications that go with it are built.

In addition to Qt's hundreds of classes, there are add-ons that extend Qt's scope and power. Some of these products, like Qt Script for Applications (QSA) and the Qt Solutions components, are available from Trolltech, while others are supplied by other companies and by the open source community. See http://www.trolltech.com/products/3rdparty/ for information on Qt add-ons. Qt also has a well-established and thriving user community that uses the qt-interest mailing list; see http://lists.trolltech.com/ for details.

If you spot errors in the book, have suggestions for the next edition, or want to give us feedback, we would be delighted to hear from you. You can reach us at qt-book@trolltech.com. The errata will be placed on http://doc.trolltech.com/qt-book-errata.html.

Acknowledgments

Our first acknowledgment is of Eirik Chambe-Eng, Trolltech's president. Eirik not only enthusiastically encouraged us to write the Qt 3 edition of the book, he also allowed us to spend a considerable amount of our work time writing it. Eirik and Trolltech CEO Haavard Nord both read the manuscript and provided valuable feedback. Their generosity and foresight was aided and abetted by Matthias Ettrich, Trolltech's lead developer. Matthias cheerfully accepted our neglect of duty as we obsessed over the writing of the first edition of this book and gave us a lot of advice on good Qt programming style.

For the Qt 3 edition, we asked two Qt customers, Paul Curtis and Klaus Schmidinger, to be our external reviewers. Both are Qt experts with an amazing attention to technical detail, which they proved by spotting some very subtle errors in our manuscript and suggesting numerous improvements. And within Trolltech, alongside Matthias, our most stalwart reviewer was Reginald Stadlbauer. His technical insight was invaluable, and he taught us how to do some things in Qt that we didn't even know were possible.

For this Qt 4 edition, we have continued to benefit from the unstinting help and support of Eirik, Haavard, and Matthias. Klaus Schmidinger continued to give valuable feedback, and within Trolltech, our key reviewers were Andreas Aardal Hanssen, Henrik Hartz, Vivi Glückstad Karlsen, Trenton Schulz, Andy Shaw, and Pål de Vibe.

In addition to the reviewers mentioned above, we received expert help from Harald Fernengel (databases), Volker Hilsheimer (ActiveX), Bradley Hughes (multithreading), Trond Kjernåsen (3D graphics and databases), Lars Knoll (2D graphics and internationalization), Sam Magnuson (qmake), Marius Bugge Monsen (item view classes), Dimitri Papadopoulos (Qt/X11), Paul Olav Tvete (custom widgets and embedded programming), Rainer Schmid (networking and XML), Amrit Pal Singh (introduction to C++), and Gunnar Sletta (2D graphics and event processing).

Extra thanks are due to Trolltech's documentation and support teams for handling documentation-related issues while the book consumed so much of our time, and to Trolltech's system administrators for keeping our machines running and our networks communicating throughout the project.

On the production side, Trenton Schulz created the accompanying CD, and Trolltech's Cathrine Bore handled the contracts and legalities on our behalf. Thanks also to Nathan Clement for the Troll illustrations. And last but not least, thanks to Lara Wysong from Pearson, for handling the production practicalities so well.

A Brief History of Qt

The Qt framework first became publicly available in May 1995. It was initially developed by Haavard Nord (Trolltech's CEO) and Eirik Chambe-Eng (Trolltech's president). Haavard and Eirik met at the Norwegian Institute of Technology in Trondheim, where they both graduated with master's degrees in computer science.

Haavard's interest in C++ GUI development began in 1988 when he was commissioned by a Swedish company to develop a C++ GUI framework. A couple of years later, in the summer of 1990, Haavard and Eirik were working together on a C++ database application for ultrasound images. The system needed to be able to run with a GUI on Unix, Macintosh, and Windows. One day that summer, Haavard and Eirik went outside to enjoy the sunshine, and as they sat on a park bench, Haavard said, "We need an object-oriented display system." The resulting discussion laid the intellectual foundation for the object-oriented cross-platform GUI framework they would soon go on to build.

In 1991, Haavard started writing the classes that eventually became Qt, collaborating with Eirik on the design. The following year, Eirik came up with the idea for "signals and slots", a simple but powerful GUI programming paradigm that has now been embraced by several other toolkits. Haavard took the idea and produced a hand-coded implementation. By 1993, Haavard and Eirik had developed Qt's first graphics kernel and were able to implement their own widgets. At the end of the year, Haavard suggested that they go into business together to build "the world's best C++ GUI framework".

The year 1994 began inauspiciously with the two young programmers wanting to enter a well-established market, with no customers, an unfinished product, and no money. Fortunately, both their wives were employed and therefore able to support their husbands for the two years Eirik and Haavard expected to need to develop the product and start earning an income.

The letter 'Q' was chosen as the class prefix because the letter looked beautiful in Haavard's Emacs font. The 't' was added to stand for "toolkit", inspired by Xt, the X Toolkit. The company was incorporated on March 4, 1994, originally as Quasar Technologies, then as Troll Tech, and today as Trolltech.

In April 1995, thanks to a contact made through one of Haavard's university professors, the Norwegian company Metis gave them a contract to develop software based on Qt. Around this time, Trolltech hired Arnt Gulbrandsen, who during his six years at Trolltech devised and implemented an ingenious documentation system as well as contributing to Qt's code.

On May 20, 1995, Qt 0.90 was uploaded to sunsite.unc.edu. Six days later, the release was announced on comp.os.linux.announce. This was Qt's first public release. Qt could be used for both Windows and Unix development, offering the same API on both platforms. Qt was available under two licenses from day one: A commercial license was required for commercial development, and a free software edition was available for open source development. The Metis contract kept Trolltech afloat, while for ten long months no one bought a commercial Qt license.

In March 1996, the European Space Agency became the second Qt customer, with a purchase of ten commercial licenses. With unwavering faith, Eirik and Haavard hired another developer. Qt 0.97 was released at the end of May, and on September 24, 1996, Qt 1.0 came out. By the end of the year, Qt had reached version 1.1; eight customers, each in a different country, had bought 18 licenses between them. This year also saw the founding of the KDE project, led by Matthias Ettrich.

Qt 1.2 was released in April 1997. Matthias Ettrich's decision to use Qt to build KDE helped Qt become the de facto standard for C++ GUI development on Linux. Qt 1.3 was released in September 1997.

Matthias joined Trolltech in 1998, and the last major Qt 1 release, 1.40, was made in September of that year. Qt 2.0 was released in June 1999. Qt 2 had a new open source license, the Q Public License (QPL), which complied with the Open Source Definition. In August 1999, Qt won the LinuxWorld award for best library/tool. Around this time, Trolltech Pty Ltd (Australia) was established.

Trolltech released Qtopia Core (then called Qt/Embedded) in 2000. It was designed to run on embedded Linux devices and provided its own window system as a lightweight replacement for X11. Both Qt/X11 and Qtopia Core were now offered under the widely used GNU General Public License (GPL) as well as under commercial licenses. By the end of 2000, Trolltech had established Trolltech Inc. (USA) and had released the first version of Qtopia, an application platform for mobile phones and PDAs. Qtopia Core won the LinuxWorld "Best Embedded Linux Solution" award in both 2001 and 2002, and Qtopia Phone achieved the same distinction in 2004.

Qt 3.0 was released in 2001. Qt was now available on Windows, Mac OS X, Unix, and Linux (desktop and embedded). Qt 3 provided 42 new classes and its code exceeded 500,000 lines. Qt 3 was a major step forward from Qt 2, including considerably improved locale and Unicode support, a completely new text viewing and editing widget, and a Perl-like regular expression class. Qt 3 won the Software Development Times "Jolt Productivity Award" in 2002.

In the summer of 2005, Qt 4.0 was released. With about 500 classes and more than 9000 functions, Qt 4 is larger and richer than any previous version, and it has been split into several libraries so that developers only need to link against the parts of Qt that they need. Qt 4 is a huge advance on previous versions with improvements that include a completely new set of efficient and easy-to-use template containers, advanced model/view functionality, a fast and flexible 2D painting framework, and powerful Unicode text viewing and editing classes, not to mention thousands of smaller enhancements across the complete range of Qt classes. Qt 4 is the first Qt edition to be available for both commercial and open source development on all the platforms it supports.

Also in 2005, Trolltech opened a representative office in Beijing to provide customers in China and the region with sales services, training, and technical support for Qtopia.

Since Trolltech's birth, Qt's popularity has grown unabated and continues to grow to this day. This success is a reflection both of the quality of Qt and of how enjoyable it is to use. In the last decade, Qt has gone from being a product used by a select few "in the know" to one that is used daily by thousands of customers and tens of thousands of open source developers all around the world.

Part I

Basic Qt

- ◆ *Hello Qt*
- ◆ *Making Connections*
- ◆ *Laying Out Widgets*
- ◆ *Using the Reference Documentation*

1. Getting Started

This chapter shows how to combine basic C++ with the functionality provided by Qt to create a few small graphical user interface (GUI) applications. This chapter also introduces two key Qt ideas: "signals and slots" and layouts. In Chapter 2, we will go into more depth, and in Chapter 3, we will start building a more realistic application.

If you already know Java or C# but have limited experience with C++, you might want to start by reading the C++ introduction in Appendix B.

Hello Qt

Let's start with a very simple Qt program. We will first study it line by line, then we will see how to compile and run it.

```
1  #include <QApplication>
2  #include <QLabel>

3  int main(int argc, char *argv[])
4  {
5      QApplication app(argc, argv);
6      QLabel *label = new QLabel("Hello Qt!");
7      label->show();
8      return app.exec();
9  }
```

Lines 1 and 2 include the definitions of the QApplication and QLabel classes. For every Qt class, there is a header file with the same name (and capitalization) as the class that contains the class's definition.

Line 5 creates a QApplication object to manage application-wide resources. The QApplication constructor requires argc and argv because Qt supports a few command-line arguments of its own.

Line 6 creates a QLabel widget that displays "Hello Qt!". In Qt and Unix terminology, a *widget* is a visual element in a user interface. The term stems from

3

"window gadget" and is the equivalent of both "control" and "container" in Windows terminology. Buttons, menus, scroll bars, and frames are all examples of widgets. Widgets can contain other widgets; for example, an application window is usually a widget that contains a QMenuBar, a few QToolBars, a QStatusBar, and some other widgets. Most applications use a QMainWindow or a QDialog as the application window, but Qt is so flexible that any widget can be a window. In this example, the QLabel widget is the application window.

Line 7 makes the label visible. Widgets are always created hidden, so that we can customize them before showing them, thereby avoiding flicker.

Line 8 passes control of the application on to Qt. At this point, the program enters the event loop. This is a kind of stand-by mode where the program waits for user actions such as mouse clicks and key presses. User actions generate *events* (also called "messages") to which the program can respond, usually by executing one or more functions. For example, when the user clicks a widget, a "mouse press" and a "mouse release" event are generated. In this respect, GUI applications differ drastically from conventional batch programs, which typically process input, produce results, and terminate without human intervention.

For simplicity, we don't bother calling delete on the QLabel object at the end of the main() function. This memory leak is harmless in such a small program, since the memory will be reclaimed by the operating system when the program terminates.

Figure 1.1. Hello on Linux

It is now possible to try the program on your own machine. First, you will need to install Qt 4.1.1 (or a later Qt 4 release), a process that is explained in Appendix A. From now on, we will assume that you have a correctly installed copy of Qt 4 and that Qt's bin directory is in your PATH environment variable. (On Windows, this is done automatically by the Qt installation program.) You will also need the program's source code in a file called hello.cpp in a directory called hello. You can type in hello.cpp yourself, or copy it from the CD provided with this book, where it is available as /examples/chap01/hello/hello.cpp.

From a command prompt, change the directory to hello, then type

```
qmake -project
```

to create a platform-independent project file (hello.pro), then type

```
qmake hello.pro
```

to create a platform-specific makefile from the project file.

Type make to build the program.* Run it by typing hello on Windows, ./hello on Unix, and open hello.app on Mac OS X. To terminate the program, click the close button in the window's title bar.

If you are using Windows and have installed the Qt Open Source Edition and the MinGW compiler, you will have a shortcut to a DOS Prompt window that has all the environment variables correctly set up for Qt. If you start this window, you can compile Qt applications within it using qmake and make as described above. The executables produced are put in the application's debug or release folder, for example, C:\qt-book\hello\release\hello.exe.

If you are using Microsoft Visual C++, you will need to run nmake instead of make. Alternatively, you can create a Visual Studio project file from hello.pro by typing

```
qmake -tp vc hello.pro
```

and then build the program in Visual Studio. If you are using Xcode on Mac OS X, you can generate an Xcode project using the command

```
qmake -spec macx-xcode
```

Figure 1.2. A label with basic HTML formatting

Before we go on to the next example, let's have some fun: Replace the line

```
QLabel *label = new QLabel("Hello Qt!");
```

with

```
QLabel *label = new QLabel("<h2><i>Hello</i> "
                           "<font color=red>Qt!</font></h2>");
```

and rebuild the application. As the example illustrates, it's easy to brighten up a Qt application's user interface using some simple HTML-style formatting.

Making Connections

The second example shows how to respond to user actions. The application consists of a button that the user can click to quit. The source code is very similar to Hello, except that we are using a QPushButton instead of a QLabel as our main widget, and we are connecting a user action (clicking a button) to a piece of code.

---

*If you get a compiler error on the <QApplication> include, it probably means that you are using an older version of Qt. Make sure that you are using Qt 4.1.1 or a later Qt 4 release.

This application's source code is on the CD in the file /examples/chap01/quit/ quit.cpp. Here's the contents of the file:

```
 1  #include <QApplication>
 2  #include <QPushButton>

 3  int main(int argc, char *argv[])
 4  {
 5      QApplication app(argc, argv);
 6      QPushButton *button = new QPushButton("Quit");
 7      QObject::connect(button, SIGNAL(clicked()),
 8                       &app, SLOT(quit()));
 9      button->show();
10      return app.exec();
11  }
```

Qt's widgets emit *signals* to indicate that a user action or a change of state has occurred.* For instance, QPushButton emits a clicked() signal when the user clicks the button. A signal can be connected to a function (called a *slot* in that context), so that when the signal is emitted, the slot is automatically executed. In our example, we connect the button's clicked() signal to the QApplication object's quit() slot. The SIGNAL() and SLOT() macros are part of the syntax; they are explained in more detail in the next chapter.

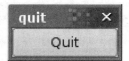

Figure 1.3. The Quit application

We will now build the application. We assume that you have created a directory called quit containing quit.cpp. Run qmake in the quit directory to generate the project file, then run it again to generate a makefile, as follows:

```
qmake -project
qmake quit.pro
```

Now build the application, and run it. If you click Quit, or press Space (which presses the button), the application will terminate.

Laying Out Widgets

In this section, we will create a small example application that demonstrates how to use layouts to manage the geometry of widgets in a window and how to use signals and slots to synchronize two widgets. The application asks for the user's age, which the user can enter by manipulating either a spin box or a slider.

---

*Qt signals are unrelated to Unix signals. In this book, we are only concerned with Qt signals.

The application consists of three widgets: a QSpinBox, a QSlider, and a QWidget. The QWidget is the application's main window. The QSpinBox and the QSlider are rendered inside the QWidget; they are *children* of the QWidget. Alternatively, we can say that the QWidget is the *parent* of the QSpinBox and the QSlider. The QWidget has no parent itself because it is being used as a top-level window. The constructors for QWidget and all of its subclasses take a QWidget * parameter that specifies the parent widget.

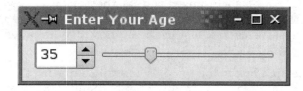

Figure 1.4. The Age application

Here's the source code:

```
1   #include <QApplication>
2   #include <QHBoxLayout>
3   #include <QSlider>
4   #include <QSpinBox>

5   int main(int argc, char *argv[])
6   {
7       QApplication app(argc, argv);

8       QWidget *window = new QWidget;
9       window->setWindowTitle("Enter Your Age");

10      QSpinBox *spinBox = new QSpinBox;
11      QSlider *slider = new QSlider(Qt::Horizontal);
12      spinBox->setRange(0, 130);
13      slider->setRange(0, 130);

14      QObject::connect(spinBox, SIGNAL(valueChanged(int)),
15                       slider, SLOT(setValue(int)));
16      QObject::connect(slider, SIGNAL(valueChanged(int)),
17                       spinBox, SLOT(setValue(int)));
18      spinBox->setValue(35);

19      QHBoxLayout *layout = new QHBoxLayout;
20      layout->addWidget(spinBox);
21      layout->addWidget(slider);
22      window->setLayout(layout);

23      window->show();

24      return app.exec();
25  }
```

Lines 8 and 9 set up the QWidget that will serve as the application's main window. We call setWindowTitle() to set the text displayed in the window's title bar.

Lines 10 and 11 create a `QSpinBox` and a `QSlider`, and lines 12 and 13 set their valid ranges. We can safely assume that the user is at most 130 years old. We could pass `window` to the `QSpinBox` and `QSlider` constructors, specifying that these widgets should have `window` as their parent, but it isn't necessary here because the layout system will figure this out by itself and automatically set the parent of the spin box and the slider, as we will see shortly.

The two `QObject::connect()` calls shown in lines 14 to 17 ensure that the spin box and the slider are synchronized so that they always show the same value. Whenever the value of one widget changes, its `valueChanged(int)` signal is emitted, and the `setValue(int)` slot of the other widget is called with the new value.

Line 18 sets the spin box value to 35. When this happens, the `QSpinBox` emits the `valueChanged(int)` signal with an `int` argument of 35. This argument is passed to the `QSlider`'s `setValue(int)` slot, which sets the slider value to 35. The slider then emits the `valueChanged(int)` signal, because its own value changed, triggering the spin box's `setValue(int)` slot. But at this point, `setValue(int)` doesn't emit any signal, since the spin box value is already 35. This prevents infinite recursion. Figure 1.5 summarizes the situation.

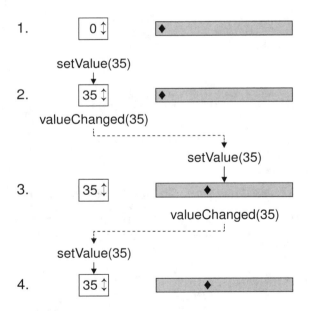

Figure 1.5. Changing one widget's value changes both

In lines 19 to 22, we lay out the spin box and slider widgets using a *layout manager*. A layout manager is an object that sets the size and position of the widgets that lie under its responsibility. Qt has three main layout manager classes:

- QHBoxLayout lays out widgets horizontally from left to right (right to left for some cultures).

- QVBoxLayout lays out widgets vertically from top to bottom.

- QGridLayout lays out widgets in a grid.

The call to QWidget::setLayout() on line 22 installs the layout manager on the window. Behind the scenes, the QSpinBox and QSlider are "reparented" to be children of the widget on which the layout is installed, and for this reason we don't need to specify an explicit parent when we construct a widget that will be put in a layout.

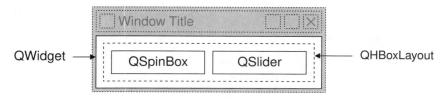

Figure 1.6. The Age application's widgets

Even though we didn't set the position or size of any widget explicitly, the QSpinBox and QSlider appear nicely laid out side by side. This is because QHBoxLayout automatically assigns reasonable positions and sizes to the widgets for which it is responsible, based on their needs. The layout managers free us from the chore of hard-coding screen positions in our applications and ensure that windows resize smoothly.

Qt's approach to building user interfaces is simple to understand and very flexible. The most common pattern that Qt programmers use is to instantiate the required widgets and then set their properties as necessary. Programmers add the widgets to layouts, which automatically take care of sizing and positioning. User interface behavior is managed by connecting widgets together using Qt's signals and slots mechanism.

Using the Reference Documentation

Qt's reference documentation is an essential tool for any Qt developer, since it covers every class and function in Qt. This book makes use of many Qt classes and functions, but it does not cover all of them, nor does it provide every detail of those that are mentioned. To get the most benefit from Qt, you should familiarize yourself with the Qt reference documentation as quickly as possible.

The documentation is available in HTML format in Qt's doc/html directory and can be read using any web browser. You can also use *Qt Assistant*, the Qt help browser, which has powerful searching and indexing features that make it quicker and easier to use than a web browser. To launch *Qt Assistant*, click

Qt by Trolltech v4.x.y|Assistant in the Start menu on Windows, type `assistant` on the command line on Unix, or double-click Assistant in the Mac OS X Finder.

The links in the "API Reference" section on the home page provide different ways of navigating Qt's classes. The "All Classes" page lists every class in Qt's API. The "Main Classes" page lists only the most commonly used Qt classes. As an exercise, you might want to look up the classes and functions that we have used in this chapter.

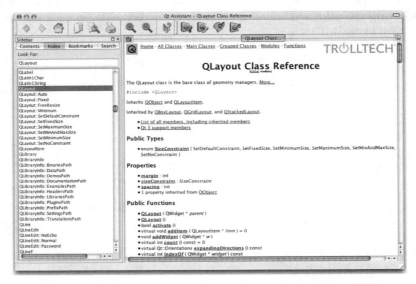

Figure 1.7. Qt's documentation in *Qt Assistant* on Mac OS X

Note that inherited functions are documented in the base class; for example, `QPushButton` has no `show()` function of its own, but it inherits one from its ancestor `QWidget`. Figure 1.8 shows how the classes we have seen so far relate to each other.

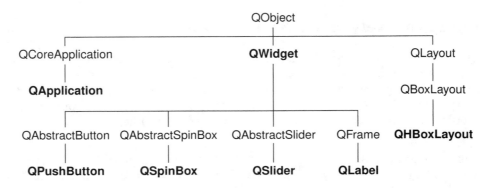

Figure 1.8. Inheritance tree for the Qt classes seen so far

The reference documentation for the current version of Qt and for some earlier versions is available online at http://doc.trolltech.com/. This site also has selected articles from *Qt Quarterly*, the Qt programmers' newsletter sent to all commercial licensees.

Widget Styles

The screenshots we have seen so far have been taken on Linux, but Qt applications look native on every supported platform. Qt achieves this by emulating the platform's look and feel, rather than wrapping a particular platform or toolkit's widget set.

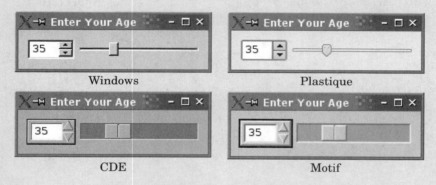

Figure 1.9. Styles available everywhere

With Qt/X11 and Qtopia Core, the default style is Plastique, which uses gradients and anti-aliasing to provide a modern look and feel. Qt application users can override the default style by using the -style command-line option. For example, to launch the Age application using the Motif style on X11, simply type

```
./age -style motif
```

on the command line.

Figure 1.10. Platform-specific styles

Unlike the other styles, the Windows XP and Mac styles are only available on their native platforms, since they rely on the platforms' theme engines.

This chapter has introduced the key concepts of signal–slot connections and layouts. It has also begun to reveal Qt's consistent and fully object-oriented approach to the construction and use of widgets. If you browse through Qt's documentation, you will find a uniformity of approach that makes it straightforward to learn how to use new widgets, and you will also find that Qt's carefully chosen names for functions, parameters, enums, and so on, make programming in Qt surprisingly pleasant and easy.

The following chapters of Part I build on the fundamentals covered here, showing how to create complete GUI applications with menus, toolbars, document windows, a status bar, and dialogs, along with the underlying functionality to read, process, and write files.

- ◆ *Subclassing QDialog*
- ◆ *Signals and Slots in Depth*
- ◆ *Rapid Dialog Design*
- ◆ *Shape-Changing Dialogs*
- ◆ *Dynamic Dialogs*
- ◆ *Built-in Widget and Dialog Classes*

2. Creating Dialogs

This chapter will teach you how to create dialog boxes using Qt. Dialog boxes present users with options and choices, and allow them to set the options to their preferred values and to make their choices. They are called dialog boxes, or simply "dialogs", because they provide a means by which users and applications can "talk to" each other.

Most GUI applications consist of a main window with a menu bar and toolbar, along with dozens of dialogs that complement the main window. It is also possible to create dialog applications that respond directly to the user's choices by performing the appropriate actions (for example, a calculator application).

We will create our first dialog purely by writing code to show how it is done. Then we will see how to build dialogs using *Qt Designer*, Qt's visual design tool. Using *Qt Designer* is a lot faster than hand-coding and makes it easy to test different designs and to change designs later.

Subclassing QDialog

Our first example is a Find dialog written entirely in C++. We will implement the dialog as a class in its own right. By doing so, we make it an independent, self-contained component, with its own signals and slots.

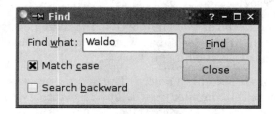

Figure 2.1. The Find dialog

The source code is spread across two files: `finddialog.h` and `finddialog.cpp`. We will start with `finddialog.h`.

```
1  #ifndef FINDDIALOG_H
2  #define FINDDIALOG_H

3  #include <QDialog>

4  class QCheckBox;
5  class QLabel;
6  class QLineEdit;
7  class QPushButton;
```

Lines 1 and 2 (and 27) protect the header file against multiple inclusions.

Line 3 includes the definition of `QDialog`, the base class for dialogs in Qt. `QDialog` inherits `QWidget`.

Lines 4 to 7 are forward declarations of the Qt classes that we will use to implement the dialog. A *forward declaration* tells the C++ compiler that a class exists, without giving all the detail that a class definition (usually located in a header file of its own) provides. We will say more about this shortly.

Next, we define `FindDialog` as a subclass of `QDialog`:

```
8   class FindDialog : public QDialog
9   {
10      Q_OBJECT

11  public:
12      FindDialog(QWidget *parent = 0);
```

The `Q_OBJECT` macro at the beginning of the class definition is necessary for all classes that define signals or slots.

The `FindDialog` constructor is typical of Qt widget classes. The `parent` parameter specifies the parent widget. The default is a null pointer, meaning that the dialog has no parent.

```
13  signals:
14      void findNext(const QString &str, Qt::CaseSensitivity cs);
15      void findPrevious(const QString &str, Qt::CaseSensitivity cs);
```

The `signals` section declares two signals that the dialog emits when the user clicks the Find button. If the Search backward option is enabled, the dialog emits `findPrevious()`; otherwise, it emits `findNext()`.

The `signals` keyword is actually a macro. The C++ preprocessor converts it into standard C++ before the compiler sees it. `Qt::CaseSensitivity` is an enum type that can take the values `Qt::CaseSensitive` and `Qt::CaseInsensitive`.

```
16  private slots:
17      void findClicked();
18      void enableFindButton(const QString &text);

19  private:
```

```
20      QLabel *label;
21      QLineEdit *lineEdit;
22      QCheckBox *caseCheckBox;
23      QCheckBox *backwardCheckBox;
24      QPushButton *findButton;
25      QPushButton *closeButton;
26  };
```

```
27  #endif
```

In the class's private section, we declare two slots. To implement the slots, we will need to access most of the dialog's child widgets, so we keep pointers to them as well. The slots keyword is, like signals, a macro that expands into a construct that the C++ compiler can digest.

For the private variables, we used forward declarations of their classes. This was possible because they are all pointers and we don't access them in the header file, so the compiler doesn't need the full class definitions. We could have included the relevant header files (<QCheckBox>, <QLabel>, etc.), but using forward declarations when it is possible makes compiling somewhat faster.

We will now look at finddialog.cpp, which contains the implementation of the FindDialog class.

```
1  #include <QtGui>
```

```
2  #include "finddialog.h"
```

First, we include <QtGui>, a header file that contains the definition of Qt's GUI classes. Qt consists of several modules, each of which lives in its own library. The most important modules are *QtCore*, *QtGui*, *QtNetwork*, *QtOpenGL*, *QtSql*, *QtSvg*, and *QtXml*. The <QtGui> header file contains the definition of all the classes that are part of the *QtCore* and *QtGui* modules. Including this header saves us the bother of including every class individually.

In filedialog.h, instead of including <QDialog> and using forward declarations for QCheckBox, QLabel, QLineEdit, and QPushButton, we could simply have included <QtGui>. However, it is generally bad style to include such a big header file from another header file, especially in larger applications.

```
3  FindDialog::FindDialog(QWidget *parent)
4      : QDialog(parent)
5  {
6      label = new QLabel(tr("Find &what:"));
7      lineEdit = new QLineEdit;
8      label->setBuddy(lineEdit);

9      caseCheckBox = new QCheckBox(tr("Match &case"));
10     backwardCheckBox = new QCheckBox(tr("Search &backward"));

11     findButton = new QPushButton(tr("&Find"));
12     findButton->setDefault(true);
13     findButton->setEnabled(false);

14     closeButton = new QPushButton(tr("Close"));
```

On line 4, we pass on the parent parameter to the base class constructor. Then we create the child widgets. The tr() function calls around the string literals mark them for translation to other languages. The function is declared in QObject and every subclass that contains the Q_OBJECT macro. It's a good habit to surround user-visible strings with tr(), even if you don't have immediate plans for translating your applications to other languages. Translating Qt applications is covered in Chapter 17.

In the string literals, we use ampersands ('&') to indicate shortcut keys. For example, line 11 creates a F̲ind button, which the user can activate by pressing Alt+F on platforms that support shortcut keys. Ampersands can also be used to control focus: On line 6 we create a label with a shortcut key (Alt+W), and on line 8 we set the label's buddy to be the line editor. A *buddy* is a widget that accepts the focus when the label's shortcut key is pressed. So when the user presses Alt+W (the label's shortcut), the focus goes to the line editor (the label's buddy).

On line 12, we make the Find button the dialog's default button by calling set-Default(true). The default button is the button that is pressed when the user hits Enter. On line 13, we disable the Find button. When a widget is disabled, it is usually shown grayed out and will not respond to user interaction.

```
15      connect(lineEdit, SIGNAL(textChanged(const QString &)),
16              this, SLOT(enableFindButton(const QString &)));
17      connect(findButton, SIGNAL(clicked()),
18              this, SLOT(findClicked()));
19      connect(closeButton, SIGNAL(clicked()),
20              this, SLOT(close()));
```

The private slot enableFindButton(const QString &) is called whenever the text in the line editor changes. The private slot findClicked() is called when the user clicks the Find button. The dialog closes itself when the user clicks Close. The close() slot is inherited from QWidget, and its default behavior is to hide the widget from view (without deleting it). We will look at the code for the enableFindButton() and findClicked() slots later on.

Since QObject is one of FindDialog's ancestors, we can omit the QObject:: prefix in front of the connect() calls.

```
21      QHBoxLayout *topLeftLayout = new QHBoxLayout;
22      topLeftLayout->addWidget(label);
23      topLeftLayout->addWidget(lineEdit);

24      QVBoxLayout *leftLayout = new QVBoxLayout;
25      leftLayout->addLayout(topLeftLayout);
26      leftLayout->addWidget(caseCheckBox);
27      leftLayout->addWidget(backwardCheckBox);

28      QVBoxLayout *rightLayout = new QVBoxLayout;
29      rightLayout->addWidget(findButton);
30      rightLayout->addWidget(closeButton);
31      rightLayout->addStretch();
```

```
32       QHBoxLayout *mainLayout = new QHBoxLayout;
33       mainLayout->addLayout(leftLayout);
34       mainLayout->addLayout(rightLayout);
35       setLayout(mainLayout);
```

Next, we lay out the child widgets using layout managers. Layouts can contain both widgets and other layouts. By nesting QHBoxLayouts, QVBoxLayouts, and QGridLayouts in various combinations, it is possible to build very sophisticated dialogs.

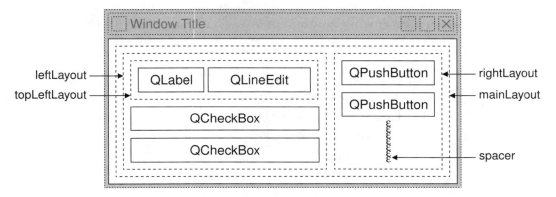

Figure 2.2. The Find dialog's layouts

For the Find dialog, we use two QHBoxLayouts and two QVBoxLayouts, as shown in Figure 2.2. The outer layout is the main layout; it is installed on the FindDialog on line 35 and is responsible for the dialog's entire area. The other three layouts are sub-layouts. The little "spring" at the bottom right of Figure 2.2 is a spacer item (or "stretch"). It uses up the empty space below the Find and Close buttons, ensuring that these buttons occupy the top of their layout.

One subtle aspect of the layout manager classes is that they are not widgets. Instead, they inherit QLayout, which in turn inherits QObject. In the figure, widgets are represented by solid outlines and layouts are represented by dashed outlines to highlight the difference between them. In a running application, layouts are invisible.

When the sub-layouts are added to the parent layout (lines 25, 33, and 34), the sub-layouts are automatically reparented. Then, when the main layout is installed on the dialog (line 35), it becomes a child of the dialog, and all the widgets in the layouts are reparented to become children of the dialog. The resulting parent–child hierarchy is depicted in Figure 2.3.

```
36       setWindowTitle(tr("Find"));
37       setFixedHeight(sizeHint().height());
38   }
```

Finally, we set the title to be shown in the dialog's title bar and we set the window to have a fixed height, since there aren't any widgets in the dialog that can meaningfully occupy any extra vertical space. The `QWidget::sizeHint()` function returns a widget's "ideal" size.

This completes the review of `FindDialog`'s constructor. Since we used `new` to create the dialog's widgets and layouts, it would seem that we need to write a destructor that calls `delete` on each of the widgets and layouts we created. But this isn't necessary, since Qt automatically deletes child objects when the parent is destroyed, and the child widgets and layouts are all descendants of the `FindDialog`.

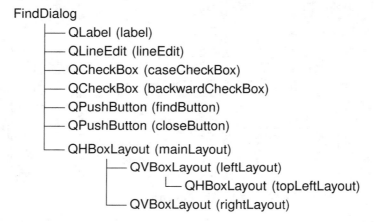

FindDialog
├── QLabel (label)
├── QLineEdit (lineEdit)
├── QCheckBox (caseCheckBox)
├── QCheckBox (backwardCheckBox)
├── QPushButton (findButton)
├── QPushButton (closeButton)
└── QHBoxLayout (mainLayout)
      ├── QVBoxLayout (leftLayout)
      │   └── QHBoxLayout (topLeftLayout)
      └── QVBoxLayout (rightLayout)

Figure 2.3. The Find dialog's parent–child relationships

Now we will look at the dialog's slots:

```
39  void FindDialog::findClicked()
40  {
41      QString text = lineEdit->text();
42      Qt::CaseSensitivity cs =
43              caseCheckBox->isChecked() ? Qt::CaseSensitive
44                                        : Qt::CaseInsensitive;
45      if (backwardCheckBox->isChecked()) {
46          emit findPrevious(text, cs);
47      } else {
48          emit findNext(text, cs);
49      }
50  }

51  void FindDialog::enableFindButton(const QString &text)
52  {
53      findButton->setEnabled(!text.isEmpty());
54  }
```

The `findClicked()` slot is called when the user clicks the Find button. It emits the `findPrevious()` or the `findNext()` signal, depending on the Search backward option. The `emit` keyword is specific to Qt; like other Qt extensions it is converted into standard C++ by the C++ preprocessor.

The `enableFindButton()` slot is called whenever the user changes the text in the line editor. It enables the button if there is some text in the editor, and disables it otherwise.

These two slots complete the dialog. We can now create a `main.cpp` file to test our `FindDialog` widget:

```
1  #include <QApplication>

2  #include "finddialog.h"

3  int main(int argc, char *argv[])
4  {
5      QApplication app(argc, argv);
6      FindDialog *dialog = new FindDialog;
7      dialog->show();
8      return app.exec();
9  }
```

To compile the program, run qmake as usual. Since the `FindDialog` class definition contains the `Q_OBJECT` macro, the makefile generated by qmake will include special rules to run moc, Qt's meta-object compiler. (Qt's meta-object system is covered in the next section.)

For moc to work correctly, we must put the class definition in a header file, separate from the implementation file. The code generated by moc includes this header file and adds some C++ magic of its own.

Classes that use the `Q_OBJECT` macro must have moc run on them. This isn't a problem because qmake automatically adds the necessary rules to the makefile. But if you forget to regenerate your makefile using qmake and moc isn't run, the linker will complain that some functions are declared but not implemented. The messages can be fairly obscure. GCC produces warnings like this one:

```
finddialog.o: In function 'FindDialog::tr(char const*, char const*)':
/usr/lib/qt/src/corelib/global/qglobal.h:1430: undefined reference to
'FindDialog::staticMetaObject'
```

Visual C++'s output starts like this:

```
finddialog.obj : error LNK2001: unresolved external symbol
"public:~virtual int __thiscall MyClass::qt_metacall(enum QMetaObject
::Call,int,void * *)"
```

If this ever happens to you, run qmake again to update the makefile, then rebuild the application.

Now run the program. If shortcut keys are shown on your platform, verify that the shortcut keys Alt+W, Alt+C, Alt+B, and Alt+F trigger the correct behavior. Press Tab to navigate through the widgets with the keyboard. The default tab order is the order in which the widgets were created. This can be changed using `QWidget::setTabOrder()`.

Providing a sensible tab order and keyboard shortcuts ensures that users who don't want to (or cannot) use a mouse are able to make full use of the application. Full keyboard control is also appreciated by fast typists.

In Chapter 3, we will use the Find dialog inside a real application, and we will connect the `findPrevious()` and `findNext()` signals to some slots.

Signals and Slots in Depth

The signals and slots mechanism is fundamental to Qt programming. It enables the application programmer to bind objects together without the objects knowing anything about each other. We have already connected some signals and slots together, declared our own signals and slots, implemented our own slots, and emitted our own signals. Let's take a moment to look at the mechanism more closely.

Slots are almost identical to ordinary C++ member functions. They can be virtual; they can be overloaded; they can be public; protected, or private, they can be directly invoked like any other C++ member functions; and their parameters can be of any types. The difference is that a slot can also be connected to a signal, in which case it is automatically called each time the signal is emitted.

The `connect()` statement looks like this:

```
connect(sender, SIGNAL(signal), receiver, SLOT(slot));
```

where `sender` and `receiver` are pointers to QObjects and where `signal` and `slot` are function signatures without parameter names. The `SIGNAL()` and `SLOT()` macros essentially convert their argument to a string.

In the examples we have seen so far, we have always connected different signals to different slots. There are other possibilities to consider.

- **One signal can be connected to many slots:**

  ```
  connect(slider, SIGNAL(valueChanged(int)),
          spinBox, SLOT(setValue(int)));
  connect(slider, SIGNAL(valueChanged(int)),
          this, SLOT(updateStatusBarIndicator(int)));
  ```

  When the signal is emitted, the slots are called one after the other, in an unspecified order.

- **Many signals can be connected to the same slot:**

  ```
  connect(lcd, SIGNAL(overflow()),
          this, SLOT(handleMathError()));
  connect(calculator, SIGNAL(divisionByZero()),
          this, SLOT(handleMathError()));
  ```

  When either signal is emitted, the slot is called.

- **A signal can be connected to another signal:**

```
connect(lineEdit, SIGNAL(textChanged(const QString &)),
        this, SIGNAL(updateRecord(const QString &)));
```

When the first signal is emitted, the second signal is emitted as well. Apart from that, signal–signal connections are indistinguishable from signal–slot connections.

- **Connections can be removed:**

```
disconnect(lcd, SIGNAL(overflow()),
           this, SLOT(handleMathError()));
```

This is rarely needed, because Qt automatically removes all connections involving an object when that object is deleted.

To successfully connect a signal to a slot (or to another signal), they must have the same parameter types in the same order:

```
connect(ftp, SIGNAL(rawCommandReply(int, const QString &)),
        this, SLOT(processReply(int, const QString &)));
```

Exceptionally, if a signal has more parameters than the slot it is connected to, the additional parameters are simply ignored:

```
connect(ftp, SIGNAL(rawCommandReply(int, const QString &)),
        this, SLOT(checkErrorCode(int)));
```

If the parameter types are incompatible, or if the signal or the slot doesn't exist, Qt will issue a warning at run-time if the application is built in debug mode. Similarly, Qt will give a warning if parameter names are included in the signal or slot signatures.

So far, we have only used signals and slots with widgets. But the mechanism itself is implemented in QObject and isn't limited to GUI programming. The mechanism can be used by any QObject subclass:

```
class Employee : public QObject
{
    Q_OBJECT

public:
    Employee() { mySalary = 0; }

    int salary() const { return mySalary; }

public slots:
    void setSalary(int newSalary);

signals:
    void salaryChanged(int newSalary);

private:
    int mySalary;
};
```

```
void Employee::setSalary(int newSalary)
{
    if (newSalary != mySalary) {
        mySalary = newSalary;
        emit salaryChanged(mySalary);
    }
}
```

Notice how the `setSalary()` slot is implemented. We only emit the `salary-Changed()` signal if `newSalary != mySalary`. This ensures that cyclic connections don't lead to infinite loops.

Qt's Meta-Object System

One of Qt's major achievements has been the extension of C++ with a mechanism for creating independent software components that can be bound together without any component knowing anything about the other components it is connected to.

The mechanism is called the *meta-object system*, and it provides two key services: signals–slots and introspection. The introspection functionality is necessary for implementing signals and slots, and allows application programmers to obtain "meta-information" about `QObject` subclasses at run-time, including the list of signals and slots supported by the object and its class name. The mechanism also supports properties (for *Qt Designer*) and text translation (for internationalization), and it lays the foundation for Qt Script for Applications (QSA).

Standard C++ doesn't provide support for the dynamic meta-information needed by Qt's meta-object system. Qt solves this problem by providing a separate tool, `moc`, that parses `Q_OBJECT` class definitions and makes the information available through C++ functions. Since `moc` implements all its functionality using pure C++, Qt's meta-object system works with any C++ compiler.

The mechanism works as follows:

- The `Q_OBJECT` macro declares some introspection functions that must be implemented in every `QObject` subclass: `metaObject()`, `tr()`, `qt_metacall()`, and a few more.

- Qt's `moc` tool generates implementations for the functions declared by `Q_OBJECT` and for all the signals.

- `QObject` member functions such as `connect()` and `disconnect()` use the introspection functions to do their work.

All of this is handled automatically by `qmake`, `moc`, and `QObject`, so you rarely need to think about it. But if you are curious, you can check out the `QMetaObject` class documentation and have a look at the C++ source files generated by `moc` to see how the implementation works.

Rapid Dialog Design

Qt is designed to be pleasant and intuitive to hand-code, and it is not unusual for programmers to develop entire Qt applications purely by writing C++ source code. Still, many programmers prefer to use a visual approach for designing forms, because they find it more natural and faster than hand-coding, and they want to be able to experiment with and change designs more quickly and easily than is possible with hand-coded forms.

Qt Designer expands the options available to programmers by providing a visual design capability. *Qt Designer* can be used to develop all or just some of an application's forms. Forms that are created using *Qt Designer* end up as C++ code, so *Qt Designer* can be used with a conventional tool chain and imposes no special requirements on the compiler.

In this section, we will use *Qt Designer* to create the Go-to-Cell dialog shown in Figure 2.4. And whether we do it in code or in *Qt Designer*, creating a dialog always involves the same fundamental steps:

- Create and initialize the child widgets.
- Put the child widgets in layouts.
- Set the tab order.
- Establish signal–slot connections.
- Implement the dialog's custom slots.

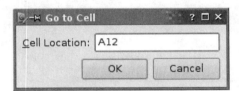

Figure 2.4. The Go-to-Cell dialog

To launch *Qt Designer*, click Qt by Trolltech v4.x.y|Designer in the Start menu on Windows, type designer on the command line on Unix, or double-click Designer in the Mac OS X Finder. When *Qt Designer* starts, it will pop up a list of templates. Click the "Widget" template, then click OK. (The "Dialog with Buttons Bottom" template might look tempting, but for this example we will create the OK and Cancel buttons by hand to show how it is done.) You should now have a window called "Untitled".

By default, *Qt Designer*'s user interface consists of several top-level windows. If you prefer an MDI-style interface, with one top-level window and several sub-windows, click Edit|User Interface Mode|Docked Window.

The first step is to create the child widgets and place them on the form. Create one label, one line editor, one horizontal spacer, and two push buttons. For each item, drag its name or icon from *Qt Designer*'s widget box and drop the item roughly where it should go on the form. The spacer item, which is invisible in the final form, is shown in *Qt Designer* as a blue spring.

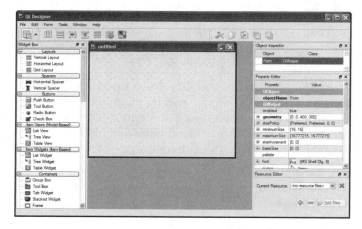

Figure 2.5. *Qt Designer* in docked window mode on Windows

Now drag the bottom of the form up to make it shorter. This should produce a form that is similar to Figure 2.6. Don't spend too much time positioning the items on the form; Qt's layout managers will lay them out precisely later on.

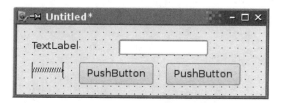

Figure 2.6. The form with some widgets

Set each widget's properties using *Qt Designer*'s property editor:

1. Click the text label. Make sure that its `objectName` property is "label" and set the `text` property to "&Cell Location:".

2. Click the line editor. Make sure that the `objectName` property is "lineEdit".

3. Click the first button. Set the `objectName` property to "okButton", the `enabled` property to "false", the `text` property to "OK", and the `default` property to "true".

4. Click the second button. Set the `objectName` property to "cancelButton" and the `text` property to "Cancel".

5. Click the form's background to select the form itself. Set `objectName` to "GoToCellDialog" and `windowTitle` to "Go to Cell".

All the widgets look fine now, except the text label, which shows &Cell Location. Click Edit|Edit Buddies to enter a special mode that allows you to set buddies. Next, click the label and drag the red arrow line to the line editor, then release. The label should now show C̲ell Location and have the line editor as its buddy. Click Edit|Edit Widgets to leave buddy mode.

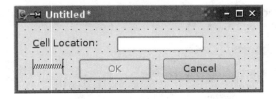

Figure 2.7. The form with properties set

The next step is to lay out the widgets on the form:

1. Click the Cell Location label and press Shift as you click the line editor next to it so that they are both selected. Click Form|Lay Out Horizontally.

2. Click the spacer, then hold Shift as you click the form's OK and Cancel buttons. Click Form|Lay Out Horizontally.

3. Click the background of the form to deselect any selected items, then click Form|Lay Out Vertically.

4. Click Form|Adjust Size to resize the form to its preferred size.

The red lines that appear on the form show the layouts that have been created. They don't appear when the form is run.

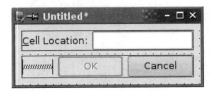

Figure 2.8. The form with the layouts

Now click Edit|Edit Tab Order. A number in a blue rectangle will appear next to every widget that can accept focus. Click each widget in turn in the order you want them to accept focus, then click Edit|Edit Widgets to leave tab order mode.

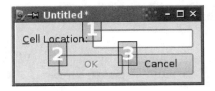

Figure 2.9. Setting the form's tab order

To preview the dialog, click the Form|Preview menu option. Check the tab order by pressing Tab repeatedly. Close the dialog using the close button in the title bar.

Save the dialog as gotocelldialog.ui in a directory called gotocell, and create a main.cpp file in the same directory using a plain text editor:

```
#include <QApplication>
#include <QDialog>

#include "ui_gotocelldialog.h"

int main(int argc, char *argv[])
{
    QApplication app(argc, argv);

    Ui::GoToCellDialog ui;
    QDialog *dialog = new QDialog;
    ui.setupUi(dialog);
    dialog->show();

    return app.exec();
}
```

Now run qmake to create a .pro file and a makefile (qmake -project; qmake gotocell.pro). The qmake tool is smart enough to detect the user interface file gotocelldialog.ui and to generate the appropriate makefile rules to invoke uic, Qt's user interface compiler. The uic tool converts gotocelldialog.ui into C++ and puts the result in ui_gotocelldialog.h.

The generated ui_gotocelldialog.h file contains the definition of the Ui::GoToCellDialog class, which is a C++ equivalent of the gotocelldialog.ui file. The class declares member variables that store the form's child widgets and layouts, and a setupUi() function that initializes the form. The generated class looks like this:

```
class Ui::GoToCellDialog
{
public:
    QLabel *label;
    QLineEdit *lineEdit;
    QSpacerItem *spacerItem;
    QPushButton *okButton;
    QPushButton *cancelButton;
    ...

    void setupUi(QWidget *widget) {
        ...
    }
};
```

The generated class doesn't inherit any Qt class. When we use the form in main.cpp, we create a QDialog and pass it to setupUi().

If you run the program now, the dialog will work, but it doesn't function exactly as we want:

- The OK button is always disabled.
- The Cancel button does nothing.
- The line editor accepts any text, instead of only accepting valid cell locations.

We can make the dialog function properly by writing some code. The cleanest approach is to create a new class that inherits both QDialog and Ui::GoToCell-Dialog and that implements the missing functionality (thus proving the adage that any software problem can be solved simply by adding another layer of indirection). Our naming convention is to give this new class the same name as the uic-generated class but without the Ui:: prefix.

Using a text editor, create a file called gotocelldialog.h that contains the following code:

```
#ifndef GOTOCELLDIALOG_H
#define GOTOCELLDIALOG_H

#include <QDialog>

#include "ui_gotocelldialog.h"

class GoToCellDialog : public QDialog, public Ui::GoToCellDialog
{
    Q_OBJECT

public:
    GoToCellDialog(QWidget *parent = 0);

private slots:
    void on_lineEdit_textChanged();
};

#endif
```

The implementation belongs in gotocelldialog.cpp:

```
#include <QtGui>

#include "gotocelldialog.h"

GoToCellDialog::GoToCellDialog(QWidget *parent)
    : QDialog(parent)
{
    setupUi(this);

    QRegExp regExp("[A-Za-z][1-9][0-9]{0,2}");
    lineEdit->setValidator(new QRegExpValidator(regExp, this));

    connect(okButton, SIGNAL(clicked()), this, SLOT(accept()));
    connect(cancelButton, SIGNAL(clicked()), this, SLOT(reject()));
}
```

```
void GoToCellDialog::on_lineEdit_textChanged()
{
    okButton->setEnabled(lineEdit->hasAcceptableInput());
}
```

In the constructor, we call setupUi() to initialize the form. Thanks to multiple inheritance, we can access Ui::GoToCellDialog's members directly. After creating the user interface, setupUi() will also automatically connect any slots that follow the naming convention on_objectName_signalName() to the corresponding objectName's signalName() signal. In our example, this means that setupUi() will establish the following signal–slot connection:

```
connect(lineEdit, SIGNAL(textChanged(const QString &)),
        this, SLOT(on_lineEdit_textChanged()));
```

Also in the constructor, we set up a validator to restrict the range of the input. Qt provides three built-in validator classes: QIntValidator, QDoubleValidator, and QRegExpValidator. Here we use a QRegExpValidator with the regular expression "[A-Za-z][1-9][0-9]{0,2}", which means: Allow one uppercase or lowercase letter, followed by one digit in the range 1 to 9, followed by zero, one, or two digits each in the range 0 to 9. (For an introduction to regular expressions, see the QRegExp class documentation.)

By passing this to the QRegExpValidator constructor, we make it a child of the GoToCellDialog object. By doing so, we don't have to worry about deleting the QRegExpValidator later; it will be deleted automatically when its parent is deleted.

Qt's parent–child mechanism is implemented in QObject. When we create an object (a widget, validator, or any other kind) with a parent, the parent adds the object to the list of its children. When the parent is deleted, it walks through its list of children and deletes each child. The children themselves then delete all of their children, and so on recursively until none remain.

The parent–child mechanism greatly simplifies memory management, reducing the risk of memory leaks. The only objects we must delete explicitly are the objects we create with new and that have no parent. And if we delete a child object before its parent, Qt will automatically remove that object from the parent's list of children.

For widgets, the parent has an additional meaning: Child widgets are shown within the parent's area. When we delete the parent widget, not only does the child vanish from memory, it also vanishes from the screen.

At the end of the constructor, we connect the OK button to QDialog's accept() slot and the Cancel button to the reject() slot. Both slots close the dialog, but accept() sets the dialog's result value to QDialog::Accepted (which equals 1), and reject() sets the value to QDialog::Rejected (which equals 0). When we use this dialog, we can use the result value to see if the user clicked OK and act accordingly.

The on_lineEdit_textChanged() slot enables or disables the OK button, according to whether the line edit contains a valid cell location. QLineEdit::hasAcceptableInput() uses the validator we set in the constructor.

This completes the dialog. We can now rewrite main.cpp to use it:

```
#include <QApplication>

#include "gotocelldialog.h"

int main(int argc, char *argv[])
{
    QApplication app(argc, argv);
    GoToCellDialog *dialog = new GoToCellDialog;
    dialog->show();
    return app.exec();
}
```

Rebuild the application (qmake -project; qmake gotocell.pro) and run it again. Type "A12" in the line edit, and notice that the OK button becomes enabled. Try typing some random text to see how the validator does its job. Click Cancel to close the dialog.

One of the beauties of using *Qt Designer* is that it allows programmers great freedom to modify their form designs without being forced to change their source code. When you develop a form purely by writing C++ code, changes to the design can be quite time-consuming. With *Qt Designer*, no time is lost since uic simply regenerates the source code for any forms that have changed. The dialog's user interface is saved in a .ui file (an XML-based file format), while custom functionality is implemented by subclassing the uic-generated class.

Shape-Changing Dialogs

We have seen how to create dialogs that always show the same widgets whenever they are used. In some cases, it is desirable to provide dialogs that can change shape. The two most common kinds of shape-changing dialogs are *extension dialogs* and *multi-page dialogs*. Both types of dialog can be implemented in Qt, either purely in code or using *Qt Designer*.

Extension dialogs usually present a simple appearance but have a toggle button that allows the user to switch between the dialog's simple and extended appearances. Extension dialogs are commonly used for applications that are trying to cater for both casual and power users, hiding the advanced options unless the user explicitly asks to see them. In this section, we will use *Qt Designer* to create the extension dialog shown in Figure 2.10.

The dialog is a Sort dialog in a spreadsheet application, where the user can select one or several columns to sort on. The dialog's simple appearance allows the user to enter a single sort key, and its extended appearance provides for two extra sort keys. A More button lets the user switch between the simple and extended appearances.

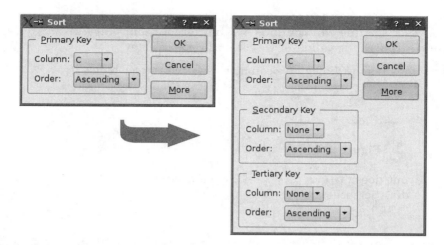

Figure 2.10. The Sort dialog with simple and extended appearances

We will create the widget with its extended appearance in *Qt Designer*, and hide the secondary and tertiary keys at run-time as needed. The widget looks complicated, but it's fairly easy to do in *Qt Designer*. The trick is to do the primary key part first, then duplicate it twice to obtain the secondary and tertiary keys:

1. Click File|New Form and choose the "Dialog with Buttons Right" template.

2. Create the More button and drag it into the vertical layout, below the vertical spacer. Set the More button's text property to "&More", and its checkable property to "true". Set the OK button's default property to "true".

3. Create a group box, two labels, two comboboxes, and one horizontal spacer, and put them anywhere on the form.

4. Drag the bottom right corner of the group box to make it larger. Then move the other widgets into the group box and position them approximately as shown in Figure 2.11 (a).

5. Drag the right edge of the second combobox to make it about twice as wide as the first combobox.

6. Set the group box's title property to "&Primary Key", the first label's text property to "Column:", and the second label's text property to "Order:".

7. Right-click the first combobox and choose Edit Items from the context menu to pop up *Qt Designer*'s combobox editor. Create one item with the text "None".

8. Right-click the second combobox and choose Edit Items. Create an "Ascending" item and a "Descending" item.

9. Click the group box, then click Form|Lay Out in a Grid. Click the group box again and click Form|Adjust Size. This will produce the layout shown in Figure 2.11 (b).

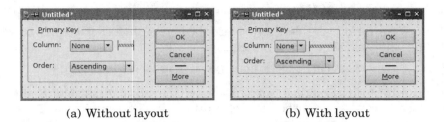

(a) Without layout	(b) With layout

Figure 2.11. Laying out the group box's children in a grid

If a layout doesn't turn out quite right or if you make a mistake, you can always click Edit|Undo or Form|Break Layout, then reposition the widgets and try again.

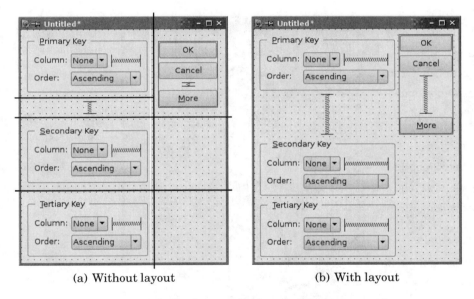

(a) Without layout	(b) With layout

Figure 2.12. Laying out the form's children in a grid

We will now add the Secondary Key and Tertiary Key group boxes:

1. Make the dialog window tall enough for the extra parts.

2. Hold down the Ctrl key (Alt on the Mac) and click the Primary Key group box to create a copy of the group box (and its contents) on top of the original. Drag the copy below the original group box, while still pressing Ctrl (or Alt). Repeat this process to create a third group box, dragging it below the second group box.

3. Change their `title` properties to "&Secondary Key" and "&Tertiary Key".

4. Create one vertical spacer and place it between the primary key group box and the secondary key group box.

5. Arrange the widgets in the grid-like pattern shown in Figure 2.12 (a).

6. Click the form to deselect any selected widgets, then click Form|Lay Out in a Grid. The form should now match Figure 2.12 (b).

7. Set the two vertical spacer items' sizeHint property to [20, 0].

The resulting grid layout has two columns and four rows, giving a total of eight cells. The Primary Key group box, the leftmost vertical spacer item, the Secondary Key group box, and the Tertiary Key group box each occupy a single cell. The vertical layout that contains the OK, Cancel, and More buttons occupies two cells. That leaves two empty cells in the bottom-right of the dialog. If this isn't what you have, undo the layout, reposition the widgets, and try again.

Rename the form "SortDialog" and change the window title to "Sort". Set the names of the child widgets to those shown in Figure 2.13.

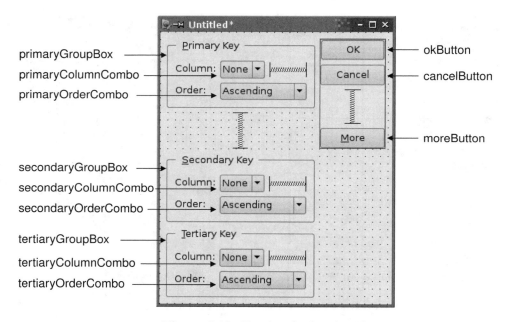

Figure 2.13. Naming the form's widgets

Click Edit|Edit Tab Order. Click each combobox in turn from topmost to bottommost, then click the OK, Cancel, and More buttons on the right side. Click Edit|Edit Widgets to leave tab order mode.

Now that the form has been designed, we are ready to make it functional by setting up some signal–slot connections. *Qt Designer* allows us to establish connections between widgets that are part of the same form. We need to establish two connections.

Click Edit|Edit Signals/Slots to enter *Qt Designer*'s connection mode. Connections are represented by blue arrows between the form's widgets. Because we chose the "Dialog with Buttons Right" template, the OK and Cancel buttons are already connected to QDialog's accept() and reject() slots. Connections are also listed in *Qt Designer*'s signal/slot editor window.

To establish a connection between two widgets, click the sender widget and drag the red arrow line to the receiver widget, then release. This pops up a dialog that allows you to choose the signal and the slot to connect.

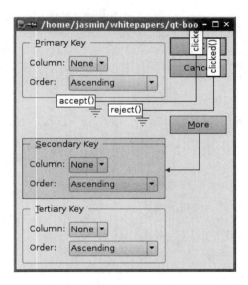

Figure 2.14. Connecting the form's widgets

The first connection to establish is between the moreButton and the secondary-GroupBox. Drag the red arrow line between these two widgets, then choose toggled(bool) as the signal and setVisible(bool) as the slot. By default, *Qt Designer* doesn't list setVisible(bool) in the list of slots, but it will appear if you enable the Show all signals and slots option.

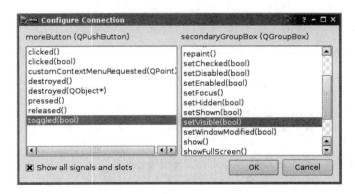

Figure 2.15. *Qt Designer*'s connection editor

The second connection is between the moreButton's toggled(bool) signal and the tertiaryGroupBox's setVisible(bool) slot. Once the connections have been made, click Edit|Edit Widgets to leave connection mode.

Save the dialog as sortdialog.ui in a directory called sort. To add code to the form, we will use the same multiple inheritance approach that we used for the Go-to-Cell dialog in the previous section.

First, create a sortdialog.h file with the following contents:

```
#ifndef SORTDIALOG_H
#define SORTDIALOG_H

#include <QDialog>

#include "ui_sortdialog.h"

class SortDialog : public QDialog, public Ui::SortDialog
{
    Q_OBJECT

public:
    SortDialog(QWidget *parent = 0);

    void setColumnRange(QChar first, QChar last);
};

#endif
```

Then create sortdialog.cpp:

```
1  #include <QtGui>

2  #include "sortdialog.h"

3  SortDialog::SortDialog(QWidget *parent)
4      : QDialog(parent)
5  {
6      setupUi(this);

7      secondaryGroupBox->hide();
8      tertiaryGroupBox->hide();
9      layout()->setSizeConstraint(QLayout::SetFixedSize);

10     setColumnRange('A', 'Z');
11 }

12 void SortDialog::setColumnRange(QChar first, QChar last)
13 {
14     primaryColumnCombo->clear();
15     secondaryColumnCombo->clear();
16     tertiaryColumnCombo->clear();

17     secondaryColumnCombo->addItem(tr("None"));
18     tertiaryColumnCombo->addItem(tr("None"));

19     primaryColumnCombo->setMinimumSize(
20             secondaryColumnCombo->sizeHint());
```

```
21    QChar ch = first;
22    while (ch <= last) {
23        primaryColumnCombo->addItem(QString(ch));
24        secondaryColumnCombo->addItem(QString(ch));
25        tertiaryColumnCombo->addItem(QString(ch));
26        ch = ch.unicode() + 1;
27    }
28 }
```

The constructor hides the secondary and tertiary parts of the dialog. It also sets the `sizeConstraint` property of the form's layout to `QLayout::SetFixedSize`, making the dialog non-resizable by the user. The layout then takes over the responsibility for resizing, and resizes the dialog automatically when child widgets are shown or hidden, ensuring that the dialog is always displayed at its optimal size.

The `setColumnRange()` slot initializes the contents of the comboboxes based on the selected columns in the spreadsheet. We insert a "None" item in the comboboxes for the (optional) secondary and tertiary keys.

Lines 19 and 20 present a subtle layout idiom. The `QWidget::sizeHint()` function returns a widget's "ideal" size, which the layout system tries to honor. This explains why different kinds of widgets, or similar widgets with different contents, may be assigned different sizes by the layout system. For comboboxes, this means that the secondary and tertiary comboboxes, which contain "None", end up larger than the primary combobox, which contains only single-letter entries. To avoid this inconsistency, we set the primary combobox's minimum size to the *secondary* combobox's ideal size.

Here is a `main()` test function that sets the range to include columns 'C' to 'F' and then shows the dialog:

```
#include <QApplication>

#include "sortdialog.h"

int main(int argc, char *argv[])
{
    QApplication app(argc, argv);
    SortDialog *dialog = new SortDialog;
    dialog->setColumnRange('C', 'F');
    dialog->show();
    return app.exec();
}
```

That completes the extension dialog. As the example illustrates, an extension dialog isn't much more difficult to design than a plain dialog: All we needed was a toggle button, a few extra signal–slot connections, and a non-resizable layout. In production applications, it is quite common for the button that controls the extension to show the text Advanced >>> when only the basic dialog is visible and Advanced <<< when the extension is shown. This is easy to achieve in Qt by calling `setText()` on the `QPushButton` whenever it is clicked.

The other common type of shape-changing dialogs, multi-page dialogs, are even easier to create in Qt, either in code or using *Qt Designer*. Such dialogs can be built in many different ways.

- A QTabWidget can be used in its own right. It provides a tab bar along the top that controls a built-in QStackedWidget.

- A QListWidget and a QStackedWidget can be used together, with the QListWidget's current item determining which page the QStackedWidget shows, by connecting the QListWidget::currentRowChanged() signal to the QStackedWidget::setCurrentIndex() slot.

- A QTreeWidget can be used with a QStackedWidget in a similar way to a QListWidget.

The QStackedWidget class is covered in Chapter 6 (Layout Management).

Dynamic Dialogs

Dynamic dialogs are dialogs that are created from *Qt Designer* .ui files at run-time. Instead of converting the .ui file to C++ code using uic, we can load the file at run-time using the QUiLoader class:

```
QUiLoader uiLoader;
QFile file("sortdialog.ui");
QWidget *sortDialog = uiLoader.load(&file);
if (sortDialog) {
    ...
}
```

We can access the form's child widgets using QObject::findChild<T>():

```
QComboBox *primaryColumnCombo =
        sortDialog->findChild<QComboBox *>("primaryColumnCombo");
if (primaryColumnCombo) {
    ...
}
```

The findChild<T>() function is a template member function that returns the child object that matches the given name and type. Because of a compiler limitation, it is not available for MSVC 6. If you need to use the MSVC 6 compiler, call the qFindChild<T>() global function instead, which works exactly the same way.

The QUiLoader class is located in a separate library. To use QUiLoader from a Qt application, we must add this line to the application's .pro file:

```
CONFIG      += uitools
```

Dynamic dialogs make it possible to change the layout of a form without recompiling the application. They can also be used to create thin-client applications, where the executable merely has a front-end form built-in and all other forms are created as required.

Built-in Widget and Dialog Classes

Qt provides a complete set of built-in widgets and common dialogs that cater for most situations. In this section, we present screenshots of almost all of them. A few specialized widgets are deferred until later: Main window widgets such as QMenuBar, QToolBar, and QStatusBar are covered in Chapter 3, and layout-related widgets such as QSplitter and QScrollArea are covered in Chapter 6. Most of the built-in widgets and dialogs are used in the examples presented in this book. In the screenshots below, the widgets are shown using the Plastique style.

| QPushButton | QToolButton | QCheckBox | QRadioButton |

Figure 2.16. Qt's button widgets

Qt provides four kinds of "buttons": QPushButton, QToolButton, QCheckBox, and QRadioButton. QPushButton and QToolButton are most commonly used to initiate an action when they are clicked, but they can also behave like toggle buttons (click to press down, click to restore). QCheckBox can be used for independent on/off options, whereas QRadioButtons are normally mutually exclusive.

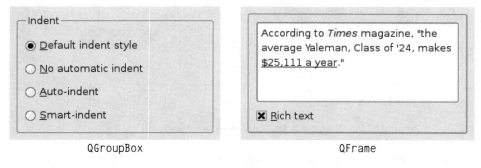

| QGroupBox | QFrame |

Figure 2.17. Qt's single-page container widgets

Qt's container widgets are widgets that contain other widgets. QFrame can also be used on its own to simply draw lines and is inherited by many other widget classes, including QToolBox and QLabel.

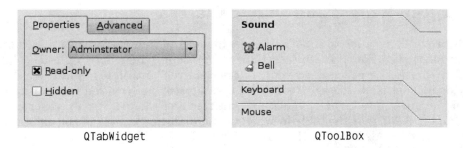

QTabWidget   QToolBox

Figure 2.18. Qt's multi-page container widgets

QTabWidget and QToolBox are multi-page widgets. Each page is a child widget, and the pages are numbered from 0.

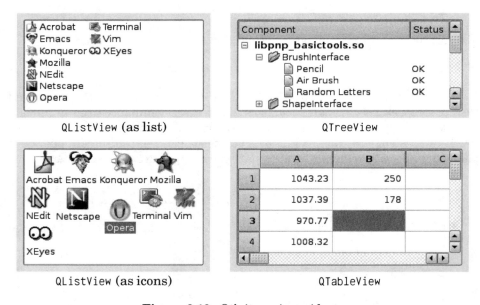

QListView (as list)   QTreeView

QListView (as icons)   QTableView

Figure 2.19. Qt's item view widgets

The item views are optimized for handling large amounts of data and often use scroll bars. The scroll bar mechanism is implemented in QAbstractScrollArea, a base class for item views and other kinds of scrollable widgets.

Qt provides a few widgets that are used purely for displaying information. QLabel is the most important of these, and it can be used for showing rich text (using a simple HTML-like syntax) and images.

QTextBrowser is a read-only QTextEdit subclass that has basic HTML support including lists, tables, images, and hypertext links. *Qt Assistant* uses QTextBrowser to present documentation to the user.

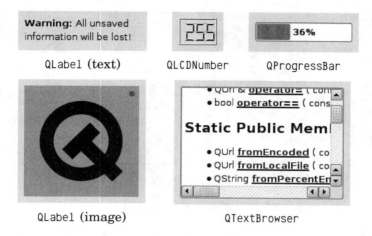

Figure 2.20. Qt's display widgets

Qt provides several widgets for data entry. QLineEdit can restrict its input using an input mask or a validator. QTextEdit is a QAbstractScrollArea subclass capable of editing large amounts of text.

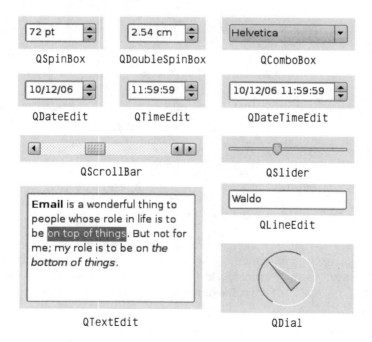

Figure 2.21. Qt's input widgets

Qt provides the standard set of common dialogs that make it easy to ask the user to select a color, font, or file, or to print a document.

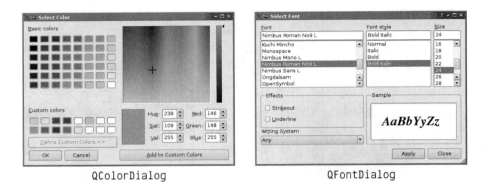

QColorDialog   QFontDialog

Figure 2.22. Qt's color dialog and font dialog

On Windows and Mac OS X, Qt uses the native dialogs rather than its own common dialogs when possible.

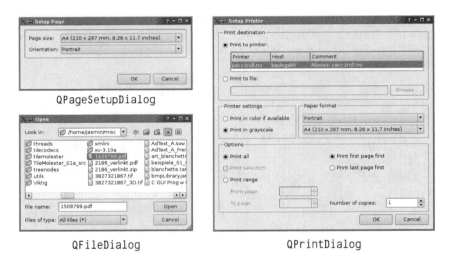

QPageSetupDialog

QFileDialog   QPrintDialog

Figure 2.23. Qt's file and print dialogs

Qt provides a versatile message box and an error dialog that remembers which messages it has shown. The progress of time-consuming operations can be indicated using QProgressDialog or using the QProgressBar shown earlier. QInputDialog is very convenient when a single line of text or a single number is required from the user.

A lot of ready-to-use functionality is provided by the built-in widgets and common dialogs. More specialized requirements can often be satisfied by setting widget properties, or by connecting signals to slots and implementing custom behavior in the slots.

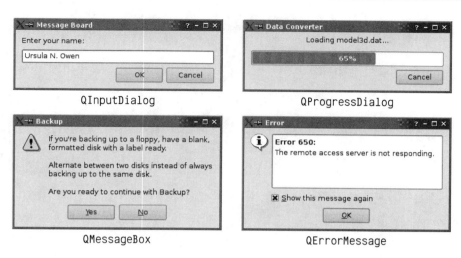

Figure 2.24. Qt's feedback dialogs

In some situations, it may be desirable to create a custom widget from scratch. Qt makes this straightforward, and custom widgets can access all the same platform-independent drawing functionality as Qt's built-in widgets. Custom widgets can even be integrated with *Qt Designer* so that they can be used in the same way as Qt's built-in widgets. Chapter 5 explains how to create custom widgets.

♦ *Subclassing QMainWindow*
♦ *Creating Menus and Toolbars*
♦ *Setting Up the Status Bar*
♦ *Implementing the File Menu*
♦ *Using Dialogs*
♦ *Storing Settings*
♦ *Multiple Documents*
♦ *Splash Screens*

3. Creating Main Windows

This chapter will teach you how to create main windows using Qt. By the end, you will be able to build an application's entire user interface, complete with menus, toolbars, status bar, and as many dialogs as the application requires.

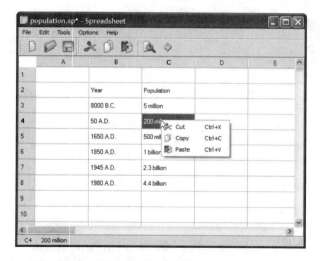

Figure 3.1. Spreadsheet application

An application's main window provides the framework upon which the application's user interface is built. The main window for the Spreadsheet application shown in Figure 3.1 will form the basis of this chapter. The Spreadsheet application makes use of the Find, Go-to-Cell, and Sort dialogs that we created in Chapter 2.

Behind most GUI applications lies a body of code that provides the underlying functionality—for example, code to read and write files or to process the data presented in the user interface. In Chapter 4, we will see how to implement such functionality, again using the Spreadsheet application as our example.

43

Subclassing QMainWindow

An application's main window is created by subclassing QMainWindow. Many of the techniques we saw in Chapter 2 for creating dialogs are also relevant for creating main windows, since both QDialog and QMainWindow inherit from QWidget.

Main windows can be created using *Qt Designer*, but in this chapter we will do everything in code to demonstrate how it's done. If you prefer the more visual approach, see the "Creating Main Windows in *Qt Designer*" chapter in *Qt Designer*'s online manual.

The source code for the Spreadsheet application's main window is spread across mainwindow.h and mainwindow.cpp. Let's start with the header file:

```
#ifndef MAINWINDOW_H
#define MAINWINDOW_H

#include <QMainWindow>

class QAction;
class QLabel;
class FindDialog;
class Spreadsheet;

class MainWindow : public QMainWindow
{
    Q_OBJECT

public:
    MainWindow();

protected:
    void closeEvent(QCloseEvent *event);
```

We define the class MainWindow as a subclass of QMainWindow. It contains the Q_OBJECT macro since it provides its own signals and slots.

The closeEvent() function is a virtual function in QWidget that is automatically called when the user closes the window. It is reimplemented in MainWindow so that we can ask the user the standard question "Do you want to save your changes?" and to save user preferences to disk.

```
private slots:
    void newFile();
    void open();
    bool save();
    bool saveAs();
    void find();
    void goToCell();
    void sort();
    void about();
```

Some menu options, like File|New and Help|About, are implemented as private slots in MainWindow. Most slots have void as their return value, but save() and saveAs() return a bool. The return value is ignored when a slot is executed in response to a signal, but when we call a slot as a function the return value is available to us just as it is when we call any ordinary C++ function.

```
    void openRecentFile();
    void updateStatusBar();
    void spreadsheetModified();

private:
    void createActions();
    void createMenus();
    void createContextMenu();
    void createToolBars();
    void createStatusBar();
    void readSettings();
    void writeSettings();
    bool okToContinue();
    bool loadFile(const QString &fileName);
    bool saveFile(const QString &fileName);
    void setCurrentFile(const QString &fileName);
    void updateRecentFileActions();
    QString strippedName(const QString &fullFileName);
```

The main window needs some more private slots and several private functions to support the user interface.

```
    Spreadsheet *spreadsheet;
    FindDialog *findDialog;
    QLabel *locationLabel;
    QLabel *formulaLabel;
    QStringList recentFiles;
    QString curFile;

    enum { MaxRecentFiles = 5 };
    QAction *recentFileActions[MaxRecentFiles];
    QAction *separatorAction;

    QMenu *fileMenu;
    QMenu *editMenu;
    ...
    QToolBar *fileToolBar;
    QToolBar *editToolBar;
    QAction *newAction;
    QAction *openAction;
    ...
    QAction *aboutQtAction;
};

#endif
```

In addition to its private slots and private functions, MainWindow also has lots of private variables. All of these will be explained as we use them.

We will now review the implementation:

```
#include <QtGui>
```

```
#include "finddialog.h"
#include "gotocelldialog.h"
#include "mainwindow.h"
#include "sortdialog.h"
#include "spreadsheet.h"
```

We include the <QtGui> header file, which contains the definition of all the Qt classes used in our subclass. We also include some custom header files, notably finddialog.h, gotocelldialog.h, and sortdialog.h from Chapter 2.

```
MainWindow::MainWindow()
{
    spreadsheet = new Spreadsheet;
    setCentralWidget(spreadsheet);

    createActions();
    createMenus();
    createContextMenu();
    createToolBars();
    createStatusBar();

    readSettings();

    findDialog = 0;

    setWindowIcon(QIcon(":/images/icon.png"));
    setCurrentFile("");
}
```

In the constructor, we begin by creating a Spreadsheet widget and setting it to be the main window's central widget. The central widget occupies the middle of the main window (see Figure 3.2). The Spreadsheet class is a QTableWidget subclass with some spreadsheet capabilities, such as support for spreadsheet formulas. We will implement it in Chapter 4.

We call the private functions createActions(), createMenus(), createContext-Menu(), createToolBars(), and createStatusBar() to set up the rest of the main window. We also call the private function readSettings() to read the application's stored settings.

We initialize the findDialog pointer to be a null pointer; the first time MainWindow::find() is called, we will create the FindDialog object.

At the end of the constructor, we set the window's icon to icon.png, a PNG file. Qt supports many image formats, including BMP, GIF,* JPEG, PNG, PNM, XBM, and XPM. Calling QWidget::setWindowIcon() sets the icon shown in the top-left corner of the window. Unfortunately, there is no platform-independent way of setting the application icon that appears on the desktop. Platform-specific procedures are explained at http://doc.trolltech.com/4.1/appicon.html.

---

*GIF support is disabled in Qt by default because the decompression algorithm used by GIF files was patented in some countries where software patents are recognized. We believe that this patent has now expired worldwide. To enable GIF support in Qt, pass the -qt-gif command-line option to the configure script or set the appropriate option in the Qt installer.

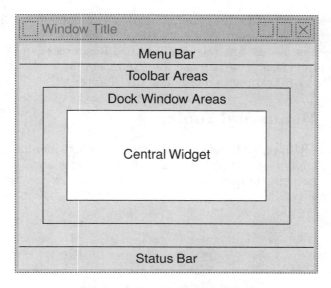

Figure 3.2. QMainWindow's areas

GUI applications generally use many images. There are several methods for providing images to the application. The most common are:

- Storing images in files and loading them at run-time.
- Including XPM files in the source code. (This works because XPM files are also valid C++ files.)
- Using Qt's resource mechanism.

Here we use Qt's resource mechanism because it is more convenient than loading files at run-time, and it works with any supported image file format. We have chosen to store the images in the source tree in a subdirectory called images.

To make use of Qt's resource system, we must create a resource file and add a line to the .pro file that identifies the resource file. In this example, we have called the resource file spreadsheet.qrc, so we put the following line in the .pro file:

```
RESOURCES     = spreadsheet.qrc
```

The resource file itself uses a simple XML format. Here's an extract from the one we have used:

```
<!DOCTYPE RCC><RCC version="1.0">
<qresource>
    <file>images/icon.png</file>
    ...
    <file>images/gotocell.png</file>
</qresource>
</RCC>
```

Resource files are compiled into the application's executable, so they can't get lost. When we refer to resources, we use the path prefix :/ (colon slash), which is why the icon is specified as :/images/icon.png. Resources can be any kind of file (not just images), and we can use them in most places where Qt expects a file name. They are covered in more detail in Chapter 12.

Creating Menus and Toolbars

Most modern GUI applications provide menus, context menus, and toolbars. The menus enable users to explore the application and learn how to do new things, while the context menus and toolbars provide quick access to frequently used functionality.

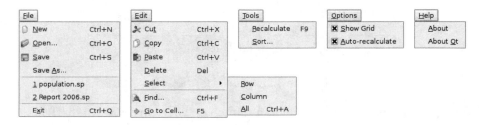

Figure 3.3. The Spreadsheet application's menus

Qt simplifies the programming of menus and toolbars through its action concept. An *action* is an item that can be added to any number of menus and toolbars. Creating menus and toolbars in Qt involves these steps:

- Create and set up the actions.
- Create menus and populate them with the actions.
- Create toolbars and populate them with the actions.

In the Spreadsheet application, actions are created in createActions():

```
void MainWindow::createActions()
{
    newAction = new QAction(tr("&New"), this);
    newAction->setIcon(QIcon(":/images/new.png"));
    newAction->setShortcut(tr("Ctrl+N"));
    newAction->setStatusTip(tr("Create a new spreadsheet file"));
    connect(newAction, SIGNAL(triggered()), this, SLOT(newFile()));
```

The New action has an accelerator (<u>N</u>ew), a parent (the main window), an icon (new.png), a shortcut key (Ctrl+N), and a status tip. We connect the action's triggered() signal to the main window's private newFile() slot, which we will implement in the next section. This connection ensures that when the user chooses the File|New menu item, clicks the New toolbar button, or presses Ctrl+N, the newFile() slot is called.

The Open, Save, and Save As actions are very similar to the New action, so we will skip directly to the "recently opened files" part of the File menu:

```
    ...
for (int i = 0; i < MaxRecentFiles; ++i) {
    recentFileActions[i] = new QAction(this);
    recentFileActions[i]->setVisible(false);
    connect(recentFileActions[i], SIGNAL(triggered()),
            this, SLOT(openRecentFile()));
}
```

We populate the recentFileActions array with actions. Each action is hidden and connected to the openRecentFile() slot. Later on, we will see how the recent file actions are made visible and used.

We can now skip to the Select All action:

```
    ...
selectAllAction = new QAction(tr("&All"), this);
selectAllAction->setShortcut(tr("Ctrl+A"));
selectAllAction->setStatusTip(tr("Select all the cells in the "
                                 "spreadsheet"));
connect(selectAllAction, SIGNAL(triggered()),
        spreadsheet, SLOT(selectAll()));
```

The selectAll() slot is provided by one of QTableWidget's ancestors, QAbstract-ItemView, so we do not have to implement it ourselves.

Let's skip further to the Show Grid action in the Options menu:

```
    ...
showGridAction = new QAction(tr("&Show Grid"), this);
showGridAction->setCheckable(true);
showGridAction->setChecked(spreadsheet->showGrid());
showGridAction->setStatusTip(tr("Show or hide the spreadsheet's "
                                "grid"));
connect(showGridAction, SIGNAL(toggled(bool)),
        spreadsheet, SLOT(setShowGrid(bool)));
```

Show Grid is a checkable action. It is rendered with a checkmark in the menu and implemented as a toggle button in the toolbar. When the action is turned on, the Spreadsheet component displays a grid. We initialize the action with the default for the Spreadsheet component, so that they are synchronized at start-up. Then we connect the Show Grid action's toggled(bool) signal to the Spread-sheet component's setShowGrid(bool) slot, which it inherits from QTableWidget. Once this action is added to a menu or toolbar, the user can toggle the grid on and off.

The Show Grid and Auto-Recalculate actions are independent checkable actions. Qt also supports mutually exclusive actions through the QActionGroup class.

```
    ...
aboutQtAction = new QAction(tr("About &Qt"), this);
aboutQtAction->setStatusTip(tr("Show the Qt library's About box"));
```

```
    connect(aboutQtAction, SIGNAL(triggered()), qApp, SLOT(aboutQt()));
}
```

For the About Qt action, we use the `QApplication` object's `aboutQt()` slot, accessible through the `qApp` global variable.

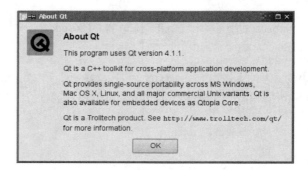

Figure 3.4. About Qt

Now that we have created the actions, we can move on to building a menu system containing them:

```
void MainWindow::createMenus()
{
    fileMenu = menuBar()->addMenu(tr("&File"));
    fileMenu->addAction(newAction);
    fileMenu->addAction(openAction);
    fileMenu->addAction(saveAction);
    fileMenu->addAction(saveAsAction);
    separatorAction = fileMenu->addSeparator();
    for (int i = 0; i < MaxRecentFiles; ++i)
        fileMenu->addAction(recentFileActions[i]);
    fileMenu->addSeparator();
    fileMenu->addAction(exitAction);
```

In Qt, menus are instances of `QMenu`. The `addMenu()` function creates a `QMenu` widget with the specified text and adds it to the menu bar. The `QMainWindow::menuBar()` function returns a pointer to a `QMenuBar`. The menu bar is created the first time `menuBar()` is called.

We start by creating the File menu and then add the New, Open, Save, and Save As actions to it. We insert a separator to visually group closely related items together. We use a `for` loop to add the (initially hidden) actions from the `recentFileActions` array, and then add the `exitAction` action at the end.

We have kept a pointer to one of the separators. This will allow us to hide the separator (if there are no recent files) or to show it, since we do not want to show two separators with nothing in between.

```
    editMenu = menuBar()->addMenu(tr("&Edit"));
    editMenu->addAction(cutAction);
    editMenu->addAction(copyAction);
```

```
editMenu->addAction(pasteAction);
editMenu->addAction(deleteAction);

selectSubMenu = editMenu->addMenu(tr("&Select"));
selectSubMenu->addAction(selectRowAction);
selectSubMenu->addAction(selectColumnAction);
selectSubMenu->addAction(selectAllAction);

editMenu->addSeparator();
editMenu->addAction(findAction);
editMenu->addAction(goToCellAction);
```

Now we create the Edit menu, adding actions with `QMenu::addAction()` as we did for the File menu, and adding the submenu with `QMenu::addMenu()` at the position where we want it to appear. The submenu, like the menu it belongs to, is a `QMenu`.

```
toolsMenu = menuBar()->addMenu(tr("&Tools"));
toolsMenu->addAction(recalculateAction);
toolsMenu->addAction(sortAction);

optionsMenu = menuBar()->addMenu(tr("&Options"));
optionsMenu->addAction(showGridAction);
optionsMenu->addAction(autoRecalcAction);

menuBar()->addSeparator();

helpMenu = menuBar()->addMenu(tr("&Help"));
helpMenu->addAction(aboutAction);
helpMenu->addAction(aboutQtAction);
}
```

We create the Tools, Options, and Help menus in a similar fashion. We insert a separator between the Options and Help menu. In Motif and CDE styles, the separator pushes the Help menu to the right; in other styles, the separator is ignored.

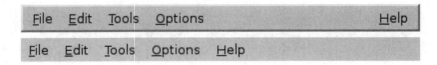

Figure 3.5. Menu bar in Motif and Windows styles

```
void MainWindow::createContextMenu()
{
    spreadsheet->addAction(cutAction);
    spreadsheet->addAction(copyAction);
    spreadsheet->addAction(pasteAction);
    spreadsheet->setContextMenuPolicy(Qt::ActionsContextMenu);
}
```

Any Qt widget can have a list of `QActions` associated with it. To provide a context menu for the application, we add the desired actions to the `Spreadsheet` widget and set that widget's context menu policy to show a context menu with these actions. Context menus are invoked by right-clicking a widget or by pressing a platform-specific key.

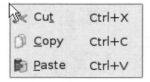

Figure 3.6. The Spreadsheet application's context menu

A more sophisticated way of providing context menus is to reimplement the QWidget::contextMenuEvent() function, create a QMenu widget, populate it with the desired actions, and call exec() on it.

```
void MainWindow::createToolBars()
{
    fileToolBar = addToolBar(tr("&File"));
    fileToolBar->addAction(newAction);
    fileToolBar->addAction(openAction);
    fileToolBar->addAction(saveAction);

    editToolBar = addToolBar(tr("&Edit"));
    editToolBar->addAction(cutAction);
    editToolBar->addAction(copyAction);
    editToolBar->addAction(pasteAction);
    editToolBar->addSeparator();
    editToolBar->addAction(findAction);
    editToolBar->addAction(goToCellAction);
}
```

Creating toolbars is very similar to creating menus. We create a File toolbar and an Edit toolbar. Just like a menu, a toolbar can have separators.

Figure 3.7. The Spreadsheet application's toolbars

Setting Up the Status Bar

With the menus and toolbars complete, we are ready to tackle the Spreadsheet application's status bar.

In its normal state, the status bar contains two indicators: the current cell's location and the current cell's formula. The status bar is also used to display status tips and other temporary messages.

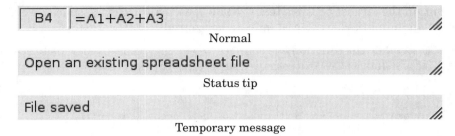

Figure 3.8. The Spreadsheet application's status bar

The MainWindow constructor calls createStatusBar() to set up the status bar:

```
void MainWindow::createStatusBar()
{
    locationLabel = new QLabel(" W999 ");
    locationLabel->setAlignment(Qt::AlignHCenter);
    locationLabel->setMinimumSize(locationLabel->sizeHint());

    formulaLabel = new QLabel;
    formulaLabel->setIndent(3);

    statusBar()->addWidget(locationLabel);
    statusBar()->addWidget(formulaLabel, 1);

    connect(spreadsheet, SIGNAL(currentCellChanged(int, int, int, int)),
            this, SLOT(updateStatusBar()));
    connect(spreadsheet, SIGNAL(modified()),
            this, SLOT(spreadsheetModified()));

    updateStatusBar();
}
```

The QMainWindow::statusBar() function returns a pointer to the status bar. (The status bar is created the first time statusBar() is called.) The status indicators are simply QLabels whose text we change whenever necessary. We have added an indent to the formulaLabel so that the text shown in it is offset slightly from the left edge. When the QLabels are added to the status bar, they are automatically reparented to make them children of the status bar.

Figure 3.8 shows that the two labels have different space requirements. The cell location indicator requires very little space, and when the window is resized, any extra space should go to the cell formula indicator on the right. This is achieved by specifying a stretch factor of 1 in the formula label's QStatusBar::addWidget() call. The location indicator has the default stretch factor of 0, meaning that it prefers not to be stretched.

When QStatusBar lays out indicator widgets, it tries to respect each widget's ideal size as given by QWidget::sizeHint() and then stretches any stretchable widgets to fill the available space. A widget's ideal size is itself dependent on the widget's contents and varies as we change the contents. To avoid constant resizing of the location indicator, we set its minimum size to be wide enough to contain the largest possible text ("W999"), with a little extra space. We also set its alignment to `Qt::AlignHCenter` to horizontally center the text.

Near the end of the function, we connect two of `Spreadsheet`'s signals to two of `MainWindow`'s slots: `updateStatusBar()` and `spreadsheetModified()`.

```
void MainWindow::updateStatusBar()
{
    locationLabel->setText(spreadsheet->currentLocation());
    formulaLabel->setText(spreadsheet->currentFormula());
}
```

The `updateStatusBar()` slot updates the cell location and the cell formula indicators. It is called whenever the user moves the cell cursor to a new cell. The slot is also used as an ordinary function at the end of `createStatusBar()` to initialize the indicators. This is necessary because `Spreadsheet` doesn't emit the `currentCellChanged()` signal at startup.

```
void MainWindow::spreadsheetModified()
{
    setWindowModified(true);
    updateStatusBar();
}
```

The `spreadsheetModified()` slot sets the `windowModified` property to `true`, updating the title bar. The function also updates the location and formula indicators so that they reflect the current state of affairs.

Implementing the File Menu

In this section, we will implement the slots and private functions necessary to make the File menu options work and to manage the recently opened files list.

```
void MainWindow::newFile()
{
    if (okToContinue()) {
        spreadsheet->clear();
        setCurrentFile("");
    }
}
```

The `newFile()` slot is called when the user clicks the File|New menu option or clicks the New toolbar button. The `okToContinue()` private function asks the user "Do you want to save your changes?" if there are unsaved changes. It returns `true` if the user chooses either Yes or No (saving the document on Yes), and it returns `false` if the user chooses Cancel. The `Spreadsheet::clear()` function clears all the spreadsheet's cells and formulas. The `setCurrentFile()` private function updates the window title to indicate that an untitled document is being edited, in addition to setting the `curFile` private variable and updating the recently opened files list.

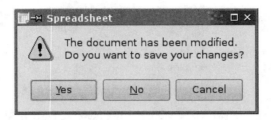

Figure 3.9. "Do you want to save your changes?"

```
bool MainWindow::okToContinue()
{
    if (isWindowModified()) {
        int r = QMessageBox::warning(this, tr("Spreadsheet"),
                        tr("The document has been modified.\n"
                           "Do you want to save your changes?"),
                        QMessageBox::Yes | QMessageBox::Default,
                        QMessageBox::No,
                        QMessageBox::Cancel | QMessageBox::Escape);
        if (r == QMessageBox::Yes) {
            return save();
        } else if (r == QMessageBox::Cancel) {
            return false;
        }
    }
    return true;
}
```

In `okToContinue()`, we check the state of the `windowModified` property. If it is true, we display the message box shown in Figure 3.9. The message box has a Yes, a No, and a Cancel button. The `QMessageBox::Default` modifier makes Yes the default button. The `QMessageBox::Escape` modifier makes the Esc key a synonym for Cancel.

The call to `warning()` may look a bit intimidating at first sight, but the general syntax is straightforward:

```
QMessageBox::warning(parent, title, message, button0, button1, ...);
```

`QMessageBox` also provides `information()`, `question()`, and `critical()`, each of which has its own particular icon.

Information   Question   Warning   Critical

Figure 3.10. Message box icons

```
void MainWindow::open()
{
    if (okToContinue()) {
```

```
        QString fileName = QFileDialog::getOpenFileName(this,
                              tr("Open Spreadsheet"), ".",
                              tr("Spreadsheet files (*.sp)"));
        if (!fileName.isEmpty())
            loadFile(fileName);
    }
}
```

The open() slot corresponds to File|Open. Like newFile(), it first calls okToContinue() to handle any unsaved changes. Then it uses the static convenience function QFileDialog::getOpenFileName() to obtain a new file name from the user. The function pops up a file dialog, lets the user choose a file, and returns the file name—or an empty string if the user clicked Cancel.

The first argument to QFileDialog::getOpenFileName() is the parent widget. The parent–child relationship doesn't mean the same thing for dialogs as for other widgets. A dialog is always a window in its own right, but if it has a parent, it is centered on top of the parent by default. A child dialog also shares its parent's taskbar entry.

The second argument is the title the dialog should use. The third argument tells it which directory it should start from, in our case the current directory.

The fourth argument specifies the file filters. A file filter consists of a descriptive text and a wildcard pattern. Had we supported comma-separated values files and Lotus 1-2-3 files in addition to Spreadsheet's native file format, we would have used the following filter:

```
tr("Spreadsheet files (*.sp)\n"
   "Comma-separated values files (*.csv)\n"
   "Lotus 1-2-3 files (*.wk1 *.wks)")
```

The loadFile() private function was called in open() to load the file. We make it an independent function because we will need the same functionality to load recently opened files:

```
bool MainWindow::loadFile(const QString &fileName)
{
    if (!spreadsheet->readFile(fileName)) {
        statusBar()->showMessage(tr("Loading canceled"), 2000);
        return false;
    }

    setCurrentFile(fileName);
    statusBar()->showMessage(tr("File loaded"), 2000);
    return true;
}
```

We use Spreadsheet::readFile() to read the file from disk. If loading is successful, we call setCurrentFile() to update the window title; otherwise, Spreadsheet::readFile() will have already notified the user of the problem through a message box. In general, it is good practice to let the lower-level components issue error messages, since they can provide the precise details of what went wrong.

In both cases, we display a message in the status bar for 2 seconds (2000 milliseconds) to keep the user informed about what the application is doing.

```
bool MainWindow::save()
{
    if (curFile.isEmpty()) {
        return saveAs();
    } else {
        return saveFile(curFile);
    }
}

bool MainWindow::saveFile(const QString &fileName)
{
    if (!spreadsheet->writeFile(fileName)) {
        statusBar()->showMessage(tr("Saving canceled"), 2000);
        return false;
    }

    setCurrentFile(fileName);
    statusBar()->showMessage(tr("File saved"), 2000);
    return true;
}
```

The save() slot corresponds to File|Save. If the file already has a name because it was opened before or has already been saved, save() calls saveFile() with that name; otherwise, it simply calls saveAs().

```
bool MainWindow::saveAs()
{
    QString fileName = QFileDialog::getSaveFileName(this,
                           tr("Save Spreadsheet"), ".",
                           tr("Spreadsheet files (*.sp)"));
    if (fileName.isEmpty())
        return false;

    return saveFile(fileName);
}
```

The saveAs() slot corresponds to File|Save As. We call QFileDialog::getSaveFile-Name() to obtain a file name from the user. If the user clicks Cancel, we return false, which is propagated up to its caller (save() or okToContinue()).

If the file already exists, the getSaveFileName() function will ask the user to confirm that they want to overwrite. This behavior can be changed by passing QFileDialog::DontConfirmOverwrite as an additional argument to getSaveFile-Name().

```
void MainWindow::closeEvent(QCloseEvent *event)
{
    if (okToContinue()) {
        writeSettings();
```

```
            event->accept();
        } else {
            event->ignore();
        }
    }
```

When the user clicks File|Exit or clicks the close button in the window's title bar, the QWidget::close() slot is called. This sends a "close" event to the widget. By reimplementing QWidget::closeEvent(), we can intercept attempts to close the main window and decide whether we want the window to actually close or not.

If there are unsaved changes and the user chooses Cancel, we "ignore" the event and leave the window unaffected by it. In the normal case, we accept the event, resulting in Qt hiding the window. We also call the private function writeSettings() to save the application's current settings.

When the last window is closed, the application terminates. If needed, we can disable this behavior by setting QApplication's quitOnLastWindowClosed property to false, in which case the application keeps running until we call QApplication::quit().

```
    void MainWindow::setCurrentFile(const QString &fileName)
    {
        curFile = fileName;
        setWindowModified(false);

        QString shownName = "Untitled";
        if (!curFile.isEmpty()) {
            shownName = strippedName(curFile);
            recentFiles.removeAll(curFile);
            recentFiles.prepend(curFile);
            updateRecentFileActions();
        }

        setWindowTitle(tr("%1[*] - %2").arg(shownName)
                                       .arg(tr("Spreadsheet")));
    }

    QString MainWindow::strippedName(const QString &fullFileName)
    {
        return QFileInfo(fullFileName).fileName();
    }
```

In setCurrentFile(), we set the curFile private variable that stores the name of the file being edited. Before we show the file name in the title bar, we remove the file's path with strippedName() to make it more user-friendly.

Every QWidget has a windowModified property that should be set to true if the window's document has unsaved changes, and to false otherwise. On Mac OS X, unsaved documents are indicated by a dot in the close button of the window's title bar; on other platforms, they are indicated by an asterisk following the file name. Qt takes care of this behavior automatically, as long as we keep the `windowModified` property up-to-date and place the marker "[*]" in the window title where we want the asterisk to appear when it is required.

The text we passed to the `setWindowTitle()` function was

```
tr("%1[*] - %2").arg(shownName)
                .arg(tr("Spreadsheet"))
```

The `QString::arg()` function replaces the lowest-numbered "*%n*" parameter with its argument and returns the resulting string. In this case, `arg()` is used with two "*%n*" parameters. The first call to `arg()` replaces "%1"; the second call replaces "%2". If the file name is "budget.sp" and no translation file is loaded, the resulting string would be "budget.sp[*] – Spreadsheet". It would have been easier to write

```
setWindowTitle(shownName + tr("[*] - Spreadsheet"));
```

but using `arg()` provides more flexibility for translators.

If there is a file name, we update `recentFiles`, the application's recently opened files list. We call `removeAll()` to remove any occurrences of the file name in the list, to avoid duplicates; then we call `prepend()` to add the file name as the first item. After updating the list, we call the private function `updateRecentFileActions()` to update the entries in the File menu.

```
void MainWindow::updateRecentFileActions()
{
    QMutableStringListIterator i(recentFiles);
    while (i.hasNext()) {
        if (!QFile::exists(i.next()))
            i.remove();
    }

    for (int j = 0; j < MaxRecentFiles; ++j) {
        if (j < recentFiles.count()) {
            QString text = tr("&%1 %2")
                           .arg(j + 1)
                           .arg(strippedName(recentFiles[j]));
            recentFileActions[j]->setText(text);
            recentFileActions[j]->setData(recentFiles[j]);
            recentFileActions[j]->setVisible(true);
        } else {
            recentFileActions[j]->setVisible(false);
        }
    }
    separatorAction->setVisible(!recentFiles.isEmpty());
}
```

We begin by removing any files that no longer exist using a Java-style iterator. Some files might have been used in a previous session, but have since been deleted. The `recentFiles` variable is of type `QStringList` (list of `QString`s). Chapter 11 explains container classes such as `QStringList` in detail, showing how they relate to the C++ Standard Template Library (STL), and the use of Qt's Java-style iterator classes.

We then go through the list of files again, this time using array-style indexing. For each file, we create a string consisting of an ampersand, a digit (j + 1), a space, and the file name (without its path). We set the corresponding action to use this text. For example, if the first file was C:\My Documents\tab04.sp, the first action's text would be "&1 tab04.sp".

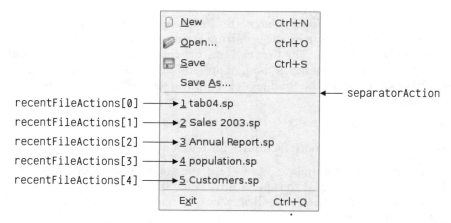

Figure 3.11. File menu with recently opened files

Every action can have an associated "data" item of type QVariant. The QVariant type can hold values of many C++ and Qt types; it is covered in Chapter 11. Here, we store the full name of the file in the action's "data" item so that we can easily retrieve it later. We also set the action to be visible.

If there are more file actions than recent files, we simply hide the extra actions. Finally, if there is at least one recent file, we set the separator to be visible.

```
void MainWindow::openRecentFile()
{
    if (okToContinue()) {
        QAction *action = qobject_cast<QAction *>(sender());
        if (action)
            loadFile(action->data().toString());
    }
}
```

When the user chooses a recent file, the openRecentFile() slot is called. The okToContinue() function is used in case there are any unsaved changes, and providing the user did not cancel, we find out which particular action invoked the slot using QObject::sender().

The qobject_cast<T>() function performs a dynamic cast based on the meta-information generated by moc, Qt's meta-object compiler. It returns a pointer of the requested QObject subclass, or 0 if the object cannot be cast to that type. Unlike the Standard C++ dynamic_cast<T>(), Qt's qobject_cast<T>() works correctly across dynamic library boundaries. In our example, we use qobject_cast<T>() to cast a QObject pointer to a QAction pointer. If the cast is successful (it should be), we call `loadFile()` with the full file name that we extract from the action's data.

Incidentally, since we know that the sender is a `QAction`, the program would still work if we used `static_cast<T>()` or a traditional C-style cast instead. Refer to the "Type Conversions" section of Appendix B for an overview of the different C++ casts.

Using Dialogs

In this section, we will explain how to use dialogs in Qt—how to create and initialize them, run them, and respond to choices made by the user interacting with them. We will make use of the Find, Go-to-Cell, and Sort dialogs that we created in Chapter 2. We will also create a simple About box.

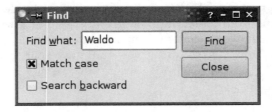

Figure 3.12. The Spreadsheet application's Find dialog

We will begin with the Find dialog. Since we want the user to be able to switch between the main Spreadsheet window and the Find dialog at will, the Find dialog must be modeless. A *modeless* window is one that runs independently of any other windows in the application.

When modeless dialogs are created, they normally have their signals connected to slots that respond to the user's interactions.

```
void MainWindow::find()
{
    if (!findDialog) {
        findDialog = new FindDialog(this);
        connect(findDialog, SIGNAL(findNext(const QString &,
                                            Qt::CaseSensitivity)),
                spreadsheet, SLOT(findNext(const QString &,
                                           Qt::CaseSensitivity)));
        connect(findDialog, SIGNAL(findPrevious(const QString &,
                                                Qt::CaseSensitivity)),
                spreadsheet, SLOT(findPrevious(const QString &,
                                               Qt::CaseSensitivity)));
    }

    findDialog->show();
    findDialog->activateWindow();
}
```

The Find dialog is a window that enables the user to search for text in the spreadsheet. The `find()` slot is called when the user clicks Edit|Find to pop up the Find dialog. At that point, several scenarios are possible:

- This is the first time the user has invoked the Find dialog.
- The Find dialog was invoked before, but the user closed it.
- The Find dialog was invoked before and is still visible.

If the Find dialog doesn't already exist, we create it and connect its `findNext()` and `findPrevious()` signals to the corresponding `Spreadsheet` slots. We could also have created the dialog in the `MainWindow` constructor, but delaying its creation makes startup faster. Also, if the dialog is never used, it is never created, saving both time and memory.

Then we call `show()` and `activateWindow()` to ensure that the window is visible and active. A call to `show()` alone is sufficient to make a hidden window visible and active, but the Find dialog may be invoked when its window is already visible, in which case `show()` does nothing and `activateWindow()` is necessary to make the window active. An alternative would have been to write

```
if (findDialog->isHidden()) {
    findDialog->show();
} else {
    findDialog->activateWindow();
}
```

which is the programming equivalent of looking both ways before crossing a one-way street.

We will now look at the Go-to-Cell dialog. We want the user to pop it up, use it, and close it without being able to switch to any other window in the application. This means that the Go-to-Cell dialog must be modal. A *modal* window is a window that pops up when invoked and blocks the application, preventing any other processing or interactions from taking place until the window is closed. The file dialogs and message boxes we used earlier were modal.

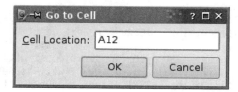

Figure 3.13. The Spreadsheet application's Go-to-Cell dialog

A dialog is modeless if it's invoked using `show()` (unless we call `setModal()` beforehand to make it modal); it is modal if it's invoked using `exec()`.

```
void MainWindow::goToCell()
{
    GoToCellDialog dialog(this);
```

```
        if (dialog.exec()) {
            QString str = dialog.lineEdit->text().toUpper();
            spreadsheet->setCurrentCell(str.mid(1).toInt() - 1,
                                        str[0].unicode() - 'A');
        }
    }
```

The `QDialog::exec()` function returns a true value (`QDialog::Accepted`) if the dialog is accepted, and a false value (`QDialog::Rejected`) otherwise. Recall that when we created the Go-to-Cell dialog using *Qt Designer* in Chapter 2, we connected OK to `accept()` and Cancel to `reject()`. If the user chooses OK, we set the current cell to the value in the line editor.

The `QTableWidget::setCurrentCell()` function expects two arguments: a row index and a column index. In the Spreadsheet application, cell A1 is cell $(0, 0)$ and cell B27 is cell $(26, 1)$. To obtain the row index from the `QString` returned by `QLineEdit::text()`, we extract the row number using `QString::mid()` (which returns a substring from the start position to the end of the string), convert it to an int using `QString::toInt()`, and subtract 1. For the column number, we subtract the numeric value of 'A' from the numeric value of the string's uppercased first character. We know that the string will have the correct format because the `QRegExpValidator` we created for the dialog only allows the OK button to be enabled if we have a letter followed by up to three digits.

The `goToCell()` function differs from all the code seen so far in that it creates a widget (a `GoToCellDialog`) as a variable on the stack. At the cost of one extra line, we could just as easily have used `new` and `delete`:

```
    void MainWindow::goToCell()
    {
        GoToCellDialog *dialog = new GoToCellDialog(this);
        if (dialog->exec()) {
            QString str = dialog->lineEdit->text().toUpper();
            spreadsheet->setCurrentCell(str.mid(1).toInt() - 1,
                                        str[0].unicode() - 'A');
        }
        delete dialog;
    }
```

Creating modal dialogs (and context menus in `QWidget::contextMenuEvent()` reimplementations) on the stack is a common programming pattern since we usually don't need the dialog (or menu) after we have used it, and it will automatically be destroyed at the end of the enclosing scope.

We will now turn to the Sort dialog. The Sort dialog is a modal dialog that allows the user to sort the currently selected area by the columns they specify. Figure 3.14 shows an example of sorting, with column B as the primary sort key and column A as the secondary sort key (both ascending).

	A	B	C	
1	George	Washington	1789-1797	
2	John	Adams	1797-1801	
3	Thomas	Jefferson	1801-1809	
4	James	Madison	1809-1817	
5	James	Monroe	1817-1825	
6	John Quincy	Adams	1825-1829	
7	Andrew	Jackson	1829-1837	
8				

	A	B	C	
1	John	Adams	1797-1801	
2	John Quincy	Adams	1825-1829	
3	Andrew	Jackson	1829-1837	
4	Thomas	Jefferson	1801-1809	
5	James	Madison	1809-1817	
6	James	Monroe	1817-1825	
7	George	Washington	1789-1797	
8				

(a) Before sort   (b) After sort

Figure 3.14. Sorting the spreadsheet's selected area

```
void MainWindow::sort()
{
    SortDialog dialog(this);
    QTableWidgetSelectionRange range = spreadsheet->selectedRange();
    dialog.setColumnRange('A' + range.leftColumn(),
                          'A' + range.rightColumn());

    if (dialog.exec()) {
        SpreadsheetCompare compare;
        compare.keys[0] =
            dialog.primaryColumnCombo->currentIndex();
        compare.keys[1] =
            dialog.secondaryColumnCombo->currentIndex() - 1;
        compare.keys[2] =
            dialog.tertiaryColumnCombo->currentIndex() - 1;
        compare.ascending[0] =
            (dialog.primaryOrderCombo->currentIndex() == 0);
        compare.ascending[1] =
            (dialog.secondaryOrderCombo->currentIndex() == 0);
        compare.ascending[2] =
            (dialog.tertiaryOrderCombo->currentIndex() == 0);
        spreadsheet->sort(compare);
    }
}
```

The code in sort() follows a similar pattern to that used for goToCell():

- We create the dialog on the stack and initialize it.

- We pop up the dialog using exec().

- If the user clicks OK, we extract the values entered by the user from the dialog's widgets and make use of them.

The setColumnRange() call sets the columns available for sorting to the columns that are selected. For example, using the selection shown in Figure 3.14, range. leftColumn() would yield 0, giving 'A' + 0 = 'A', and range.rightColumn() would yield 2, giving 'A' + 2 = 'C'.

The compare object stores the primary, secondary, and tertiary sort keys and their sort orders. (We will see the definition of the SpreadsheetCompare class in the next chapter.) The object is used by Spreadsheet::sort() to compare two rows. The keys array stores the column numbers of the keys. For example, if the selection extends from C2 to E5, column C has position 0. The ascending array stores the order associated with each key as a bool. QComboBox::current-Index() returns the index of the currently selected item, starting at 0. For the secondary and tertiary keys, we subtract one from the current item to account for the "None" item.

The sort() function does the job, but it is a bit fragile. It assumes that the Sort dialog is implemented in a particular way, with comboboxes and "None" items. This means that if we redesign the Sort dialog, we may also need to rewrite this code. While this approach is adequate for a dialog that is only called from one place, it opens the door to maintenance nightmares if the dialog is used in several places.

A more robust approach is to make the SortDialog class smarter by having it create a SpreadsheetCompare object itself, which can then be accessed by its caller. This simplifies MainWindow::sort() significantly:

```
void MainWindow::sort()
{
    SortDialog dialog(this);
    QTableWidgetSelectionRange range = spreadsheet->selectedRange();
    dialog.setColumnRange('A' + range.leftColumn(),
                          'A' + range.rightColumn());

    if (dialog.exec())
        spreadsheet->performSort(dialog.comparisonObject());
}
```

This approach leads to loosely coupled components and is almost always the right choice for dialogs that will be called from more than one place.

A more radical approach would be to pass a pointer to the Spreadsheet object when initializing the SortDialog object and to allow the dialog to operate directly on the Spreadsheet. This makes the SortDialog much less general, since it will only work on a certain type of widget, but it simplifies the code even further by eliminating the SortDialog::setColumnRange() function. The MainWindow::sort() function then becomes

```
void MainWindow::sort()
{
    SortDialog dialog(this);
    dialog.setSpreadsheet(spreadsheet);
    dialog.exec();
}
```

This approach mirrors the first: Instead of the caller needing intimate knowledge of the dialog, the dialog needs intimate knowledge of the data structures supplied by the caller. This approach may be useful where the dialog needs to apply changes live. But just as the caller code is fragile using the first approach, this third approach breaks if the data structures change.

Some developers choose just one approach to using dialogs and stick with that. This has the benefit of familiarity and simplicity since all their dialog usages follow the same pattern, but it also misses the benefits of the approaches that are not used. Ideally, the approach to use should be decided on a per-dialog basis.

We will round off this section with the About box. We could create a custom dialog like we did for the Find or Go-to-Cell dialogs to present the information about the application, but since most About boxes are highly stylized, Qt provides a simpler solution.

```
void MainWindow::about()
{
    QMessageBox::about(this, tr("About Spreadsheet"),
            tr("<h2>Spreadsheet 1.1</h2>"
               "<p>Copyright &copy; 2006 Software Inc."
               "<p>Spreadsheet is a small application that "
               "demonstrates QAction, QMainWindow, QMenuBar, "
               "QStatusBar, QTableWidget, QToolBar, and many other "
               "Qt classes."));
}
```

The About box is obtained by calling `QMessageBox::about()`, a static convenience function. The function is very similar to `QMessageBox::warning()`, except that it uses the parent window's icon instead of the standard "warning" icon.

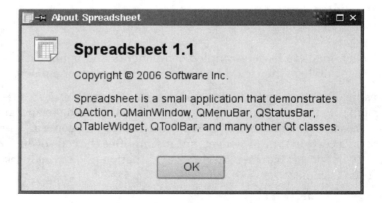

Figure 3.15. About Spreadsheet

So far we have used several convenience static functions from both `QMessageBox` and `QFileDialog`. These functions create a dialog, initialize it, and call `exec()` on it. It is also possible, although less convenient, to create a `QMessageBox` or a `QFileDialog` widget like any other widget and explicitly call `exec()`, or even `show()`, on it.

Storing Settings

In the MainWindow constructor, we called readSettings() to load the application's stored settings. Similarly, in closeEvent(), we called writeSettings() to save the settings. These two functions are the last MainWindow member functions that need to be implemented.

```cpp
void MainWindow::writeSettings()
{
    QSettings settings("Software Inc.", "Spreadsheet");

    settings.setValue("geometry", geometry());
    settings.setValue("recentFiles", recentFiles);
    settings.setValue("showGrid", showGridAction->isChecked());
    settings.setValue("autoRecalc", autoRecalcAction->isChecked());
}
```

The writeSettings() function saves the main window's geometry (position and size), the list of recently opened files, and the Show Grid and Auto-Recalculate options.

By default, QSettings stores the application's settings in platform-specific locations. On Windows, it uses the system registry; on Unix, it stores the data in text files; on Mac OS X, it uses the Core Foundation Preferences API.

The constructor arguments specify the organization's name and the application's name. This information is used in a platform-specific way to find a location for the settings.

QSettings stores settings as *key–value* pairs. The *key* is similar to a file system path. Subkeys can be specified using a path-like syntax (for example, findDialog/matchCase) or using beginGroup() and endGroup():

```cpp
settings.beginGroup("findDialog");
settings.setValue("matchCase", caseCheckBox->isChecked());
settings.setValue("searchBackward", backwardCheckBox->isChecked());
settings.endGroup();
```

The *value* can be an int, a bool, a double, a QString, a QStringList, or any other type supported by QVariant, including registered custom types.

```cpp
void MainWindow::readSettings()
{
    QSettings settings("Software Inc.", "Spreadsheet");

    QRect rect = settings.value("geometry",
                                QRect(200, 200, 400, 400)).toRect();
    move(rect.topLeft());
    resize(rect.size());

    recentFiles = settings.value("recentFiles").toStringList();
    updateRecentFileActions();

    bool showGrid = settings.value("showGrid", true).toBool();
    showGridAction->setChecked(showGrid);
```

```
        bool autoRecalc = settings.value("autoRecalc", true).toBool();
        autoRecalcAction->setChecked(autoRecalc);
}
```

The readSettings() function loads the settings that were saved by writeSettings(). The second argument to the value() function specifies a default value, in case there are no settings available. The default values are used the first time the application is run. Since no second argument is given for the recent files list, it will be set to an empty list on the first run.

Qt provides a QWidget::setGeometry() function to complement QWidget::geometry(), but it doesn't always work as we would expect on X11 because of limitations in many window managers. For that reason, we use move() and resize() instead. (See http://doc.trolltech.com/4.1/geometry.html for a detailed explanation.)

The arrangement we opted for in MainWindow, with all the QSettings-related code in readSettings() and writeSettings(), is just one of many possible approaches. A QSettings object can be created to query or modify some setting at any time during the execution of the application and from anywhere in the code.

We have now completed the Spreadsheet's MainWindow implementation. In the following sections, we will discuss how the Spreadsheet application can be modified to handle multiple documents and how to implement a splash screen. We will complete its functionality, including handling formulas and sorting, in the next chapter.

Multiple Documents

We are now ready to code the Spreadsheet application's main() function:

```
#include <QApplication>

#include "mainwindow.h"

int main(int argc, char *argv[])
{
    QApplication app(argc, argv);
    MainWindow mainWin;
    mainWin.show();
    return app.exec();
}
```

This main() function is a little bit different from those we have written so far: We have created the MainWindow instance as a variable on the stack instead of using new. The MainWindow instance is then automatically destroyed when the function terminates.

With the main() function shown above, the Spreadsheet application provides a single main window and can only handle one document at a time. If we want to edit multiple documents at the same time, we could start multiple instances of the Spreadsheet application. But this isn't as convenient for users as having a single instance of the application providing multiple main windows, just as one instance of a web browser can provide multiple browser windows simultaneously.

We will modify the Spreadsheet application so that it can handle multiple documents. First, we need a slightly different File menu:

- File|New creates a new main window with an empty document, instead of reusing the existing main window.
- File|Close closes the current main window.
- File|Exit closes all windows.

In the original version of the File menu, there was no Close option because that would have been the same as Exit.

Figure 3.16. The new File menu

This is the new `main()` function:

```
int main(int argc, char *argv[])
{
    QApplication app(argc, argv);
    MainWindow *mainWin = new MainWindow;
    mainWin->show();
    return app.exec();
}
```

With multiple windows, it now makes sense to create `MainWindow` with `new`, because then we can use `delete` on a main window when we have finished with it to save memory.

This is the new `MainWindow::newFile()` slot:

```
void MainWindow::newFile()
{
    MainWindow *mainWin = new MainWindow;
    mainWin->show();
}
```

We simply create a new `MainWindow` instance. It may seem odd that we don't keep any pointer to the new window, but that isn't a problem since Qt keeps track of all the windows for us.

These are the actions for Close and Exit:

```
void MainWindow::createActions()
{
    ...
    closeAction = new QAction(tr("&Close"), this);
    closeAction->setShortcut(tr("Ctrl+W"));
    closeAction->setStatusTip(tr("Close this window"));
    connect(closeAction, SIGNAL(triggered()), this, SLOT(close()));

    exitAction = new QAction(tr("E&xit"), this);
    exitAction->setShortcut(tr("Ctrl+Q"));
    exitAction->setStatusTip(tr("Exit the application"));
    connect(exitAction, SIGNAL(triggered()),
            qApp, SLOT(closeAllWindows()));
    ...
}
```

The `QApplication::closeAllWindows()` slot closes all of the application's windows, unless one of them rejects the close event. This is exactly the behavior we need here. We don't have to worry about unsaved changes because that's handled in `MainWindow::closeEvent()` whenever a window is closed.

It looks as if we have finished making the application capable of handling multiple windows. Unfortunately, there is a hidden problem lurking: If the user keeps creating and closing main windows, the machine might eventually run out of memory. This is because we keep creating `MainWindow` widgets in `newFile()` but we never delete them. When the user closes a main window, the default behavior is to hide it, so it still remains in memory. With many main windows, this can be a problem.

The solution is to set the `Qt::WA_DeleteOnClose` attribute in the constructor:

```
MainWindow::MainWindow()
{
    ...
    setAttribute(Qt::WA_DeleteOnClose);
    ...
}
```

This tells Qt to delete the window when it is closed. The `Qt::WA_DeleteOnClose` attribute is one of many flags that can be set on a `QWidget` to influence its behavior.

Memory leaking isn't the only problem that we must deal with. Our original application design included an implied assumption that we would only have one main window. With multiple windows, each main window has its own recently opened files list and its own options. Clearly, the recently opened files list should be global to the whole application. We can achieve this quite easily by declaring the `recentFiles` variable static, so that only one instance of it exists for the whole application. But then we must ensure that wherever we called `updateRecentFileActions()` to update the File menu, we must call it on all main windows. Here's the code to achieve this:

```
foreach (QWidget *win, QApplication::topLevelWidgets()) {
    if (MainWindow *mainWin = qobject_cast<MainWindow *>(win))
        mainWin->updateRecentFileActions();
}
```

The code uses Qt's `foreach` construct (explained in Chapter 11) to iterate over all the application's windows and calls `updateRecentFileActions()` on all widgets of type `MainWindow`. Similar code can be used for synchronizing the Show Grid and Auto-Recalculate options, or to make sure that the same file isn't loaded twice.

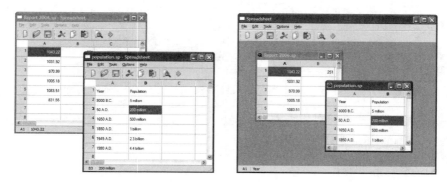

Figure 3.17. SDI versus MDI

Applications that provide one document per main window are said to be SDI (single document interface) applications. A common alternative on Windows is MDI (multiple document interface), where the application has a single main window that manages multiple document windows within its central area. Qt can be used to create both SDI and MDI applications on all its supported platforms. Figure 3.17 shows the Spreadsheet application using both approaches. MDI is explained in Chapter 6 (Layout Management).

Splash Screens

Many applications present a splash screen at startup. Some developers use a splash screen to disguise a slow startup, while others do it to satisfy their marketing departments. Adding a splash screen to Qt applications is very easy using the `QSplashScreen` class.

The `QSplashScreen` class shows an image before the main window appears. It can also write messages on the image to inform the user about the progress of the application's initialization process. Typically, the splash screen code is located in `main()`, before the call to `QApplication::exec()`.

Next is an example `main()` function that uses `QSplashScreen` to present a splash screen in an application that loads modules and establishes network connections at startup.

```
int main(int argc, char *argv[])
{
    QApplication app(argc, argv);

    QSplashScreen *splash = new QSplashScreen;
    splash->setPixmap(QPixmap(":/images/splash.png"));
    splash->show();

    Qt::Alignment topRight = Qt::AlignRight | Qt::AlignTop;

    splash->showMessage(QObject::tr("Setting up the main window..."),
                        topRight, Qt::white);
    MainWindow mainWin;

    splash->showMessage(QObject::tr("Loading modules..."),
                        topRight, Qt::white);
    loadModules();

    splash->showMessage(QObject::tr("Establishing connections..."),
                        topRight, Qt::white);
    establishConnections();

    mainWin.show();
    splash->finish(&mainWin);
    delete splash;

    return app.exec();
}
```

Figure 3.18. A splash screen

We have now completed the Spreadsheet application's user interface. In the next chapter, we will complete the application by implementing the core spreadsheet functionality.

4. Implementing Application Functionality

In the previous two chapters, we explained how to create the Spreadsheet application's user interface. In this chapter, we will complete the program by coding its underlying functionality. Among other things, we will see how to load and save files, how to store data in memory, how to implement clipboard operations, and how to add support for spreadsheet formulas to QTableWidget.

The Central Widget

The central area of a QMainWindow can be occupied by any kind of widget. Here's an overview of the possibilities:

1. Use a standard Qt widget.

A standard widget like QTableWidget or QTextEdit can be used as a central widget. In this case, the application's functionality, such as loading and saving files, must be implemented elsewhere (for example, in a QMainWindow subclass).

2. Use a custom widget.

Specialized applications often need to show data in a custom widget. For example, an icon editor program would have an IconEditor widget as its central widget. Chapter 5 explains how to write custom widgets in Qt.

3. Use a plain QWidget with a layout manager.

Sometimes the application's central area is occupied by many widgets. This can be done by using a QWidget as the parent of all the other widgets, and using layout managers to size and position the child widgets.

4. Use a splitter.

Another way of using multiple widgets together is to use a QSplitter. The QSplitter arranges its child widgets horizontally or vertically, with splitter handles to give some sizing control to the user. Splitters can contain all kinds of widgets, including other splitters.

5. Use an MDI workspace.

If the application uses MDI, the central area is occupied by a QWorkspace widget, and each of the MDI windows is a child of that widget.

Layouts, splitters, and MDI workspaces can be combined with standard Qt widgets or with custom widgets. Chapter 6 covers these classes in depth.

For the Spreadsheet application, a QTableWidget subclass is used as the central widget. The QTableWidget class already provides most of the spreadsheet capability we need, but it doesn't support clipboard operations and doesn't understand spreadsheet formulas like "=A1+A2+A3". We will implement this missing functionality in the Spreadsheet class.

Subclassing QTableWidget

The Spreadsheet class inherits from QTableWidget. A QTableWidget is effectively a grid that represents a two-dimensional sparse array. It displays whichever cells the user scrolls to, within its specified dimensions. When the user enters some text into an empty cell, QTableWidget automatically creates a QTableWidgetItem to store the text.

Let's start implementing Spreadsheet, beginning with the header file:

```
#ifndef SPREADSHEET_H
#define SPREADSHEET_H

#include <QTableWidget>

class Cell;
class SpreadsheetCompare;
```

The header starts with forward declarations for the Cell and SpreadsheetCompare classes.

Figure 4.1. Inheritance trees for Spreadsheet and Cell

The attributes of a QTableWidget cell, such as its text and its alignment, are stored in a QTableWidgetItem. Unlike QTableWidget, QTableWidgetItem isn't a widget class; it is a pure data class. The Cell class inherits QTableWidgetItem and is explained when its implementation is shown in this chapter's last section.

```cpp
class Spreadsheet : public QTableWidget
{
    Q_OBJECT

public:
    Spreadsheet(QWidget *parent = 0);

    bool autoRecalculate() const { return autoRecalc; }
    QString currentLocation() const;
    QString currentFormula() const;
    QTableWidgetSelectionRange selectedRange() const;
    void clear();
    bool readFile(const QString &fileName);
    bool writeFile(const QString &fileName);
    void sort(const SpreadsheetCompare &compare);
```

The autoRecalculate() function is implemented inline since it just returns whether or not auto-recalculation is in force.

In Chapter 3, we relied on some public functions in Spreadsheet when we implemented MainWindow. For example, we called clear() from MainWindow::newFile() to reset the spreadsheet. We also used some functions inherited from QTableWidget, notably setCurrentCell() and setShowGrid().

```cpp
public slots:
    void cut();
    void copy();
    void paste();
    void del();
    void selectCurrentRow();
    void selectCurrentColumn();
    void recalculate();
    void setAutoRecalculate(bool recalc);
    void findNext(const QString &str, Qt::CaseSensitivity cs);
    void findPrevious(const QString &str, Qt::CaseSensitivity cs);

signals:
    void modified();
```

Spreadsheet provides many slots that implement actions from the Edit, Tools, and Options menus, and it provides one signal, modified(), to announce any change that has occurred.

```cpp
private slots:
    void somethingChanged();
```

We define one private slot used internally by the Spreadsheet class.

```cpp
private:
    enum { MagicNumber = 0x7F51C883, RowCount = 999, ColumnCount = 26 };
```

```
    Cell *cell(int row, int column) const;
    QString text(int row, int column) const;
    QString formula(int row, int column) const;
    void setFormula(int row, int column, const QString &formula);

    bool autoRecalc;
};
```

In the class's private section, we declare three constants, four functions, and one variable.

```
class SpreadsheetCompare
{
public:
    bool operator()(const QStringList &row1,
                    const QStringList &row2) const;

    enum { KeyCount = 3 };
    int keys[KeyCount];
    bool ascending[KeyCount];
};

#endif
```

The header file ends with the `SpreadsheetCompare` class definition. We will explain this when we review `Spreadsheet::sort()`.

We will now look at the implementation:

```
#include <QtGui>

#include "cell.h"
#include "spreadsheet.h"

Spreadsheet::Spreadsheet(QWidget *parent)
    : QTableWidget(parent)
{
    autoRecalc = true;

    setItemPrototype(new Cell);
    setSelectionMode(ContiguousSelection);

    connect(this, SIGNAL(itemChanged(QTableWidgetItem *)),
            this, SLOT(somethingChanged()));

    clear();
}
```

Normally, when the user enters some text on an empty cell, the `QTableWidget` will automatically create a `QTableWidgetItem` to hold the text. In our spreadsheet, we want `Cell` items to be created instead. This is achieved by the set-ItemPrototype() call in the constructor. Internally, `QTableWidget` clones the item passed as a prototype every time a new item is required.

Also in the constructor, we set the selection mode to `QAbstractItemView::ContiguousSelection` to allow a single rectangular selection. We connect the table widget's `itemChanged()` signal to the private `somethingChanged()` slot; this ensures that when the user edits a cell, the somethingChanged() slot is called. Finally, we call clear() to resize the table and to set the column headings.

```
void Spreadsheet::clear()
{
    setRowCount(0);
    setColumnCount(0);
    setRowCount(RowCount);
    setColumnCount(ColumnCount);

    for (int i = 0; i < ColumnCount; ++i) {
        QTableWidgetItem *item = new QTableWidgetItem;
        item->setText(QString(QChar('A' + i)));
        setHorizontalHeaderItem(i, item);
    }

    setCurrentCell(0, 0);
}
```

The clear() function is called from the Spreadsheet constructor to initialize the spreadsheet. It is also called from MainWindow::newFile().

We could have used QTableWidget::clear() to clear all the items and any selections, but that would have left the headers at their current size. Instead, we resize the table down to 0 × 0. This clears the entire spreadsheet, including the headers. We then resize the table to ColumnCount × RowCount (26 × 999) and populate the horizontal header with QTableWidgetItems containing the column names "A", "B", ..., "Z". We don't need to set the vertical header labels, because these default to "1", "2", ..., "999". At the end, we move the cell cursor to cell A1.

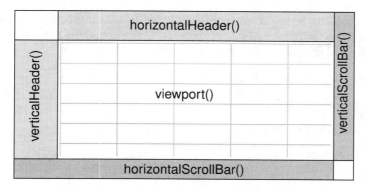

Figure 4.2. QTableWidget's constituent widgets

A QTableWidget is composed of several child widgets. It has a horizontal QHeaderView at the top, a vertical QHeaderView on the left, and two QScrollBars. The area in the middle is occupied by a special widget called the *viewport*, on which QTableWidget draws the cells. The different child widgets are accessible through functions inherited from QTableView and QAbstractScrollArea (see Figure 4.2). QAbstractScrollArea provides a scrollable viewport and two scroll bars, which can be turned on and off. Its QScrollArea subclass is covered in Chapter 6.

Storing Data as Items

In the Spreadsheet application, every non-empty cell is stored in memory as an individual `QTableWidgetItem` object. Storing data as items is an approach that is also used by `QListWidget` and `QTreeWidget`, which operate on `QListWidgetItems` and `QTreeWidgetItems`.

Qt's item classes can be used out of the box as data holders. For example, a `QTableWidgetItem` already stores a few attributes, including a string, font, color, and icon, and a pointer back to the `QTableWidget`. The items can also hold data (`QVariants`), including registered custom types, and by subclassing the item class we can provide additional functionality.

Other toolkits provide a `void` pointer in their item classes to store custom data. In Qt, the more natural approach is to use `setData()` with a `QVariant`, but if a `void` pointer is required, it can be trivially achieved by subclassing an item class and adding a `void` pointer member variable.

For more challenging data handling requirements, such as large data sets, complex data items, database integration, and multiple data views, Qt provides a set of model/view classes that separate the data from their visual representation. These are covered in Chapter 10.

```
Cell *Spreadsheet::cell(int row, int column) const
{
    return static_cast<Cell *>(item(row, column));
}
```

The `cell()` private function returns the `Cell` object for a given row and column. It is almost the same as `QTableWidget::item()`, except that it returns a `Cell` pointer instead of a `QTableWidgetItem` pointer.

```
QString Spreadsheet::text(int row, int column) const
{
    Cell *c = cell(row, column);
    if (c) {
        return c->text();
    } else {
        return "";
    }
}
```

The `text()` private function returns the text for a given cell. If `cell()` returns a null pointer, the cell is empty, so we return an empty string.

```
QString Spreadsheet::formula(int row, int column) const
{
    Cell *c = cell(row, column);
    if (c) {
        return c->formula();
    } else {
        return "";
```

```
        }
    }
```

The `formula()` function returns the cell's formula. In many cases, the formula and the text are the same; for example, the formula "Hello" evaluates to the string "Hello", so if the user types "Hello" into a cell and presses Enter, that cell will show the text "Hello". But there are a few exceptions:

- If the formula is a number, it is interpreted as such. For example, the formula "1.50" evaluates to the `double` value 1.5, which is rendered as a right-aligned "1.5" in the spreadsheet.

- If the formula starts with a single quote, the rest of the formula is interpreted as text. For example, the formula "'12345" evaluates to the string "12345".

- If the formula starts with an equals sign ('='), the formula is interpreted as an arithmetic formula. For example, if cell A1 contains "12" and cell A2 contains "6", the formula "=A1+A2" evaluates to 18.

The task of converting a formula into a value is performed by the `Cell` class. For the moment, the thing to bear in mind is that the text shown in the cell is the result of evaluating the formula, not the formula itself.

```cpp
void Spreadsheet::setFormula(int row, int column,
                             const QString &formula)
{
    Cell *c = cell(row, column);
    if (!c) {
        c = new Cell;
        setItem(row, column, c);
    }
    c->setFormula(formula);
}
```

The `setFormula()` private function sets the formula for a given cell. If the cell already has a `Cell` object, we reuse it. Otherwise, we create a new `Cell` object and call `QTableWidget::setItem()` to insert it into the table. At the end, we call the cell's own `setFormula()` function, which will cause the cell to be repainted if it's shown on screen. We don't need to worry about deleting the `Cell` object later on; `QTableWidget` takes ownership of the cell and will delete it automatically at the right time.

```cpp
QString Spreadsheet::currentLocation() const
{
    return QChar('A' + currentColumn())
           + QString::number(currentRow() + 1);
}
```

The `currentLocation()` function returns the current cell's location in the usual spreadsheet format of column letter followed by row number. `MainWindow::updateStatusBar()` uses it to show the location in the status bar.

```
QString Spreadsheet::currentFormula() const
{
    return formula(currentRow(), currentColumn());
}
```

The `currentFormula()` function returns the current cell's formula. It is called from `MainWindow::updateStatusBar()`.

```
void Spreadsheet::somethingChanged()
{
    if (autoRecalc)
        recalculate();
    emit modified();
}
```

The `somethingChanged()` private slot recalculates the whole spreadsheet if "auto-recalculate" is enabled. It also emits the `modified()` signal.

Loading and Saving

We will now implement the loading and saving of Spreadsheet files using a custom binary format. We will do this using `QFile` and `QDataStream`, which together provide platform-independent binary I/O.

We will start with writing a Spreadsheet file:

```
bool Spreadsheet::writeFile(const QString &fileName)
{
    QFile file(fileName);
    if (!file.open(QIODevice::WriteOnly)) {
        QMessageBox::warning(this, tr("Spreadsheet"),
                             tr("Cannot write file %1:\n%2.")
                             .arg(file.fileName())
                             .arg(file.errorString()));
        return false;
    }

    QDataStream out(&file);
    out.setVersion(QDataStream::Qt_4_1);

    out << quint32(MagicNumber);

    QApplication::setOverrideCursor(Qt::WaitCursor);
    for (int row = 0; row < RowCount; ++row) {
        for (int column = 0; column < ColumnCount; ++column) {
            QString str = formula(row, column);
            if (!str.isEmpty())
                out << quint16(row) << quint16(column) << str;
        }
    }
    QApplication::restoreOverrideCursor();
    return true;
}
```

The writeFile() function is called from MainWindow::saveFile() to write the file to disk. It returns true on success, false on error.

We create a QFile object with the given file name and call open() to open the file for writing. We also create a QDataStream object that operates on the QFile and use it to write out the data.

Just before we write the data, we change the application's cursor to the standard wait cursor (usually an hourglass) and restore the normal cursor once all the data is written. At the end of the function, the file is automatically closed by QFile's destructor.

QDataStream supports basic C++ types as well as many of Qt's types. The syntax is modeled after the Standard C++ <iostream> classes. For example,

```
out << x << y << z;
```

writes the variables x, y, and z to a stream, and

```
in >> x >> y >> z;
```

reads them from a stream. Because the C++ basic types char, short, int, long, and long long may have different sizes on different platforms, it is safest to cast these values to one of qint8, quint8, qint16, quint16, qint32, quint32, qint64, and quint64, which are guaranteed to be of the size they advertise (in bits).

The Spreadsheet application's file format is fairly simple. A Spreadsheet file starts with a 32-bit number that identifies the file format (MagicNumber, defined as 0x7F51C883 in spreadsheet.h, an arbitrary random number.) Then comes a series of blocks, each of which contains a single cell's row, column, and formula. To save space, we don't write out empty cells.

Figure 4.3. The Spreadsheet file format

The precise binary representation of the data types is determined by QDataStream. For example, a quint16 is stored as two bytes in big-endian order, and a QString as the string's length followed by the Unicode characters.

The binary representation of Qt types has evolved quite a lot since Qt 1.0. It is likely to continue evolving in future Qt releases to keep pace with the evolution of existing types and to allow for new Qt types. By default, QDataStream uses the most recent version of the binary format (version 7 in Qt 4.1), but it can be set to read older versions. To avoid any compatibility problems if the application is recompiled later using a newer Qt release, we explicitly tell QDataStream to use version 7 irrespective of the version of Qt we are compiling against. (QDataStream::Qt_4_1 is a convenience constant that equals 7.)

QDataStream is very versatile. It can be used on a QFile, and also on a QBuffer, a QProcess, a QTcpSocket, or a QUdpSocket. Qt also offers a QTextStream class that can be used instead of QDataStream for reading and writing text files. Chapter 12 explains these classes in depth, and also describes various approaches to handling different QDataStream versions.

```
bool Spreadsheet::readFile(const QString &fileName)
{
    QFile file(fileName);
    if (!file.open(QIODevice::ReadOnly)) {
        QMessageBox::warning(this, tr("Spreadsheet"),
                             tr("Cannot read file %1:\n%2.")
                             .arg(file.fileName())
                             .arg(file.errorString()));
        return false;
    }

    QDataStream in(&file);
    in.setVersion(QDataStream::Qt_4_1);

    quint32 magic;
    in >> magic;
    if (magic != MagicNumber) {
        QMessageBox::warning(this, tr("Spreadsheet"),
                             tr("The file is not a Spreadsheet file."));
        return false;
    }

    clear();

    quint16 row;
    quint16 column;
    QString str;

    QApplication::setOverrideCursor(Qt::WaitCursor);
    while (!in.atEnd()) {
        in >> row >> column >> str;
        setFormula(row, column, str);
    }
    QApplication::restoreOverrideCursor();
    return true;
}
```

The readFile() function is very similar to writeFile(). We use QFile to read in the file, but this time using the QIODevice::ReadOnly flag rather than QIODevice::WriteOnly. Then we set the QDataStream version to 7. The format for reading must always be the same as for writing.

If the file has the correct magic number at the beginning, we call clear() to blank out all the cells in the spreadsheet, and we read in the cell data. Since the file only contains the data for non-empty cells, and it is very unlikely that every cell in the spreadsheet will be set, we must ensure that all cells are cleared before reading.

Implementing the Edit Menu

We are now ready to implement the slots that correspond to the application's Edit menu.

```
void Spreadsheet::cut()
{
    copy();
    del();
}
```

The `cut()` slot corresponds to Edit|Cut. The implementation is simple since Cut is the same as Copy followed by Delete.

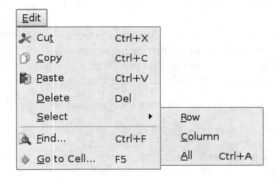

Figure 4.4. The Spreadsheet application's Edit menu

```
void Spreadsheet::copy()
{
    QTableWidgetSelectionRange range = selectedRange();
    QString str;

    for (int i = 0; i < range.rowCount(); ++i) {
        if (i > 0)
            str += "\n";
        for (int j = 0; j < range.columnCount(); ++j) {
            if (j > 0)
                str += "\t";
            str += formula(range.topRow() + i, range.leftColumn() + j);
        }
    }
    QApplication::clipboard()->setText(str);
}
```

The `copy()` slot corresponds to Edit|Copy. It iterates over the current selection (which is simply the current cell if there is no explicit selection). Each selected cell's formula is added to a `QString`, with rows separated by newline characters and columns separated by tab characters.

The system clipboard is available in Qt through the `QApplication::clipboard()` static function. By calling `QClipboard::setText()`, we make the text available on the clipboard, both to this application and to other applications that support plain text. Our format with tab and newline characters as separators is understood by a variety of applications, including Microsoft Excel.

"Red\t Green\t Blue\n Cyan\t Magenta\t Yellow"

Figure 4.5. Copying a selection onto the clipboard

The `QTableWidget::selectedRanges()` function returns a list of selection ranges. We know there cannot be more than one because we set the selection mode to `QAbstractItemView::ContiguousSelection` in the constructor. For our convenience, we define a `selectedRange()` function that returns the selection range:

```
QTableWidgetSelectionRange Spreadsheet::selectedRange() const
{
    QList<QTableWidgetSelectionRange> ranges = selectedRanges();
    if (ranges.isEmpty())
        return QTableWidgetSelectionRange();
    return ranges.first();
}
```

If there is a selection at all, we simply return the first (and only) one. The case where there is no selection should never happen since the `ContiguousSelection` mode treats the current cell as being selected. But to protect against the possibility of a bug in our program that makes no cell current, we handle this case.

```
void Spreadsheet::paste()
{
    QTableWidgetSelectionRange range = selectedRange();
    QString str = QApplication::clipboard()->text();
    QStringList rows = str.split('\n');
    int numRows = rows.count();
    int numColumns = rows.first().count('\t') + 1;

    if (range.rowCount() * range.columnCount() != 1
            && (range.rowCount() != numRows
                || range.columnCount() != numColumns)) {
        QMessageBox::information(this, tr("Spreadsheet"),
                tr("The information cannot be pasted because the copy "
                    "and paste areas aren't the same size."));
        return;
    }

    for (int i = 0; i < numRows; ++i) {
        QStringList columns = rows[i].split('\t');
        for (int j = 0; j < numColumns; ++j) {
```

```
                int row = range.topRow() + i;
                int column = range.leftColumn() + j;
                if (row < RowCount && column < ColumnCount)
                    setFormula(row, column, columns[j]);
            }
        }
        somethingChanged();
    }
```

The paste() slot corresponds to Edit|Paste. We fetch the text on the clipboard and call the static function QString::split() to break the string into a QStringList. Each row becomes one string in the list.

Next, we determine the dimension of the copy area. The number of rows is the number of strings in the QStringList; the number of columns is the number of tab characters in the first row, plus 1. If only one cell is selected, we use that cell as the top-left corner of the paste area; otherwise, we use the current selection as the paste area.

To perform the paste, we iterate over the rows and split each of them into cells by using QString::split() again, but this time using tab as the separator. Figure 4.6 illustrates the steps.

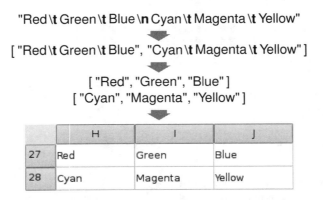

Figure 4.6. Pasting clipboard text into the spreadsheet

```
void Spreadsheet::del()
{
    foreach (QTableWidgetItem *item, selectedItems())
        delete item;
}
```

The del() slot corresponds to Edit|Delete. It is sufficient to use delete on each of the Cell objects in the selection to clear the cells. The QTableWidget notices when its QTableWidgetItems are deleted and automatically repaints itself if any of the items were visible. If we call cell() with the location of a deleted cell, it will return a null pointer.

```
void Spreadsheet::selectCurrentRow()
{
    selectRow(currentRow());
}

void Spreadsheet::selectCurrentColumn()
{
    selectColumn(currentColumn());
}
```

The selectCurrentRow() and selectCurrentColumn() functions correspond to the Edit|Select|Row and Edit|Select|Column menu options. The implementations rely on QTableWidget's selectRow() and selectColumn() functions. We do not need to implement the functionality behind Edit|Select|All, since that is provided by QTableWidget's inherited function QAbstractItemView::selectAll().

```
void Spreadsheet::findNext(const QString &str, Qt::CaseSensitivity cs)
{
    int row = currentRow();
    int column = currentColumn() + 1;

    while (row < RowCount) {
        while (column < ColumnCount) {
            if (text(row, column).contains(str, cs)) {
                clearSelection();
                setCurrentCell(row, column);
                activateWindow();
                return;
            }
            ++column;
        }
        column = 0;
        ++row;
    }
    QApplication::beep();
}
```

The findNext() slot iterates through the cells starting from the cell to the right of the cursor and moving right until the last column is reached, then continues from the first column in the row below, and so on until the text is found or until the very last cell is reached. For example, if the current cell is cell C24, we search D24, E24, ..., Z24, then A25, B25, C25, ..., Z25, and so on until Z999. If we find a match, we clear the current selection, move the cell cursor to the cell that matched, and make the window that contains the Spreadsheet active. If no match is found, we make the application beep to indicate that the search finished unsuccessfully.

```
void Spreadsheet::findPrevious(const QString &str,
                               Qt::CaseSensitivity cs)
{
    int row = currentRow();
    int column = currentColumn() - 1;

    while (row >= 0) {
```

```
            while (column >= 0) {
                if (text(row, column).contains(str, cs)) {
                    clearSelection();
                    setCurrentCell(row, column);
                    activateWindow();
                    return;
                }
                --column;
            }
            column = ColumnCount - 1;
            --row;
        }
        QApplication::beep();
    }
```

The findPrevious() slot is similar to findNext(), except that it iterates backward and stops at cell A1.

Implementing the Other Menus

We will now implement the slots for the Tools and Options menus.

Figure 4.7. The Spreadsheet application's Tools and Options menus

```
void Spreadsheet::recalculate()
{
    for (int row = 0; row < RowCount; ++row) {
        for (int column = 0; column < ColumnCount; ++column) {
            if (cell(row, column))
                cell(row, column)->setDirty();
        }
    }
    viewport()->update();
}
```

The recalculate() slot corresponds to Tools|Recalculate. It is also called automatically by Spreadsheet when necessary.

We iterate over all the cells and call setDirty() on every cell to mark each one as requiring recalculation. The next time QTableWidget calls text() on a Cell to obtain the value to show in the spreadsheet, the value will be recalculated.

Then we call update() on the viewport to repaint the whole spreadsheet. The repaint code in QTableWidget then calls text() on each visible cell to obtain the value to display. Because we called setDirty() on every cell, the calls to text() will use a freshly calculated value. The calculation may require non-visible cells to be recalculated, cascading the calculation until every cell that needs to be recalculated to display the correct text in the viewport has been freshly calculated. The calculation is performed by the `Cell` class.

```
void Spreadsheet::setAutoRecalculate(bool recalc)
{
    autoRecalc = recalc;
    if (autoRecalc)
        recalculate();
}
```

The `setAutoRecalculate()` slot corresponds to Options|Auto-Recalculate. If the feature is being turned on, we recalculate the whole spreadsheet immediately to make sure that it's up to date; afterward, `recalculate()` is called automatically from `somethingChanged()`.

We don't need to implement anything for Options|Show Grid because `QTableWidget` already has a `setShowGrid()` slot, which it inherits from its base class `QTableView`. All that remains is `Spreadsheet::sort()`, which is called from `MainWindow::sort()`:

```
void Spreadsheet::sort(const SpreadsheetCompare &compare)
{
    QList<QStringList> rows;
    QTableWidgetSelectionRange range = selectedRange();
    int i;

    for (i = 0; i < range.rowCount(); ++i) {
        QStringList row;
        for (int j = 0; j < range.columnCount(); ++j)
            row.append(formula(range.topRow() + i,
                               range.leftColumn() + j));
        rows.append(row);
    }

    qStableSort(rows.begin(), rows.end(), compare);

    for (i = 0; i < range.rowCount(); ++i) {
        for (int j = 0; j < range.columnCount(); ++j)
            setFormula(range.topRow() + i, range.leftColumn() + j,
                       rows[i][j]);
    }

    clearSelection();
    somethingChanged();
}
```

Sorting operates on the current selection and reorders the rows according to the sort keys and sort orders stored in the `compare` object. We represent each row of data with a `QStringList` and store the selection as a list of rows. We use Qt's `qStableSort()` algorithm, and for simplicity sort by formula rather than by value. Qt's standard algorithms and data structures are covered in Chapter 11 (Container Classes).

	C	D	E
2	Edsger	Dijkstra	1930-05-11
3	Tony	Hoare	1934-01-11
4	Niklaus	Wirth	1934-02-15
5	Donald	Knuth	1938-01-10

index	value
0	["Edsger", "Dijkstra", "1930-05-11"]
1	["Tony", "Hoare", "1934-01-11"]
2	["Niklaus", "Wirth", "1934-02-15"]
3	["Donald", "Knuth", "1938-01-10"]

Figure 4.8. Storing the selection as a list of rows

The `qStableSort()` function accepts a begin iterator, an end iterator, and a comparison function. The comparison function is a function that takes two arguments (two `QStringLists`) and that returns `true` if the first argument is "less than" the second argument, `false` otherwise. The `compare` object we pass as the comparison function isn't really a function, but it can be used as one, as we will see shortly.

index	value
0	["Donald", "Knuth", "1938-01-10"]
1	["Edsger", "Dijkstra", "1930-05-11"]
2	["Niklaus", "Wirth", "1934-02-15"]
3	["Tony", "Hoare", "1934-01-11"]

	C	D	E
2	Donald	Knuth	1938-01-10
3	Edsger	Dijkstra	1930-05-11
4	Niklaus	Wirth	1934-02-15
5	Tony	Hoare	1934-01-11

Figure 4.9. Putting the data back into the table after sorting

After performing the `qStableSort()`, we move the data back into the table, clear the selection, and call `somethingChanged()`.

In `spreadsheet.h`, the `SpreadsheetCompare` class was defined like this:

```
class SpreadsheetCompare
{
public:
    bool operator()(const QStringList &row1,
                    const QStringList &row2) const;

    enum { KeyCount = 3 };
    int keys[KeyCount];
    bool ascending[KeyCount];
};
```

The `SpreadsheetCompare` class is special because it implements a `()` operator. This allows us to use the class as if it were a function. Such classes are called function objects, or functors. To understand how functors work, we will start with a simple example:

```
class Square
{
public:
    int operator()(int x) const { return x * x; }
}
```

The `Square` class provides one function, `operator()(int)`, that returns the square of its parameter. By naming the function `operator()(int)` rather than, say, `compute(int)`, we gain the capability of using an object of type `Square` as if it were a function:

```
Square square;
int y = square(5);
```

Now let's see an example involving `SpreadsheetCompare`:

```
QStringList row1, row2;
QSpreadsheetCompare compare;
...
if (compare(row1, row2)) {
    // row1 is less than row2
}
```

The `compare` object can be used just as if it had been a plain `compare()` function. Additionally, its implementation can access all the sort keys and sort orders, which are stored as member variables.

An alternative to this scheme would have been to store the sort keys and sort orders in global variables and use a plain `compare()` function. However, communicating through global variables is inelegant and can lead to subtle bugs. Functors are a more powerful idiom for interfacing with template functions such as `qStableSort()`.

Here is the implementation of the function that is used to compare two spreadsheet rows:

```
bool SpreadsheetCompare::operator()(const QStringList &row1,
                                    const QStringList &row2) const
{
    for (int i = 0; i < KeyCount; ++i) {
        int column = keys[i];
        if (column != -1) {
            if (row1[column] != row2[column]) {
                if (ascending[i]) {
                    return row1[column] < row2[column];
                } else {
                    return row1[column] > row2[column];
                }
            }
        }
    }
    return false;
}
```

The operator returns `true` if the first row is less than the second row; otherwise, it returns `false`. The `qStableSort()` function uses the result of this function to perform the sort.

The SpreadsheetCompare object's keys and ascending arrays are populated in the MainWindow::sort() function (shown in Chapter 2). Each key holds a column index, or –1 ("None").

We compare the corresponding cell entries in the two rows for each key in order. As soon as we find a difference, we return an appropriate true or false value. If all the comparisons turn out to be equal, we return false. The qStableSort() function uses the order before the sort to resolve tie situations; if row1 preceded row2 originally and neither compares as "less than" the other, row1 will still precede row2 in the result. This is what distinguishes qStableSort() from its unstable cousin qSort().

We have now completed the Spreadsheet class. In the next section, we will review the Cell class. This class is used to hold cell formulas and provides a reimplementation of the QTableWidgetItem::data() function that Spreadsheet calls indirectly, through the QTableWidgetItem::text() function, to display the result of calculating a cell's formula.

Subclassing QTableWidgetItem

The Cell class inherits from QTableWidgetItem. The class is designed to work well with Spreadsheet, but it has no specific dependencies on that class and could in theory be used in any QTableWidget. Here's the header file:

```
#ifndef CELL_H
#define CELL_H

#include <QTableWidgetItem>

class Cell : public QTableWidgetItem
{
public:
    Cell();

    QTableWidgetItem *clone() const;
    void setData(int role, const QVariant &value);
    QVariant data(int role) const;
    void setFormula(const QString &formula);
    QString formula() const;
    void setDirty();

private:
    QVariant value() const;
    QVariant evalExpression(const QString &str, int &pos) const;
    QVariant evalTerm(const QString &str, int &pos) const;
    QVariant evalFactor(const QString &str, int &pos) const;

    mutable QVariant cachedValue;
    mutable bool cacheIsDirty;
};

#endif
```

The `Cell` class extends `QTableWidgetItem` by adding two private variables:

- `cachedValue` caches the cell's value as a `QVariant`.
- `cacheIsDirty` is `true` if the cached value isn't up to date.

We use `QVariant` because some cells have a `double` value, while others have a `QString` value.

The `cachedValue` and `cacheIsDirty` variables are declared with the C++ `mutable` keyword. This allows us to modify these variables in const functions. Alternatively, we could recalculate the value each time `text()` is called, but that would be needlessly inefficient.

Notice that there is no `Q_OBJECT` macro in the class definition. `Cell` is a plain C++ class, with no signals or slots. In fact, because `QTableWidgetItem` doesn't inherit from `QObject`, we cannot have signals and slots in `Cell` as it stands. Qt's item classes don't inherit from `QObject` to keep their overhead to the barest minimum. If signals and slots are needed, they can be implemented in the widget that contains the items or, exceptionally, using multiple inheritance with `QObject`.

Here's the start of `cell.cpp`:

```
#include <QtGui>

#include "cell.h"

Cell::Cell()
{
    setDirty();
}
```

In the constructor, we only need to set the cache as dirty. There is no need to pass a parent; when the cell is inserted into a `QTableWidget` with `setItem()`, the `QTableWidget` will automatically take ownership of it.

Every `QTableWidgetItem` can hold some data, up to one `QVariant` for each data "role". The most commonly used roles are `Qt::EditRole` and `Qt::DisplayRole`. The edit role is used for data that is to be edited, and the display role is for data that is to be displayed. Often the data for both is the same, but in `Cell` the edit role corresponds to the cell's formula and the display role corresponds to the cell's value (the result of evaluating the formula).

```
QTableWidgetItem *Cell::clone() const
{
    return new Cell(*this);
}
```

The `clone()` function is called by `QTableWidget` when it needs to create a new cell—for example, when the user starts typing into an empty cell that has not been used before. The instance passed to `QTableWidget::setItemPrototype()` is the item that is cloned. Since member-wise copying is sufficient for `Cell`, we are relying on the default copy constructor automatically created by C++ to create new `Cell` instances in the `clone()` function.

```
void Cell::setFormula(const QString &formula)
{
    setData(Qt::EditRole, formula);
}
```

The `setFormula()` function sets the cell's formula. It is simply a convenience function for calling `setData()` with the edit role. It is called from `Spreadsheet::setFormula()`.

```
QString Cell::formula() const
{
    return data(Qt::EditRole).toString();
}
```

The `formula()` function is called from `Spreadsheet::formula()`. Like `setFormula()` it is a convenience function, this time retrieving the item's `EditRole` data.

```
void Cell::setData(int role, const QVariant &value)
{
    QTableWidgetItem::setData(role, value);
    if (role == Qt::EditRole)
        setDirty();
}
```

If we have a new formula, we set `cacheIsDirty` to `true` to ensure that the cell is recalculated the next time `text()` is called.

There is no `text()` function defined in `Cell`, although we call `text()` on `Cell` instances in `Spreadsheet::text()`. The `text()` function is a convenience function provided by `QTableWidgetItem`; it is the equivalent of calling `data(Qt::DisplayRole).toString()`.

```
void Cell::setDirty()
{
    cacheIsDirty = true;
}
```

The `setDirty()` function is called to force a recalculation of the cell's value. It simply sets `cacheIsDirty` to `true`, meaning that `cachedValue` is no longer up to date. The recalculation isn't performed until it is necessary.

```
QVariant Cell::data(int role) const
{
    if (role == Qt::DisplayRole) {
        if (value().isValid()) {
            return value().toString();
        } else {
            return "####";
        }
    } else if (role == Qt::TextAlignmentRole) {
        if (value().type() == QVariant::String) {
            return int(Qt::AlignLeft | Qt::AlignVCenter);
```

```
        } else {
            return int(Qt::AlignRight | Qt::AlignVCenter);
        }
    } else {
        return QTableWidgetItem::data(role);
    }
}
```

The data() function is reimplemented from QTableWidgetItem. It returns the text that should be shown in the spreadsheet if called with Qt::DisplayRole, and the formula if called with Qt::EditRole. It returns a suitable alignment if called with Qt::TextAlignmentRole. In the DisplayRole case, it relies on value() to compute the cell's value. If the value is invalid (because the formula is wrong), we return "####".

The Cell::value() function used in data() returns a QVariant. A QVariant can store values of different types, such as double and QString, and provides functions to convert the variant to other types. For example, calling toString() on a variant that holds a double value produces a string representation of the double. A QVariant constructed using the default constructor is an "invalid" variant.

```
const QVariant Invalid;

QVariant Cell::value() const
{
    if (cacheIsDirty) {
        cacheIsDirty = false;

        QString formulaStr = formula();
        if (formulaStr.startsWith('\'')) {
            cachedValue = formulaStr.mid(1);
        } else if (formulaStr.startsWith('=')) {
            cachedValue = Invalid;
            QString expr = formulaStr.mid(1);
            expr.replace(" ", "");
            expr.append(QChar::Null);

            int pos = 0;
            cachedValue = evalExpression(expr, pos);
            if (expr[pos] != QChar::Null)
                cachedValue = Invalid;
        } else {
            bool ok;
            double d = formulaStr.toDouble(&ok);
            if (ok) {
                cachedValue = d;
            } else {
                cachedValue = formulaStr;
            }
        }
    }
    return cachedValue;
}
```

The value() private function returns the cell's value. If cacheIsDirty is true, we need to recalculate the value.

If the formula starts with a single quote (for example, "'12345"), the single quote occupies position 0 and the value is the string from position 1 to the end.

If the formula starts with an equals sign ('='), we take the string from position 1 and remove any spaces it may contain. Then we call evalExpression() to compute the value of the expression. The pos argument is passed by reference; it indicates the position of the character where parsing should begin. After the call to evalExpression(), the character at position pos should be the QChar::Null character we appended, if it was successfully parsed. If the parse failed before the end, we set cachedValue to be Invalid.

If the formula doesn't begin with a single quote or an equals sign, we attempt to convert it to a floating-point value using toDouble(). If the conversion works, we set cachedValue to be the resulting number; otherwise, we set cachedValue to be the formula string. For example, a formula of "1.50" causes toDouble() to set ok to true and return 1.5, while a formula of "World Population" causes toDouble() to set ok to false and return 0.0.

By giving toDouble() a pointer to a bool, we are able to distinguish between the conversion of a string that represents the numeric value 0.0 and a conversion error (where 0.0 is also returned but the bool is set to false). Sometimes the returning of a zero value on conversion failure is exactly what we need, in which case we do not bother passing a pointer to a bool. For performance and portability reasons, Qt never uses C++ exceptions to report failure. This doesn't prevent you from using them in Qt programs, providing your compiler supports them.

The value() function is declared const. We had to declare cachedValue and cacheIsValid as mutable variables so that the compiler will allow us to modify them in const functions. It might be tempting to make value() non-const and remove the mutable keywords, but that would not compile because we call value() from data(), a const function.

We have now completed the Spreadsheet application, apart from parsing formulas. The rest of this section covers evalExpression() and the two helper functions evalTerm() and evalFactor(). The code is a bit complicated, but it is included here to make the application complete. Since the code is not related to GUI programming, you can safely skip it and continue reading from Chapter 5.

The evalExpression() function returns the value of a spreadsheet expression. An expression is defined as one or more terms separated by '+' or '–' operators. The terms themselves are defined as one or more factors separated by '*' or '/' operators. By breaking down expressions into terms and terms into factors, we ensure that the operators are applied with the correct precedence.

For example, "2∗C5+D6" is an expression with "2∗C5" as its first term and "D6" as its second term. The term "2∗C5" has "2" as its first factor and "C5" as its second factor, and the term "D6" consists of the single factor "D6". A factor can be a number ("2"), a cell location ("C5"), or an expression in parentheses, optionally preceded by a unary minus.

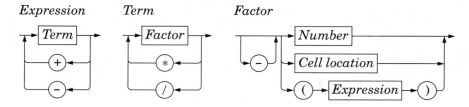

Figure 4.10. Syntax diagram for spreadsheet expressions

The syntax of spreadsheet expressions is defined in Figure 4.10. For each symbol in the grammar (*Expression, Term,* and *Factor*), there is a corresponding member function that parses it and whose structure closely follows the grammar. Parsers written this way are called recursive-descent parsers.

Let's start with evalExpression(), the function that parses an *Expression*:

```
QVariant Cell::evalExpression(const QString &str, int &pos) const
{
    QVariant result = evalTerm(str, pos);
    while (str[pos] != QChar::Null) {
        QChar op = str[pos];
        if (op != '+' && op != '-')
            return result;
        ++pos;

        QVariant term = evalTerm(str, pos);
        if (result.type() == QVariant::Double
                && term.type() == QVariant::Double) {
            if (op == '+') {
                result = result.toDouble() + term.toDouble();
            } else {
                result = result.toDouble() - term.toDouble();
            }
        } else {
            result = Invalid;
        }
    }
    return result;
}
```

First, we call evalTerm() to get the value of the first term. If the following character is '+' or '−', we continue by calling evalTerm() a second time; otherwise, the expression consists of a single term, and we return its value as the value of the whole expression. After we have the value of the first two terms, we compute the result of the operation, depending on the operator. If both terms evaluated to a double, we compute the result as a double; otherwise, we set the result to be Invalid.

We continue like this until there are no more terms. This works correctly because addition and subtraction are left-associative; that is, "1–2–3" means "(1–2)–3", not "1–(2–3)".

```cpp
QVariant Cell::evalTerm(const QString &str, int &pos) const
{
    QVariant result = evalFactor(str, pos);
    while (str[pos] != QChar::Null) {
        QChar op = str[pos];
        if (op != '*' && op != '/')
            return result;
        ++pos;

        QVariant factor = evalFactor(str, pos);
        if (result.type() == QVariant::Double
                && factor.type() == QVariant::Double) {
            if (op == '*') {
                result = result.toDouble() * factor.toDouble();
            } else {
                if (factor.toDouble() == 0.0) {
                    result = Invalid;
                } else {
                    result = result.toDouble() / factor.toDouble();
                }
            }
        } else {
            result = Invalid;
        }
    }
    return result;
}
```

The evalTerm() function is very similar to evalExpression(), except that it deals with multiplication and division. The only subtlety in evalTerm() is that we must avoid division by zero, since it is an error on some processors. While it is generally inadvisable to test floating-point values for equality because of rounding errors, it is safe to test for equality against 0.0 to prevent division by zero.

```cpp
QVariant Cell::evalFactor(const QString &str, int &pos) const
{
    QVariant result;
    bool negative = false;

    if (str[pos] == '-') {
        negative = true;
        ++pos;
    }

    if (str[pos] == '(') {
        ++pos;
        result = evalExpression(str, pos);
```

```
            if (str[pos] != ')')
                result = Invalid;
            ++pos;
        } else {
            QRegExp regExp("[A-Za-z][1-9][0-9]{0,2}");
            QString token;

            while (str[pos].isLetterOrNumber() || str[pos] == '.') {
                token += str[pos];
                ++pos;
            }

            if (regExp.exactMatch(token)) {
                int column = token[0].toUpper().unicode() - 'A';
                int row = token.mid(1).toInt() - 1;

                Cell *c = static_cast<Cell *>(
                                    tableWidget()->item(row, column));
                if (c) {
                    result = c->value();
                } else {
                    result = 0.0;
                }
            } else {
                bool ok;
                result = token.toDouble(&ok);
                if (!ok)
                    result = Invalid;
            }
        }

        if (negative) {
            if (result.type() == QVariant::Double) {
                result = -result.toDouble();
            } else {
                result = Invalid;
            }
        }
        return result;
    }
```

The evalFactor() function is a bit more complicated than evalExpression() and evalTerm(). We start by noting whether the factor is negated. We then see if it begins with an open parenthesis. If it does, we evaluate the contents of the parentheses as an expression by calling evalExpression(). When parsing a parenthesized expression, evalExpression() calls evalTerm(), which calls eval-Factor(), which calls evalExpression() again. This is where recursion occurs in the parser.

If the factor isn't a nested expression, we extract the next token, which should be a cell location or a number. If the token matches the QRegExp, we take it to be a cell reference and we call value() on the cell at the given location. The cell could be anywhere in the spreadsheet, and it could have dependencies on other cells. The dependencies are not a problem; they will simply trigger more `value()` calls and (for "dirty" cells) more parsing until all the dependent cell values are calculated. If the token isn't a cell location, we take it to be a number.

What happens if cell A1 contains the formula "=A1"? Or if cell A1 contains "=A2" and cell A2 contains "=A1"? Although we have not written any special code to detect circular dependencies, the parser handles these cases gracefully by returning an invalid `QVariant`. This works because we set `cacheIsDirty` to `false` and `cachedValue` to `Invalid` in `value()` before we call `evalExpression()`. If `evalExpression()` recursively calls `value()` on the same cell, it returns `Invalid` immediately, and the whole expression then evaluates to `Invalid`.

We have now completed the formula parser. It would be straightforward to extend it to handle predefined spreadsheet functions, like "sum()" and "avg()", by extending the grammatical definition of *Factor*. Another easy extension is to implement the '+' operator with string operands (as concatenation); this requires no changes to the grammar.

5. Creating Custom Widgets

This chapter explains how to develop custom widgets using Qt. Custom widgets can be created by subclassing an existing Qt widget or by subclassing `QWidget` directly. We will demonstrate both approaches, and we will also see how to integrate a custom widget with *Qt Designer* so that it can be used just like a built-in Qt widget. We will round off the chapter by presenting a custom widget that uses double buffering, a powerful technique for high-speed drawing.

Customizing Qt Widgets

In some cases, we find that a Qt widget requires more customization than is possible by setting its properties in *Qt Designer* or by calling its functions. A simple and direct solution is to subclass the relevant widget class and adapt it to suit our needs.

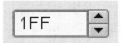

Figure 5.1. The `HexSpinBox` widget

In this section, we will develop a hexadecimal spin box to show how this works. `QSpinBox` only supports decimal integers, but by subclassing it's quite easy to make it accept and display hexadecimal values.

```
#ifndef HEXSPINBOX_H
#define HEXSPINBOX_H

#include <QSpinBox>

class QRegExpValidator;

class HexSpinBox : public QSpinBox
{
    Q_OBJECT
```

```
public:
    HexSpinBox(QWidget *parent = 0);

protected:
    QValidator::State validate(QString &text, int &pos) const;
    int valueFromText(const QString &text) const;
    QString textFromValue(int value) const;

private:
    QRegExpValidator *validator;
};

#endif
```

The HexSpinBox inherits most of its functionality from QSpinBox. It provides a typical constructor and reimplements three virtual functions from QSpinBox.

```
#include <QtGui>

#include "hexspinbox.h"

HexSpinBox::HexSpinBox(QWidget *parent)
    : QSpinBox(parent)
{
    setRange(0, 255);
    validator = new QRegExpValidator(QRegExp("[0-9A-Fa-f]{1,8}"), this);
}
```

We set the default range to be 0 to 255 (0x00 to 0xFF), which is more appropriate for a hexadecimal spin box than QSpinBox's default of 0 to 99.

The user can modify a spin box's current value either by clicking its up and down arrows or by typing a value into the spin box's line editor. In the latter case, we want to restrict the user's input to legitimate hexadecimal numbers. To achieve this, we use a QRegExpValidator that accepts between one and eight characters, each of which must be in one of the sets, '0' to '9', 'A' to 'F', and 'a' to 'f'.

```
QValidator::State HexSpinBox::validate(QString &text, int &pos) const
{
    return validator->validate(text, pos);
}
```

This function is called by QSpinBox to see if the text entered so far is valid. There are three possible results: Invalid (the text doesn't match the regular expression), Intermediate (the text is a plausible part of a valid value), and Acceptable (the text is valid). The QRegExpValidator has a suitable validate() function, so we simply return the result of calling it. In theory, we should return Invalid or Intermediate for values that lie outside the spin box's range, but QSpinBox is smart enough to detect that condition without any help.

```
QString HexSpinBox::textFromValue(int value) const
{
    return QString::number(value, 16).toUpper();
}
```

The `textFromValue()` function converts an integer value to a string. `QSpinBox` calls it to update the editor part of the spin box when the user presses the spin box's up or down arrows. We use the static function `QString::number()` with a second argument of 16 to convert the value to lowercase hexadecimal, and call `QString::toUpper()` on the result to make it uppercase.

```
int HexSpinBox::valueFromText(const QString &text) const
{
    bool ok;
    return text.toInt(&ok, 16);
}
```

The `valueFromText()` function performs the reverse conversion, from a string to an integer value. It is called by `QSpinBox` when the user types a value into the editor part of the spin box and presses Enter. We use the `QString::toInt()` function to attempt to convert the current text to an integer value, again using base 16. If the string is not valid hexadecimal, `ok` is set to `false` and `toInt()` returns 0. Here, we don't have to consider this possibility because the validator only permits valid hexadecimal strings to be entered. Instead of passing the address of a dummy variable (`ok`), we could instead pass a null pointer as the first argument to `toInt()`.

We have now finished the hexadecimal spin box. Customizing other Qt widgets follows the same pattern: Pick a suitable Qt widget, subclass it, and reimplement some virtual functions to change its behavior.

Subclassing QWidget

Many custom widgets are simply a combination of existing widgets, whether they are built-in Qt widgets or other custom widgets such as `HexSpinBox`. Custom widgets that are built by composing existing widgets can usually be developed in *Qt Designer*:

- Create a new form using the "Widget" template.
- Add the necessary widgets to the form, and lay them out.
- Set up the signals and slots connections.
- If behavior beyond what can be achieved through signals and slots is required, write the necessary code in a class that inherits both `QWidget` and the uic-generated class.

Naturally, combining existing widgets can also be done entirely in code. Whichever approach is taken, the resulting class inherits directly from `QWidget`.

If the widget has no signals and slots of its own and doesn't reimplement any virtual functions, it is even possible to simply assemble the widget by combining existing widgets without a subclass. That's the approach we used in Chapter 1 to create the Age application, with a `QWidget`, a `QSpinBox`, and a

QSlider. Even so, we could just as easily have subclassed QWidget and created the QSpinBox and QSlider in the subclass's constructor.

When none of Qt's widgets are suitable for the task at hand, and when there's no way to combine or adapt existing widgets to obtain the desired result, we can still create the widget we want. This is achieved by subclassing QWidget and reimplementing a few event handlers to paint the widget and to respond to mouse clicks. This approach gives us complete freedom to define and control both the appearance and the behavior of our widget. Qt's built-in widgets, like QLabel, QPushButton, and QTableWidget, are implemented this way. If they didn't exist in Qt, it would still be possible to create them ourselves using the public functions provided by QWidget in a completely platform-independent manner.

To demonstrate how to write a custom widget using this approach, we will create the IconEditor widget shown in Figure 5.2. The IconEditor is a widget that could be used in an icon editing program.

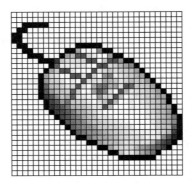

Figure 5.2. The IconEditor widget

Let's begin by reviewing the header file.

```
#ifndef ICONEDITOR_H
#define ICONEDITOR_H

#include <QColor>
#include <QImage>
#include <QWidget>

class IconEditor : public QWidget
{
    Q_OBJECT
    Q_PROPERTY(QColor penColor READ penColor WRITE setPenColor)
    Q_PROPERTY(QImage iconImage READ iconImage WRITE setIconImage)
    Q_PROPERTY(int zoomFactor READ zoomFactor WRITE setZoomFactor)

public:
    IconEditor(QWidget *parent = 0);

    void setPenColor(const QColor &newColor);
    QColor penColor() const { return curColor; }
```

```
    void setZoomFactor(int newZoom);
    int zoomFactor() const { return zoom; }
    void setIconImage(const QImage &newImage);
    QImage iconImage() const { return image; }
    QSize sizeHint() const;
```

The IconEditor class uses the Q_PROPERTY() macro to declare three custom properties: penColor, iconImage, and zoomFactor. Each property has a data type, a "read" function, and an optional "write" function. For example, the penColor property is of type QColor and can be read and written using the penColor() and setPenColor() functions.

When we make use of the widget in *Qt Designer*, custom properties appear in *Qt Designer's* property editor below the properties inherited from QWidget. Properties may be of any type supported by QVariant. The Q_OBJECT macro is necessary for classes that define properties.

```
protected:
    void mousePressEvent(QMouseEvent *event);
    void mouseMoveEvent(QMouseEvent *event);
    void paintEvent(QPaintEvent *event);

private:
    void setImagePixel(const QPoint &pos, bool opaque);
    QRect pixelRect(int i, int j) const;

    QColor curColor;
    QImage image;
    int zoom;
};

#endif
```

IconEditor reimplements three protected functions from QWidget and has a few private functions and variables. The three private variables hold the values of the three properties.

The implementation file begins with the IconEditor's constructor:

```
#include <QtGui>

#include "iconeditor.h"

IconEditor::IconEditor(QWidget *parent)
    : QWidget(parent)
{
    setAttribute(Qt::WA_StaticContents);
    setSizePolicy(QSizePolicy::Minimum, QSizePolicy::Minimum);

    curColor = Qt::black;
    zoom = 8;

    image = QImage(16, 16, QImage::Format_ARGB32);
    image.fill(qRgba(0, 0, 0, 0));
}
```

The constructor has some subtle aspects such as the `Qt::WA_StaticContents` attribute and the `setSizePolicy()` call. We will discuss them shortly.

The pen color is set to black. The zoom factor is set to 8, meaning that each pixel in the icon will be rendered as an 8×8 square.

The icon data is stored in the `image` member variable and can be accessed through the `setIconImage()` and `iconImage()` functions. An icon editor program would typically call `setIconImage()` when the user opens an icon file and `iconImage()` to retrieve the icon when the user wants to save it. The `image` variable is of type `QImage`. We initialize it to 16×16 pixels and 32-bit ARGB format, a format that supports semi-transparency. We clear the image data by filling it with a transparent color.

The `QImage` class stores an image in a hardware-independent fashion. It can be set to use a 1-bit, 8-bit, or 32-bit depth. An image with 32-bit depth uses 8 bits for each of the red, green, and blue components of a pixel. The remaining 8 bits store the pixel's alpha component (opacity). For example, a pure red color's red, green, blue, and alpha components have the values 255, 0, 0, and 255. In Qt, this color can be specified as

```
QRgb red = qRgba(255, 0, 0, 255);
```

or, since the color is opaque, as

```
QRgb red = qRgb(255, 0, 0);
```

`QRgb` is simply a typedef for `unsigned int`, and `qRgb()` and `qRgba()` are inline functions that combine their arguments into one 32-bit integer value. It is also possible to write

```
QRgb red = 0xFFFF0000;
```

where the first `FF` corresponds to the alpha component and the second `FF` to the red component. In the `IconEditor` constructor, we fill the `QImage` with a transparent color by using 0 as the alpha component.

Qt provides two types for storing colors: `QRgb` and `QColor`. While `QRgb` is only a typedef used in `QImage` to store 32-bit pixel data, `QColor` is a class with many useful functions and is widely used in Qt to store colors. In the `IconEditor` widget, we only use `QRgb` when dealing with the `QImage`; we use `QColor` for everything else, including the `penColor` property.

```
QSize IconEditor::sizeHint() const
{
    QSize size = zoom * image.size();
    if (zoom >= 3)
        size += QSize(1, 1);
    return size;
}
```

The `sizeHint()` function is reimplemented from `QWidget` and returns the ideal size of a widget. Here, we take the image size multiplied by the zoom factor, with one extra pixel in each direction to accommodate a grid if the zoom factor is 3 or more. (We don't show a grid if the zoom factor is 2 or 1, because the grid would then hardly leave any room for the icon's pixels.)

A widget's size hint is mostly useful in conjunction with layouts. Qt's layout managers try as much as possible to respect a widget's size hint when they lay out a form's child widgets. For `IconEditor` to be a good layout citizen, it must report a credible size hint.

In addition to the size hint, widgets have a size policy that tells the layout system whether they like to be stretched and shrunk. By calling `setSizePolicy()` in the constructor with `QSizePolicy::Minimum` as horizontal and vertical policies, we tell any layout manager that is responsible for this widget that the widget's size hint is really its minimum size. In other words, the widget can be stretched if required, but it should never shrink below the size hint. This can be overridden in *Qt Designer* by setting the widget's `sizePolicy` property. The meaning of the various size policies is explained in Chapter 6 (Layout Management).

```cpp
void IconEditor::setPenColor(const QColor &newColor)
{
    curColor = newColor;
}
```

The `setPenColor()` function sets the current pen color. The color will be used for newly drawn pixels.

```cpp
void IconEditor::setIconImage(const QImage &newImage)
{
    if (newImage != image) {
        image = newImage.convertToFormat(QImage::Format_ARGB32);
        update();
        updateGeometry();
    }
}
```

The `setIconImage()` function sets the image to edit. We call `convertToFormat()` to make the image 32-bit with an alpha buffer, if it isn't already. Elsewhere in the code, we will assume that the image data is stored as 32-bit ARGB values.

After setting the `image` variable, we call `QWidget::update()` to force a repainting of the widget using the new image. Next, we call `QWidget::updateGeometry()` to tell any layout that contains the widget that the widget's size hint has changed. The layout will then automatically adapt to the new size hint.

```cpp
void IconEditor::setZoomFactor(int newZoom)
{
    if (newZoom < 1)
        newZoom = 1;

    if (newZoom != zoom) {
        zoom = newZoom;
        update();
        updateGeometry();
```

```
        }
    }
```

The setZoomFactor() function sets the zoom factor for the image. To prevent division by zero elsewhere, we correct any value below 1. Again, we call update() and updateGeometry() to repaint the widget and to notify any managing layout about the size hint change.

The penColor(), iconImage(), and zoomFactor() functions are implemented as inline functions in the header file.

We will now review the code for the paintEvent() function. This function is IconEditor's most important function. It is called whenever the widget needs repainting. The default implementation in QWidget does nothing, leaving the widget blank.

Just like closeEvent(), which we met in Chapter 3, paintEvent() is an event handler. Qt has many other event handlers, each of which corresponds to a different type of event. Chapter 7 covers event processing in depth.

There are many situations when a paint event is generated and paintEvent() is called:

- When a widget is shown for the first time, the system automatically generates a paint event to force the widget to paint itself.

- When a widget is resized, the system generates a paint event.

- If the widget is obscured by another window and then revealed again, a paint event is generated for the area that was hidden (unless the window system stored the area).

We can also force a paint event by calling QWidget::update() or QWidget::repaint(). The difference between these two functions is that repaint() forces an immediate repaint, whereas update() simply schedules a paint event for when Qt next processes events. (Both functions do nothing if the widget isn't visible on screen.) If update() is called multiple times, Qt compresses the consecutive paint events into a single paint event to avoid flicker. In IconEditor, we always use update().

Here's the code:

```
    void IconEditor::paintEvent(QPaintEvent *event)
    {
        QPainter painter(this);

        if (zoom >= 3) {
            painter.setPen(palette().foreground().color());
            for (int i = 0; i <= image.width(); ++i)
                painter.drawLine(zoom * i, 0,
                                 zoom * i, zoom * image.height());
            for (int j = 0; j <= image.height(); ++j)
                painter.drawLine(0, zoom * j,
                                 zoom * image.width(), zoom * j);
        }
```

```
    for (int i = 0; i < image.width(); ++i) {
        for (int j = 0; j < image.height(); ++j) {
            QRect rect = pixelRect(i, j);
            if (!event->region().intersect(rect).isEmpty()) {
                QColor color = QColor::fromRgba(image.pixel(i, j));
                painter.fillRect(rect, color);
            }
        }
    }
}
```

We start by constructing a QPainter object on the widget. If the zoom factor is 3 or more, we draw the horizontal and vertical lines that form the grid using the QPainter::drawLine() function.

A call to QPainter::drawLine() has the following syntax:

```
    painter.drawLine(x1, y1, x2, y2);
```

where (x1, y1) is the position of one end of the line and (x2, y2) is the position of the other end. There is also an overloaded version of the function that takes two QPoints instead of four ints.

The top-left pixel of a Qt widget is located at position (0, 0), and the bottom-right pixel is located at (width() – 1, height() – 1). This is similar to the conventional Cartesian coordinate system, but upside down. We can change QPainter's coordinate system by using transformations, such as translation, scaling, rotation, and shearing. This is covered in Chapter 8 (2D and 3D Graphics).

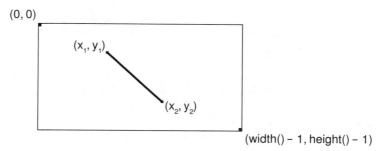

Figure 5.3. Drawing a line using QPainter

Before we call drawLine() on the QPainter, we set the line's color using setPen(). We could hard-code a color, like black or gray, but a better approach is to use the widget's palette.

Every widget is equipped with a palette that specifies which colors should be used for what. For example, there is a palette entry for the background color of widgets (usually light gray) and one for the color of text on that background (usually black). By default, a widget's palette adopts the window system's color scheme. By using colors from the palette, we ensure that IconEditor respects the user's preferences.

A widget's palette consists of three color groups: active, inactive, and disabled. Which color group should be used depends on the widget's current state:

- The `Active` group is used for widgets in the currently active window.
- The `Inactive` group is used for widgets in the other windows.
- The `Disabled` group is used for disabled widgets in any window.

The `QWidget::palette()` function returns the widget's palette as a `QPalette` object. Color groups are specified as enums of type `QPalette::ColorGroup`.

When we want to get an appropriate brush or color for drawing, the correct approach is to use the current palette, obtained from `QWidget::palette()`, and the required role, for example, `QPalette::foreground()`. Each role function returns a brush, which is normally what we want, but if we just need the color we can extract it from the brush, as we did in the `paintEvent()`. By default, the brushes returned are those appropriate to the widget's state, so we do not need to specify a color group.

The `paintEvent()` function finishes by drawing the image itself. The call to `IconEditor::pixelRect()` returns a `QRect` that defines the region to repaint. As an easy optimization, we don't redraw pixels that fall outside this region.

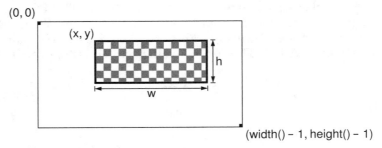

Figure 5.4. Drawing a rectangle using `QPainter`

We call `QPainter::fillRect()` to draw a zoomed pixel. `QPainter::fillRect()` takes a `QRect` and a `QBrush`. By passing a `QColor` as the brush, we obtain a solid fill pattern.

```
QRect IconEditor::pixelRect(int i, int j) const
{
    if (zoom >= 3) {
        return QRect(zoom * i + 1, zoom * j + 1, zoom - 1, zoom - 1);
    } else {
        return QRect(zoom * i, zoom * j, zoom, zoom);
    }
}
```

The `pixelRect()` function returns a `QRect` suitable for `QPainter::fillRect()`. The i and j parameters are pixel coordinates in the `QImage`—not in the widget. If the zoom factor is 1, the two coordinate systems coincide exactly.

The QRect constructor has the syntax QRect(x, y, width, height), where (x, y) is the position of the top-left corner of the rectangle and width × height is the size of the rectangle. If the zoom factor is 3 or more, we reduce the size of the rectangle by one pixel horizontally and vertically so that the fill does not draw over the grid lines.

```cpp
void IconEditor::mousePressEvent(QMouseEvent *event)
{
    if (event->button() == Qt::LeftButton) {
        setImagePixel(event->pos(), true);
    } else if (event->button() == Qt::RightButton) {
        setImagePixel(event->pos(), false);
    }
}
```

When the user presses a mouse button, the system generates a "mouse press" event. By reimplementing QWidget::mousePressEvent(), we can respond to this event and set or clear the image pixel under the mouse cursor.

If the user pressed the left mouse button, we call the private function setImagePixel() with true as the second argument, telling it to set the pixel to the current pen color. If the user pressed the right mouse button, we also call setImagePixel(), but pass false to clear the pixel.

```cpp
void IconEditor::mouseMoveEvent(QMouseEvent *event)
{
    if (event->buttons() & Qt::LeftButton) {
        setImagePixel(event->pos(), true);
    } else if (event->buttons() & Qt::RightButton) {
        setImagePixel(event->pos(), false);
    }
}
```

The mouseMoveEvent() handles "mouse move" events. By default, these events are only generated when the user is holding down a button. It is possible to change this behavior by calling QWidget::setMouseTracking(), but we don't need to do so for this example.

Just as pressing the left or right mouse button sets or clears a pixel, keeping it pressed and hovering over a pixel is also enough to set or clear a pixel. Since it's possible to hold more than one button pressed down at a time, the value returned by QMouseEvent::buttons() is a bitwise OR of the mouse buttons. We test whether a certain button is pressed down using the & operator, and if this is the case we call setImagePixel().

```cpp
void IconEditor::setImagePixel(const QPoint &pos, bool opaque)
{
    int i = pos.x() / zoom;
    int j = pos.y() / zoom;

    if (image.rect().contains(i, j)) {
        if (opaque) {
            image.setPixel(i, j, penColor().rgba());
```

```
        } else {
            image.setPixel(i, j, qRgba(0, 0, 0, 0));
        }

        update(pixelRect(i, j));
    }
}
```

The `setImagePixel()` function is called from `mousePressEvent()` and `mouseMove-Event()` to set or clear a pixel. The `pos` parameter is the position of the mouse on the widget.

The first step is to convert the mouse position from widget coordinates to image coordinates. This is done by dividing the `x()` and `y()` components of the mouse position by the zoom factor. Next, we check whether the point is within the correct range. The check is easily made using `QImage::rect()` and `QRect::contains()`; this effectively checks that i is between 0 and `image.width()` – 1 and that j is between 0 and `image.height()` – 1.

Depending on the `opaque` parameter, we set or clear the pixel in the image. Clearing a pixel is really setting it to be transparent. We must convert the pen `QColor` to an 32-bit ARGB value for the `QImage::setPixel()` call. At the end, we call `update()` with a `QRect` of the area that needs to be repainted.

Now that we have reviewed the member functions, we will return to the `Qt::WA_StaticContents` attribute that we used in the constructor. This attribute tells Qt that the widget's content doesn't change when the widget is resized and that the content stays rooted to the widget's top-left corner. Qt uses this information to avoid needlessly repainting areas that are already shown when resizing the widget.

Normally, when a widget is resized, Qt generates a paint event for the widget's entire visible area. But if the widget is created with the `Qt::WA_StaticContents` attribute, the paint event's region is restricted to the pixels that were not previously shown. This implies that if the widget is resized to a smaller size, no paint event is generated at all.

Figure 5.5. Resizing a `Qt::WA_StaticContents` widget

The `IconEditor` widget is now complete. Using the information and examples from earlier chapters, we could write code that uses the `IconEditor` as a window in its own right, as a central widget in a `QMainWindow`, as a child widget inside a layout, or as a child widget inside a `QScrollArea` (p. 148). In the next section, we will see how to integrate it with *Qt Designer*.

Integrating Custom Widgets with Qt Designer

Before we can use custom widgets in *Qt Designer*, we must make *Qt Designer* aware of them. There are two techniques for doing this: the "promotion" approach and the plugin approach.

The promotion approach is the quickest and easiest. It consists of choosing a built-in Qt widget that has a similar API to the one we want our custom widget to have and completing a dialog box in *Qt Designer* with some information about the custom widget. The widget can then be used in forms developed with *Qt Designer*, although it will be represented by the associated built-in Qt widget while the form is edited or previewed.

Here's how to insert a HexSpinBox widget into a form using this approach:

1. Create a QSpinBox by dragging it from *Qt Designer*'s widget box onto the form.
2. Right-click the spin box and choose Promote to Custom Widget from the context menu.
3. Fill in the dialog that pops up with "HexSpinBox" as the class name and "hexspinbox.h" as the header file.

Voilà! The code generated by uic will include hexspinbox.h instead of <QSpinBox> and instantiate a HexSpinBox. In *Qt Designer*, the HexSpinBox widget will be represented by a QSpinBox, allowing us to set all the properties of a QSpinBox (for example, the range and the current value).

Figure 5.6. *Qt Designer*'s custom widget dialog

The drawbacks of the promotion approach are that properties that are specific to the custom widget aren't accessible in *Qt Designer* and that the widget isn't rendered as itself. Both these problems can be solved by using the plugin approach.

The plugin approach requires the creation of a plugin library that *Qt Designer* can load at run-time and use to create instances of the widget. The real widget is then used by *Qt Designer* when editing the form and for previewing, and thanks to Qt's meta-object system, *Qt Designer* can dynamically obtain the list of its properties. To show how this works, we will integrate the IconEditor from the previous section as a plugin.

First, we must subclass QDesignerCustomWidgetInterface and reimplement some
virtual functions. We will assume that the plugin source code is located in a
directory called iconeditorplugin and that the IconEditor source code is located
in a parallel directory called iconeditor.

Here's the class definition:

```
#include <QDesignerCustomWidgetInterface>

class IconEditorPlugin : public QObject,
                         public QDesignerCustomWidgetInterface
{
    Q_OBJECT
    Q_INTERFACES(QDesignerCustomWidgetInterface)
public:
    IconEditorPlugin(QObject *parent = 0);

    QString name() const;
    QString includeFile() const;
    QString group() const;
    QIcon icon() const;
    QString toolTip() const;
    QString whatsThis() const;
    bool isContainer() const;
    QWidget *createWidget(QWidget *parent);
};
```

The IconEditorPlugin subclass is a factory class that encapsulates the IconEditor widget. It inherits both QObject and QDesignerCustomWidgetIterface and
uses the Q_INTERFACES() macro to tell moc that the second base class is a plugin
interface. The functions are used by *Qt Designer* to create instances of the class
and to obtain information about it.

```
IconEditorPlugin::IconEditorPlugin(QObject *parent)
    : QObject(parent)
{
}
```

The constructor is trivial.

```
QString IconEditorPlugin::name() const
{
    return "IconEditor";
}
```

The name() function returns the name of the widget provided by the plugin.

```
QString IconEditorPlugin::includeFile() const
{
    return "iconeditor.h";
}
```

The includeFile() function returns the name of the header file for the specified
widget encapsulated by the plugin. The header file is included in the code
generated by the uic tool.

```
QString IconEditorPlugin::group() const
{
    return tr("Image Manipulation Widgets");
}
```

The group() function returns the name of the widget box group this custom widget should belong to. If the name isn't already in use, *Qt Designer* will create a new group for the widget.

```
QIcon IconEditorPlugin::icon() const
{
    return QIcon(":/images/iconeditor.png");
}
```

The icon() function returns the icon to use to represent the custom widget in *Qt Designer*'s widget box. Here, we assume that the IconEditorPlugin has an associated Qt resource file with a suitable entry for the icon editor image.

```
QString IconEditorPlugin::toolTip() const
{
    return tr("An icon editor widget");
}
```

The toolTip() function returns the tooltip to show when the mouse hovers over the custom widget in *Qt Designer*'s widget box.

```
QString IconEditorPlugin::whatsThis() const
{
    return tr("This widget is presented in Chapter 5 of <i>C++ GUI "
             "Programming with Qt 4</i> as an example of a custom Qt "
             "widget.");
}
```

The whatsThis() function returns the "What's This?" text for *Qt Designer* to display.

```
bool IconEditorPlugin::isContainer() const
{
    return false;
}
```

The isContainer() function returns true if the widget can contain other widgets; otherwise, it returns false. For example, QFrame is a widget that can contain other widgets. In general, any Qt widget can contain other widgets, but *Qt Designer* disallows this when isContainer() returns false.

```
QWidget *IconEditorPlugin::createWidget(QWidget *parent)
{
    return new IconEditor(parent);
}
```

The create() function is called by *Qt Designer* to create an instance of a widget class with the given parent.

```
Q_EXPORT_PLUGIN2(iconeditorplugin, IconEditorPlugin)
```

At the end of the source file that implements the plugin class, we must use the Q_EXPORT_PLUGIN2() macro to make the plugin available to *Qt Designer*. The first argument is the name we want to give the plugin; the second argument is the name of the class that implements it.

The .pro file for building the plugin looks like this:

```
TEMPLATE     = lib
CONFIG       += designer plugin release
HEADERS      = ../iconeditor/iconeditor.h \
               iconeditorplugin.h
SOURCES      = ../iconeditor/iconeditor.cpp \
               iconeditorplugin.cpp
RESOURCES    = iconeditorplugin.qrc
DESTDIR      = $(QTDIR)/plugins/designer
```

The .pro file assumes that the QTDIR environment variable is set to the directory where Qt is installed. When you type make or nmake to build the plugin, it will automatically install itself in *Qt Designer*'s plugins directory. Once the plugin is built, the IconEditor widget can be used in *Qt Designer* in the same way as any of Qt's built-in widgets.

If you want to integrate several custom widgets with *Qt Designer*, you can either create one plugin for each one of them or combine them into a single plugin by deriving from QDesignerCustomWidgetCollectionInterface.

Double Buffering

Double buffering is a GUI programming technique that consists of rendering a widget to an off-screen pixmap and copying the pixmap onto the display. With earlier versions of Qt, this technique was frequently used to eliminate flicker and to provide a snappier user interface.

In Qt 4, QWidget handles this automatically, so we rarely need to worry about widgets flickering. Still, explicit double buffering remains beneficial if the widget's rendering is complex and needed repeatedly. We can then store a pixmap permanently with the widget, always ready for the next paint event, and copy the pixmap to the widget whenever we receive a paint event. It is especially helpful when we want to do small modifications, such as drawing a rubber band, without recomputing the whole widget's rendering over and over.

We will round off this chapter by reviewing the Plotter custom widget. This widget uses double buffering and also demonstrates some other aspects of Qt programming, including keyboard event handling, manual layout, and coordinate systems.

The Plotter widget displays one or more curves specified as vectors of coordinates. The user can draw a rubber band on the image, and the Plotter will zoom in on the area enclosed by the rubber band. The user draws the rubber band by clicking a point on the graph, dragging the mouse to another position with the left mouse button held down, and releasing the mouse button.

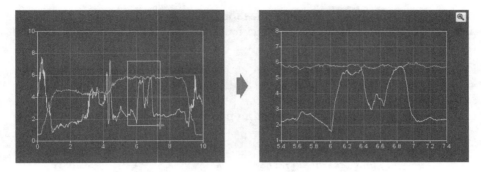

Figure 5.7. Zooming in on the `Plotter` widget

The user can zoom in repeatedly by drawing a rubber band multiple times, zooming out using the Zoom Out button, and then zooming back in using the Zoom In button. The Zoom In and Zoom Out buttons appear the first time they become available, so that they don't clutter the display if the user doesn't zoom the graph.

The `Plotter` widget can hold the data for any number of curves. It also maintains a stack of `PlotSettings` objects, each of which corresponds to a particular zoom level.

Let's review the class, starting with `plotter.h`:

```cpp
#ifndef PLOTTER_H
#define PLOTTER_H

#include <QMap>
#include <QPixmap>
#include <QVector>
#include <QWidget>

class QToolButton;
class PlotSettings;

class Plotter : public QWidget
{
    Q_OBJECT

public:
    Plotter(QWidget *parent = 0);

    void setPlotSettings(const PlotSettings &settings);
    void setCurveData(int id, const QVector<QPointF> &data);
    void clearCurve(int id);
    QSize minimumSizeHint() const;
    QSize sizeHint() const;

public slots:
    void zoomIn();
    void zoomOut();
```

We start by including the header files for the Qt classes that are used in the plotter file's header, and forward declaring the classes that have pointers or references in the header.

In the Plotter class, we provide three public functions for setting up the plot, and two public slots for zooming in and out. We also reimplement minimum-SizeHint() and sizeHint() from QWidget. We store a curve's points as a QVector<QPointF>, where QPointF is a floating-point version of QPoint.

```
protected:
    void paintEvent(QPaintEvent *event);
    void resizeEvent(QResizeEvent *event);
    void mousePressEvent(QMouseEvent *event);
    void mouseMoveEvent(QMouseEvent *event);
    void mouseReleaseEvent(QMouseEvent *event);
    void keyPressEvent(QKeyEvent *event);
    void wheelEvent(QWheelEvent *event);
```

In the protected section of the class, we declare all the QWidget event handlers that we want to reimplement.

```
private:
    void updateRubberBandRegion();
    void refreshPixmap();
    void drawGrid(QPainter *painter);
    void drawCurves(QPainter *painter);

    enum { Margin = 50 };

    QToolButton *zoomInButton;
    QToolButton *zoomOutButton;
    QMap<int, QVector<QPointF> > curveMap;
    QVector<PlotSettings> zoomStack;
    int curZoom;
    bool rubberBandIsShown;
    QRect rubberBandRect;
    QPixmap pixmap;
};
```

In the private section of the class, we declare a few functions for painting the widget, a constant, and several member variables. The Margin constant is used to provide some spacing around the graph.

Among the member variables is pixmap of type QPixmap. This variable holds a copy of the whole widget's rendering, identical to what is shown on screen. The plot is always drawn onto this off-screen pixmap first; then the pixmap is copied onto the widget.

```
class PlotSettings
{
public:
    PlotSettings();

    void scroll(int dx, int dy);
    void adjust();
```

```
    double spanX() const { return maxX - minX; }
    double spanY() const { return maxY - minY; }

    double minX;
    double maxX;
    int numXTicks;
    double minY;
    double maxY;
    int numYTicks;

private:
    static void adjustAxis(double &min, double &max, int &numTicks);
};

#endif
```

The `PlotSettings` class specifies the range of the *x* and *y* axes and the number of ticks for these axes. Figure 5.8 shows the correspondence between a `PlotSettings` object and a `Plotter` widget.

By convention, `numXTicks` and `numYTicks` are off by one; if `numXTicks` is 5, `Plotter` will actually draw 6 tick marks on the *x* axis. This simplifies the calculations later on.

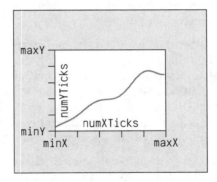

Figure 5.8. `PlotSettings`'s member variables

Now let's review the implementation file:

```
#include <QtGui>
#include <cmath>

#include "plotter.h"
```

We include the expected header files and import all the `std` namespace's symbols into the global namespace. This allows us to access the functions that are declared in <cmath> without prefixing them with `std::` (for example, `floor()` instead of `std::floor()`).

```
Plotter::Plotter(QWidget *parent)
    : QWidget(parent)
{
    setBackgroundRole(QPalette::Dark);
```

```
    setAutoFillBackground(true);
    setSizePolicy(QSizePolicy::Expanding, QSizePolicy::Expanding);
    setFocusPolicy(Qt::StrongFocus);
    rubberBandIsShown = false;

    zoomInButton = new QToolButton(this);
    zoomInButton->setIcon(QIcon(":/images/zoomin.png"));
    zoomInButton->adjustSize();
    connect(zoomInButton, SIGNAL(clicked()), this, SLOT(zoomIn()));

    zoomOutButton = new QToolButton(this);
    zoomOutButton->setIcon(QIcon(":/images/zoomout.png"));
    zoomOutButton->adjustSize();
    connect(zoomOutButton, SIGNAL(clicked()), this, SLOT(zoomOut()));

    setPlotSettings(PlotSettings());
}
```

The setBackgroundRole() call tells QWidget to use the "dark" component of the palette as the color for erasing the widget, instead of the "window" component. This gives Qt a default color that it can use to fill any newly revealed pixels when the widget is resized to a larger size, before paintEvent() even has the chance to paint the new pixels. We also need to call setAutoFillBackground(true) to enable this mechanism. (By default, child widgets inherit the background from their parent widget.)

The setSizePolicy() call sets the widget's size policy to QSizePolicy::Expanding in both directions. This tells any layout manager that is responsible for the widget that the widget is especially willing to grow, but can also shrink. This setting is typical for widgets that can take up a lot of screen space. The default is QSizePolicy::Preferred in both directions, which means that the widget prefers to be the size of its size hint, but it can be shrunk down to its minimum size hint or expanded indefinitely if necessary.

The setFocusPolicy(Qt::StrongFocus) call makes the widget accept focus by clicking or by pressing Tab. When the Plotter has focus, it will receive events for key presses. The Plotter widget understands a few keys: + to zoom in; – to zoom out; and the arrow keys to scroll up, down, left, and right.

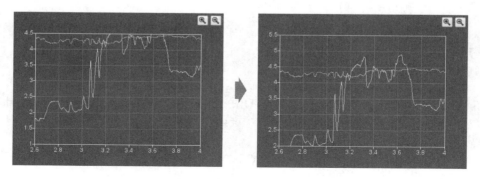

Figure 5.9. Scrolling the Plotter widget

Still in the constructor, we create two QToolButtons, each with an icon. These buttons allow the user to zoom in and out. The button's icons are stored in a resource file, so any application that uses the Plotter widget will need this entry in its .pro file:

```
RESOURCES     = plotter.qrc
```

The resource file is similar to the one we have used for the Spreadsheet application:

```
<!DOCTYPE RCC><RCC version="1.0">
<qresource>
    <file>images/zoomin.png</file>
    <file>images/zoomout.png</file>
</qresource>
</RCC>
```

The adjustSize() calls on the buttons set their sizes to be that of their size hints. The buttons are not put in a layout; instead, we will position them manually in the Plotter's resize event. Since we are not using any layouts, we must specify the buttons' parent explicitly by passing this to the QPushButton constructor.

The call to setPlotSettings() at the end completes the initialization.

```
void Plotter::setPlotSettings(const PlotSettings &settings)
{
    zoomStack.clear();
    zoomStack.append(settings);
    curZoom = 0;
    zoomInButton->hide();
    zoomOutButton->hide();
    refreshPixmap();
}
```

The setPlotSettings() function is used to specify the PlotSettings to use for displaying the plot. It is called by the Plotter constructor and can be called by users of the class. The plotter starts out at its default zoom level. Each time the user zooms in, a new PlotSettings instance is created and put onto the zoom stack. The zoom stack is represented by two member variables:

- zoomStack holds the different zoom settings as a QVector<PlotSettings>.
- curZoom holds the current PlotSettings's index in the zoomStack.

After the call to setPlotSettings(), the zoom stack contains only one entry, and the Zoom In and Zoom Out buttons are hidden. These buttons will not be shown until we call show() on them in the zoomIn() and zoomOut() slots. (Normally, it is sufficient to call show() on the top-level widget to show all the children. But when we explicitly call hide() on a child widget, it is hidden until we call show() on it.)

The call to refreshPixmap() is necessary to update the display. Usually, we would call update(), but here we do things slightly differently because we want to keep a QPixmap up to date at all times. After regenerating the pixmap, refreshPixmap() calls update() to copy the pixmap onto the widget.

```
void Plotter::zoomOut()
{
    if (curZoom > 0) {
        --curZoom;
        zoomOutButton->setEnabled(curZoom > 0);
        zoomInButton->setEnabled(true);
        zoomInButton->show();
        refreshPixmap();
    }
}
```

The zoomOut() slot zooms out if the graph is zoomed in. It decrements the current zoom level and enables the Zoom Out button depending on whether the graph can be zoomed out any more or not. The Zoom In button is enabled and shown, and the display is updated with a call to refreshPixmap().

```
void Plotter::zoomIn()
{
    if (curZoom < zoomStack.count() - 1) {
        ++curZoom;
        zoomInButton->setEnabled(curZoom < zoomStack.count() - 1);
        zoomOutButton->setEnabled(true);
        zoomOutButton->show();
        refreshPixmap();
    }
}
```

If the user has previously zoomed in and then out again, the PlotSettings for the next zoom level will be in the zoom stack, and we can zoom in. (Otherwise, it is still possible to zoom in using a rubber band.)

The slot increments curZoom to move one level deeper into the zoom stack, sets the Zoom In button enabled or disabled depending on whether it's possible to zoom in any further, and enables and shows the Zoom Out button. Again, we call refreshPixmap() to make the plotter use the latest zoom settings.

```
void Plotter::setCurveData(int id, const QVector<QPointF> &data)
{
    curveMap[id] = data;
    refreshPixmap();
}
```

The setCurveData() function sets the curve data for a given curve ID. If a curve with the same ID already exists in curveMap, it is replaced with the new curve data; otherwise, the new curve is simply inserted. The curveMap member variable is of type QMap<int, QVector<QPointF>>.

```
void Plotter::clearCurve(int id)
{
    curveMap.remove(id);
```

```
        refreshPixmap();
    }
```

The `clearCurve()` function removes the specified curve from the curve map.

```
    QSize Plotter::minimumSizeHint() const
    {
        return QSize(6 * Margin, 4 * Margin);
    }
```

The `minimumSizeHint()` function is similar to `sizeHint()`; just as `sizeHint()` specifies a widget's ideal size, `minimumSizeHint()` specifies a widget's ideal minimum size. A layout never resizes a widget below its minimum size hint.

The value we return is 300×200 (since `Margin` equals 50) to allow for the margin on all four sides and some space for the plot itself. Below that size, the plot would be too small to be useful.

```
    QSize Plotter::sizeHint() const
    {
        return QSize(12 * Margin, 8 * Margin);
    }
```

In `sizeHint()`, we return an "ideal" size in proportion to the `Margin` constant and with the same pleasing 3:2 aspect ratio we used for the `minimumSizeHint()`.

This finishes the review of the `Plotter`'s public functions and slots. Now let's review the protected event handlers.

```
    void Plotter::paintEvent(QPaintEvent * /* event */)
    {
        QStylePainter painter(this);
        painter.drawPixmap(0, 0, pixmap);

        if (rubberBandIsShown) {
            painter.setPen(palette().light().color());
            painter.drawRect(rubberBandRect.normalized()
                                           .adjusted(0, 0, -1, -1));
        }

        if (hasFocus()) {
            QStyleOptionFocusRect option;
            option.initFrom(this);
            option.backgroundColor = palette().dark().color();
            painter.drawPrimitive(QStyle::PE_FrameFocusRect, option);
        }
    }
```

Normally, `paintEvent()` is the place where we perform all the drawing. But here all the plot drawing is done beforehand in `refreshPixmap()`, so we can render the entire plot simply by copying the pixmap onto the widget at position (0, 0).

If the rubber band is visible, we draw it on top of the plot. We use the "light" component from the widget's current color group as the pen color to ensure good contrast with the "dark" background. Notice that we draw directly on the widget, leaving the off-screen pixmap untouched. Using `QRect::normalized()`

ensures that the rubber band rectangle has positive width and height (swapping coordinates if necessary), and adjusted() reduces the size of the rectangle by one pixel to allow for its own 1-pixel-wide outline.

If the Plotter has focus, a focus rectangle is drawn using the widget style's draw-Primitive() function with QStyle::PE_FrameFocusRect as its first argument and a QStyleOptionFocusRect object as its second argument. The focus rectangle's drawing options are inherited from the Plotter widget (by the initFrom() call). The background color must be specified explicitly.

When we want to paint using the current style, we can either call a QStyle function directly, for example,

```
style()->drawPrimitive(QStyle::PE_FrameFocusRect, &option, &painter,
                       this);
```

or we can use a QStylePainter instead of a normal QPainter, as we have done in Plotter, and paint more conveniently using that.

The QWidget::style() function returns the style that should be used to draw the widget. In Qt, a widget style is a subclass of QStyle. The built-in styles include QWindowsStyle, QWindowsXPStyle, QMotifStyle, QCDEStyle, QMacStyle, and QPlastiqueStyle. Each of these styles reimplements the virtual functions in QStyle to perform the drawing in the correct way for the platform the style is emulating. QStylePainter's drawPrimitive() function calls the QStyle function of the same name, which can be used for drawing "primitive elements" like panels, buttons, and focus rectangles. The widget style is usually the same for all widgets in an application (QApplication::style()), but it can be overridden on a per-widget basis using QWidget::setStyle().

By subclassing QStyle, it is possible to define a custom style. This can be done to give a distinctive look to an application or a suite of applications. While it is generally advisable to use the target platform's native look and feel, Qt offers a lot of flexibility if you want to be adventurous.

Qt's built-in widgets rely almost exclusively on QStyle to paint themselves. This is why they look like native widgets on all platforms supported by Qt. Custom widgets can be made style-aware either by using QStyle to paint themselves or by using built-in Qt widgets as child widgets. For Plotter, we use a combination of both approaches: The focus rectangle is drawn using QStyle (via a QStylePainter), and the Zoom In and Zoom Out buttons are built-in Qt widgets.

```
void Plotter::resizeEvent(QResizeEvent * /* event */)
{
    int x = width() - (zoomInButton->width()
                       + zoomOutButton->width() + 10);
    zoomInButton->move(x, 5);
    zoomOutButton->move(x + zoomInButton->width() + 5, 5);
    refreshPixmap();
}
```

Whenever the Plotter widget is resized, Qt generates a "resize" event. Here, we reimplement resizeEvent() to place the Zoom In and Zoom Out buttons at the top right of the Plotter widget.

We move the Zoom In button and the Zoom Out button to be side by side, separated by a 5-pixel gap and with a 5-pixel offset from the top and right edges of the parent widget.

If we wanted the buttons to stay rooted to the top-left corner, whose coordinates are (0, 0), we would simply have moved them there in the Plotter constructor. But we want to track the top-right corner, whose coordinates depend on the size of the widget. Because of this, it's necessary to reimplement resizeEvent() and to set the buttons' position there.

We didn't set any positions for the buttons in the Plotter constructor. This isn't a problem, since Qt always generates a resize event before a widget is shown for the first time.

An alternative to reimplementing resizeEvent() and laying out the child widgets manually would have been to use a layout manager (for example, QGridLayout). Using a layout would have been a little more complicated and would have consumed more resources; on the other hand, it would gracefully handle right-to-left layouts, necessary for languages such as Arabic and Hebrew.

At the end, we call refreshPixmap() to redraw the pixmap at the new size.

```
void Plotter::mousePressEvent(QMouseEvent *event)
{
    QRect rect(Margin, Margin,
               width() - 2 * Margin, height() - 2 * Margin);

    if (event->button() == Qt::LeftButton) {
        if (rect.contains(event->pos())) {
            rubberBandIsShown = true;
            rubberBandRect.setTopLeft(event->pos());
            rubberBandRect.setBottomRight(event->pos());
            updateRubberBandRegion();
            setCursor(Qt::CrossCursor);
        }
    }
}
```

When the user presses the left mouse button, we start displaying a rubber band. This involves setting rubberBandIsShown to true, initializing the rubberBandRect member variable with the current mouse pointer position, scheduling a paint event to paint the rubber band, and changing the mouse cursor to have a crosshair shape.

The rubberBandRect variable is of type QRect. A QRect can be defined either as an $(x, y, width, height)$ quadruple—where (x, y) is the position of the top-left corner and $width \times height$ is the size of the rectangle—or as a top-left and a bottom-right coordinate pair. Here, we have used the coordinate pair representation. We set the point where the user clicked as both the top-left corner and as the bottom-right corner. Then we call updateRubberBandRegion() to force a repaint of the (tiny) area covered by the rubber band.

Qt provides two mechanisms for controlling the mouse cursor's shape:

- QWidget::setCursor() sets the cursor shape to use when the mouse hovers over a particular widget. If no cursor is set for a widget, the parent widget's cursor is used. The default for top-level widgets is an arrow cursor.

- QApplication::setOverrideCursor() sets the cursor shape for the entire application, overriding the cursors set by individual widgets until restore-OverrideCursor() is called.

In Chapter 4, we called QApplication::setOverrideCursor() with Qt::WaitCursor to change the application's cursor to the standard wait cursor.

```
void Plotter::mouseMoveEvent(QMouseEvent *event)
{
    if (rubberBandIsShown) {
        updateRubberBandRegion();
        rubberBandRect.setBottomRight(event->pos());
        updateRubberBandRegion();
    }
}
```

When the user moves the mouse cursor while holding the left button, we first call updateRubberBandRegion() to schedule a paint event to repaint the area where the rubber band was, then we recompute rubberBandRect to account for the mouse move, and finally we call updateRubberBandRegion() a second time to repaint the area where the rubber band has moved to. This effectively erases the rubber band and redraws it at the new coordinates.

If the user moves the mouse upward or leftward, it's likely that rubberBand-Rect's nominal bottom-right corner will end up above or to the left of its top-left corner. If this occurs, the QRect will have a negative width or height. We used QRect::normalized() in paintEvent() to ensure that the top-left and bottom-right coordinates are adjusted to obtain a nonnegative width and height.

```
void Plotter::mouseReleaseEvent(QMouseEvent *event)
{
    if ((event->button() == Qt::LeftButton) && rubberBandIsShown) {
        rubberBandIsShown = false;
        updateRubberBandRegion();
        unsetCursor();

        QRect rect = rubberBandRect.normalized();
        if (rect.width() < 4 || rect.height() < 4)
            return;
        rect.translate(-Margin, -Margin);

        PlotSettings prevSettings = zoomStack[curZoom];
        PlotSettings settings;
        double dx = prevSettings.spanX() / (width() - 2 * Margin);
        double dy = prevSettings.spanY() / (height() - 2 * Margin);
```

```
settings.minX = prevSettings.minX + dx * rect.left();
settings.maxX = prevSettings.minX + dx * rect.right();
settings.minY = prevSettings.maxY - dy * rect.bottom();
settings.maxY = prevSettings.maxY - dy * rect.top();
settings.adjust();

zoomStack.resize(curZoom + 1);
zoomStack.append(settings);
zoomIn();
    }
}
```

When the user releases the left mouse button, we erase the rubber band and restore the standard arrow cursor. If the rubber band is at least 4 × 4, we perform the zoom. If the rubber band is smaller than that, it's likely that the user clicked the widget by mistake or to give it focus, so we do nothing.

The code to perform the zoom is a bit complicated. This is because we deal with widget coordinates and plotter coordinates at the same time. Most of the work we perform here is to convert the rubberBandRect from widget coordinates to plotter coordinates. Once we have done the conversion, we call PlotSettings:: adjust() to round the numbers and find a sensible number of ticks for each axis. Figures 5.10 and 5.11 depict the situation.

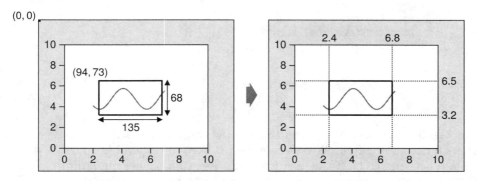

Figure 5.10. Converting the rubber band from widget to plotter coordinates

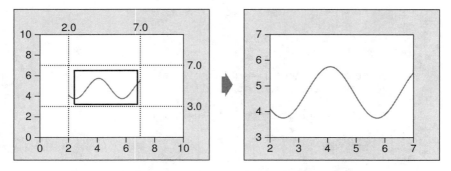

Figure 5.11. Adjusting plotter coordinates and zooming in on the rubber band

Then we perform the zoom. The zoom is achieved by pushing the new PlotSettings that we have just calculated on top of the zoom stack and calling zoomIn() to do the job.

```cpp
void Plotter::keyPressEvent(QKeyEvent *event)
{
    switch (event->key()) {
    case Qt::Key_Plus:
        zoomIn();
        break;
    case Qt::Key_Minus:
        zoomOut();
        break;
    case Qt::Key_Left:
        zoomStack[curZoom].scroll(-1, 0);
        refreshPixmap();
        break;
    case Qt::Key_Right:
        zoomStack[curZoom].scroll(+1, 0);
        refreshPixmap();
        break;
    case Qt::Key_Down:
        zoomStack[curZoom].scroll(0, -1);
        refreshPixmap();
        break;
    case Qt::Key_Up:
        zoomStack[curZoom].scroll(0, +1);
        refreshPixmap();
        break;
    default:
        QWidget::keyPressEvent(event);
    }
}
```

When the user presses a key and the Plotter widget has focus, the keyPressEvent() function is called. We reimplement it here to respond to six keys: +, -, Up, Down, Left, and Right. If the user pressed a key that we are not handling, we call the base class implementation. For simplicity, we ignore the Shift, Ctrl, and Alt modifier keys, which are available through QKeyEvent::modifiers().

```cpp
void Plotter::wheelEvent(QWheelEvent *event)
{
    int numDegrees = event->delta() / 8;
    int numTicks = numDegrees / 15;

    if (event->orientation() == Qt::Horizontal) {
        zoomStack[curZoom].scroll(numTicks, 0);
    } else {
        zoomStack[curZoom].scroll(0, numTicks);
    }
    refreshPixmap();
}
```

Wheel events occur when a mouse wheel is turned. Most mice only provide a vertical wheel, but some also have a horizontal wheel. Qt supports both kinds of wheel. Wheel events go to the widget that has the focus. The delta() function returns the distance the wheel was rotated in eighths of a degree. Mice typically work in steps of 15 degrees. Here, we scroll by the requested number of ticks by modifying the topmost item on the zoom stack and update the display using refreshPixmap().

The most common use of the wheel mouse is to scroll a scroll bar. When we use QScrollArea (covered in Chapter 6) to provide scroll bars, QScrollArea handles the wheel mouse events automatically, so we don't need to reimplement wheelEvent() ourselves.

This finishes the implementation of the event handlers. Now let's review the private functions.

```
void Plotter::updateRubberBandRegion()
{
    QRect rect = rubberBandRect.normalized();
    update(rect.left(), rect.top(), rect.width(), 1);
    update(rect.left(), rect.top(), 1, rect.height());
    update(rect.left(), rect.bottom(), rect.width(), 1);
    update(rect.right(), rect.top(), 1, rect.height());
}
```

The updateRubberBand() function is called from mousePressEvent(), mouseMove-Event(), and mouseReleaseEvent() to erase or redraw the rubber band. It consists of four calls to update() that schedule a paint event for the four small rectangular areas that are covered by the rubber band (two vertical and two horizontal lines). Qt provides the QRubberBand class for drawing rubber bands, but here, hand-coding provided finer control.

```
void Plotter::refreshPixmap()
{
    pixmap = QPixmap(size());
    pixmap.fill(this, 0, 0);

    QPainter painter(&pixmap);
    painter.initFrom(this);
    drawGrid(&painter);
    drawCurves(&painter);
    update();
}
```

The refreshPixmap() function redraws the plot onto the off-screen pixmap and updates the display. We resize the pixmap to have the same size as the widget and fill it with the widget's erase color. This color is the "dark" component of the palette, because of the call to setBackgroundRole() in the Plotter constructor. If the background is a non-solid brush, QPixmap::fill() needs to know the offset in the widget where the pixmap will end up to align the brush pattern correctly. Here, the pixmap corresponds to the entire widget, so we specify position (0, 0).

Then we create a QPainter to draw on the pixmap. The initFrom() call sets the painter's pen, background, and font to the same ones as the Plotter widget. Next we call drawGrid() and drawCurves() to perform the drawing. At the end, we call update() to schedule a paint event for the whole widget. The pixmap is copied to the widget in the paintEvent() function (p. 123).

```
void Plotter::drawGrid(QPainter *painter)
{
    QRect rect(Margin, Margin,
               width() - 2 * Margin, height() - 2 * Margin);
    if (!rect.isValid())
        return;

    PlotSettings settings = zoomStack[curZoom];
    QPen quiteDark = palette().dark().color().light();
    QPen light = palette().light().color();

    for (int i = 0; i <= settings.numXTicks; ++i) {
        int x = rect.left() + (i * (rect.width() - 1)
                                 / settings.numXTicks);
        double label = settings.minX + (i * settings.spanX()
                                          / settings.numXTicks);
        painter->setPen(quiteDark);
        painter->drawLine(x, rect.top(), x, rect.bottom());
        painter->setPen(light);
        painter->drawLine(x, rect.bottom(), x, rect.bottom() + 5);
        painter->drawText(x - 50, rect.bottom() + 5, 100, 15,
                          Qt::AlignHCenter | Qt::AlignTop,
                          QString::number(label));
    }
    for (int j = 0; j <= settings.numYTicks; ++j) {
        int y = rect.bottom() - (j * (rect.height() - 1)
                                   / settings.numYTicks);
        double label = settings.minY + (j * settings.spanY()
                                          / settings.numYTicks);
        painter->setPen(quiteDark);
        painter->drawLine(rect.left(), y, rect.right(), y);
        painter->setPen(light);
        painter->drawLine(rect.left() - 5, y, rect.left(), y);
        painter->drawText(rect.left() - Margin, y - 10, Margin - 5, 20,
                          Qt::AlignRight | Qt::AlignVCenter,
                          QString::number(label));
    }
    painter->drawRect(rect.adjusted(0, 0, -1, -1));
}
```

The drawGrid() function draws the grid behind the curves and the axes. The area on which we draw the grid is specified by rect. If the widget isn't large enough to accommodate the graph, we return immediately.

The first for loop draws the grid's vertical lines and the ticks along the *x* axis. The second for loop draws the grid's horizontal lines and the ticks along the *y* axis. At the end, we draw a rectangle along the margins. The drawText()

function is used to draw the numbers corresponding to the tick marks on both axes.

The calls to drawText() have the following syntax:

```
painter->drawText(x, y, width, height, alignment, text);
```

where (x, y, width, height) define a rectangle, alignment the position of the text within that rectangle, and text the text to draw.

```
void Plotter::drawCurves(QPainter *painter)
{
    static const QColor colorForIds[6] = {
        Qt::red, Qt::green, Qt::blue, Qt::cyan, Qt::magenta, Qt::yellow
    };
    PlotSettings settings = zoomStack[curZoom];
    QRect rect(Margin, Margin,
               width() - 2 * Margin, height() - 2 * Margin);
    if (!rect.isValid())
        return;

    painter->setClipRect(rect.adjusted(+1, +1, -1, -1));

    QMapIterator<int, QVector<QPointF> > i(curveMap);
    while (i.hasNext()) {
        i.next();

        int id = i.key();
        const QVector<QPointF> &data = i.value();
        QPolygonF polyline(data.count());

        for (int j = 0; j < data.count(); ++j) {
            double dx = data[j].x() - settings.minX;
            double dy = data[j].y() - settings.minY;
            double x = rect.left() + (dx * (rect.width() - 1)
                                         / settings.spanX());
            double y = rect.bottom() - (dy * (rect.height() - 1)
                                           / settings.spanY());
            polyline[j] = QPointF(x, y);
        }
        painter->setPen(colorForIds[uint(id) % 6]);
        painter->drawPolyline(polyline);
    }
}
```

The drawCurves() function draws the curves on top of the grid. We start by calling setClipRect() to set the QPainter's clip region to the rectangle that contains the curves (excluding the margins and the frame around the graph). QPainter will then ignore drawing operations on pixels outside the area.

Next, we iterate over all the curves using a Java-style iterator, and for each curve, we iterate over its constituent QPointFs. The key() function gives the curve's ID, and the value() function gives the corresponding curve data as a QVector<QPointF>. The inner for loop converts each QPointF from plotter coordinates to widget coordinates and stores them in the polyline variable.

Once we have converted all the points of a curve to widget coordinates, we set the pen color for the curve (using one of a set of predefined colors) and call drawPolyline() to draw a line that goes through all the curve's points.

This is the complete Plotter class. All that remains are a few functions in PlotSettings.

```
PlotSettings::PlotSettings()
{
    minX = 0.0;
    maxX = 10.0;
    numXTicks = 5;

    minY = 0.0;
    maxY = 10.0;
    numYTicks = 5;
}
```

The PlotSettings constructor initializes both axes to the range 0 to 10 with 5 tick marks.

```
void PlotSettings::scroll(int dx, int dy)
{
    double stepX = spanX() / numXTicks;
    minX += dx * stepX;
    maxX += dx * stepX;

    double stepY = spanY() / numYTicks;
    minY += dy * stepY;
    maxY += dy * stepY;
}
```

The scroll() function increments (or decrements) minX, maxX, minY, and maxY by the interval between two ticks times a given number. This function is used to implement scrolling in Plotter::keyPressEvent().

```
void PlotSettings::adjust()
{
    adjustAxis(minX, maxX, numXTicks);
    adjustAxis(minY, maxY, numYTicks);
}
```

The adjust() function is called from mouseReleaseEvent() to round the minX, maxX, minY, and maxY values to "nice" values and to determine the number of ticks appropriate for each axis. The private function adjustAxis() does its work one axis at a time.

```
void PlotSettings::adjustAxis(double &min, double &max,
                              int &numTicks)
{
    const int MinTicks = 4;
    double grossStep = (max - min) / MinTicks;
    double step = pow(10.0, floor(log10(grossStep)));

    if (5 * step < grossStep) {
        step *= 5;
```

```
        } else if (2 * step < grossStep) {
            step *= 2;
        }

        numTicks = int(ceil(max / step) - floor(min / step));
        if (numTicks < MinTicks)
            numTicks = MinTicks;
        min = floor(min / step) * step;
        max = ceil(max / step) * step;
    }
```

The adjustAxis() function converts its min and max parameters into "nice" numbers and sets its numTicks parameter to the number of ticks it calculates to be appropriate for the given [min, max] range. Because adjustAxis() needs to modify the actual variables (minX, maxX, numXTicks, etc.) and not just copies, its parameters are non-const references.

Most of the code in adjustAxis() simply attempts to determine an appropriate value for the interval between two ticks (the "step"). To obtain nice numbers along the axis, we must select the step with care. For example, a step value of 3.8 would lead to an axis with multiples of 3.8, which is difficult for people to relate to. For axes labeled in decimal notation, "nice" step values are numbers of the form 10^n, $2 \cdot 10^n$, or $5 \cdot 10^n$.

We start by computing the "gross step", a kind of maximum for the step value. Then we find the corresponding number of the form 10^n that is smaller than or equal to the gross step. We do this by taking the decimal logarithm of the gross step, rounding that value down to a whole number, then raising 10 to the power of this rounded number. For example, if the gross step is 236, we compute log 236 = 2.37291...; then we round it down to 2 and obtain $10^2 = 100$ as the candidate step value of the form 10^n.

Once we have the first candidate step value, we can use it to calculate the other two candidates: $2 \cdot 10^n$ and $5 \cdot 10^n$. For the example above, the two other candidates are 200 and 500. The 500 candidate is larger than the gross step, so we can't use it. But 200 is smaller than 236, so we use 200 for the step size in this example.

It's fairly easy to derive numTicks, min, and max from the step value. The new min value is obtained by rounding the original min down to the nearest multiple of the step, and the new max value is obtained by rounding up to the nearest multiple of the step. The new numTicks is the number of intervals between the rounded min and max values. For example, if min is 240 and max is 1184 upon entering the function, the new range becomes [200, 1200], with 5 tick marks.

This algorithm will give suboptimal results in some cases. A more sophisticated algorithm is described in Paul S. Heckbert's article "Nice Numbers for Graph Labels" published in *Graphics Gems* (ISBN 0-12-286166-3).

This chapter has brought us to the end of Part I. It has explained how to customize an existing Qt widget and how to build a widget from the ground up using QWidget as the base class. We have already seen how to compose a widget from existing widgets in Chapter 2, and we will explore the theme further in Chapter 6.

At this point, we know enough to write complete GUI applications using Qt. In Parts II and III, we will explore Qt in greater depth so that we can make full use of Qt's power.

Part II

Intermediate Qt

6. Layout Management

Every widget that is placed on a form must be given an appropriate size and position. Qt provides several classes that lay out widgets on a form: `QHBoxLayout`, `QVBoxLayout`, `QGridLayout`, and `QStackLayout`. These classes are so convenient and easy to use that almost every Qt developer uses them, either directly in source code or through *Qt Designer*.

Another reason to use Qt's layout classes is that they ensure that forms adapt automatically to different fonts, languages, and platforms. If the user changes the system's font settings, the application's forms will respond immediately, resizing themselves if necessary. And if you translate the application's user interface to other languages, the layout classes take into consideration the widgets' translated contents to avoid text truncation.

Other classes that perform layout management include `QSplitter`, `QScrollArea`, `QMainWindow`, and `QWorkspace`. What these classes have in common is that they provide a flexible layout that the user can manipulate. For example, `QSplitter` provides a splitter bar that the user can drag to resize widgets, and `QWorkspace` provides support for MDI (multiple document interface), a means of showing many documents simultaneously within an application's main window. Because they are often used as alternatives to the layout classes proper, they are covered in this chapter.

Laying Out Widgets on a Form

There are three basic ways of managing the layout of child widgets on a form: absolute positioning, manual layout, and layout managers. We will look at each of these approaches in turn, using the Find File dialog shown in Figure 6.1 as our example.

Figure 6.1. The Find File dialog

Absolute positioning is the crudest way of laying out widgets. It is achieved by assigning hard-coded sizes and positions to the form's child widgets and a fixed size to the form. Here's what the FindFileDialog constructor looks like using absolute positioning:

```
FindFileDialog::FindFileDialog(QWidget *parent)
    : QDialog(parent)
{
    ...
    namedLabel->setGeometry(9, 9, 50, 25);
    namedLineEdit->setGeometry(65, 9, 200, 25);
    lookInLabel->setGeometry(9, 40, 50, 25);
    lookInLineEdit->setGeometry(65, 40, 200, 25);
    subfoldersCheckBox->setGeometry(9, 71, 256, 23);
    tableWidget->setGeometry(9, 100, 256, 100);
    messageLabel->setGeometry(9, 206, 256, 25);
    findButton->setGeometry(271, 9, 85, 32);
    stopButton->setGeometry(271, 47, 85, 32);
    closeButton->setGeometry(271, 84, 85, 32);
    helpButton->setGeometry(271, 199, 85, 32);

    setWindowTitle(tr("Find Files or Folders"));
    setFixedSize(365, 240);
}
```

Absolute positioning has many disadvantages:

- The user cannot resize the window.

- Some text may be truncated if the user chooses an unusually large font or if the application is translated into another language.

- The widgets might have inappropriate sizes for some styles.

- The positions and sizes must be calculated manually. This is tedious and error-prone, and makes maintenance painful.

An alternative to absolute positioning is manual layout. With manual layout, the widgets are still given absolute positions, but their sizes are made proportional to the size of the window rather than being entirely hard-coded. This can be achieved by reimplementing the form's `resizeEvent()` function to set its child widgets' geometries:

```
FindFileDialog::FindFileDialog(QWidget *parent)
    : QDialog(parent)
{
    ...
    setMinimumSize(265, 190);
    resize(365, 240);
}

void FindFileDialog::resizeEvent(QResizeEvent * /* event */)
{
    int extraWidth = width() - minimumWidth();
    int extraHeight = height() - minimumHeight();

    namedLabel->setGeometry(9, 9, 50, 25);
    namedLineEdit->setGeometry(65, 9, 100 + extraWidth, 25);
    lookInLabel->setGeometry(9, 40, 50, 25);
    lookInLineEdit->setGeometry(65, 40, 100 + extraWidth, 25);
    subfoldersCheckBox->setGeometry(9, 71, 156 + extraWidth, 23);

    tableWidget->setGeometry(9, 100, 156 + extraWidth,
                             50 + extraHeight);
    messageLabel->setGeometry(9, 156 + extraHeight, 156 + extraWidth,
                              25);
    findButton->setGeometry(171 + extraWidth, 9, 85, 32);
    stopButton->setGeometry(171 + extraWidth, 47, 85, 32);
    closeButton->setGeometry(171 + extraWidth, 84, 85, 32);
    helpButton->setGeometry(171 + extraWidth, 149 + extraHeight, 85,
                            32);
}
```

In the `FindFileDialog` constructor, we set the form's minimum size to 265×190 and the initial size to 365×240. In the `resizeEvent()` handler, we give any extra space to the widgets that we want to grow. This ensures that the form scales smoothly when the user resizes it.

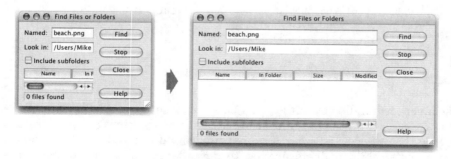

Figure 6.2. Resizing a resizable dialog

Just like absolute positioning, manual layout requires a lot of hard-coded constants to be calculated by the programmer. Writing code like this is tiresome, especially if the design changes. And there is still the risk of text truncation. We can avoid this risk by taking account of the child widgets' size hints, but that would complicate the code even further.

The most convenient solution for laying out widgets on a form is to use Qt's layout managers. The layout managers provide sensible defaults for every type of widget and take into account each widget's size hint, which in turn typically depends on the widget's font, style, and contents. Layout managers also respect minimum and maximum sizes, and automatically adjust the layout in response to font changes, content changes, and window resizing.

The three most important layout managers are QHBoxLayout, QVBoxLayout, and QGridLayout. These classes inherit QLayout, which provides the basic framework for layouts. All three classes are fully supported by *Qt Designer* and can also be used directly in code.

Here's the FindFileDialog code using layout managers:

```
FindFileDialog::FindFileDialog(QWidget *parent)
    : QDialog(parent)
{
    ...
    QGridLayout *leftLayout = new QGridLayout;
    leftLayout->addWidget(namedLabel, 0, 0);
    leftLayout->addWidget(namedLineEdit, 0, 1);
    leftLayout->addWidget(lookInLabel, 1, 0);
    leftLayout->addWidget(lookInLineEdit, 1, 1);
    leftLayout->addWidget(subfoldersCheckBox, 2, 0, 1, 2);
    leftLayout->addWidget(tableWidget, 3, 0, 1, 2);
    leftLayout->addWidget(messageLabel, 4, 0, 1, 2);

    QVBoxLayout *rightLayout = new QVBoxLayout;
    rightLayout->addWidget(findButton);
    rightLayout->addWidget(stopButton);
    rightLayout->addWidget(closeButton);
    rightLayout->addStretch();
    rightLayout->addWidget(helpButton);

    QHBoxLayout *mainLayout = new QHBoxLayout;
    mainLayout->addLayout(leftLayout);
    mainLayout->addLayout(rightLayout);
    setLayout(mainLayout);

    setWindowTitle(tr("Find Files or Folders"));
}
```

The layout is handled by one QHBoxLayout, one QGridLayout, and one QVBoxLayout. The QGridLayout on the left and the QVBoxLayout on the right are placed side by side by the outer QHBoxLayout. The margin around the dialog and the spacing between the child widgets are set to default values based on the current widget style; they can be changed using QLayout::setMargin() and QLayout::setSpacing().

The same dialog could be created visually in *Qt Designer* by placing the child widgets in their approximate positions; selecting those that need to be laid out together; and clicking Form|Lay Out Horizontally, Form|Lay Out Vertically, or Form|Lay Out in a Grid. We used this approach in Chapter 2 for creating the Spreadsheet application's Go-to-Cell and Sort dialogs.

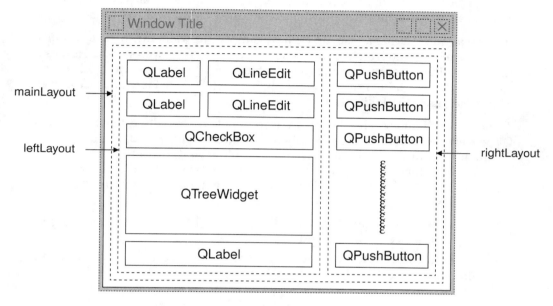

Figure 6.3. The Find File dialog's layout

Using `QHBoxLayout` and `QVBoxLayout` is fairly straightforward, but using `QGrid-Layout` is a bit more involved. `QGridLayout` works on a two-dimensional grid of cells. The `QLabel` in the top-left corner of the layout is at position (0, 0), and the corresponding `QLineEdit` is at position (0, 1). The `QCheckBox` spans two columns; it occupies the cells in positions (2, 0) and (2, 1). The `QTreeWidget` and the `QLabel` beneath it also span two columns. The calls to `addWidget()` have the following syntax:

```
layout->addWidget(widget, row, column, rowSpan, columnSpan);
```

Here, `widget` is the child widget to insert into the layout, (`row`, `column`) is the top-left cell occupied by the widget, `rowSpan` is the number of rows occupied by the widget, and `columnSpan` is the number of columns occupied by the widget. If omitted, the `rowSpan` and `columnSpan` parameters default to 1.

The `addStretch()` call tells the layout manager to consume space at that point in the layout. By adding a stretch item, we have told the layout manager to put any excess space between the Close button and the Help button. In *Qt Designer*, we can achieve the same effect by inserting a spacer. Spacers appear in *Qt Designer* as blue "springs".

Using layout managers provides additional benefits to those we have discussed so far. If we add a widget to a layout or remove a widget from a layout, the layout will automatically adapt to the new situation. The same applies if we call `hide()` or `show()` on a child widget. If a child widget's size hint changes, the layout will be automatically redone, taking into account the new size hint. Also, layout managers automatically set a minimum size for the form as a whole, based on the form's child widgets' minimum sizes and size hints.

In the examples presented so far, we have simply put widgets into layouts and used spacer items (stretches) to consume any excess space. In some cases, this isn't sufficient to make the layout look exactly the way we want. In these situations, we can adjust the layout by changing the size policies and size hints of the widgets being laid out.

A widget's size policy tells the layout system how it should stretch or shrink. Qt provides sensible default size policies for all its built-in widgets, but since no single default can account for every possible layout, it is still common for developers to change the size policies for one or two widgets on a form. A `QSizePolicy` has both a horizontal and a vertical component. Here are the most useful values:

- `Fixed` means that the widget cannot grow or shrink. The widget always stays at the size of its size hint.

- `Minimum` means that the widget's size hint is its minimum size. The widget cannot shrink below the size hint, but it can grow to fill available space if necessary.

- `Maximum` means that the widget's size hint is its maximum size. The widget can be shrunk down to its minimum size hint.

- `Preferred` means that the widget's size hint is its preferred size, but that the widget can still shrink or grow if necessary.

- `Expanding` means that the widget can shrink or grow and that it is especially willing to grow.

Figure 6.4 summarizes the meaning of the different size policies, using a `QLabel` showing the text "Some Text" as an example.

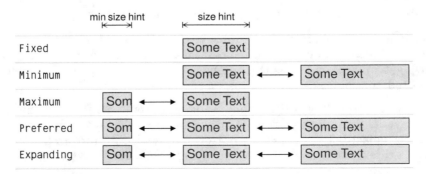

Figure 6.4. The meaning of the different size policies

In the figure, `Preferred` and `Expanding` are depicted the same way. So what is the difference? When a form that contains both `Preferred` and `Expanding` widgets is resized, extra space is given to the `Expanding` widgets, while the `Preferred` widgets stay at their size hint.

There are two other size policies: `MinimumExpanding` and `Ignored`. The former was necessary in a few rare cases in older versions of **Qt**, but it isn't useful anymore; the preferred approach is to use `Expanding` and reimplement `minimumSizeHint()` appropriately. The latter is similar to `Expanding`, except that it ignores the widget's size hint and minimum size hint.

In addition to the size policy's horizontal and vertical components, the `QSizePolicy` class stores a horizontal and a vertical stretch factor. These stretch factors can be used to indicate that different child widgets should grow at different rates when the form expands. For example, if we have a `QTreeWidget` above a `QTextEdit` and we want the `QTextEdit` to be twice as tall as the `QTreeWidget`, we can set the `QTextEdit`'s vertical stretch factor to 2 and the `QTreeWidget`'s vertical stretch factor to 1.

Yet another way of influencing a layout is to set a minimum size, a maximum size, or a fixed size on the child widgets. The layout manager will respect these constraints when laying out the widgets. And if this isn't sufficient, we can always derive from the child widget's class and reimplement `sizeHint()` to obtain the size hint we need.

Stacked Layouts

The `QStackedLayout` class lays out a set of child widgets, or "pages", and shows only one at a time, hiding the others from the user. The `QStackedLayout` itself is invisible and provides no intrinsic means for the user to change page. The small arrows and the dark gray frame in Figure 6.5 are provided by *Qt Designer* to make the layout easier to design with. For convenience, **Qt** also includes `QStackedWidget`, which provides a `QWidget` with a built-in `QStackedLayout`.

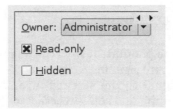

Figure 6.5. `QStackedLayout`

The pages are numbered from 0. To make a specific child widget visible, we can call `setCurrentIndex()` with a page number. The page number for a child widget is available using `indexOf()`.

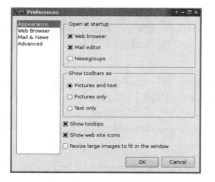 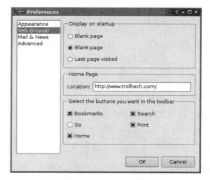

Figure 6.6. Two pages of the Preferences dialog

The Preferences dialog shown in Figure 6.6 is an example that uses QStacked-Layout. The dialog consists of a QListWidget on the left and a QStackedLayout on the right. Each item in the QListWidget corresponds to a different page in the QStackedLayout. Here's the relevant code from the dialog's constructor:

```
PreferenceDialog::PreferenceDialog(QWidget *parent)
    : QDialog(parent)
{
    ...
    listWidget = new QListWidget;
    listWidget->addItem(tr("Appearance"));
    listWidget->addItem(tr("Web Browser"));
    listWidget->addItem(tr("Mail & News"));
    listWidget->addItem(tr("Advanced"));

    stackedLayout = new QStackedLayout;
    stackedLayout->addWidget(appearancePage);
    stackedLayout->addWidget(webBrowserPage);
    stackedLayout->addWidget(mailAndNewsPage);
    stackedLayout->addWidget(advancedPage);
    connect(listWidget, SIGNAL(currentRowChanged(int)),
            stackedLayout, SLOT(setCurrentIndex(int)));
    ...
    listWidget->setCurrentRow(0);
}
```

We create a QListWidget and populate it with the page names. Then we create a QStackedLayout and call addWidget() for each page. We connect the list widget's currentRowChanged(int) signal to the stacked layout's setCurrentIndex(int) to implement the page switching and call setCurrentRow() on the list widget at the end of the constructor to start on page 0.

Forms like this are also very easy to create using *Qt Designer*:

1. Create a new form based on the "Dialog" or the "Widget" template.

2. Add a QListWidget and a QStackedWidget to the form.

3. Fill each page with child widgets and layouts.

(To create a new page, right-click and choose Insert Page; to switch pages, click the tiny left or right arrow located at the top-right of the `QStackedWidget`.)

4. Lay the widgets out side by side using a horizontal layout.

5. Connect the list widget's `currentRowChanged(int)` signal to the stacked widget's `setCurrentIndex(int)` slot.

6. Set the value of the list widget's `currentRow` property to 0.

Since we have implemented page switching using predefined signals and slots, the dialog will exhibit the correct behavior when previewed in *Qt Designer*.

Splitters

A `QSplitter` is a widget that contains other widgets. The widgets in a splitter are separated by splitter handles. Users can change the sizes of a splitter's child widgets by dragging the handles. Splitters can often be used as an alternative to layout managers, to give more control to the user.

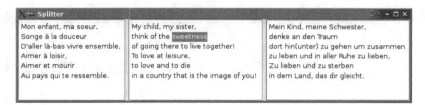

Figure 6.7. The Splitter application

The child widgets of a `QSplitter` are automatically placed side by side (or one below the other) in the order in which they are created, with splitter bars between adjacent widgets. Here's the code for creating the window depicted in Figure 6.7:

```
int main(int argc, char *argv[])
{
    QApplication app(argc, argv);

    QTextEdit *editor1 = new QTextEdit;
    QTextEdit *editor2 = new QTextEdit;
    QTextEdit *editor3 = new QTextEdit;

    QSplitter splitter(Qt::Horizontal);
    splitter.addWidget(editor1);
    splitter.addWidget(editor2);
    splitter.addWidget(editor3);
    ...
    splitter.show();
    return app.exec();
}
```

The example consists of three `QTextEdits` laid out horizontally by a `QSplitter` widget. Unlike layout managers, which simply lay out a form's child widgets and have no visual representation, `QSplitter` inherits from `QWidget` and can be used like any other widget.

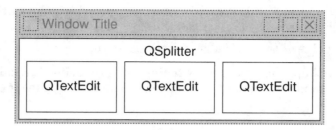

Figure 6.8. The Splitter application's widgets

Complex layouts can be achieved by nesting horizontal and vertical `QSplitters`. For example, the Mail Client application shown in Figure 6.9 consists of a horizontal `QSplitter` that contains a vertical `QSplitter` on its right side.

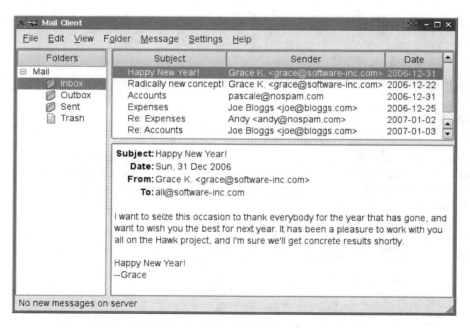

Figure 6.9. The Mail Client application on Mac OS X

Here's the code in the constructor of the Mail Client application's `QMainWindow` subclass:

```
MailClient::MailClient()
{
    ...
```

```
        rightSplitter = new QSplitter(Qt::Vertical);
        rightSplitter->addWidget(messagesTreeWidget);
        rightSplitter->addWidget(textEdit);
        rightSplitter->setStretchFactor(1, 1);

        mainSplitter = new QSplitter(Qt::Horizontal);
        mainSplitter->addWidget(foldersTreeWidget);
        mainSplitter->addWidget(rightSplitter);
        mainSplitter->setStretchFactor(1, 1);
        setCentralWidget(mainSplitter);

        setWindowTitle(tr("Mail Client"));
        readSettings();
    }
```

After creating the three widgets that we want to display, we create a vertical splitter, rightSplitter, and add the two widgets we want on the right. Then we create a horizontal splitter, mainSplitter, and add the widget we want it to display on the left and rightSplitter whose widgets we want shown on the right. We make mainSplitter the QMainWindow's central widget.

When the user resizes a window, QSplitter normally distributes the space so that the relative sizes of the child widgets stay the same. In the Mail Client example, we don't want this behavior; instead, we want the QTreeWidget and the QTableWidget to keep their sizes and we want to give any extra space to the QTextEdit. This is achieved by the two setStretchFactor() calls. The first argument is the 0-based index of the splitter's child widget, and the second argument is the stretch factor we want to set; the default is 0.

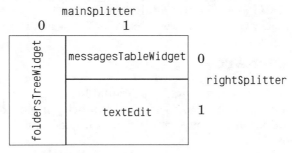

Figure 6.10. The Mail Client's splitter indexing

The first setStretchFactor() call is on rightSplitter, and it sets the widget at position 1 (textEdit) to have a stretch factor of 1. The second setStretchFactor() call is on mainSplitter, and it sets the widget at position 1 (rightSplitter) to have a stretch factor of 1. This ensures that the textEdit will get any additional space that is available.

When the application is started, QSplitter gives the child widgets appropriate sizes based on their initial sizes (or based on their size hint if no initial size is specified). We can move the splitter handles programmatically by calling QSplitter::setSizes(). The QSplitter class also provides a means of saving and restoring its state the next time the application is run. Here's the writeSettings() function that saves the Mail Client's settings:

```
void MailClient::writeSettings()
{
    QSettings settings("Software Inc.", "Mail Client");

    settings.beginGroup("mainWindow");
    settings.setValue("size", size());
    settings.setValue("mainSplitter", mainSplitter->saveState());
    settings.setValue("rightSplitter", rightSplitter->saveState());
    settings.endGroup();
}
```

Here's the corresponding readSettings() function:

```
void MailClient::readSettings()
{
    QSettings settings("Software Inc.", "Mail Client");

    settings.beginGroup("mainWindow");
    resize(settings.value("size", QSize(480, 360)).toSize());
    mainSplitter->restoreState(
            settings.value("mainSplitter").toByteArray());
    rightSplitter->restoreState(
            settings.value("rightSplitter").toByteArray());
    settings.endGroup();
}
```

QSplitter is fully supported by *Qt Designer*. To put widgets into a splitter, place the child widgets approximately in their desired positions, select them, and click Form|Lay Out Horizontally in Splitter or Form|Lay Out Vertically in Splitter.

Scrolling Areas

The QScrollArea class provides a scrollable viewport and two scroll bars. If we want to add scroll bars to a widget, it is much simpler to use a QScrollArea than to instantiate our own QScrollBars and implement the scrolling functionality ourselves.

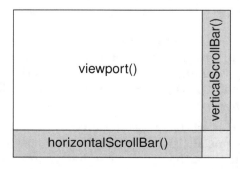

Figure 6.11. QScrollArea's constituent widgets

The way to use QScrollArea is to call setWidget() with the widget we want to add scroll bars to. QScrollArea automatically reparents the widget to make it a child of the viewport (accessible through QScrollArea::viewport()) if it isn't already. For example, if we want scroll bars around the IconEditor widget we developed in Chapter 5, we can write this:

```
int main(int argc, char *argv[])
{
    QApplication app(argc, argv);

    IconEditor *iconEditor = new IconEditor;
    iconEditor->setIconImage(QImage(":/images/mouse.png"));

    QScrollArea scrollArea;
    scrollArea.setWidget(iconEditor);
    scrollArea.viewport()->setBackgroundRole(QPalette::Dark);
    scrollArea.viewport()->setAutoFillBackground(true);
    scrollArea.setWindowTitle(QObject::tr("Icon Editor"));

    scrollArea.show();
    return app.exec();
}
```

The QScrollArea presents the widget at its current size or uses the size hint if the widget hasn't been resized yet. By calling setWidgetResizable(true), we can tell QScrollArea to automatically resize the widget to take advantage of any extra space beyond its size hint.

By default, the scroll bars are only displayed when the viewport is smaller than the child widget. We can force the scroll bars to always be shown by setting scroll bar policies:

```
scrollArea.setHorizontalScrollBarPolicy(Qt::ScrollBarAlwaysOn);
scrollArea.setVerticalScrollBarPolicy(Qt::ScrollBarAlwaysOn);
```

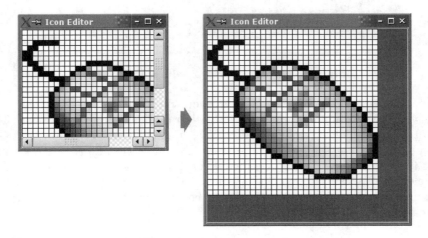

Figure 6.12. Resizing a QScrollArea

QScrollArea inherits much of its functionality from QAbstractScrollArea. Classes like QTextEdit and QAbstractItemView (the base class of Qt's item view classes) derive from QAbstractScrollArea, so we don't need to wrap them in a QScrollArea to get scroll bars.

Dock Widgets and Toolbars

Dock widgets are widgets that can be docked inside a QMainWindow or floated as independent windows. QMainWindow provides four dock widget areas: one above, one below, one to the left, and one to the right of the central widget. Applications like Microsoft Visual Studio and *Qt Linguist* make extensive use of dock windows to provide a very flexible user interface. In Qt, dock widgets are instances of QDockWidget.

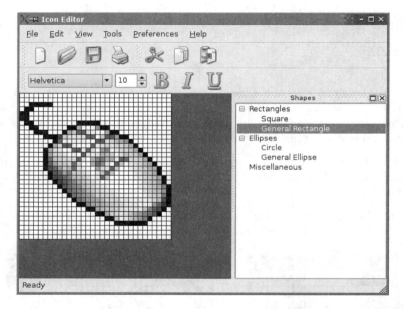

Figure 6.13. A QMainWindow with a dock widget

Every dock widget has its own title bar, even when it is docked. Users can move dock windows from one dock area to another by dragging the title bar. They can also detach a dock window from an area and let the dock window float as an independent window by dragging the dock window outside of any dock area. Free-floating dock windows are always "on top" of their main window. Users can close a QDockWidget by clicking the close button in the widget's title bar. Any combination of these features can be disabled by calling QDockWidget::setFeatures().

In earlier versions of Qt, toolbars were treated like dock widgets and shared the same dock areas. Starting with Qt 4, toolbars occupy their own areas around the central widget (as shown in Figure 6.14) and can't be undocked. If a floating toolbar is required, we can simply put it inside a `QDockWindow`.

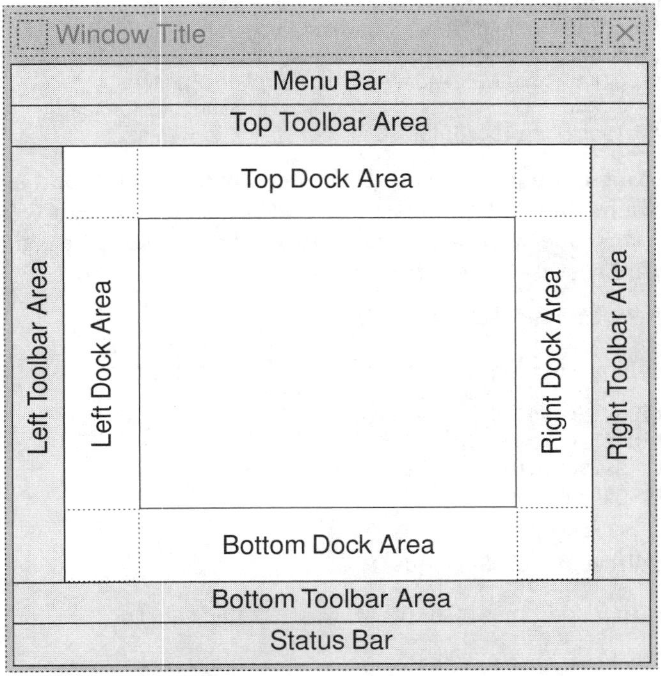

Figure 6.14. `QMainWindow`'s dock and toolbar areas

The corners indicated with dotted lines can belong to either of their two adjoining dock areas. For example, we could make the top-left corner belong to the left dock area by calling `QMainWindow::setCorner(Qt::TopLeftCorner, Qt::LeftDockWidgetArea)`.

The following code snippet shows how to wrap an existing widget (in this case, a `QTreeWidget`) in a `QDockWidget` and insert it into the right dock area:

```
QDockWidget *shapesDockWidget = new QDockWidget(tr("Shapes"));
shapesDockWidget->setWidget(treeWidget);
shapesDockWidget->setAllowedAreas(Qt::LeftDockWidgetArea
                                  | Qt::RightDockWidgetArea);
addDockWidget(Qt::RightDockWidgetArea, shapesDockWidget);
```

The `setAllowedAreas()` call specifies constraints on which dock areas can accept the dock window. Here, we only allow the user to drag the dock widget into the left and right dock areas, where there is enough vertical space for it to be displayed sensibly. If no allowed areas are explicitly set, the user can drag the dock widget to any of the four areas.

Here's how to create a toolbar containing a `QComboBox`, a `QSpinBox`, and a few `QToolButtons` from a `QMainWindow` subclass's constructor:

```
QToolBar *fontToolBar = new QToolBar(tr("Font"));
fontToolBar->addWidget(familyComboBox);
fontToolBar->addWidget(sizeSpinBox);
fontToolBar->addAction(boldAction);
fontToolBar->addAction(italicAction);
fontToolBar->addAction(underlineAction);
fontToolBar->setAllowedAreas(Qt::TopToolBarArea
                                | Qt::BottomToolBarArea);
addToolBar(fontToolBar);
```

If we want to save the position of all the dock widgets and toolbars so that we can restore them the next time the application is run, we can write code that is similar to the code we used to save a QSplitter's state, using QMainWindow's saveState() and restoreState() functions:

```
void MainWindow::writeSettings()
{
    QSettings settings("Software Inc.", "Icon Editor");

    settings.beginGroup("mainWindow");
    settings.setValue("size", size());
    settings.setValue("state", saveState());
    settings.endGroup();
}

void MainWindow::readSettings()
{
    QSettings settings("Software Inc.", "Icon Editor");

    settings.beginGroup("mainWindow");
    resize(settings.value("size").toSize());
    restoreState(settings.value("state").toByteArray());
    settings.endGroup();
}
```

Finally, QMainWindow provides a context menu that lists all the dock windows and toolbars. The user can close and restore dock windows and hide and restore toolbars using this menu.

Figure 6.15. A QMainWindow context menu

Multiple Document Interface

Applications that provide multiple documents within the main window's central area are called multiple document interface applications, or MDI applications. In Qt, an MDI application is created by using the QWorkspace class

as the central widget and by making each document window a child of the
QWorkspace.

It is conventional for MDI applications to provide a Window menu that includes
some commands for managing the windows and the list of windows. The active
window is identified with a checkmark. The user can make any window active
by clicking its entry in the Window menu.

In this section, we will develop the MDI Editor application shown in Figure 6.16 to demonstrate how to create an MDI application and how to implement its Window menu.

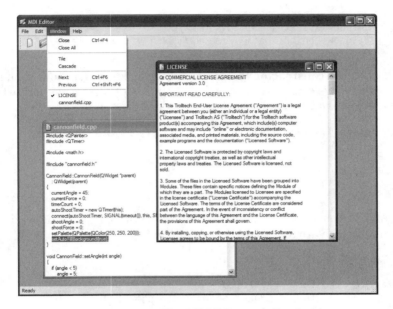

Figure 6.16. The MDI Editor application

The application consists of two classes: MainWindow and Editor. The code is
on the CD, and since most of it is the same or similar to the Spreadsheet
application from Part I, we will only present the new code.

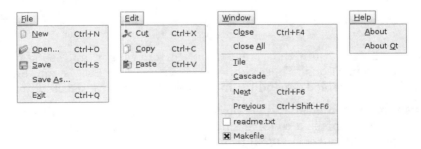

Figure 6.17. The MDI Editor application's menus

Let's start with the MainWindow class.

```
MainWindow::MainWindow()
{
    workspace = new QWorkspace;
    setCentralWidget(workspace);
    connect(workspace, SIGNAL(windowActivated(QWidget *)),
            this, SLOT(updateMenus()));

    createActions();
    createMenus();
    createToolBars();
    createStatusBar();

    setWindowTitle(tr("MDI Editor"));
    setWindowIcon(QPixmap(":/images/icon.png"));
}
```

In the MainWindow constructor, we create a QWorkspace widget and make it the
central widget. We connect the QWorkspace's windowActivated() signal to the slot
we will use to keep the window menu up to date.

```
void MainWindow::newFile()
{
    Editor *editor = createEditor();
    editor->newFile();
    editor->show();
}
```

The newFile() slot corresponds to the File|New menu option. It depends on the
createEditor() private function to create a child Editor widget.

```
Editor *MainWindow::createEditor()
{
    Editor *editor = new Editor;
    connect(editor, SIGNAL(copyAvailable(bool)),
            cutAction, SLOT(setEnabled(bool)));
    connect(editor, SIGNAL(copyAvailable(bool)),
            copyAction, SLOT(setEnabled(bool)));

    workspace->addWindow(editor);
    windowMenu->addAction(editor->windowMenuAction());
    windowActionGroup->addAction(editor->windowMenuAction());

    return editor;
}
```

The createEditor() function creates an Editor widget and sets up two
signal–slot connections. These connections ensure that Edit|Cut and Edit|Copy
are enabled or disabled depending on whether there is any selected text.

Because we are using MDI, it is possible that there will be multiple Editor
widgets in use. This is a concern since we are only interested in responding
to the copyAvailable(bool) signal from the active Editor window, not from the
others. But these signals can only ever be emitted by the active window, so this
isn't a problem in practice.

Once we have set up the Editor, we add a QAction representing the window to the Window menu. The action is provided by the Editor class, which we will cover in a moment. We also add the action to a QActionGroup object. The QActionGroup ensures that only one Window menu item is checked at a time.

```
void MainWindow::open()
{
    Editor *editor = createEditor();
    if (editor->open()) {
        editor->show();
    } else {
        editor->close();
    }
}
```

The open() function corresponds to File|Open. It creates an Editor for the new document and calls open() on the Editor. It makes more sense to implement the file operations in the Editor class than in the MainWindow class, because each Editor needs to maintain its own independent state.

If the open() fails, we simply close the editor since the user will have already been notified of the error. We don't need to explicitly delete the Editor object ourselves; this is done automatically by Editor through the Qt::WA_DeleteOn-Close widget attribute, which is set in the Editor constructor.

```
void MainWindow::save()
{
    if (activeEditor())
        activeEditor()->save();
}
```

The save() slot calls Editor::save() on the active editor, if there is one. Again, the code that performs the real work is located in the Editor class.

```
Editor *MainWindow::activeEditor()
{
    return qobject_cast<Editor *>(workspace->activeWindow());
}
```

The activeEditor() private function returns the active child window as an Editor pointer, or a null pointer if there isn't one.

```
void MainWindow::cut()
{
    if (activeEditor())
        activeEditor()->cut();
}
```

The cut() slot calls Editor::cut() on the active editor. We don't show the copy() and paste() slots because they follow the same pattern.

```
void MainWindow::updateMenus()
{
    bool hasEditor = (activeEditor() != 0);
```

```
        bool hasSelection = activeEditor()
                        && activeEditor()->textCursor().hasSelection();

    saveAction->setEnabled(hasEditor);
    saveAsAction->setEnabled(hasEditor);
    pasteAction->setEnabled(hasEditor);
    cutAction->setEnabled(hasSelection);
    copyAction->setEnabled(hasSelection);
    closeAction->setEnabled(hasEditor);
    closeAllAction->setEnabled(hasEditor);
    tileAction->setEnabled(hasEditor);
    cascadeAction->setEnabled(hasEditor);
    nextAction->setEnabled(hasEditor);
    previousAction->setEnabled(hasEditor);
    separatorAction->setVisible(hasEditor);

    if (activeEditor())
        activeEditor()->windowMenuAction()->setChecked(true);
}
```

The updateMenus() slot is called whenever a window is activated (and when the last window is closed) to update the menu system, due to the signal–slot connection we put in the MainWindow constructor.

Most menu options only make sense if there is an active window, so we disable them if there isn't one. At the end, we call setChecked() on the QAction representing the active window. Thanks to the QActionGroup, we don't need to explicitly uncheck the previously active window.

```
    void MainWindow::createMenus()
    {
        ...
        windowMenu = menuBar()->addMenu(tr("&Window"));
        windowMenu->addAction(closeAction);
        windowMenu->addAction(closeAllAction);
        windowMenu->addSeparator();
        windowMenu->addAction(tileAction);
        windowMenu->addAction(cascadeAction);
        windowMenu->addSeparator();
        windowMenu->addAction(nextAction);
        windowMenu->addAction(previousAction);
        windowMenu->addAction(separatorAction);
        ...
    }
```

The createMenus() private function fills the Window menu with actions. The actions are all typical of such menus and are easily implemented using QWorkspace's closeActiveWindow(), closeAllWindows(), tile(), and cascade() slots. Every time the user opens a new window, it is added to the Window menu's list of actions. (This is done in the createEditor() function that we saw on page 154.) When the user closes an editor window, its action in the Window menu is deleted (since the action is owned by the editor window), and so the action is automatically removed from the Window menu.

```
void MainWindow::closeEvent(QCloseEvent *event)
{
    workspace->closeAllWindows();
    if (activeEditor()) {
        event->ignore();
    } else {
        event->accept();
    }
}
```

The closeEvent() function is reimplemented to close all child windows, causing each child to receive a close event. If one of the child widgets "ignores" its close event (because the user canceled an "unsaved changes" message box), we ignore the close event for the MainWindow; otherwise, we accept it, resulting in Qt closing the entire window. If we didn't reimplement closeEvent() in MainWindow, the user would not be given the opportunity to save unsaved changes.

We have now finished our review of MainWindow, so we can move on to the Editor implementation. The Editor class represents one child window. It inherits QTextEdit, which provides the text editing functionality. Just as any Qt widget can be used as a stand-alone window, any Qt widget can be used as a child window in an MDI workspace.

Here's the class definition:

```
class Editor : public QTextEdit
{
    Q_OBJECT

public:
    Editor(QWidget *parent = 0);

    void newFile();
    bool open();
    bool openFile(const QString &fileName);
    bool save();
    bool saveAs();
    QSize sizeHint() const;
    QAction *windowMenuAction() const { return action; }

protected:
    void closeEvent(QCloseEvent *event);

private slots:
    void documentWasModified();

private:
    bool okToContinue();
    bool saveFile(const QString &fileName);
    void setCurrentFile(const QString &fileName);
    bool readFile(const QString &fileName);
    bool writeFile(const QString &fileName);
    QString strippedName(const QString &fullFileName);

    QString curFile;
    bool isUntitled;
```

```
        QString fileFilters;
        QAction *action;
    };
```

Four of the private functions that were in the Spreadsheet application's Main-
Window class (p. 57) are also present in the Editor class: okToContinue(), save-
File(), setCurrentFile(), and strippedName().

```
    Editor::Editor(QWidget *parent)
        : QTextEdit(parent)
    {
        action = new QAction(this);
        action->setCheckable(true);
        connect(action, SIGNAL(triggered()), this, SLOT(show()));
        connect(action, SIGNAL(triggered()), this, SLOT(setFocus()));

        isUntitled = true;
        fileFilters = tr("Text files (*.txt)\n"
                         "All files (*)");

        connect(document(), SIGNAL(contentsChanged()),
                this, SLOT(documentWasModified()));

        setWindowIcon(QPixmap(":/images/document.png"));
        setAttribute(Qt::WA_DeleteOnClose);
    }
```

First, we create a QAction representing the editor in the application's Window
menu and connect that action to the show() and setFocus() slots.

Since we allow users to create any number of editor windows, we must make
some provision for naming them so that they can be distinguished before they
have been saved for the first time. One common way of handling this is to
allocate names that include a number (for example, document1.txt). We use the
isUntitled variable to distinguish between names supplied by the user and
names we have created programmatically.

We connect the text document's contentsChanged() signal to the private docu-
mentWasModified() slot. This slot simply calls setWindowModified(true).

Finally, we set the Qt::WA_DeleteOnClose attribute to prevent memory leaks
when the user closes an Editor window.

After the constructor, we expect either newFile() or open() to be called.

```
    void Editor::newFile()
    {
        static int documentNumber = 1;

        curFile = tr("document%1.txt").arg(documentNumber);
        setWindowTitle(curFile + "[*]");
        action->setText(curFile);
        isUntitled = true;
        ++documentNumber;
    }
```

The newFile() function generates a name like document1.txt for the new document. The code belongs in newFile(), rather than the constructor, because we don't want to consume numbers when we call open() to open an existing document in a newly created Editor. Since documentNumber is declared static, it is shared across all Editor instances.

The "[*]" marker in the window title is a place marker for where we want the asterisk to appear when the file has unsaved changes on platforms other than Mac OS X. We covered this place marker in Chapter 3 (p. 58).

```cpp
bool Editor::open()
{
    QString fileName =
            QFileDialog::getOpenFileName(this, tr("Open"), ".",
                                         fileFilters);
    if (fileName.isEmpty())
        return false;

    return openFile(fileName);
}
```

The open() function tries to open an existing file using openFile().

```cpp
bool Editor::save()
{
    if (isUntitled) {
        return saveAs();
    } else {
        return saveFile(curFile);
    }
}
```

The save() function uses the isUntitled variable to determine whether it should call saveFile() or saveAs().

```cpp
void Editor::closeEvent(QCloseEvent *event)
{
    if (okToContinue()) {
        event->accept();
    } else {
        event->ignore();
    }
}
```

The closeEvent() function is reimplemented to allow the user to save unsaved changes. The logic is coded in the okToContinue() function, which pops up a message box that asks, "Do you want to save your changes?" If okToContinue() returns true, we accept the close event; otherwise, we "ignore" it and leave the window unaffected by it.

```cpp
void Editor::setCurrentFile(const QString &fileName)
{
    curFile = fileName;
    isUntitled = false;
    action->setText(strippedName(curFile));
```

```
        document()->setModified(false);
        setWindowTitle(strippedName(curFile) + "[*]");
        setWindowModified(false);
    }
```

The `setCurrentFile()` function is called from `openFile()` and `saveFile()` to update the `curFile` and `isUntitled` variables, to set the window title and action text, and to set the document's "modified" flag to `false`. Whenever the user modifies the text in the editor, the underlying `QTextDocument` emits the `contents-Changed()` signal and sets its internal "modified" flag to `true`.

```
    QSize Editor::sizeHint() const
    {
        return QSize(72 * fontMetrics().width('x'),
                     25 * fontMetrics().lineSpacing());
    }
```

The `sizeHint()` function returns a size based on the width of the letter 'x' and the height of a text line. `QWorkspace` uses the size hint to give an initial size to the window.

Here's the MDI Editor application's `main.cpp` file:

```
    #include <QApplication>

    #include "mainwindow.h"

    int main(int argc, char *argv[])
    {
        QApplication app(argc, argv);
        QStringList args = app.arguments();

        MainWindow mainWin;
        if (args.count() > 1) {
            for (int i = 1; i < args.count(); ++i)
                mainWin.openFile(args[i]);
        } else {
            mainWin.newFile();
        }

        mainWin.show();
        return app.exec();
    }
```

If the user specifies any files on the command line, we attempt to load them. Otherwise, we start with an empty document. Qt-specific command-line options, such as `-style` and `-font`, are automatically removed from the argument list by the `QApplication` constructor. So if we write

```
    mdieditor -style motif readme.txt
```

on the command line, `QApplication::arguments()` returns a `QStringList` containing two items ("mdieditor" and "readme.txt"), and the MDI Editor application starts up with the document `readme.txt`.

MDI is one way of handling multiple documents simultaneously. On Mac OS X, the preferred approach is to use multiple top-level windows. This approach is covered in the "Multiple Documents" section of Chapter 3.

7. Event Processing

Events are generated by the window system or by Qt itself in response to various occurrences. When the user presses or releases a key or mouse button, a key or mouse event is generated; when a window is shown for the first time, a paint event is generated to tell the newly visible window that it needs to draw itself. Most events are generated in response to user actions, but some, like timer events, are generated independently by the system.

When we program with Qt, we seldom need to think about events, because Qt widgets emit signals when something significant occurs. Events become useful when we write our own custom widgets or when we want to modify the behavior of existing Qt widgets.

Events should not be confused with signals. As a rule, signals are useful when *using* a widget, whereas events are useful when *implementing* a widget. For example, when we are using QPushButton, we are more interested in its clicked() signal than in the low-level mouse or key events that caused the signal to be emitted. But if we are implementing a class like QPushButton, we need to write code to handle mouse and key events and emit the clicked() signal when necessary.

Reimplementing Event Handlers

In Qt, an event is an object that inherits QEvent. Qt handles more than a hundred types of event, each identified by an enum value. For example, QEvent::type() returns QEvent::MouseButtonPress for mouse press events.

Many event types require more information than can be stored in a plain QEvent object; for example, mouse press events need to store which mouse button triggered the event as well as where the mouse pointer was positioned when the event occurred. This additional information is stored in dedicated QEvent subclasses, such as QMouseEvent.

Events are notified to objects through their event() function, inherited from QObject. The event() implementation in QWidget forwards the most common types of event to specific event handlers, such as mousePressEvent(), keyPress-Event(), and paintEvent().

We have already seen many event handlers when implementing MainWindow, IconEditor, and Plotter in earlier chapters. There are many other types of event listed in the QEvent reference documentation, and it is also possible to create custom event types and to dispatch events ourselves. Here, we will review two common event types that deserve more explanation: key events and timer events.

Key events are handled by reimplementing keyPressEvent() and keyRelease-Event(). The Plotter widget reimplements keyPressEvent(). Normally, we only need to reimplement keyPressEvent() since the only keys for which release is important are the modifier keys Ctrl, Shift, and Alt, and these can be checked for in a keyPressEvent() using QKeyEvent::modifiers(). For example, if we were implementing a CodeEditor widget, its stripped-down keyPressEvent() that distinguishes between Home and Ctrl+Home would look like this:

```
void CodeEditor::keyPressEvent(QKeyEvent *event)
{
    switch (event->key()) {
    case Qt::Key_Home:
        if (event->modifiers() & Qt::ControlModifier) {
            goToBeginningOfDocument();
        } else {
            goToBeginningOfLine();
        }
        break;
    case Qt::Key_End:
        ...
    default:
        QWidget::keyPressEvent(event);
    }
}
```

The Tab and Backtab (Shift+Tab) keys are special cases. They are handled by QWidget::event() before it calls keyPressEvent(), with the semantic of passing the focus to the next or previous widget in the focus chain. This behavior is usually what we want, but in a CodeEditor widget, we might prefer to make Tab indent a line. The event() reimplementation would then look like this:

```
bool CodeEditor::event(QEvent *event)
{
    if (event->type() == QEvent::KeyPress) {
        QKeyEvent *keyEvent = static_cast<QKeyEvent *>(event);
        if (keyEvent->key() == Qt::Key_Tab) {
            insertAtCurrentPosition('\t');
            return true;
        }
    }
```

```
        return QWidget::event(event);
}
```

If the event is a key press, we cast the QEvent object to a QKeyEvent and check which key was pressed. If the key is Tab, we do some processing and return true to tell Qt that we have handled the event. If we returned false, Qt would propagate the event to the parent widget.

A higher-level approach for implementing key bindings is to use a QAction. For example, if goToBeginningOfLine() and goToBeginningOfDocument() are public slots in the CodeEditor widget, and the CodeEditor is used as the central widget in a MainWindow class, we could add the key bindings with the following code:

```
MainWindow::MainWindow()
{
    editor = new CodeEditor;
    setCentralWidget(editor);

    goToBeginningOfLineAction =
            new QAction(tr("Go to Beginning of Line"), this);
    goToBeginningOfLineAction->setShortcut(tr("Home"));
    connect(goToBeginningOfLineAction, SIGNAL(activated()),
            editor, SLOT(goToBeginningOfLine()));

    goToBeginningOfDocumentAction =
            new QAction(tr("Go to Beginning of Document"), this);
    goToBeginningOfDocumentAction->setShortcut(tr("Ctrl+Home"));
    connect(goToBeginningOfDocumentAction, SIGNAL(activated()),
            editor, SLOT(goToBeginningOfDocument()));
    ...
}
```

This makes it easy to add the commands to a menu or a toolbar, as we saw in Chapter 3. If the commands don't appear in the user interface, the QAction objects could be replaced with a QShortcut object, the class used by QAction internally to support key bindings.

By default, key bindings set using QAction or QShortcut on a widget are enabled whenever the window that contains the widget is active. This can be changed using QAction::setShortcutContext() or QShortcut::setContext().

Another common type of event is the timer event. While most other event types occur as a result of a user action, timer events allow applications to perform processing at regular time intervals. Timer events can be used to implement blinking cursors and other animations, or simply to refresh the display.

To demonstrate timer events, we will implement a Ticker widget. This widget shows a text banner that scrolls left by one pixel every 30 milliseconds. If the widget is wider than the text, the text is repeated as often as necessary to fill the entire width of the widget.

ɔ say ++ How long it lasted was impossible to say ++ Hoⱱ

Figure 7.1. The Ticker widget

Here's the header file:

```
#ifndef TICKER_H
#define TICKER_H

#include <QWidget>

class Ticker : public QWidget
{
    Q_OBJECT
    Q_PROPERTY(QString text READ text WRITE setText)

public:
    Ticker(QWidget *parent = 0);

    void setText(const QString &newText);
    QString text() const { return myText; }
    QSize sizeHint() const;

protected:
    void paintEvent(QPaintEvent *event);
    void timerEvent(QTimerEvent *event);
    void showEvent(QShowEvent *event);
    void hideEvent(QHideEvent *event);

private:
    QString myText;
    int offset;
    int myTimerId;
};

#endif
```

We reimplement four event handlers in Ticker, three of which we have not seen before: timerEvent(), showEvent(), and hideEvent().

Now let's review the implementation:

```
#include <QtGui>

#include "ticker.h"

Ticker::Ticker(QWidget *parent)
    : QWidget(parent)
{
    offset = 0;
    myTimerId = 0;
}
```

The constructor initializes the offset variable to 0. The *x* coordinate at which the text is drawn is derived from the offset value. Timer IDs are always non-zero, so we use 0 to indicate that no timer has been started.

```
void Ticker::setText(const QString &newText)
{
    myText = newText;
    update();
    updateGeometry();
}
```

The setText() function sets the text to display. It calls update() to request a repaint and updateGeometry() to notify any layout manager responsible for the Ticker widget about a size hint change.

```
QSize Ticker::sizeHint() const
{
    return fontMetrics().size(0, text());
}
```

The sizeHint() function returns the space needed by the text as the widget's ideal size. QWidget::fontMetrics() returns a QFontMetrics object that can be queried to obtain information relating to the widget's font. In this case, we ask for the size required by the given text. (The first argument to QFontMetrics:: size() is a flag that isn't needed for simple strings, so we just pass 0.)

```
void Ticker::paintEvent(QPaintEvent * /* event */)
{
    QPainter painter(this);

    int textWidth = fontMetrics().width(text());
    if (textWidth < 1)
        return;
    int x = -offset;
    while (x < width()) {
        painter.drawText(x, 0, textWidth, height(),
                         Qt::AlignLeft | Qt::AlignVCenter, text());
        x += textWidth;
    }
}
```

The paintEvent() function draws the text using QPainter::drawText(). It uses fontMetrics() to ascertain how much horizontal space the text requires, and then draws the text as many times as necessary to fill the entire width of the widget, taking offset into account.

```
void Ticker::showEvent(QShowEvent * /* event */)
{
    myTimerId = startTimer(30);
}
```

The showEvent() function starts a timer. The call to QObject::startTimer() returns an ID number, which we can use later to identify the timer. QObject supports multiple independent timers, each with its own time interval. After the call to startTimer(), Qt will generate a timer event approximately every 30 milliseconds; the accuracy depends on the underlying operating system.

We could have called `startTimer()` in the `Ticker` constructor, but we save some resources by having **Qt** generate timer events only when the widget is actually visible.

```
void Ticker::timerEvent(QTimerEvent *event)
{
    if (event->timerId() == myTimerId) {
        ++offset;
        if (offset >= fontMetrics().width(text()))
            offset = 0;
        scroll(-1, 0);
    } else {
        QWidget::timerEvent(event);
    }
}
```

The `timerEvent()` function is called at intervals by the system. It increments `offset` by 1 to simulate movement, wrapping at the width of the text. Then it scrolls the contents of the widget one pixel to the left using `QWidget::scroll()`. It would have been sufficient to call `update()` instead of `scroll()`, but `scroll()` is more efficient because it simply moves the existing pixels on screen and only generates a paint event for the widget's newly revealed area (a 1-pixel-wide strip in this case).

If the timer event isn't for the timer we are interested in, we pass it on to our base class.

```
void Ticker::hideEvent(QHideEvent * /* event */)
{
    killTimer(myTimerId);
}
```

The `hideEvent()` function calls `QObject::killTimer()` to stop the timer.

Timer events are low level, and if we need multiple timers, it can become cumbersome to keep track of all the timer IDs. In such situations, it is usually easier to create a `QTimer` object for each timer. `QTimer` emits the `timeout()` signal at each time interval. `QTimer` also provides a convenient interface for single-shot timers (timers that time out just once).

Installing Event Filters

One really powerful feature of Qt's event model is that a `QObject` instance can be set to monitor the events of another `QObject` instance before the latter object even sees them.

Let's suppose that we have a `CustomerInfoDialog` widget composed of several `QLineEdit`s and that we want to use the Space key to move the focus to the next `QLineEdit`. This non-standard behavior might be appropriate for an in-house application whose users are trained in its use. A straightforward solution is to subclass `QLineEdit` and reimplement `keyPressEvent()` to call `focusNextChild()`, like this:

```
void MyLineEdit::keyPressEvent(QKeyEvent *event)
{
    if (event->key() == Qt::Key_Space) {
        focusNextChild();
    } else {
        QLineEdit::keyPressEvent(event);
    }
}
```

This approach has one main disadvantage: If we use several different kinds of widgets in the form (for example, QComboBoxes and QSpinBoxes), we must also subclass them to make them exhibit the same behavior. A better solution is to make CustomerInfoDialog monitor its child widgets' key press events and implement the required behavior in the monitoring code. This can be achieved using event filters. Setting up an event filter involves two steps:

1. Register the monitoring object with the target object by calling install-EventFilter() on the target.

2. Handle the target object's events in the monitor's eventFilter() function.

A good place to register the monitoring object is in the CustomerInfoDialog constructor:

```
CustomerInfoDialog::CustomerInfoDialog(QWidget *parent)
    : QDialog(parent)
{
    ...
    firstNameEdit->installEventFilter(this);
    lastNameEdit->installEventFilter(this);
    cityEdit->installEventFilter(this);
    phoneNumberEdit->installEventFilter(this);
}
```

Once the event filter is registered, the events that are sent to the firstName-Edit, lastNameEdit, cityEdit, and phoneNumberEdit widgets are first sent to the CustomerInfoDialog's eventFilter() function before they are sent on to their intended destination.

Here's the eventFilter() function that receives the events:

```
bool CustomerInfoDialog::eventFilter(QObject *target, QEvent *event)
{
    if (target == firstNameEdit || target == lastNameEdit
            || target == cityEdit || target == phoneNumberEdit) {
        if (event->type() == QEvent::KeyPress) {
            QKeyEvent *keyEvent = static_cast<QKeyEvent *>(event);
            if (keyEvent->key() == Qt::Key_Space) {
                focusNextChild();
                return true;
            }
        }
    }
    return QDialog::eventFilter(target, event);
}
```

First, we check to see if the target widget is one of the QLineEdits. If the event was a key press, we cast it to QKeyEvent and check which key was pressed. If the pressed key was Space, we call focusNextChild() to pass focus on to the next widget in the focus chain, and we return true to tell Qt that we have handled the event. If we returned false, Qt would send the event to its intended target, resulting in a spurious space being inserted into the QLineEdit.

If the target widget isn't a QLineEdit, or if the event isn't a Space key press, we pass control to the base class's implementation of eventFilter(). The target widget could also be some widget that the base class, QDialog, is monitoring. (In Qt 4.1, this is not the case for QDialog. However, other Qt widget classes, such as QScrollArea, do monitor some of their child widgets for various reasons.)

Qt offers five levels at which events can be processed and filtered:

1. **We can reimplement a specific event handler.**

   Reimplementing event handlers such as mousePressEvent(), keyPress-Event(), and paintEvent() is by far the most common way to process events. We have already seen many examples of this.

2. **We can reimplement QObject::event().**

   By reimplementing the event() function, we can process events before they reach the specific event handlers. This approach is mostly needed to override the default meaning of the Tab key, as shown earlier (p. 164). This is also used to handle rare types of event for which no specific event handler exists (for example, QEvent::HoverEnter). When we reimplement event(), we must call the base class's event() function for handling the cases we don't explicitly handle.

3. **We can install an event filter on a single QObject.**

   Once an object has been registered using installEventFilter(), all the events for the target object are first sent to the monitoring object's event-Filter() function. If multiple event filters are installed on the same object, the filters are activated in turn, from the most recently installed back to the first installed.

4. **We can install an event filter on the QApplication object.**

   Once an event filter has been registered for qApp (the unique QApplication object), every event for every object in the application is sent to the event-Filter() function before it is sent to any other event filter. This approach is mostly useful for debugging. It can also be used to handle mouse events sent to disabled widgets, which QApplication normally discards.

5. **We can subclass QApplication and reimplement notify().**

   Qt calls QApplication::notify() to send out an event. Reimplementing this function is the only way to get all the events, before any event filters get the opportunity to look at them. Event filters are generally more useful, because there can be any number of concurrent event filters, but only one notify() function.

Many event types, including mouse and key events, can be propagated. If the event has not been handled on the way to its target object or by the target object itself, the whole event processing process is repeated, but this time with the target object's parent as the new target. This continues, going from parent to parent, until either the event is handled or the top-level object is reached.

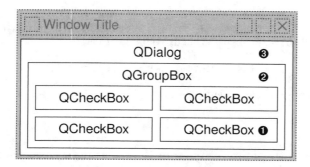

Figure 7.2. Event propagation in a dialog

Figure 7.2 shows how a key press event is propagated from child to parent in a dialog. When the user presses a key, the event is first sent to the widget that has focus, in this case the bottom-right QCheckBox. If the QCheckBox doesn't handle the event, Qt sends it to the QGroupBox, and finally to the QDialog object.

Staying Responsive During Intensive Processing

When we call QApplication::exec(), we start Qt's event loop. Qt issues a few events on startup to show and paint the widgets. After that, the event loop is running, constantly checking to see if any events have occurred and dispatching these events to QObjects in the application.

While one event is being processed, additional events may be generated and appended to Qt's event queue. If we spend too much time processing a particular event, the user interface will become unresponsive. For example, any events generated by the window system while the application is saving a file to disk will not be processed until the file is saved. During the save, the application will not respond to requests from the window system to repaint itself.

One solution is to use multiple threads: one thread for the application's user interface and another thread to perform file saving (or any other time-consuming operation). This way, the application's user interface will stay responsive while the file is being saved. We will see how to achieve this in Chapter 18.

A simpler solution is to make frequent calls to QApplication::processEvents() in the file saving code. This function tells Qt to process any pending events, and then returns control to the caller. In fact, `QApplication::exec()` is little more than a `while` loop around a `processEvents()` function call.

Here's an example of how we can keep the user interface responsive using `processEvents()`, based on the file saving code for `Spreadsheet` (p. 80):

```
bool Spreadsheet::writeFile(const QString &fileName)
{
    QFile file(fileName);
    ...
    for (int row = 0; row < RowCount; ++row) {
        for (int column = 0; column < ColumnCount; ++column) {
            QString str = formula(row, column);
            if (!str.isEmpty())
                out << quint16(row) << quint16(column) << str;
        }
        qApp->processEvents();
    }
    return true;
}
```

One danger with this approach is that the user might close the main window while the application is still saving, or even click File|Save a second time, resulting in undefined behavior. The easiest solution to this problem is to replace

```
qApp->processEvents();
```

with

```
qApp->processEvents(QEventLoop::ExcludeUserInputEvents);
```

telling Qt to ignore mouse and key events.

Often, we want to show a `QProgressDialog` while a long-running operation is taking place. `QProgressDialog` has a progress bar that keeps the user informed about the progress being made by the application. `QProgressDialog` also provides a Cancel button that allows the user to abort the operation. Here's the code for saving a Spreadsheet file using this approach:

```
bool Spreadsheet::writeFile(const QString &fileName)
{
    QFile file(fileName);
    ...
    QProgressDialog progress(this);
    progress.setLabelText(tr("Saving %1").arg(fileName));
    progress.setRange(0, RowCount);
    progress.setModal(true);

    for (int row = 0; row < RowCount; ++row) {
        progress.setValue(row);
        qApp->processEvents();
        if (progress.wasCanceled()) {
            file.remove();
            return false;
        }
```

```
        for (int column = 0; column < ColumnCount; ++column) {
            QString str = formula(row, column);
            if (!str.isEmpty())
                out << quint16(row) << quint16(column) << str;
        }
    }
    return true;
}
```

We create a `QProgressDialog` with `NumRows` as the total number of steps. Then, for each row, we call `setValue()` to update the progress bar. `QProgressDialog` automatically computes a percentage by dividing the current progress value by the total number of steps. We call `QApplication::processEvents()` to process any repaint events or any user clicks or key presses (for example, to allow the user to click Cancel). If the user clicks Cancel, we abort the save and remove the file.

We don't call `show()` on the `QProgressDialog` because progress dialogs do that for themselves. If the operation turns out to be short, presumably because the file to save is small or because the machine is fast, `QProgressDialog` will detect this and will not show itself at all.

In addition to multithreading and using `QProgressDialog`, there is a completely different way of dealing with long-running operations: Instead of performing the processing when the user requests, we can defer the processing until the application is idle. This can work if the processing can be safely interrupted and resumed, since we cannot predict how long the application will be idle.

In Qt, this approach can be implemented by using a 0-millisecond timer. These timers time out whenever there are no pending events. Here's an example `timerEvent()` implementation that shows the idle processing approach:

```
void Spreadsheet::timerEvent(QTimerEvent *event)
{
    if (event->timerId() == myTimerId) {
        while (step < MaxStep && !qApp->hasPendingEvents()) {
            performStep(step);
            ++step;
        }
    } else {
        QTableWidget::timerEvent(event);
    }
}
```

If `hasPendingEvents()` returns `true`, we stop processing and give control back to Qt. The processing will resume when Qt has handled all its pending events.

♦ *Painting with QPainter*

♦ *Painter Transformations*

♦ *High-Quality Rendering with QImage*

♦ *Printing*

♦ *Graphics with OpenGL*

8. 2D and 3D Graphics

Qt's 2D graphics engine is based on the QPainter class. QPainter can draw geometric shapes (points, lines, rectangles, ellipses, arcs, chords, pie segments, polygons, and Bézier curves), as well as pixmaps, images, and text. Furthermore, QPainter supports advanced features such as antialiasing (for text and shape edges), alpha blending, gradient filling, and vector paths. QPainter also supports transformations, which makes it possible to draw resolution-independent 2D graphics.

QPainter can be used to draw on a "paint device", such as a QWidget, a QPixmap, or a QImage. It is useful when we write custom widgets or custom item classes with their own look and feel. QPainter can also be used in conjunction with QPrinter for printing and for generating PDFs. This means that we can often use the same code to display data on screen and to produce printed reports.

An alternative to QPainter is to use OpenGL. OpenGL is a standard library for drawing 2D and 3D graphics. The *QtOpenGL* module makes it very easy to integrate OpenGL code into Qt applications.

Painting with QPainter

To start painting to a paint device (typically a widget), we simply create a QPainter and pass a pointer to the device. For example:

```
void MyWidget::paintEvent(QPaintEvent *event)
{
    QPainter painter(this);
    ...
}
```

We can draw various shapes using QPainter's draw...() functions. Figure 8.1 lists the most important ones. The way the drawing is performed is influenced by QPainter's settings. Some of these are adopted from the device, others are initialized to default values. The three main painter settings are the pen, the brush, and the font:

- The *pen* is used for drawing lines and shape outlines. It consists of a color, a width, a line style, a cap style, and a join style.

- The *brush* is the pattern used for filling geometric shapes. It normally consists of a color and a style, but can also be a texture (a pixmap that is repeated infinitely) or a gradient.

- The *font* is used for drawing text. A font has many attributes, including a family and a point size.

These settings can be modified at any time by calling `setPen()`, `setBrush()`, and `setFont()` with a `QPen`, `QBrush`, or `QFont` object.

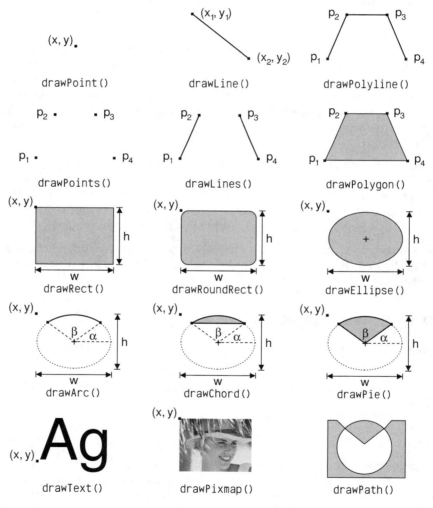

Figure 8.1. `QPainter`'s most frequently used `draw...()` functions

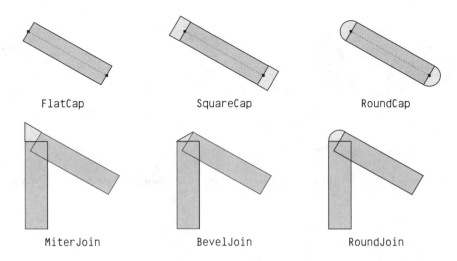

Figure 8.2. Cap and join styles

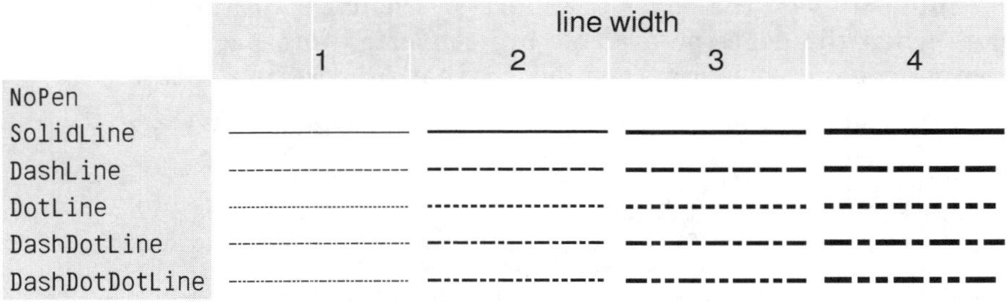

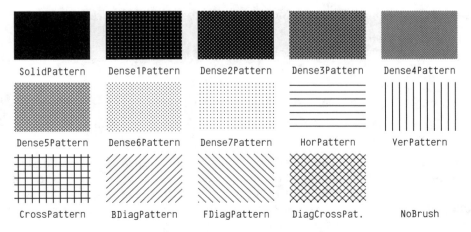

Figure 8.3. Pen styles

Figure 8.4. Predefined brush styles

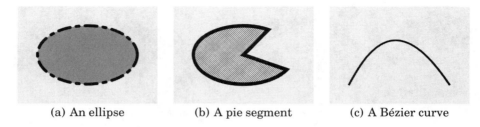

(a) An ellipse   (b) A pie segment   (c) A Bézier curve

Figure 8.5. Geometric shape examples

Let's see a few examples in practice. Here's the code to draw the ellipse shown in Figure 8.5 (a):

```
QPainter painter(this);
painter.setRenderHint(QPainter::Antialiasing, true);
painter.setPen(QPen(Qt::black, 12, Qt::DashDotLine, Qt::RoundCap));
painter.setBrush(QBrush(Qt::green, Qt::SolidPattern));
painter.drawEllipse(80, 80, 400, 240);
```

The setRenderHint() call enables antialiasing, telling QPainter to use different color intensities on the edges to reduce the visual distortion that normally occurs when the edges of a shape are converted into pixels. The result is smoother edges on platforms and devices that support this feature.

Here's the code to draw the pie segment shown in Figure 8.5 (b):

```
QPainter painter(this);
painter.setRenderHint(QPainter::Antialiasing, true);
painter.setPen(QPen(Qt::black, 15, Qt::SolidLine, Qt::RoundCap,
                    Qt::MiterJoin));
painter.setBrush(QBrush(Qt::blue, Qt::DiagCrossPattern));
painter.drawPie(80, 80, 400, 240, 60 * 16, 270 * 16);
```

The last two arguments to drawPie() are expressed in sixteenths of a degree.

Here's the code to draw the cubic Bézier curve shown in Figure 8.5 (c):

```
QPainter painter(this);
painter.setRenderHint(QPainter::Antialiasing, true);

QPainterPath path;
path.moveTo(80, 320);
path.cubicTo(200, 80, 320, 80, 480, 320);

painter.setPen(QPen(Qt::black, 8));
painter.drawPath(path);
```

The QPainterPath class can specify arbitrary vector shapes by connecting basic graphical elements together: straight lines, ellipses, polygons, arcs, quadratic and cubic Bézier curves, and other painter paths. Painter paths are the ultimate drawing primitive in the sense that any shape or combination of shapes can be expressed as a path.

A path specifies an outline, and the area described by the outline can be filled using a brush. In the example of Figure 8.5 (c), we didn't set a brush, so only the outline is drawn.

The three examples above use built-in brush patterns (`Qt::SolidPattern`, `Qt::DiagCrossPattern`, and `Qt::NoBrush`). In modern applications, gradient fills are a popular alternative to monochrome fill patterns. Gradients rely on color interpolation to obtain smooth transitions between two or more colors. They are frequently used to produce 3D effects; for example, the Plastique style uses gradients to render `QPushButtons`.

Qt supports three types of gradients: linear, conical, and radial. The Oven Timer example in the next section combines all three types of gradients in a single widget to make it look like the real thing.

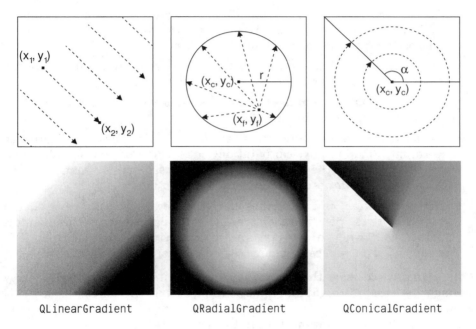

QLinearGradient   QRadialGradient   QConicalGradient

Figure 8.6. `QPainter`'s gradient brushes

- *Linear gradients* are defined by two control points and by a series of "color stops" on the line that connects these two points. For example, the linear gradient of Figure 8.6 is created using the following code:

  ```
  QLinearGradient gradient(50, 100, 300, 350);
  gradient.setColorAt(0.0, Qt::white);
  gradient.setColorAt(0.2, Qt::green);
  gradient.setColorAt(1.0, Qt::black);
  ```

  We specify three colors at three different positions between the two control points. Positions are specified as floating-point values between 0 and 1, where 0 corresponds to the first control point and 1 to the second control point. Colors between the specified stops are interpolated.

- *Radial gradients* are defined by a center point (x_c, y_c), a radius r, and a focal point (x_f, y_f), in addition to the color stops. The center point and the radius specify a circle. The colors spread outward from the focal point, which can be the center point or any other point inside the circle.

- *Conical gradients* are defined by a center point (x_c, y_c) and an angle α. The colors spread around the center point like the sweep of a watch's seconds hand.

So far we have mentioned QPainter's pen, brush, and font settings. In addition to these, QPainter has other settings that influence the way shapes and text are drawn:

- The *background brush* is used to fill the background of geometric shapes (underneath the brush pattern), text, or bitmaps when the *background mode* is Qt::OpaqueMode (the default is Qt::TransparentMode).

- The *brush origin* is the starting point for brush patterns, normally the top-left corner of the widget.

- The *clip region* is the area of the device that can be painted. Painting outside the clip region has no effect.

- The *viewport*, *window*, and *world matrix* determine how logical QPainter coordinates map to physical paint device coordinates. By default, these are set up so that the logical and physical coordinate systems coincide. Coordinate systems are covered in the next section.

- The *composition mode* specifies how the newly drawn pixels should interact with the pixels already present on the paint device. The default is "source over", where drawn pixels are drawn on top of existing pixels. This is supported only on certain devices and is covered later in this chapter.

At any time, we can save the current state of a painter on an internal stack by calling save() and restore it later on by calling restore(). This can be useful if we want to temporarily change some painter settings and then reset them to their previous values, as we will see in the next section.

Painter Transformations

With QPainter's default coordinate system, the point (0, 0) is located at the top-left corner of the paint device; x coordinates increase rightward and y coordinates increase downward. Each pixel occupies an area of size 1×1 in the default coordinate system.

One important thing to understand is that the center of a pixel lies on "half-pixel" coordinates. For example, the top-left pixel covers the area between points (0, 0) and (1, 1), and its center is located at (0.5, 0.5). If we ask QPainter to draw a pixel at, say, (100, 100), it will approximate the result by shifting the coordinate by +0.5 in both directions, resulting in the pixel centered at (100.5, 100.5) being drawn.

This distinction may seem rather academic at first, but it has important consequences in practice. First, the shifting by +0.5 only occurs if antialiasing is disabled (the default); if antialiasing is enabled and we try to draw a pixel at (100, 100) in black, QPainter will actually color the four pixels (99.5, 99.5), (99.5, 100.5), (100.5, 99.5), and (100.5, 100.5) light gray, to give the impression of a pixel lying exactly at the meeting point of the four pixels. If this effect is undesirable, we can avoid it by specifying half-pixel coordinates, for example, (100.5, 100.5).

When drawing shapes such as lines, rectangles, and ellipses, similar rules apply. Figure 8.7 shows how the result of a drawRect(2, 2, 6, 5) call varies according to the pen's width, when antialiasing is off. In particular, it is important to notice that a 6 × 5 rectangle drawn with a pen width of 1 effectively covers an area of size 7 × 6. This is different from older toolkits, including earlier versions of Qt, but it is essential for making truly scalable, resolution-independent vector graphics possible.

(0, 0)

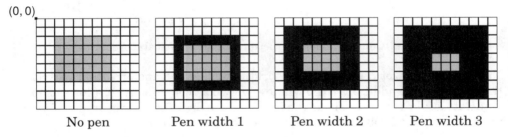

No pen   Pen width 1   Pen width 2   Pen width 3

Figure 8.7. Drawing a 6 × 5 rectangle with no antialiasing

Now that we understand the default coordinate system, we can take a closer look at how it can be changed using QPainter's viewport, window, and world matrix. (In this context, the term "window" does not refer to a window in the sense of a top-level widget, and the "viewport" has nothing to do with QScrollArea's viewport.)

The viewport and the window are tightly bound. The viewport is an arbitrary rectangle specified in physical coordinates. The window specifies the same rectangle, but in logical coordinates. When we do the painting, we specify points in logical coordinates, and those coordinates are converted into physical coordinates in a linear algebraic manner, based on the current window–viewport settings.

By default, the viewport and the window are set to the device's rectangle. For example, if the device is a 320 × 200 widget, both the viewport and the window are the same 320 × 200 rectangle with its top-left corner at position (0, 0). In this case, the logical and physical coordinate systems are the same.

The window–viewport mechanism is useful to make the drawing code independent of the size or resolution of the paint device. For example, if we want the logical coordinates to extend from (–50, –50) to (+50, +50), with (0, 0) in the middle, we can set the window as follows:

```
painter.setWindow(-50, -50, 100, 100);
```

The (–50, –50) pair specifies the origin, and the (100, 100) pair specifies the width and height. This means that the logical coordinates (–50, –50) now correspond to the physical coordinates (0, 0), and the logical coordinates (+50, +50) correspond to the physical coordinates (320, 200). In this example, we didn't change the viewport.

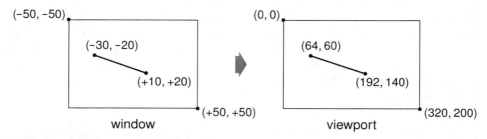

Figure 8.8. Converting logical coordinates into physical coordinates

Now comes the world matrix. The world matrix is a transformation matrix that is applied in addition to the window–viewport conversion. It allows us to translate, scale, rotate, or shear the items we are drawing. For example, if we wanted to draw text at a 45° angle, we would use this code:

```
QMatrix matrix;
matrix.rotate(45.0);
painter.setMatrix(matrix);
painter.drawText(rect, Qt::AlignCenter, tr("Revenue"));
```

The logical coordinates we pass to drawText() are transformed by the world matrix, then mapped to physical coordinates using the window–viewport settings.

If we specify multiple transformations, they are applied in the order in which they are given. For example, if we want to use the point (10, 20) as the rotation's pivot point, we can do so by translating the window, performing the rotation, and then translating the window back to its original position:

```
QMatrix matrix;
matrix.translate(-10.0, -20.0);
matrix.rotate(45.0);
matrix.translate(+10.0, +20.0);
painter.setMatrix(matrix);
painter.drawText(rect, Qt::AlignCenter, tr("Revenue"));
```

A simpler way to specify transformations is to use QPainter's translate(), scale(), rotate(), and shear() convenience functions:

```
painter.translate(-10.0, -20.0);
painter.rotate(45.0);
painter.translate(+10.0, +20.0);
painter.drawText(rect, Qt::AlignCenter, tr("Revenue"));
```

But if we want to use the same transformations repeatedly, it's more efficient to store them in a QMatrix object and set the world matrix on the painter whenever the transformations are needed.

Figure 8.9. The OvenTimer widget

To illustrate painter transformations, we will review the code of the OvenTimer widget shown in Figure 8.9. The OvenTimer widget is modeled after the kitchen timers that were used before it was common to have ovens with clocks built-in. The user can click a notch to set the duration. The wheel automatically turns counterclockwise until 0 is reached, at which point OvenTimer emits the timeout() signal.

```
class OvenTimer : public QWidget
{
    Q_OBJECT

public:
    OvenTimer(QWidget *parent = 0);

    void setDuration(int secs);
    int duration() const;
    void draw(QPainter *painter);

signals:
    void timeout();

protected:
    void paintEvent(QPaintEvent *event);
    void mousePressEvent(QMouseEvent *event);

private:
    QDateTime finishTime;
    QTimer *updateTimer;
    QTimer *finishTimer;
};
```

The `OvenTimer` class inherits `QWidget` and reimplements two virtual functions: `paintEvent()` and `mousePressEvent()`.

```
const double DegreesPerMinute = 7.0;
const double DegreesPerSecond = DegreesPerMinute / 60;
const int MaxMinutes = 45;
const int MaxSeconds = MaxMinutes * 60;
const int UpdateInterval = 1;
```

We start by defining a few constants that control the oven timer's look and feel.

```
OvenTimer::OvenTimer(QWidget *parent)
    : QWidget(parent)
{
    finishTime = QDateTime::currentDateTime();

    updateTimer = new QTimer(this);
    connect(updateTimer, SIGNAL(timeout()), this, SLOT(update()));

    finishTimer = new QTimer(this);
    finishTimer->setSingleShot(true);
    connect(finishTimer, SIGNAL(timeout()), this, SIGNAL(timeout()));
    connect(finishTimer, SIGNAL(timeout()), updateTimer, SLOT(stop()));
}
```

In the constructor, we create two `QTimer` objects: `updateTimer` is used to refresh the appearance of the widget every second, and `finishTimer` emits the widget's `timeout()` signal when the oven timer reaches 0. The `finishTimer` only needs to timeout once, so we call `setSingleShot(true)`; by default, timers fire repeatedly until they are stopped or destroyed. The last `connect()` call is an optimization to stop updating the widget every second when the timer is inactive.

```
void OvenTimer::setDuration(int secs)
{
    if (secs > MaxSeconds) {
        secs = MaxSeconds;
    } else if (secs <= 0) {
        secs = 0;
    }

    finishTime = QDateTime::currentDateTime().addSecs(secs);

    if (secs > 0) {
        updateTimer->start(UpdateInterval * 1000);
        finishTimer->start(secs * 1000);
    } else {
        updateTimer->stop();
        finishTimer->stop();
    }
    update();
}
```

The `setDuration()` function sets the duration of the oven timer to the given number of seconds. We compute the finish time by adding the duration to the current time (obtained from QDateTime::currentDateTime()) and store it in the finishTime private variable. At the end, we call update() to redraw the widget with the new duration.

The finishTime variable is of type QDateTime. Since the variable holds both a date and a time, we avoid a wrap-around bug when the current time is before midnight and the finish time is after midnight.

```
int OvenTimer::duration() const
{
    int secs = QDateTime::currentDateTime().secsTo(finishTime);
    if (secs < 0)
        secs = 0;
    return secs;
}
```

The duration() function returns the number of seconds left before the timer is due to finish. If the timer is inactive, we return 0.

```
void OvenTimer::mousePressEvent(QMouseEvent *event)
{
    QPointF point = event->pos() - rect().center();
    double theta = atan2(-point.x(), -point.y()) * 180 / 3.14159265359;
    setDuration(duration() + int(theta / DegreesPerSecond));
    update();
}
```

If the user clicks the widget, we find the closest notch using a subtle but effective mathematical formula, and we use the result to set the new duration. Then we schedule a repaint. The notch that the user clicked will now be at the top and will move counterclockwise as time passes until 0 is reached.

```
void OvenTimer::paintEvent(QPaintEvent * /* event */)
{
    QPainter painter(this);
    painter.setRenderHint(QPainter::Antialiasing, true);

    int side = qMin(width(), height());

    painter.setViewport((width() - side) / 2, (height() - side) / 2,
                        side, side);
    painter.setWindow(-50, -50, 100, 100);

    draw(&painter);
}
```

In paintEvent(), we set the viewport to be the largest square area that fits inside the widget, and we set the window to be the rectangle (–50, –50, 100, 100), that is, the 100 × 100 rectangle extending from (–50, –50) to (+50, +50). The qMin() template function returns the lowest of its two arguments. Then we call the draw() function to actually perform the drawing.

Figure 8.10. The OvenTimer widget at three different sizes

If we had not set the viewport to be a square, the oven timer would be an ellipse when the widget is resized to a non-square rectangle. To avoid such deformations, we must set the viewport and the window to rectangles with the same aspect ratio.

Now let's look at the drawing code:

```
void OvenTimer::draw(QPainter *painter)
{
    static const int triangle[3][2] = {
        { -2, -49 }, { +2, -49 }, { 0, -47 }
    };
    QPen thickPen(palette().foreground(), 1.5);
    QPen thinPen(palette().foreground(), 0.5);
    QColor niceBlue(150, 150, 200);

    painter->setPen(thinPen);
    painter->setBrush(palette().foreground());
    painter->drawPolygon(QPolygon(3, &triangle[0][0]));
```

We start by drawing the tiny triangle that marks the 0 position at the top of the widget. The triangle is specified by three hard-coded coordinates, and we use drawPolygon() to render it.

What is so convenient about the window–viewport mechanism is that we can hard-code the coordinates we use in the draw commands and still get good resizing behavior.

```
    QConicalGradient coneGradient(0, 0, -90.0);
    coneGradient.setColorAt(0.0, Qt::darkGray);
    coneGradient.setColorAt(0.2, niceBlue);
    coneGradient.setColorAt(0.5, Qt::white);
    coneGradient.setColorAt(1.0, Qt::darkGray);

    painter->setBrush(coneGradient);
    painter->drawEllipse(-46, -46, 92, 92);
```

We draw the outer circle and fill it using a conical gradient. The gradient's center point is located at (0, 0), and the angle is –90°.

```
QRadialGradient haloGradient(0, 0, 20, 0, 0);
haloGradient.setColorAt(0.0, Qt::lightGray);
haloGradient.setColorAt(0.8, Qt::darkGray);
haloGradient.setColorAt(0.9, Qt::white);
haloGradient.setColorAt(1.0, Qt::black);

painter->setPen(Qt::NoPen);
painter->setBrush(haloGradient);
painter->drawEllipse(-20, -20, 40, 40);
```

We fill the inner circle using a radial gradient. The center point and the focal point of the gradient are located at (0, 0). The radius of the gradient is 20.

```
QLinearGradient knobGradient(-7, -25, 7, -25);
knobGradient.setColorAt(0.0, Qt::black);
knobGradient.setColorAt(0.2, niceBlue);
knobGradient.setColorAt(0.3, Qt::lightGray);
knobGradient.setColorAt(0.8, Qt::white);
knobGradient.setColorAt(1.0, Qt::black);

painter->rotate(duration() * DegreesPerSecond);
painter->setBrush(knobGradient);
painter->setPen(thinPen);
painter->drawRoundRect(-7, -25, 14, 50, 150, 50);

for (int i = 0; i <= MaxMinutes; ++i) {
    if (i % 5 == 0) {
        painter->setPen(thickPen);
        painter->drawLine(0, -41, 0, -44);
        painter->drawText(-15, -41, 30, 25,
                          Qt::AlignHCenter | Qt::AlignTop,
                          QString::number(i));
    } else {
        painter->setPen(thinPen);
        painter->drawLine(0, -42, 0, -44);
    }
    painter->rotate(-DegreesPerMinute);
}
}
```

We call `rotate()` to rotate the painter's coordinate system. In the old coordinate system, the 0-minute mark was on top; now, the 0-minute mark is moved to the place that is appropriate for the time left. We draw the rectangular knob handle after the rotation, since its orientation depends on the rotation angle.

In the `for` loop, we draw the tick marks along the outer circle's edge and the numbers for each multiple of 5 minutes. The text is drawn in an invisible rectangle underneath the tick mark. At the end of each iteration, we rotate the painter clockwise by 7°, which corresponds to one minute. The next time we draw a tick mark, it will be at a different position around the circle, even though the coordinates we pass to the drawLine() and drawText() calls are always the same.

The code in the for loop suffers from a minor flaw, which would quickly become apparent if we performed more iterations. Each time we call rotate(), we effectively multiply the current world matrix with a rotation matrix, producing a new world matrix. The rounding errors associated with floating-point arithmetic add up, resulting in an increasingly inaccurate world matrix. Here's one way to rewrite the code to avoid this issue, using save() and restore() to save and reload the original transformation matrix for each iteration:

```
for (int i = 0; i <= MaxMinutes; ++i) {
    painter->save();
    painter->rotate(-i * DegreesPerMinute);

    if (i % 5 == 0) {
        painter->setPen(thickPen);
        painter->drawLine(0, -41, 0, -44);
        painter->drawText(-15, -41, 30, 25,
                          Qt::AlignHCenter | Qt::AlignTop,
                          QString::number(i));
    } else {
        painter->setPen(thinPen);
        painter->drawLine(0, -42, 0, -44);
    }
    painter->restore();
}
```

Another way of implementing an oven timer would have been to compute the (x, y) positions ourselves, using sin() and cos() to find the positions along the circle. But then we would still need to use a translation and a rotation to draw the text at an angle.

High-Quality Rendering with QImage

When drawing, we may be faced with a trade-off between speed and accuracy. For example, on X11 and Mac OS X, drawing on a QWidget or QPixmap relies on the platform's native paint engine. On X11, this ensures that communication with the X server is kept to a minimum; only paint commands are sent rather than actual image data. The main drawback of this approach is that Qt is limited by the platform's native support:

- On X11, features such as antialiasing and support for fractional coordinates are available only if the X Render extension is present on the X server.
- On Mac OS X, the native aliased graphics engine uses different algorithms for drawing polygons than X11 and Windows, with slightly different results.

When accuracy is more important than efficiency, we can draw to a QImage and copy the result onto the screen. This always uses Qt's own internal paint engine, giving identical results on all platforms. The only restriction is that the QImage on which we paint must be created with an argument of either QImage::Format_RGB32 or QImage::Format_ARGB32_Premultiplied.

The premultiplied ARGB32 format is almost identical to the conventional ARGB32 format (0xaarrggbb), the difference being that the red, green, and blue channels are "premultiplied" with the alpha channel. This means that the RGB values, which normally range from 0x00 to 0xFF, are scaled from 0x00 to the alpha value. For example, a 50%-transparent blue color is represented as 0x7F0000FF in ARGB32 format, but 0x7F00007F in premultiplied ARGB32 format, and similarly a 75%-transparent dark green of 0x3F008000 in ARGB32 format would be 0x3F002000 in premultiplied ARGB32 format.

Let's suppose we want to use antialiasing for drawing a widget, and we want to obtain good results even on X11 systems with no X Render extension. The original paintEvent() handler, which relies on X Render for the antialiasing, might look like this:

```
void MyWidget::paintEvent(QPaintEvent *event)
{
    QPainter painter(this);
    painter.setRenderHint(QPainter::Antialiasing, true);
    draw(&painter);
}
```

Here's how to rewrite the widget's paintEvent() function to use Qt's platform-independent graphics engine:

```
void MyWidget::paintEvent(QPaintEvent *event)
{
    QImage image(size(), QImage::Format_ARGB32_Premultiplied);
    QPainter imagePainter(&image);
    imagePainter.initFrom(this);
    imagePainter.setRenderHint(QPainter::Antialiasing, true);
    imagePainter.eraseRect(rect());
    draw(&imagePainter);
    imagePainter.end();

    QPainter widgetPainter(this);
    widgetPainter.drawImage(0, 0, image);
}
```

We create a QImage of the same size as the widget in premultiplied ARGB32 format, and a QPainter to draw on the image. The initFrom() call initializes the painter's pen, background, and font based on the widget. We perform the drawing using the QPainter as usual, and at the end we reuse the QPainter object to copy the image onto the widget.

This approach produces identical high-quality results on all platforms, with the exception of font rendering, which depends on the installed fonts.

One particularly powerful feature of Qt's graphics engine is its support for composition modes. These specify how a source and a destination pixel are merged together when drawing. This applies to all painting operations, including pen, brush, gradient, and image drawing.

The default composition mode is `QImage::CompositionMode_SourceOver`, meaning that the source pixel (the pixel we are drawing) is blended on top of the destination pixel (the existing pixel) in such a way that the alpha component of the source defines its translucency. Figure 8.11 shows the result of drawing a semi-transparent butterfly on top of a checker pattern with the different modes.

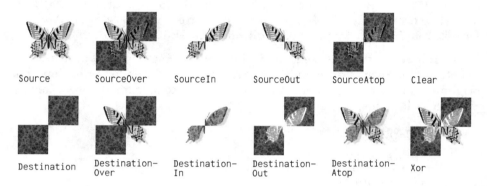

Figure 8.11. `QPainter`'s composition modes

Compositions modes are set using `QPainter::setCompositionMode()`. For example, here's how to create a `QImage` containing the XOR of the butterfly and the checker pattern:

```
QImage resultImage = checkerPatternImage;
QPainter painter(&resultImage);
painter.setCompositionMode(QPainter::CompositionMode_Xor);
painter.drawImage(0, 0, butterflyImage);
```

One issue to be aware of is that the `QImage::CompositionMode_Xor` operation applies to the alpha channel. This means that if we XOR the color white (`0xFFFFFFFF`) with itself, we obtain a transparent color (`0x00000000`), not black (`0xFF000000`).

Printing

Printing in Qt is similar to drawing on a `QWidget`, `QPixmap`, or `QImage`. It consists of the following steps:

1. Create a `QPrinter` to serve as the paint device.

2. Pop up a `QPrintDialog`, allowing the user to choose a printer and to set a few options.

3. Create a `QPainter` to operate on the `QPrinter`.

4. Draw a page using the `QPainter`.

5. Call `QPrinter::newPage()` to advance to the next page.

6. Repeat steps 4 and 5 until all the pages are printed.

On Windows and Mac OS X, `QPrinter` uses the system's printer drivers. On Unix, it generates PostScript and sends it to `lp` or `lpr` (or to the program set using `QPrinter::setPrintProgram()`). `QPrinter` can also be used to generate PDF files by calling `setOutputFormat(QPrinter::PdfFormat)`.

Figure 8.12. Printing a `QImage`

Let's start with some simple examples that all print on a single page. The first example prints a `QImage`:

```
void PrintWindow::printImage(const QImage &image)
{
    QPrintDialog printDialog(&printer, this);
    if (printDialog.exec()) {
        QPainter painter(&printer);
        QRect rect = painter.viewport();
        QSize size = image.size();
        size.scale(rect.size(), Qt::KeepAspectRatio);
        painter.setViewport(rect.x(), rect.y(),
                            size.width(), size.height());
        painter.setWindow(image.rect());
        painter.drawImage(0, 0, image);
    }
}
```

We assume that the `PrintWindow` class has a member variable called `printer` of type `QPrinter`. We could simply have created the `QPrinter` on the stack in `printImage()`, but then it would not remember the user's settings from one print run to another.

We create a `QPrintDialog` and call `exec()` to show it. It returns `true` if the user clicked the OK button; otherwise, it returns `false`. After the call to `exec()`, the `QPrinter` object is ready to use. (It is also possible to print without using a `QPrintDialog`, by directly calling `QPrinter` member functions to set things up.)

Next, we create a `QPainter` to draw on the `QPrinter`. We set the window to the image's rectangle and the viewport to a rectangle with the same aspect ratio, and we draw the image at position (0, 0).

By default, `QPainter`'s window is initialized so that the printer appears to have a similar resolution as the screen (usually somewhere between 72 and 100 dots per inch), making it easy to reuse widget painting code for printing. Here, it didn't matter, because we set our own window.

Printing items that take up no more than a single page is simple, but many applications need to print multiple pages. For those, we need to paint one page at a time and call `newPage()` to advance to the next page. This raises the problem of determining how much information we can print on each page. There are two main approaches to handling multi-page documents with Qt:

- We can convert our data to HTML and render it using `QTextDocument`, Qt's rich text engine.
- We can perform the drawing and the page breaking by hand.

We will review both approaches in turn. As an example, we will print a flower guide: a list of flower names, each with a textual description. Each entry in the guide is stored as a string of the format "*name*: *description*", for example:

```
Miltonopsis santanae: A most dangerous orchid species.
```

Since each flower's data is represented by a single string, we can represent all the flowers in the guide using one `QStringList`. Here's the function that prints a flower guide using Qt's rich text engine:

```
void PrintWindow::printFlowerGuide(const QStringList &entries)
{
    QString html;

    foreach (QString entry, entries) {
        QStringList fields = entry.split(": ");
        QString title = Qt::escape(fields[0]);
        QString body = Qt::escape(fields[1]);

        html += "<table width=\"100%\" border=1 cellspacing=0>\n"
                "<tr><td bgcolor=\"lightgray\"><font size=\"+1\">"
                "<b><i>" + title + "</i></b></font>\n<tr><td>" + body
                + "\n</table>\n<br>\n";
    }
    printHtml(html);
}
```

The first step is to convert the QStringList into HTML. Each flower becomes an HTML table with two cells. We use Qt::escape() to replace the special characters '&', '<', '>' with the corresponding HTML entities ("&", "<", ">"). Then we call printHtml() to print the text.

```cpp
void PrintWindow::printHtml(const QString &html)
{
    QPrintDialog printDialog(&printer, this);
    if (printDialog.exec()) {
        QPainter painter(&printer);
        QTextDocument textDocument;
        textDocument.setHtml(html);
        textDocument.print(&printer);
    }
}
```

The printHtml() function pops up a QPrintDialog and takes care of printing an HTML document. It can be reused "as is" in any Qt application to print arbitrary HTML pages.

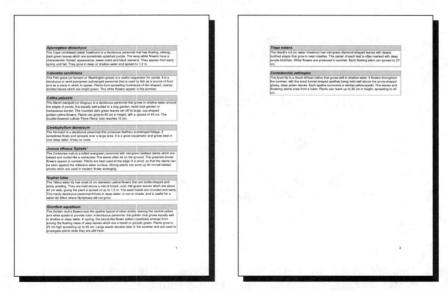

Figure 8.13. Printing a flower guide using QTextDocument

Converting a document to HTML and using QTextDocument to print it is by far the most convenient alternative for printing reports and other complex documents. In cases where we need more control, we can do the page layout and the drawing by hand. Let's now see how we can use this approach to print a flower guide. Here's the new printFlowerGuide() function:

```cpp
void PrintWindow::printFlowerGuide(const QStringList &entries)
{
    QPrintDialog printDialog(&printer, this);
    if (printDialog.exec()) {
```

```
        QPainter painter(&printer);
        QList<QStringList> pages;

        paginate(&painter, &pages, entries);
        printPages(&painter, pages);
    }
}
```

After setting up the printer and constructing the painter, we call the `paginate()` helper function to determine which entry should appear on which page. The result of this is a list of `QStringList`s, with each `QStringList` holding the entries for one page. We pass on that result to `printPages()`.

For example, let's suppose that the flower guide contains 6 entries, which we will refer to as $\mathcal{A}$, $\mathcal{B}$, $\mathcal{C}$, $\mathcal{D}$, $\mathcal{E}$, and $\mathcal{F}$. Now let's suppose that there is room for $\mathcal{A}$ and $\mathcal{B}$ on the first page; $\mathcal{C}$, $\mathcal{D}$, and $\mathcal{E}$ on the second page; and $\mathcal{F}$ on the third page. The `pages` list would then have the list $[\mathcal{A}, \mathcal{B}]$ at index position 0, the list $[\mathcal{C}, \mathcal{D}, \mathcal{E}]$ at index position 1, and the list $[\mathcal{F}]$ at index position 2.

```
void PrintWindow::paginate(QPainter *painter, QList<QStringList> *pages,
                           const QStringList &entries)
{
    QStringList currentPage;
    int pageHeight = painter->window().height() - 2 * LargeGap;
    int y = 0;

    foreach (QString entry, entries) {
        int height = entryHeight(painter, entry);
        if (y + height > pageHeight && !currentPage.empty()) {
            pages->append(currentPage);
            currentPage.clear();
            y = 0;
        }
        currentPage.append(entry);
        y += height + MediumGap;
    }
    if (!currentPage.empty())
        pages->append(currentPage);
}
```

The `paginate()` function distributes the flower guide entries into pages. It relies on the `entryHeight()` function, which computes the height of one entry. It also takes into account the vertical gaps at the top and bottom of the page, of size `LargeGap`.

We iterate through the entries and append them to the current page until we come to an entry that doesn't fit; then we append the current page to the `pages` list and start a new page.

```
int PrintWindow::entryHeight(QPainter *painter, const QString &entry)
{
    QStringList fields = entry.split(": ");
    QString title = fields[0];
    QString body = fields[1];
```

```
    int textWidth = painter->window().width() - 2 * SmallGap;
    int maxHeight = painter->window().height();

    painter->setFont(titleFont);
    QRect titleRect = painter->boundingRect(0, 0, textWidth, maxHeight,
                                       Qt::TextWordWrap, title);
    painter->setFont(bodyFont);
    QRect bodyRect = painter->boundingRect(0, 0, textWidth, maxHeight,
                                       Qt::TextWordWrap, body);
    return titleRect.height() + bodyRect.height() + 4 * SmallGap;
}
```

The `entryHeight()` function uses `QPainter::boundingRect()` to compute the vertical space needed by one entry. Figure 8.14 shows the layout of a flower entry and the meaning of the `SmallGap` and `MediumGap` constants.

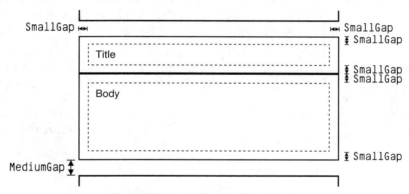

Figure 8.14. A flower entry's layout

```
void PrintWindow::printPages(QPainter *painter,
                             const QList<QStringList> &pages)
{
    int firstPage = printer.fromPage() - 1;
    if (firstPage >= pages.size())
        return;
    if (firstPage == -1)
        firstPage = 0;

    int lastPage = printer.toPage() - 1;
    if (lastPage == -1 || lastPage >= pages.size())
        lastPage = pages.size() - 1;

    int numPages = lastPage - firstPage + 1;

    for (int i = 0; i < printer.numCopies(); ++i) {
        for (int j = 0; j < numPages; ++j) {
            if (i != 0 || j != 0)
                printer.newPage();

            int index;
            if (printer.pageOrder() == QPrinter::FirstPageFirst) {
                index = firstPage + j;
            } else {
```

```
                    index = lastPage - j;
            }
            printPage(painter, pages[index], index + 1);
        }
    }
}
```

The `printPages()` function's role is to print each page using `printPage()` in the correct order and the correct amount of times. Using the `QPrintDialog`, the user might request several copies, specify a print range, or request the pages in reverse order. It is our responsibility to honor these options—or to disable them using `QPrintDialog::setEnabledOptions()`.

We start by determining the range to print. `QPrinter`'s `fromPage()` and `toPage()` functions return the page numbers selected by the user, or 0 if no range was chosen. We subtract 1 because our `pages` list is indexed from 0, and set `firstPage` and `lastPage` to cover the full range if the user didn't set any range.

Then we print each page. The outer `for` loop iterates as many times as necessary to produce the number of copies requested by the user. Most printer drivers support multiple copies, so for those `QPrinter::numCopies()` always returns 1. If the printer driver can't handle multiple copies, `numCopies()` returns the number of copies requested by the user, and the application is responsible for printing that number of copies. (In the `QImage` example earlier in this section, we ignored `numCopies()` for the sake of simplicity.)

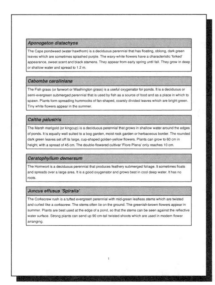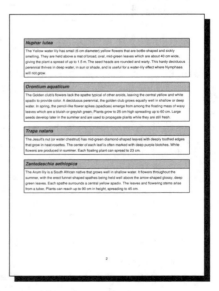

Figure 8.15. Printing a flower guide using `QPainter`

The inner `for` loop iterates through the pages. If the page isn't the first page, we call `newPage()` to flush the old page and start painting on a fresh page. We call `printPage()` to paint each page.

```
void PrintWindow::printPage(QPainter *painter,
                            const QStringList &entries, int pageNumber)
{
    painter->save();
    painter->translate(0, LargeGap);
    foreach (QString entry, entries) {
        QStringList fields = entry.split(": ");
        QString title = fields[0];
        QString body = fields[1];
        printBox(painter, title, titleFont, Qt::lightGray);
        printBox(painter, body, bodyFont, Qt::white);
        painter->translate(0, MediumGap);
    }
    painter->restore();

    painter->setFont(footerFont);
    painter->drawText(painter->window(),
                      Qt::AlignHCenter | Qt::AlignBottom,
                      QString::number(pageNumber));
}
```

The `printPage()` function iterates through all the flower guide entries and prints them using two calls to `printBox()`: one for the title (the flower's name) and one for the body (its description). It also draws the page number centered at the bottom of the page.

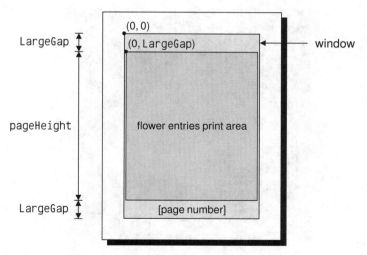

Figure 8.16. The flower guide's page layout

```
void PrintWindow::printBox(QPainter *painter, const QString &str,
                           const QFont &font, const QBrush &brush)
{
    painter->setFont(font);

    int boxWidth = painter->window().width();
    int textWidth = boxWidth - 2 * SmallGap;
    int maxHeight = painter->window().height();
```

```
    QRect textRect = painter->boundingRect(SmallGap, SmallGap,
                                           textWidth, maxHeight,
                                           Qt::TextWordWrap, str);
    int boxHeight = textRect.height() + 2 * SmallGap;

    painter->setPen(QPen(Qt::black, 2, Qt::SolidLine));
    painter->setBrush(brush);
    painter->drawRect(0, 0, boxWidth, boxHeight);
    painter->drawText(textRect, Qt::TextWordWrap, str);
    painter->translate(0, boxHeight);
}
```

The `printBox()` function draws the outline of a box, then draws the text inside the box.

Graphics with OpenGL

OpenGL is a standard API for rendering 2D and 3D graphics. Qt applications can draw 3D graphics by using the *QtOpenGL* module, which relies on the system's OpenGL library. This section assumes that you are familiar with OpenGL. If OpenGL is new to you, a good place to start learning it is `http://www.opengl.org/`.

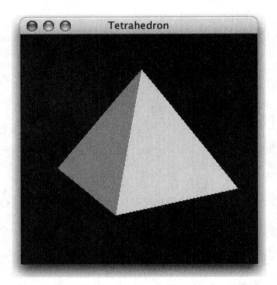

Figure 8.17. The Tetrahedron application

Drawing graphics with OpenGL from a Qt application is straightforward: We must subclass `QGLWidget`, reimplement a few virtual functions, and link the application against the *QtOpenGL* and OpenGL libraries. Because `QGLWidget` inherits from `QWidget`, most of what we already know still applies. The main difference is that we use standard OpenGL functions to perform the drawing instead of `QPainter`.

To show how this works, we will review the code of the Tetrahedron application shown in Figure 8.17. The application presents a 3D tetrahedron, or four-sided die, with each face drawn using a different color. The user can rotate the tetrahedron by pressing a mouse button and dragging. The user can set the color of a face by double-clicking it and choosing a color from the QColorDialog that pops up.

```cpp
class Tetrahedron : public QGLWidget
{
    Q_OBJECT

public:
    Tetrahedron(QWidget *parent = 0);

protected:
    void initializeGL();
    void resizeGL(int width, int height);
    void paintGL();
    void mousePressEvent(QMouseEvent *event);
    void mouseMoveEvent(QMouseEvent *event);
    void mouseDoubleClickEvent(QMouseEvent *event);

private:
    void draw();
    int faceAtPosition(const QPoint &pos);

    GLfloat rotationX;
    GLfloat rotationY;
    GLfloat rotationZ;
    QColor faceColors[4];
    QPoint lastPos;
};
```

The Tetrahedron class inherits from QGLWidget. The initializeGL(), resizeGL(), and paintGL() functions are reimplemented from QGLWidget. The mouse event handlers are reimplemented from QWidget as usual.

```cpp
Tetrahedron::Tetrahedron(QWidget *parent)
    : QGLWidget(parent)
{
    setFormat(QGLFormat(QGL::DoubleBuffer | QGL::DepthBuffer));
    rotationX = -21.0;
    rotationY = -57.0;
    rotationZ = 0.0;
    faceColors[0] = Qt::red;
    faceColors[1] = Qt::green;
    faceColors[2] = Qt::blue;
    faceColors[3] = Qt::yellow;
}
```

In the constructor, we call QGLWidget::setFormat() to specify the OpenGL display context, and we initialize the class's private variables.

```cpp
void Tetrahedron::initializeGL()
{
```

```
qglClearColor(Qt::black);
glShadeModel(GL_FLAT);
glEnable(GL_DEPTH_TEST);
glEnable(GL_CULL_FACE);
}
```

The initializeGL() function is called just once, before paintGL() is called. This is the place where we can set up the OpenGL rendering context, define display lists, and perform other initializations.

All the code is standard OpenGL, except for the call to QGLWidget's qglClear-Color() function. If we wanted to stick to standard OpenGL, we would call gl-ClearColor() in RGBA mode and glClearIndex() in color index mode instead.

```
void Tetrahedron::resizeGL(int width, int height)
{
    glViewport(0, 0, width, height);
    glMatrixMode(GL_PROJECTION);
    glLoadIdentity();
    GLfloat x = GLfloat(width) / height;
    glFrustum(-x, x, -1.0, 1.0, 4.0, 15.0);
    glMatrixMode(GL_MODELVIEW);
}
```

The resizeGL() function is called before paintGL() is called the first time, but after initializeGL() is called. It is also called whenever the widget is resized. This is the place where we can set up the OpenGL viewport, projection, and any other settings that depend on the widget's size.

```
void Tetrahedron::paintGL()
{
    glClear(GL_COLOR_BUFFER_BIT | GL_DEPTH_BUFFER_BIT);
    draw();
}
```

The paintGL() function is called whenever the widget needs to be repainted. This is similar to QWidget::paintEvent(), but instead of QPainter functions we use OpenGL functions. The actual drawing is performed by the private function draw().

```
void Tetrahedron::draw()
{
    static const GLfloat P1[3] = { 0.0, -1.0, +2.0 };
    static const GLfloat P2[3] = { +1.73205081, -1.0, -1.0 };
    static const GLfloat P3[3] = { -1.73205081, -1.0, -1.0 };
    static const GLfloat P4[3] = { 0.0, +2.0, 0.0 };

    static const GLfloat * const coords[4][3] = {
        { P1, P2, P3 }, { P1, P3, P4 }, { P1, P4, P2 }, { P2, P4, P3 }
    };

    glMatrixMode(GL_MODELVIEW);
    glLoadIdentity();
    glTranslatef(0.0, 0.0, -10.0);
    glRotatef(rotationX, 1.0, 0.0, 0.0);
```

```
        glRotatef(rotationY, 0.0, 1.0, 0.0);
        glRotatef(rotationZ, 0.0, 0.0, 1.0);

        for (int i = 0; i < 4; ++i) {
            glLoadName(i);
            glBegin(GL_TRIANGLES);
            qglColor(faceColors[i]);
            for (int j = 0; j < 3; ++j) {
                glVertex3f(coords[i][j][0], coords[i][j][1],
                           coords[i][j][2]);
            }
            glEnd();
        }
    }
```

In draw(), we draw the tetrahedron, taking into account the x, y, and z rotations and the colors stored in the faceColors array. Everything is standard OpenGL, except for the qglColor() call. We could have used one of the OpenGL functions glColor3d() or glIndex() instead, depending on the mode.

```
    void Tetrahedron::mousePressEvent(QMouseEvent *event)
    {
        lastPos = event->pos();
    }

    void Tetrahedron::mouseMoveEvent(QMouseEvent *event)
    {
        GLfloat dx = GLfloat(event->x() - lastPos.x()) / width();
        GLfloat dy = GLfloat(event->y() - lastPos.y()) / height();

        if (event->buttons() & Qt::LeftButton) {
            rotationX += 180 * dy;
            rotationY += 180 * dx;
            updateGL();
        } else if (event->buttons() & Qt::RightButton) {
            rotationX += 180 * dy;
            rotationZ += 180 * dx;
            updateGL();
        }
        lastPos = event->pos();
    }
```

The mousePressEvent() and mouseMoveEvent() functions are reimplemented from QWidget to allow the user to rotate the view by clicking and dragging. The left mouse button allows the user to rotate around the x and y axes, the right mouse button around the x and z axes.

After modifying the rotationX variable, and either the rotationY or the rotationZ variable, we call updateGL() to redraw the scene.

```
    void Tetrahedron::mouseDoubleClickEvent(QMouseEvent *event)
    {
        int face = faceAtPosition(event->pos());
        if (face != -1) {
            QColor color = QColorDialog::getColor(faceColors[face], this);
```

```
                if (color.isValid()) {
                    faceColors[face] = color;
                    updateGL();
                }
            }
        }
```

The mouseDoubleClickEvent() is reimplemented from QWidget to allow the user to set the color of a tetrahedron face by double-clicking it. We call the private function faceAtPosition() to determine which face, if any, is located under the cursor. If a face was double-clicked, we call QColorDialog::getColor() to obtain a new color for that face. Then we update the faceColors array with the new color, and we call updateGL() to redraw the scene.

```
    int Tetrahedron::faceAtPosition(const QPoint &pos)
    {
        const int MaxSize = 512;
        GLuint buffer[MaxSize];
        GLint viewport[4];

        glGetIntegerv(GL_VIEWPORT, viewport);
        glSelectBuffer(MaxSize, buffer);
        glRenderMode(GL_SELECT);

        glInitNames();
        glPushName(0);

        glMatrixMode(GL_PROJECTION);
        glPushMatrix();
        glLoadIdentity();
        gluPickMatrix(GLdouble(pos.x()), GLdouble(viewport[3] - pos.y()),
                      5.0, 5.0, viewport);
        GLfloat x = GLfloat(width()) / height();
        glFrustum(-x, x, -1.0, 1.0, 4.0, 15.0);
        draw();
        glMatrixMode(GL_PROJECTION);
        glPopMatrix();

        if (!glRenderMode(GL_RENDER))
            return -1;
        return buffer[3];
    }
```

The faceAtPosition() function returns the number of the face at a certain position on the widget, or −1 if there is no face at that position. The code for determining this in OpenGL is a bit complicated. Essentially, what we do is render the scene in GL_SELECT mode to take advantage of OpenGL's picking capabilities and then retrieve the face number (its "name") from the OpenGL hit record.

Here's main.cpp:

```
    #include <QApplication>
    #include <iostream>
```

```
#include "tetrahedron.h"

using namespace std;

int main(int argc, char *argv[])
{
    QApplication app(argc, argv);
    if (!QGLFormat::hasOpenGL()) {
        cerr << "This system has no OpenGL support" << endl;
        return 1;
    }

    Tetrahedron tetrahedron;
    tetrahedron.setWindowTitle(QObject::tr("Tetrahedron"));
    tetrahedron.resize(300, 300);
    tetrahedron.show();

    return app.exec();
}
```

If the user's system doesn't support OpenGL, we print an error message to the console and return immediately.

To link the application against the *QtOpenGL* module and the system's OpenGL library, the .pro file needs this entry:

```
QT              += opengl
```

That completes the Tetrahedron application. For more information about the *QtOpenGL* module, see the reference documentation for QGLWidget, QGLFormat, QGLContext, QGLColormap, and QGLPixelBuffer.

9. Drag and Drop

Drag and drop is a modern and intuitive way of transferring information within an application or between different applications. It is often provided in addition to clipboard support for moving and copying data.

In this chapter, we will see how to add drag and drop support to an application and how to handle custom formats. Then we will show how to reuse the drag and drop code to add clipboard support. This code reuse is possible because both mechanisms are based on QMimeData, a class that can provide data in several formats.

Enabling Drag and Drop

Drag and drop involves two distinct actions: dragging and dropping. Qt widgets can serve as drag sites, as drop sites, or as both.

Our first example shows how to make a Qt application accept a drag initiated by another application. The Qt application is a main window with a QTextEdit as its central widget. When the user drags a text file from the desktop or from a file explorer and drops it onto the application, the application loads the file into the QTextEdit.

Here's the definition of the example's MainWindow class:

```
class MainWindow : public QMainWindow
{
    Q_OBJECT

public:
    MainWindow();

protected:
    void dragEnterEvent(QDragEnterEvent *event);
    void dropEvent(QDropEvent *event);

private:
    bool readFile(const QString &fileName);
```

```
        QTextEdit *textEdit;
};
```

The `MainWindow` class reimplements `dragEnterEvent()` and `dropEvent()` from `QWidget`. Since the purpose of the example is to show drag and drop, much of the functionality we would expect to be in a main window class has been omitted.

```
MainWindow::MainWindow()
{
    textEdit = new QTextEdit;
    setCentralWidget(textEdit);

    textEdit->setAcceptDrops(false);
    setAcceptDrops(true);

    setWindowTitle(tr("Text Editor"));
}
```

In the constructor, we create a `QTextEdit` and set it as the central widget. By default, `QTextEdit` accepts textual drags from other applications, and if the user drops a file onto it, it will insert the file name into the text. Since drop events are propagated from child to parent, by disabling dropping on the `QTextEdit` and enabling it on the main window, we get the drop events for the whole window in `MainWindow`.

```
void MainWindow::dragEnterEvent(QDragEnterEvent *event)
{
    if (event->mimeData()->hasFormat("text/uri-list"))
        event->acceptProposedAction();
}
```

The `dragEnterEvent()` is called whenever the user drags an object onto a widget. If we call `acceptProposedAction()` on the event, we indicate that the user can drop the drag object on this widget. By default, the widget wouldn't accept the drag. Qt automatically changes the cursor to indicate to the user whether or not the widget is a legitimate drop site.

Here we want the user to be allowed to drag files but nothing else. To do so, we check the MIME type of the drag. The MIME type `text/uri-list` is used to store a list of universal resource identifiers (URIs), which can be file names, URLs (such as HTTP or FTP paths), or other global resource identifiers. Standard MIME types are defined by the Internet Assigned Numbers Authority (IANA). They consist of a type and a subtype separated by a slash. MIME types are used by the clipboard and by the drag and drop system to identify different types of data. The official list of MIME types is available at http://www.iana.org/assignments/media-types/.

```
void MainWindow::dropEvent(QDropEvent *event)
{
    QList<QUrl> urls = event->mimeData()->urls();
    if (urls.isEmpty())
        return;

    QString fileName = urls.first().toLocalFile();
```

```
        if (fileName.isEmpty())
            return;

        if (readFile(fileName))
            setWindowTitle(tr("%1 - %2").arg(fileName)
                                        .arg(tr("Drag File")));
    }
```

The `dropEvent()` is called when the user drops an object onto the widget. We call `QMimeData::urls()` to obtain a list of `QUrl`s. Typically, users only drag one file at a time, but it is possible for them to drag multiple files by dragging a selection. If there's more that one URL, or if the URL is not a local file name, we return immediately.

`QWidget` also provides `dragMoveEvent()` and `dragLeaveEvent()`, but for most applications they don't need to be reimplemented.

The second example illustrates how to initiate a drag and accept a drop. We will create a `QListWidget` subclass that supports drag and drop, and use it as a component in the Project Chooser application shown in Figure 9.1.

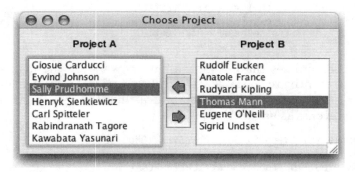

Figure 9.1. The Project Chooser application

The Project Chooser application presents the user with two list widgets, populated with names. Each list widget represents a project. The user can drag and drop the names in the list widgets to move a person from one project to another.

The drag and drop code is all located in the `QListWidget` subclass. Here's the class definition:

```
    class ProjectListWidget : public QListWidget
    {
        Q_OBJECT

    public:
        ProjectListWidget(QWidget *parent = 0);

    protected:
        void mousePressEvent(QMouseEvent *event);
        void mouseMoveEvent(QMouseEvent *event);
        void dragEnterEvent(QDragEnterEvent *event);
```

```
    void dragMoveEvent(QDragMoveEvent *event);
    void dropEvent(QDropEvent *event);

private:
    void startDrag();

    QPoint startPos;
};
```

The `ProjectListWidget` class reimplements five event handlers declared in `QWidget`.

```
ProjectListWidget::ProjectListWidget(QWidget *parent)
    : QListWidget(parent)
{
    setAcceptDrops(true);
}
```

In the constructor, we enable drops on the list widget.

```
void ProjectListWidget::mousePressEvent(QMouseEvent *event)
{
    if (event->button() == Qt::LeftButton)
        startPos = event->pos();
    QListWidget::mousePressEvent(event);
}
```

When the user presses the left mouse button, we store the mouse position in the `startPos` private variable. We call `QListWidget`'s implementation of `mousePressEvent()` to ensure that the `QListWidget` has the opportunity to process mouse press events as usual.

```
void ProjectListWidget::mouseMoveEvent(QMouseEvent *event)
{
    if (event->buttons() & Qt::LeftButton) {
        int distance = (event->pos() - startPos).manhattanLength();
        if (distance >= QApplication::startDragDistance())
            startDrag();
    }
    QListWidget::mouseMoveEvent(event);
}
```

When the user moves the mouse cursor while holding the left mouse button, we consider starting a drag. We compute the distance between the current mouse position and the position where the left mouse button was pressed. If the distance is larger than `QApplication`'s recommended drag start distance (normally 4 pixels), we call the private function `startDrag()` to start dragging. This avoids initiating a drag just because the user's hand shakes.

```
void ProjectListWidget::startDrag()
{
    QListWidgetItem *item = currentItem();
    if (item) {
        QMimeData *mimeData = new QMimeData;
        mimeData->setText(item->text());
```

```
            QDrag *drag = new QDrag(this);
            drag->setMimeData(mimeData);
            drag->setPixmap(QPixmap(":/images/person.png"));
            if (drag->start(Qt::MoveAction) == Qt::MoveAction)
                delete item;
        }
    }
```

In startDrag(), we create an object of type QDrag with this as its parent. The
QDrag object stores the data in a QMimeData object. For this example, we provide
the data as a text/plain string using QMimeData::setText(). QMimeData provides
several functions for handling the most common types of drags (images, URLs,
colors, etc.) and can handle arbitrary MIME types represented as QByteArrays.
The call to QDrag::setPixmap() sets the icon that follows the cursor while the
drag is taking place.

The QDrag::start() call starts the dragging operation and blocks until the user
drops or cancels the drag. It takes a combination of supported "drag actions"
as argument (Qt::CopyAction, Qt::MoveAction, and Qt::LinkAction) and returns
the drag action that was executed (or Qt::IgnoreAction if none was executed).
Which action is executed depends on what the source widget allows, what the
target supports, and which modifier keys are pressed when the drop occurs.
After the start() call, Qt takes ownership of the drag object and will delete it
when it is no longer required.

```
    void ProjectListWidget::dragEnterEvent(QDragEnterEvent *event)
    {
        ProjectListWidget *source =
                qobject_cast<ProjectListWidget *>(event->source());
        if (source && source != this) {
            event->setDropAction(Qt::MoveAction);
            event->accept();
        }
    }
```

The ProjectListWidget widget not only originates drags, it also accepts such
drags if they come from another ProjectListWidget in the same application.
QDragEnterEvent::source() returns a pointer to the widget that initiated the
drag if that widget is part of the same application; otherwise, it returns a
null pointer. We use qobject_cast<T>() to ensure that the drag comes from a
ProjectListWidget. If all is correct, we tell Qt that we are ready to accept the
action as a move action.

```
    void ProjectListWidget::dragMoveEvent(QDragMoveEvent *event)
    {
        ProjectListWidget *source =
                qobject_cast<ProjectListWidget *>(event->source());
        if (source && source != this) {
            event->setDropAction(Qt::MoveAction);
            event->accept();
        }
    }
```

The code in dragMoveEvent() is identical to what we did in dragEnterEvent(). It is necessary because we need to override QListWidget's (actually, QAbstractItem-View's) implementation of the function.

```
void ProjectListWidget::dropEvent(QDropEvent *event)
{
    ProjectListWidget *source =
            qobject_cast<ProjectListWidget *>(event->source());
    if (source && source != this) {
        addItem(event->mimeData()->text());
        event->setDropAction(Qt::MoveAction);
        event->accept();
    }
}
```

In dropEvent(), we retrieve the dragged text using QMimeData::text() and create an item with that text. We also need to accept the event as a "move action" to tell the source widget that it can now remove the original version of the dragged item.

Drag and drop is a powerful mechanism for transferring data between applications. But in some cases, it's possible to implement drag and drop without using Qt's drag and drop facilities. If all we want to do is to move data within one widget in one application, we can often simply reimplement mousePressEvent() and mouseReleaseEvent().

Supporting Custom Drag Types

In the examples so far, we have relied on QMimeData's support for common MIME types. Thus, we called QMimeData::setText() to create a text drag, and we used QMimeData:urls() to retrieve the contents of a text/uri-list drag. If we want to drag plain text, HTML text, images, URLs, or colors, we can use QMimeData without formality. But if we want to drag custom data, we must choose between the following alternatives:

1. We can provide arbitrary data as a QByteArray using QMimeData::setData() and extract it later using QMimeData::data().

2. We can subclass QMimeData and reimplement formats() and retrieveData() to handle our custom data types.

3. For drag and drop operations within a single application, we can subclass QMimeData and store the data using any data structure we want.

The first approach does not involve any subclassing, but does have some drawbacks: We need to convert our data structure to a QByteArray even if the drag is not ultimately accepted, and if we want to provide several MIME types to interact nicely with a wide range of applications, we need to store the data several times (once per MIME type). If the data is large, this can slow down the application needlessly. The second and third approaches can avoid or minimize these problems. They give us complete control and can be used together.

To show how these approaches work, we will show how to add drag and drop capabilities to a `QTableWidget`. The drag will support the following MIME types: text/plain, text/html, and text/csv. Using the first approach, starting a drag looks like this:

```
void MyTableWidget::mouseMoveEvent(QMouseEvent *event)
{
    if (event->buttons() & Qt::LeftButton) {
        int distance = (event->pos() - startPos).manhattanLength();
        if (distance >= QApplication::startDragDistance())
            startDrag();
    }
    QTableWidget::mouseMoveEvent(event);
}

void MyTableWidget::startDrag()
{
    QString plainText = selectionAsPlainText();
    if (plainText.isEmpty())
        return;

    QMimeData *mimeData = new QMimeData;
    mimeData->setText(plainText);
    mimeData->setHtml(toHtml(plainText));
    mimeData->setData("text/csv", toCsv(plainText).toUtf8());

    QDrag *drag = new QDrag(this);
    drag->setMimeData(mimeData);
    if (drag->start(Qt::CopyAction | Qt::MoveAction) == Qt::MoveAction)
        deleteSelection();
}
```

The `startDrag()` private function is called from `mouseMoveEvent()` to start dragging a rectangular selection. We set the text/plain and text/html MIME types using `setText()` and `setHtml()`, and we set the text/csv type using `setData()`, which takes an arbitrary MIME type and a `QByteArray`. The code for the `selectionAsString()` is more or less the same as the `Spreadsheet::copy()` function from Chapter 4 (p. 83).

```
QString MyTableWidget::toCsv(const QString &plainText)
{
    QString result = plainText;
    result.replace("\\", "\\\\");
    result.replace("\"", "\\\"");
    result.replace("\t", "\", \"");
    result.replace("\n", "\"\n\"");
    result.prepend("\"");
    result.append("\"");
    return result;
}

QString MyTableWidget::toHtml(const QString &plainText)
{
    QString result = Qt::escape(plainText);
    result.replace("\t", "<td>");
```

```
        result.replace("\n", "\n<tr><td>");
        result.prepend("<table>\n<tr><td>");
        result.append("\n</table>");
        return result;
}
```

The toCsv() and toHtml() functions convert a "tabs and newlines" string into a CSV (comma-separated values) or an HTML string. For example, the data

```
Red      Green    Blue
Cyan     Yellow   Magenta
```

is converted to

```
"Red", "Green", "Blue"
"Cyan", "Yellow", "Magenta"
```

or to

```
<table>
<tr><td>Red<td>Green<td>Blue
<tr><td>Cyan<td>Yellow<td>Magenta
</table>
```

The conversion is performed in the simplest way possible, using QString::replace(). To escape HTML special characters, we use Qt::escape().

```
void MyTableWidget::dropEvent(QDropEvent *event)
{
    if (event->mimeData()->hasFormat("text/csv")) {
        QByteArray csvData = event->mimeData()->data("text/csv");
        QString csvText = QString::fromUtf8(csvData);
        ...
        event->acceptProposedAction();
    } else if (event->mimeData()->hasFormat("text/plain")) {
        QString plainText = event->mimeData()->text();
        ...
        event->acceptProposedAction();
    }
}
```

Although we provide the data in three different formats, we only accept two of them in dropEvent(). If the user drags cells from a QTableWidget to an HTML editor, we want the cells to be converted into an HTML table. But if the user drags arbitrary HTML into a QTableWidget, we don't want to accept it.

To make this example work, we also need to call setAcceptDrops(true) and setSelectionMode(ContiguousSelection) in the MyTableWidget constructor.

We will now redo the example, but this time we will subclass QMimeData to postpone or avoid the (potentially expensive) conversions between QTableWidget-Items and QByteArray. Here's the definition of our subclass:

```
class TableMimeData : public QMimeData
{
    Q_OBJECT
```

```
public:
    TableMimeData(const QTableWidget *tableWidget,
                  const QTableWidgetSelectionRange &range);

    const QTableWidget *tableWidget() const { return myTableWidget; }
    QTableWidgetSelectionRange range() const { return myRange; }
    QStringList formats() const;

protected:
    QVariant retrieveData(const QString &format,
                          QVariant::Type preferredType) const;

private:
    static QString toHtml(const QString &plainText);
    static QString toCsv(const QString &plainText);

    QString text(int row, int column) const;
    QString rangeAsPlainText() const;

    const QTableWidget *myTableWidget;
    QTableWidgetSelectionRange myRange;
    QStringList myFormats;
};
```

Instead of storing actual data, we store a `QTableWidgetSelectionRange` that specifies which cells are being dragged and keep a pointer to the `QTableWidget`. The `formats()` and `retrieveData()` functions are reimplemented from `QMimeData`.

```
TableMimeData::TableMimeData(const QTableWidget *tableWidget,
                             const QTableWidgetSelectionRange &range)
{
    myTableWidget = tableWidget;
    myRange = range;
    myFormats << "text/csv" << "text/html" << "text/plain";
}
```

In the constructor, we initialize the private variables.

```
QStringList TableMimeData::formats() const
{
    return myFormats;
}
```

The `formats()` function returns a list of MIME types provided by the MIME data object. The precise order of the formats is usually irrelevant, but it's good practice to put the "best" formats first. Applications that support many formats will sometimes use the first one that matches.

```
QVariant TableMimeData::retrieveData(const QString &format,
                                     QVariant::Type preferredType) const
{
    if (format == "text/plain") {
        return rangeAsPlainText();
    } else if (format == "text/csv") {
        return toCsv(rangeAsPlainText());
    } else if (format == "text/html") {
```

```
            return toHtml(rangeAsPlainText());
        } else {
            return QMimeData::retrieveData(format, preferredType);
        }
    }
```

The retrieveData() function returns the data for a given MIME type as a QVariant. The value of the format parameter is normally one of the strings returned by formats(), but we cannot assume that, since not all applications check the MIME type against formats(). The getter functions text(), html(), urls(), image-Data(), colorData(), and data() provided by QMimeData are implemented in terms of retrieveData().

The preferredType parameter gives us a hint about which type we should put in the QVariant. Here, we ignore it and trust QMimeData to convert the return value into the desired type, if necessary.

```
    void MyTableWidget::dropEvent(QDropEvent *event)
    {
        const TableMimeData *tableData =
                qobject_cast<const TableMimeData *>(event->mimeData());

        if (tableData) {
            const QTableWidget *otherTable = tableData->tableWidget();
            QTableWidgetSelectionRange otherRange = tableData->range();
            ...
            event->acceptProposedAction();
        } else if (event->mimeData()->hasFormat("text/csv")) {
            QByteArray csvData = event->mimeData()->data("text/csv");
            QString csvText = QString::fromUtf8(csvData);
            ...
            event->acceptProposedAction();
        } else if (event->mimeData()->hasFormat("text/plain")) {
            QString plainText = event->mimeData()->text();
            ...
            event->acceptProposedAction();
        }
        QTableWidget::mouseMoveEvent(event);
    }
```

The dropEvent() function is similar to the one we had earlier in this section, but this time we optimize it by checking first if we can safely cast the QMimeData object to a TableMimeData. If the qobject_cast<T>() works, this means the drag was originated by a MyTableWidget in the same application, and we can directly access the table data instead of going through QMimeData's API. If the cast fails, we extract the data the standard way.

In this example, we encoded the CSV text using the UTF-8 encoding. If we want to be certain of using the right encoding, we could use the charset parameter of the text/plain MIME type to specify an explicit encoding. Here are a few examples:

```
    text/plain;charset=US-ASCII
    text/plain;charset=ISO-8859-1
```

```
text/plain;charset=Shift_JIS
text/plain;charset=UTF-8
```

Clipboard Handling

Most applications make use of Qt's built-in clipboard handling in one way or another. For example, the QTextEdit class provides cut(), copy(), and paste() slots as well as keyboard shortcuts, so little or no additional code is required.

When writing our own classes, we can access the clipboard through QApplication::clipboard(), which returns a pointer to the application's QClipboard object. Handling the system clipboard is easy: Call setText(), setImage(), or setPixmap() to put data onto the clipboard, and call text(), image(), or pixmap() to retrieve data from the clipboard. We have already seen examples of clipboard use in the Spreadsheet application from Chapter 4.

For some applications, the built-in functionality might not be sufficient. For example, we might want to provide data that isn't just text or an image, or we might want to provide data in many different formats for maximum interoperability with other applications. The issue is very similar to what we encountered earlier with drag and drop, and the answer is also similar: We can subclass QMimeData and reimplement a few virtual functions.

If our application supports drag and drop through a custom QMimeData subclass, we can simply reuse the QMimeData subclass and put it on the clipboard using the setMimeData() function. To retrieve the data, we can call mimeData() on the clipboard.

On X11, it is usually possible to paste a selection by clicking the middle button of a three-button mouse. This is done using a separate "selection" clipboard. If you want your widgets to support this kind of clipboard as well as the standard one, you must pass QClipboard::Selection as an additional argument to the various clipboard calls. For example, here's how we would reimplement mouseReleaseEvent() in a text editor to support pasting using the middle mouse button:

```cpp
void MyTextEditor::mouseReleaseEvent(QMouseEvent *event)
{
    QClipboard *clipboard = QApplication::clipboard();
    if (event->button() == Qt::MidButton
            && clipboard->supportsSelection()) {
        QString text = clipboard->text(QClipboard::Selection);
        pasteText(text);
    }
}
```

On X11, the supportsSelection() function returns true. On other platforms, it returns false.

If we want to be notified whenever the clipboard's contents change, we can connect the QClipboard::dataChanged() signal to a custom slot.

- ◆ *Using the Item View Convenience Classes*
- ◆ *Using Predefined Models*
- ◆ *Implementing Custom Models*
- ◆ *Implementing Custom Delegates*

10. Item View Classes

Many applications let the user search, view, and edit individual items that belong to a data set. The data might be held in files or accessed from a database or a network server. The standard approach to dealing with data sets like this is to use Qt's item view classes.

In earlier versions of Qt, the item view widgets were populated with the entire contents of a data set; the users would perform all their searches and edits on the data held in the widget, and at some point the changes would be written back to the data source. Although simple to understand and use, this approach doesn't scale well to very large data sets and doesn't lend itself to situations where we want to display the same data set in two or more different widgets.

The Smalltalk language popularized a flexible approach to visualizing large data sets: model–view–controller (MVC). In the MVC approach, the *model* represents the data set and is responsible for fetching the data that is needed for viewing and for writing back any changes. Each type of data set has its own model, but the API that the models provide to the views is uniform no matter what the underlying data set. The *view* presents the data to the user. With any large data set only a limited amount of data will be visible at any one time, so that is the only data that the view asks for. The *controller* mediates between the user and the view, converting user actions into requests to navigate or edit data, which the view then transmits to the model as necessary.

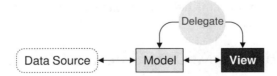

Figure 10.1. Qt's model/view architecture

Qt provides a model/view architecture inspired by the MVC approach. In Qt, the model behaves the same as it does for classic MVC. But instead of a controller, Qt uses a slightly different abstraction: the *delegate*. The delegate

217

is used to provide fine control over how items are rendered and edited. Qt provides a default delegate for every type of view. This is sufficient for most applications, so we usually don't need to care about it.

Using Qt's model/view architecture, we can use models that only fetch the data that is actually needed for display in the view. This makes handling very large data sets much faster and less memory hungry than reading all the data. And by registering a model with two or more views, we can give the user the opportunity of viewing and interacting with the data in different ways, with little overhead. Qt automatically keeps multiple views in sync, reflecting changes to one in all the others. An additional benefit of the model/view architecture is that if we decide to change how the underlying data set is stored, we just need to change the model; the views will continue to behave correctly.

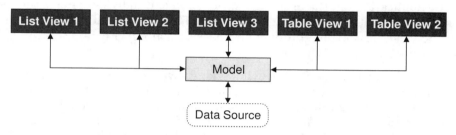

Figure 10.2. One model can serve multiple views

In many situations, we only need to present relatively small numbers of items to the user. In these common cases, we can use Qt's convenience item view classes (QListWidget, QTableWidget, and QTreeWidget) and populate them with items directly. These classes behave in a similar way to the item view classes provided by earlier versions of Qt. They store their data in "items" (for example, a QTableWidget contains QTableWidgetItems). Internally, the convenience classes use custom models that make the items visible to the views.

For large data sets, duplicating the data is often not an option. In these cases, we can use Qt's views (QListView, QTableView, and QTreeView), in conjunction with a data model, which can be a custom model or one of Qt's predefined models. For example, if the data set is held in a database, we can combine a QTableView with a QSqlTableModel.

Using the Item View Convenience Classes

Using Qt's item view convenience subclasses is usually simpler than defining a custom model and is appropriate when we don't need the benefits of separating the model and the view. We used this technique in Chapter 4 when we subclassed QTableWidget and QTableWidgetItem to implement spreadsheet functionality.

In this section, we will show how to use the convenience item view subclasses to display items. The first example shows a read-only `QListWidget`, the second example shows an editable `QTableWidget`, and the third example shows a read-only `QTreeWidget`.

We begin with a simple dialog that lets the user pick a flowchart symbol from a list. Each item consists of an icon, a text, and a unique ID.

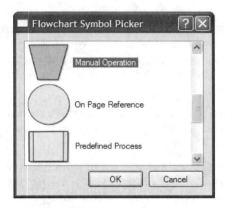

Figure 10.3. The Flowchart Symbol Picker application

Let's start with an extract from the dialog's header file:

```
class FlowChartSymbolPicker : public QDialog
{
    Q_OBJECT

public:
    FlowChartSymbolPicker(const QMap<int, QString> &symbolMap,
                          QWidget *parent = 0);

    int selectedId() const { return id; }
    void done(int result);
    ...
};
```

When we construct the dialog, we must pass it a `QMap<int, QString>`, and after it has executed we can retrieve the chosen ID (or –1 if the user didn't select any item) by calling `selectedId()`.

```
FlowChartSymbolPicker::FlowChartSymbolPicker(
        const QMap<int, QString> &symbolMap, QWidget *parent)
    : QDialog(parent)
{
    id = -1;

    listWidget = new QListWidget;
    listWidget->setIconSize(QSize(60, 60));

    QMapIterator<int, QString> i(symbolMap);
```

```
        while (i.hasNext()) {
            i.next();
            QListWidgetItem *item = new QListWidgetItem(i.value(),
                                                        listWidget);
            item->setIcon(iconForSymbol(i.value()));
            item->setData(Qt::UserRole, i.key());
        }
        ...
    }
```

We initialize id (the last selected ID) to –1. Next we construct a QListWidget, a convenience item view widget. We iterate over each item in the flowchart symbol map and create a QListWidgetItem to represent each one. The QListWidgetItem constructor takes a QString that represents the text to display, followed by the parent QListWidget.

Then we set the item's icon and we call setData() to store our arbitrary ID in the QListWidgetItem. The iconForSymbol() private function returns a QIcon for a given symbol name.

QListWidgetItem's have several roles, each of which has an associated QVariant. The most common roles are Qt::DisplayRole, Qt::EditRole, and Qt::IconRole, and for these there are convenience setter and getter functions (setText(), setIcon()), but there are several other roles. We can also define custom roles by specifying a numeric value of Qt::UserRole or higher. In our example, we use Qt::UserRole to store each item's ID.

The omitted part of the constructor is concerned with creating the buttons, laying out the widgets, and setting the window's title.

```
    void FlowChartSymbolPicker::done(int result)
    {
        id = -1;
        if (result == QDialog::Accepted) {
            QListWidgetItem *item = listWidget->currentItem();
            if (item)
                id = item->data(Qt::UserRole).toInt();
        }
        QDialog::done(result);
    }
```

The done() function is reimplemented from QDialog. It is called when the user presses OK or Cancel. If the user clicked OK, we retrieve the relevant item and extract the ID using the data() function. If we were interested in the item's text, we could retrieve it by calling item->data(Qt::DisplayRole).toString() or more conveniently, item->text().

By default, QListWidget is read-only. If we wanted the user to edit the items, we could set the view's edit triggers using QAbstractItemView::setEditTriggers(); for example, a setting of QAbstractItemView::AnyKeyPressed means that the user can begin editing an item just by starting to type. Alternatively, we could provide an Edit button (and perhaps Add and Delete buttons) and connect them to slots so that we could handle the editing operations programmatically.

Now that we have seen how to use a convenience item view class for viewing and selecting data, we will look at an example where we can edit data. Again we are using a dialog, this time one that presents a set of (x, y) coordinates that the user can edit.

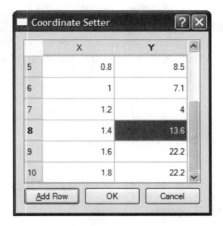

Figure 10.4. The Coordinate Setter application

As with the previous example, we will focus on the item view relevant code, starting with the constructor.

```
CoordinateSetter::CoordinateSetter(QList<QPointF> *coords,
                                   QWidget *parent)
    : QDialog(parent)
{
    coordinates = coords;

    tableWidget = new QTableWidget(0, 2);
    tableWidget->setHorizontalHeaderLabels(
            QStringList() << tr("X") << tr("Y"));

    for (int row = 0; row < coordinates->count(); ++row) {
        QPointF point = coordinates->at(row);
        addRow();
        tableWidget->item(row, 0)->setText(QString::number(point.x()));
        tableWidget->item(row, 1)->setText(QString::number(point.y()));
    }
    ...
}
```

The `QTableWidget` constructor takes the initial number of table rows and columns to display. Every item in a `QTableWidget` is represented by a `QTable-WidgetItem`, including horizontal and vertical header items. The `setHorizontal-HeaderLabels()` function sets the text for each horizontal table widget item to the corresponding text in the string list it is passed. By default, `QTableWidget` provides a vertical header with rows labeled from 1, which is exactly what we want, so we don't need to set the vertical header labels manually.

Once we have created and centered the column labels, we iterate through the coordinate data that was passed in. For every (x, y) pair, we create two QTable-WidgetItems corresponding to the x and y coordinates. The items are added to the table using QTableWidget::setItem(), which takes a row and a column in addition to the item.

By default, QTableWidget allows editing. The user can edit any cell in the table by navigating to it and then either pressing F2 or simply by typing. All changes made by the user in the view will be automatically reflected into the QTableWid-getItems. To prevent editing, we can call setEditTriggers(QAbstractItemView::NoEditTriggers).

```
void CoordinateSetter::addRow()
{
    int row = tableWidget->rowCount();

    tableWidget->insertRow(row);

    QTableWidgetItem *item0 = new QTableWidgetItem;
    item0->setTextAlignment(Qt::AlignRight | Qt::AlignVCenter);
    tableWidget->setItem(row, 0, item0);

    QTableWidgetItem *item1 = new QTableWidgetItem;
    item1->setTextAlignment(Qt::AlignRight | Qt::AlignVCenter);
    tableWidget->setItem(row, 1, item1);

    tableWidget->setCurrentItem(item0);
}
```

The addRow() slot is invoked when the user clicks the Add Row button. We append a new row using insertRow(). If the user attempts to edit a cell in the new row, the QTableWidget will automatically create a new QTableWidgetItem.

```
void CoordinateSetter::done(int result)
{
    if (result == QDialog::Accepted) {
        coordinates->clear();
        for (int row = 0; row < tableWidget->rowCount(); ++row) {
            double x = tableWidget->item(row, 0)->text().toDouble();
            double y = tableWidget->item(row, 1)->text().toDouble();
            coordinates->append(QPointF(x, y));
        }
    }
    QDialog::done(result);
}
```

Finally, when the user clicks OK, we clear the coordinates that were passed in to the dialog, and create a new set based on the coordinates in the QTableWid-get's items.

For our third and final example of Qt's convenience item view widgets, we will look at some snippets from an application that shows Qt application settings using a QTreeWidget. Read-only is the default for QTreeWidget.

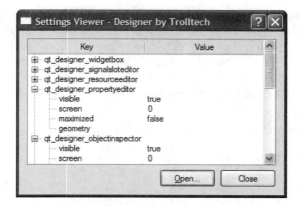

Figure 10.5. The Settings Viewer application

Here's an extract from the constructor:

```
SettingsViewer::SettingsViewer(QWidget *parent)
    : QDialog(parent)
{
    organization = "Trolltech";
    application = "Designer";

    treeWidget = new QTreeWidget;
    treeWidget->setColumnCount(2);
    treeWidget->setHeaderLabels(
            QStringList() << tr("Key") << tr("Value"));
    treeWidget->header()->setResizeMode(0, QHeaderView::Stretch);
    treeWidget->header()->setResizeMode(1, QHeaderView::Stretch);
    ...
    setWindowTitle(tr("Settings Viewer"));
    readSettings();
}
```

To access an application's settings, a QSettings object must be created with the organization's name and the application's name as parameters. We set default names ("Designer" by "Trolltech") and then construct a new QTreeWidget. At the end, we call the readSettings() function.

```
void SettingsViewer::readSettings()
{
    QSettings settings(organization, application);

    treeWidget->clear();
    addChildSettings(settings, 0, "");

    treeWidget->sortByColumn(0);
    treeWidget->setFocus();
    setWindowTitle(tr("Settings Viewer - %1 by %2")
                .arg(application).arg(organization));
}
```

Application settings are stored in a hierarchy of keys and values. The add-ChildSettings() private function takes a settings object, a parent QTreeWidgetItem, and the current "group". A group is the QSettings equivalent of a file system directory. The addChildSettings() function can call itself recursively to traverse an arbitrary tree structure. The initial call from the readSettings() function passes 0 as the parent item to represent the root.

```cpp
void SettingsViewer::addChildSettings(QSettings &settings,
        QTreeWidgetItem *parent, const QString &group)
{
    QTreeWidgetItem *item;

    settings.beginGroup(group);

    foreach (QString key, settings.childKeys()) {
        if (parent) {
            item = new QTreeWidgetItem(parent);
        } else {
            item = new QTreeWidgetItem(treeWidget);
        }
        item->setText(0, key);
        item->setText(1, settings.value(key).toString());
    }
    foreach (QString group, settings.childGroups()) {
        if (parent) {
            item = new QTreeWidgetItem(parent);
        } else {
            item = new QTreeWidgetItem(treeWidget);
        }
        item->setText(0, group);
        addChildSettings(settings, item, group);
    }
    settings.endGroup();
}
```

The addChildSettings() function is used to create all the QTreeWidgetItems. It iterates over all the keys at the current level in the settings hierarchy and creates one QTableWidgetItem per key. If 0 was passed as the parent item, we create the item as a child of the QTreeWidget itself (making it a top-level item); otherwise, we create the item as a child of parent. The first column is set to the name of the key and the second column to the corresponding value.

Next, the function iterates over every group at the current level. For each group, a new QTreeWidgetItem is created with its first column set to the group's name. The function then calls itself recursively with the group item as the parent to populate the QTreeWidget with the group's child items.

The item view widgets shown in this section allow us to use a style of programming that is very similar to that used in earlier versions of Qt: reading an entire data set into an item view widget, using item objects to represent data elements, and (if the items are editable) writing back to the data source. In the following sections, we will go beyond this simple approach and take full advantage of Qt's model/view architecture.

Using Predefined Models

Qt provides several predefined models for use with the view classes:

`QStringListModel`	Stores a list of strings
`QStandardItemModel`	Stores arbitrary hierarchical data
`QDirModel`	Encapsulates the local file system
`QSqlQueryModel`	Encapsulates an SQL result set
`QSqlTableModel`	Encapsulates an SQL table
`QSqlRelationalTableModel`	Encapsulates an SQL table with foreign keys
`QSortFilterProxyModel`	Sorts and/or filters another model

In this section, we will look at how to use the `QStringListModel`, the `QDirModel`, and the `QSortFilterProxyModel`. The SQL models are covered in Chapter 13.

Let's begin with a simple dialog that users can use to add, delete, and edit a `QStringList`, where each string represents a team leader.

Figure 10.6. The Team Leaders application

Here's the relevant extract from the constructor:

```
TeamLeadersDialog::TeamLeadersDialog(const QStringList &leaders,
                                     QWidget *parent)
    : QDialog(parent)
{
    model = new QStringListModel(this);
    model->setStringList(leaders);

    listView = new QListView;
    listView->setModel(model);
    listView->setEditTriggers(QAbstractItemView::AnyKeyPressed
                              | QAbstractItemView::DoubleClicked);
    ...
}
```

We begin by creating and populating a QStringListModel. Next we create a QListView and set its model to the one we have just created. We also set some editing triggers to allow the user to edit a string simply by starting to type on it or by double-clicking it. By default, no editing triggers are set on a QListView, making the view effectively read-only.

```
void TeamLeadersDialog::insert()
{
    int row = listView->currentIndex().row();
    model->insertRows(row, 1);

    QModelIndex index = model->index(row);
    listView->setCurrentIndex(index);
    listView->edit(index);
}
```

When the user clicks the Insert button, the insert() slot is invoked. The slot begins by retrieving the row number for the list view's current item. Every data item in a model has a corresponding "model index", which is represented by a QModelIndex object. We will look at model indexes in detail in the next section, but for now it is sufficient to know that an index has three main components: a row, a column, and a pointer to the model to which it belongs. For a one-dimensional list model, the column is always 0.

Once we have the row number, we insert one new row at that position. The insertion is performed on the model, and the model automatically updates the list view. We then set the list view's current index to the blank row we just inserted. Finally, we set the list view to editing mode on the new row, just as if the user had pressed a key or double-clicked to initiate editing.

```
void TeamLeadersDialog::del()
{
    model->removeRows(listView->currentIndex().row(), 1);
}
```

In the constructor, the Delete button's clicked() signal is connected to the del() slot. Since we are just deleting the current row, we can call removeRows() with the current index position and a row count of 1. Just like with insertion, we rely on the model to update the view accordingly.

```
QStringList TeamLeadersDialog::leaders() const
{
    return model->stringList();
}
```

Finally, the leaders() function provides a means of reading back the edited strings when the dialog is closed.

TeamLeadersDialog could be made into a generic string list editing dialog simply by parameterizing its window title. Another generic dialog that is often required is one that presents a list of files or directories to the user. The next example uses the QDirModel class, which encapsulates the computer's file system and is capable of showing (and hiding) various file attributes. This model can apply a filter to restrict the kinds of file system entries that are shown and can order the entries in various ways.

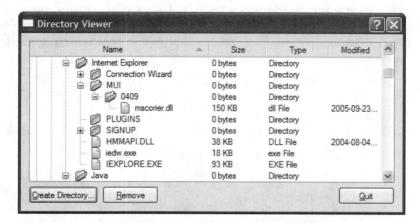

Figure 10.7. The Directory Viewer application

We will begin by looking at the creation and setting up of the model and the view in the Directory Viewer dialog's constructor.

```
DirectoryViewer::DirectoryViewer(QWidget *parent)
    : QDialog(parent)
{
    model = new QDirModel;
    model->setReadOnly(false);
    model->setSorting(QDir::DirsFirst | QDir::IgnoreCase | QDir::Name);

    treeView = new QTreeView;
    treeView->setModel(model);
    treeView->header()->setStretchLastSection(true);
    treeView->header()->setSortIndicator(0, Qt::AscendingOrder);
    treeView->header()->setSortIndicatorShown(true);
    treeView->header()->setClickable(true);

    QModelIndex index = model->index(QDir::currentPath());
    treeView->expand(index);
    treeView->scrollTo(index);
    treeView->resizeColumnToContents(0);
    ...
}
```

Once the model has been constructed, we make it editable and set various initial sort ordering attributes. We then create the QTreeView that will display the model's data. The QTreeView's header can be used to provide user-controlled sorting. By making the header clickable, the user can sort by whichever column header they click, with repeated clicks alternating between ascending and descending orders. Once the tree view's header has been set up, we get the model index of the current directory and make sure that this directory is visible by expanding its parents if necessary using expand(), and scrolling to it using scrollTo(). Then we make sure that the first column is wide enough to show all its entries without using ellipses (...).

In the part of the constructor code that isn't shown here, we connected the Create Directory and Remove buttons to slots to perform these actions. We do not need a Rename button since users can rename in-place by pressing F2 and typing.

```
void DirectoryViewer::createDirectory()
{
    QModelIndex index = treeView->currentIndex();
    if (!index.isValid())
        return;

    QString dirName = QInputDialog::getText(this,
                             tr("Create Directory"),
                             tr("Directory name"));
    if (!dirName.isEmpty()) {
        if (!model->mkdir(index, dirName).isValid())
            QMessageBox::information(this, tr("Create Directory"),
                    tr("Failed to create the directory"));
    }
}
```

If the user enters a directory name in the input dialog, we attempt to create a directory with this name as a child of the current directory. The QDirModel:: mkdir() function takes the parent directory's index and the name of the new directory, and returns the model index of the directory it created. If the operation fails, it returns an invalid model index.

```
void DirectoryViewer::remove()
{
    QModelIndex index = treeView->currentIndex();
    if (!index.isValid())
        return;

    bool ok;
    if (model->fileInfo(index).isDir()) {
        ok = model->rmdir(index);
    } else {
        ok = model->remove(index);
    }
    if (!ok)
        QMessageBox::information(this, tr("Remove"),
                tr("Failed to remove %1").arg(model->fileName(index)));
}
```

If the user clicks Remove, we attempt to remove the file or directory associated with the current item. We could use QDir to accomplish that, but QDirModel offers convenience functions that work on QModelIndexes.

The last example in this section shows how to use QSortFilterProxyModel. Unlike the other predefined models, this model encapsulates an existing model and manipulates the data that passes between the underlying model and the view. In our example, the underlying model is a QStringListModel initialized with the list of color names recognized by Qt (obtained through QColor::colorNames()). The user can type a filter string in a QLineEdit and specify how this string is to be interpreted (as a regular expression, a wildcard pattern, or a fixed string) using a combobox.

Figure 10.8. The Color Names application

Here's an extract from the ColorNamesDialog constructor:

```
ColorNamesDialog::ColorNamesDialog(QWidget *parent)
    : QDialog(parent)
{
    sourceModel = new QStringListModel(this);
    sourceModel->setStringList(QColor::colorNames());

    proxyModel = new QSortFilterProxyModel(this);
    proxyModel->setSourceModel(sourceModel);
    proxyModel->setFilterKeyColumn(0);

    listView = new QListView;
    listView->setModel(proxyModel);
    ...
    syntaxComboBox = new QComboBox;
    syntaxComboBox->addItem(tr("Regular expression"), QRegExp::RegExp);
    syntaxComboBox->addItem(tr("Wildcard"), QRegExp::Wildcard);
    syntaxComboBox->addItem(tr("Fixed string"), QRegExp::FixedString);
    ...
}
```

The QStringListModel is created and populated in the usual way. This is followed by the construction of the QSortFilterProxyModel. We pass the underlying model using setSourceModel() and tell the proxy to filter based on column 0 of the original model. The QComboBox::addItem() function accepts an optional "data" argument of type QVariant; we use this to store the QRegExp::PatternSyntax value that corresponds to each item's text.

```
void ColorNamesDialog::reapplyFilter()
{
    QRegExp::PatternSyntax syntax =
            QRegExp::PatternSyntax(syntaxComboBox->itemData(
                    syntaxComboBox->currentIndex()).toInt());
    QRegExp regExp(filterLineEdit->text(), Qt::CaseInsensitive, syntax);
    proxyModel->setFilterRegExp(regExp);
}
```

The reapplyFilter() slot is invoked whenever the user changes the filter string or the pattern syntax combobox. We create a QRegExp using the text in the line edit. Then we set its pattern syntax to the one stored in the syntax combobox's current item's data. When we call setFilterRegExp(), the new filter becomes active and the view is automatically updated.

Implementing Custom Models

Qt's predefined models offer a convenient means of handling and viewing data. However, some data sources cannot be used efficiently using the predefined models, and for these situations it is necessary to create custom models optimized for the underlying data source.

Before we embark on creating custom models, let's first review the key concepts used in Qt's model/view architecture. Every data element in a model has a model index and a set of attributes, called roles, that can take arbitrary values. We saw earlier in the chapter that the most commonly used roles are Qt::DisplayRole and Qt::EditRole. Other roles are used for supplementary data (for example, Qt::ToolTipRole, Qt::StatusTipRole, and Qt::WhatsThisRole), and yet others for controlling basic display attributes (such as Qt::FontRole, Qt::TextAlignmentRole, Qt::TextColorRole, and Qt::BackgroundColorRole).

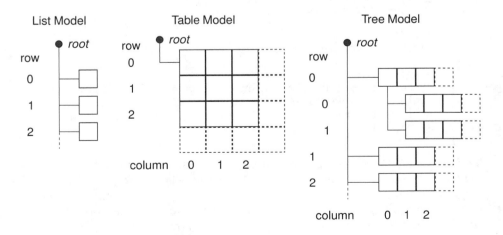

Figure 10.9. Schematic view of Qt's models

For a list model, the only relevant index component is the row number, accessible from QModelIndex::row(). For a table model, the relevant index components are the row and column numbers, accessible from QModelIndex::row() and QModelIndex::column(). For both list and table models, every item's parent is the root, which is represented by an invalid QModelIndex. The first two examples in this section show how to implement custom table models.

A tree model is similar to a table model, with the following differences. Like a table model, the parent of top-level items is the root (an invalid QModelIndex), but every other item's parent is some other item in the hierarchy. Parents are accessible from QModelIndex::parent(). Every item has its role data, and zero or more children, each an item in its own right. Since items can have other items as children, it is possible to represent recursive (tree-like) data structures, as the final example in this section will show.

The first example in this section is a read-only table model that shows currency values in relation to each other.

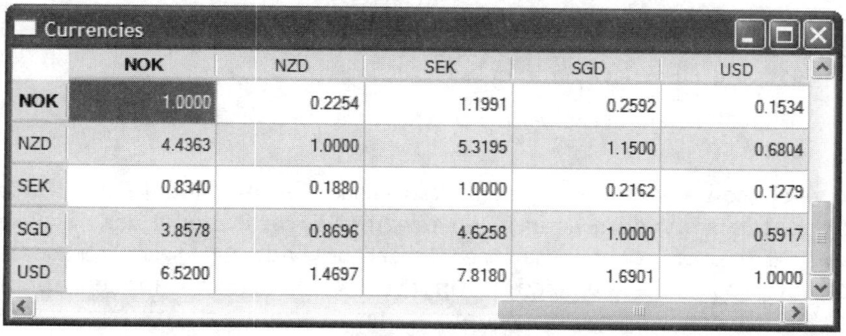

Figure 10.10. The Currencies application

	NOK	NZD	SEK	SGD	USD
NOK	1.0000	0.2254	1.1991	0.2592	0.1534
NZD	4.4363	1.0000	5.3195	1.1500	0.6804
SEK	0.8340	0.1880	1.0000	0.2162	0.1279
SGD	3.8578	0.8696	4.6258	1.0000	0.5917
USD	6.5200	1.4697	7.8180	1.6901	1.0000

The application could be implemented using a simple table, but we want to use a custom model to take advantage of certain properties of the data to minimize storage. If we were to store the 162 currently traded currencies in a table, we would need to store $162 \times 162 = 26\,244$ values; with the custom model presented below, we only need to store 162 values (the value of each currency in relation to the U.S. dollar).

The CurrencyModel class will be used with a standard QTableView. The CurrencyModel is populated with a QMap<QString, double>; each key is a currency code and each value is the value of the currency in U.S. dollars. Here's a code snippet that shows how the map is populated and how the model is used:

```
QMap<QString, double> currencyMap;
currencyMap.insert("AUD", 1.3259);
currencyMap.insert("CHF", 1.2970);
...
currencyMap.insert("SGD", 1.6901);
currencyMap.insert("USD", 1.0000);
```

```
CurrencyModel currencyModel;
currencyModel.setCurrencyMap(currencyMap);

QTableView tableView;
tableView.setModel(&currencyModel);
tableView.setAlternatingRowColors(true);
```

Now we can look at the implementation of the model, starting with its header:

```
class CurrencyModel : public QAbstractTableModel
{
public:
    CurrencyModel(QObject *parent = 0);

    void setCurrencyMap(const QMap<QString, double> &map);
    int rowCount(const QModelIndex &parent) const;
    int columnCount(const QModelIndex &parent) const;
    QVariant data(const QModelIndex &index, int role) const;
    QVariant headerData(int section, Qt::Orientation orientation,
                        int role) const;

private:
    QString currencyAt(int offset) const;

    QMap<QString, double> currencyMap;
};
```

We have chosen to subclass QAbstractTableModel for our model since that most closely matches our data source. Qt provides several model base classes, including QAbstractListModel, QAbstractTableModel, and QAbstractItemModel. The QAbstractItemModel class is used to support a wide variety of models, including those that are based on recursive data structures, while the QAbstractListModel and QAbstractTableModel classes are provided for convenience when using one-dimensional or two-dimensional data sets.

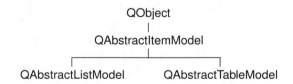

Figure 10.11. Inheritance tree for the abstract model classes

For a read-only table model, we must reimplement three functions: rowCount(), columnCount(), and data(). In this case, we have also reimplemented header-Data(), and we provide a function to initialize the data (setCurrencyMap()).

```
CurrencyModel::CurrencyModel(QObject *parent)
    : QAbstractTableModel(parent)
{
}
```

We do not need to do anything in the constructor, except pass the parent parameter to the base class.

```
int CurrencyModel::rowCount(const QModelIndex & /* parent */) const
{
    return currencyMap.count();
}

int CurrencyModel::columnCount(const QModelIndex & /* parent */) const
{
    return currencyMap.count();
}
```

For this table model, the row and column counts are the number of currencies in the currency map. The parent parameter has no meaning for a table model; it is there because rowCount() and columnCount() are inherited from the more generic QAbstractItemModel base class, which supports hierarchies.

```
QVariant CurrencyModel::data(const QModelIndex &index, int role) const
{
    if (!index.isValid())
        return QVariant();

    if (role == Qt::TextAlignmentRole) {
        return int(Qt::AlignRight | Qt::AlignVCenter);
    } else if (role == Qt::DisplayRole) {
        QString rowCurrency = currencyAt(index.row());
        QString columnCurrency = currencyAt(index.column());

        if (currencyMap.value(rowCurrency) == 0.0)
            return "####";

        double amount = currencyMap.value(columnCurrency)
                        / currencyMap.value(rowCurrency);

        return QString("%1").arg(amount, 0, 'f', 4);
    }
    return QVariant();
}
```

The data() function returns the value of any of an item's roles. The item is specified as a QModelIndex. For a table model, the interesting components of a QModelIndex are its row and column number, available using row() and column().

If the role is Qt::TextAlignmentRole, we return an alignment suitable for numbers. If the display role is Qt::DisplayRole, we look up the value for each currency and calculate the exchange rate.

We could return the calculated value as a double, but then we would have no control over how many decimal places were shown (unless we use a custom delegate). Instead, we return the value as a string, formatted as we want.

```
QVariant CurrencyModel::headerData(int section,
                                   Qt::Orientation /* orientation */,
                                   int role) const
{
    if (role != Qt::DisplayRole)
        return QVariant();
    return currencyAt(section);
}
```

The headerData() function is called by the view to populate its horizontal and vertical headers. The section parameter is the row or column number (depending on the orientation). Since the rows and columns have the same currency codes, we do not care about the orientation and simply return the code of the currency for the given section number.

```
void CurrencyModel::setCurrencyMap(const QMap<QString, double> &map)
{
    currencyMap = map;
    reset();
}
```

The caller can change the currency map using setCurrencyMap(). The QAbstract-ItemModel::reset() call tells any views that are using the model that all their data is invalid; this forces them to request fresh data for the items that are visible.

```
QString CurrencyModel::currencyAt(int offset) const
{
    return (currencyMap.begin() + offset).key();
}
```

The currencyAt() function returns the key (the currency code) at the given offset in the currency map. We use an STL-style iterator to find the item and call key() on it.

As we have just seen, it is not difficult to create read-only models, and depending on the nature of the underlying data, there are potential savings in memory and speed with a well-designed model. The next example, the Cities application, is also table-based, but this time all the data is entered by the user.

This application is used to store values indicating the distance between any two cities. Like the previous example, we could simply use a QTableWidget and store one item for every city pair. However, a custom model could be more efficient, because the distance from any city $\mathcal{A}$ to any different city $\mathcal{B}$ is the same whether traveling from $\mathcal{A}$ to $\mathcal{B}$ or from $\mathcal{B}$ to $\mathcal{A}$, so the items are mirrored along the main diagonal.

To see how a custom model compares with a simple table, let us assume that we have three cities, $\mathcal{A}$, $\mathcal{B}$, and C. If we store a value for every combination, we would need to store nine values. A carefully designed model would require only the three items $(\mathcal{A}, \mathcal{B})$, $(\mathcal{A}, C)$, and $(\mathcal{B}, C)$.

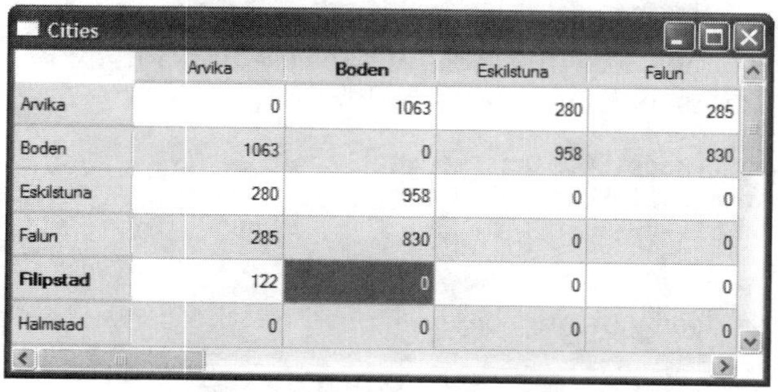

Figure 10.12. The Cities application

Here's how we set up and use the model:

```
QStringList cities;
cities << "Arvika" << "Boden" << "Eskilstuna" << "Falun"
       << "Filipstad" << "Halmstad" << "Helsingborg" << "Karlstad"
       << "Kiruna" << "Kramfors" << "Motala" << "Sandviken"
       << "Skara" << "Stockholm" << "Sundsvall" << "Trelleborg";

CityModel cityModel;
cityModel.setCities(cities);

QTableView tableView;
tableView.setModel(&cityModel);
tableView.setAlternatingRowColors(true);
```

We must reimplement the same functions as we did for the previous example. In addition, we must also reimplement setData() and flags() to make the model editable. Here is the class definition:

```
class CityModel : public QAbstractTableModel
{
    Q_OBJECT

public:
    CityModel(QObject *parent = 0);

    void setCities(const QStringList &cityNames);
    int rowCount(const QModelIndex &parent) const;
    int columnCount(const QModelIndex &parent) const;
    QVariant data(const QModelIndex &index, int role) const;
    bool setData(const QModelIndex &index, const QVariant &value,
                 int role);
    QVariant headerData(int section, Qt::Orientation orientation,
                        int role) const;
    Qt::ItemFlags flags(const QModelIndex &index) const;

private:
    int offsetOf(int row, int column) const;

    QStringList cities;
    QVector<int> distances;
};
```

For this model, we are using two data structures: cities of type QStringList
to hold the city names, and distances of type QVector<int> to hold the distance
between each unique pair of cities.

```
CityModel::CityModel(QObject *parent)
    : QAbstractTableModel(parent)
{
}
```

The constructor does nothing beyond pass on the parent parameter to the
base class.

```
int CityModel::rowCount(const QModelIndex & /* parent */) const
{
    return cities.count();
}

int CityModel::columnCount(const QModelIndex & /* parent */) const
{
    return cities.count();
}
```

Since we have a square grid of cities, the number of rows and columns is the
number of cities in our list.

```
QVariant CityModel::data(const QModelIndex &index, int role) const
{
    if (!index.isValid())
        return QVariant();

    if (role == Qt::TextAlignmentRole) {
        return int(Qt::AlignRight | Qt::AlignVCenter);
    } else if (role == Qt::DisplayRole) {
        if (index.row() == index.column())
            return 0;
        int offset = offsetOf(index.row(), index.column());
        return distances[offset];
    }
    return QVariant();
}
```

The data() function is similar to what we did in CurrencyModel. It returns 0 if
the row and column are the same, because that corresponds to the case where
the two cities are the same; otherwise, it finds the entry for the given row and
column in the distances vector and returns the distance for that particular pair
of cities.

```
QVariant CityModel::headerData(int section,
                               Qt::Orientation /* orientation */,
                               int role) const
{
    if (role == Qt::DisplayRole)
        return cities[section];
    return QVariant();
}
```

The headerData() function is simple because we have a square table with every row having an identical column header. We simply return the name of the city at the given offset in the cities string list.

```
bool CityModel::setData(const QModelIndex &index,
                        const QVariant &value, int role)
{
    if (index.isValid() && index.row() != index.column()
            && role == Qt::EditRole) {
        int offset = offsetOf(index.row(), index.column());
        distances[offset] = value.toInt();

        QModelIndex transposedIndex = createIndex(index.column(),
                                                  index.row());
        emit dataChanged(index, index);
        emit dataChanged(transposedIndex, transposedIndex);
        return true;
    }
    return false;
}
```

The setData() function is called when the user edits an item. Providing the model index is valid, the two cities are different, and the data element to modify is the Qt::EditRole, the function stores the value the user entered in the distances vector.

The createIndex() function is used to generate a model index. We need it to get the model index of the item on the other side of the main diagonal that corresponds with the item being set, since both items must show the same data. The createIndex() function takes the row before the column; here we invert the parameters to get the model index of the diagonally opposite item to the one specified by index.

We emit the dataChanged() signal with the model index of the item that was changed. The reason this signal takes two model indexes is that it is possible for a change to affect a rectangular region of more than one row and column, so the indexes passed are the index of the top left and bottom right items of those that have changed. We also emit the dataChanged() signal for the transposed index to ensure that the view will refresh the item. Finally, we return true or false to indicate whether or not the edit succeeded.

```
Qt::ItemFlags CityModel::flags(const QModelIndex &index) const
{
    Qt::ItemFlags flags = QAbstractItemModel::flags(index);
    if (index.row() != index.column())
        flags |= Qt::ItemIsEditable;
    return flags;
}
```

The flags() function is used by the model to communicate what can be done with an item (for example, whether it is editable). The default implementation from QAbstractTableModel returns Qt::ItemIsSelectable | Qt::ItemIsEnabled. We add the `Qt::ItemIsEditable` flag for all items except those lying on the diagonals (which are always 0).

```
void CityModel::setCities(const QStringList &cityNames)
{
    cities = cityNames;
    distances.resize(cities.count() * (cities.count() - 1) / 2);
    distances.fill(0);
    reset();
}
```

If a new list of cities is given, we set the private `QStringList` to the new list, resize and clear the distances vector, and call `QAbstractItemModel::reset()` to notify any views that their visible items must be refetched.

```
int CityModel::offsetOf(int row, int column) const
{
    if (row < column)
        qSwap(row, column);
    return (row * (row - 1) / 2) + column;
}
```

The `offsetOf()` private function computes the index of a given city pair in the distances vector. For example, if we had cities $\mathcal{A}$, $\mathcal{B}$, $\mathcal{C}$, and $\mathcal{D}$, and the user updated row 3, column 1, $\mathcal{B}$ to $\mathcal{D}$, the offset would be $3 \times (3 - 1)/2 + 1 = 4$. If the user had instead updated row 1, column 3, $\mathcal{D}$ to $\mathcal{B}$, thanks to the `qSwap()`, exactly the same calculation would be performed and an identical offset would be returned.

Figure 10.13. The `cities` and `distances` data structures and the table model

The last example in this section is a model that shows the parse tree for a given regular expression. A regular expression consists of one or more terms, separated by '|' characters. Thus, the regular expression "alpha | bravo | charlie" contains three terms. Each term is a sequence of one or more factors; for example, the term "bravo" consists of five factors (each letter is a factor). The factors can be further decomposed into an atom and an optional quantifier, such as '*', '+', and '?'. Since regular expressions can have parenthesized subexpressions, they can have recursive parse trees.

The regular expression shown in Figure 10.14, "ab | (cd)?e", matches an 'a' followed by a 'b', or alternatively either a 'c' followed by a 'd' followed by an 'e', or just an 'e' on its own. So it will match "ab" and "cde", but not "bc" or "cd".

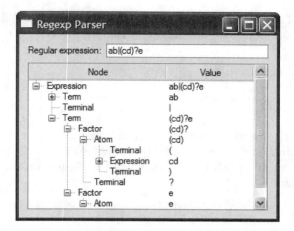

Figure 10.14. The Regexp Parser application

The Regexp Parser application consists of four classes:

- `RegExpWindow` is a window that lets the user enter a regular expression and shows the corresponding parse tree.

- `RegExpParser` generates a parse tree from a regular expression.

- `RegExpModel` is a tree model that encapsulates a parse tree.

- `Node` represents an item in a parse tree.

Let's start with the `Node` class:

```cpp
class Node
{
public:
    enum Type { RegExp, Expression, Term, Factor, Atom, Terminal };

    Node(Type type, const QString &str = "");
    ~Node();

    Type type;
    QString str;
    Node *parent;
    QList<Node *> children;
};
```

Every node has a type, a string (which may be empty), a parent (which may be 0), and a list of child nodes (which may be empty).

```cpp
Node::Node(Type type, const QString &str)
{
    this->type = type;
    this->str = str;
    parent = 0;
}
```

The constructor simply initializes the node's type and string. Because all the data is public, code that uses Node can manipulate the type, string, parent, and children directly.

```
Node::~Node()
{
    qDeleteAll(children);
}
```

The qDeleteAll() function iterates over a container of pointers and calls delete on each one. It does not set the pointers to 0, so if it is used outside of a destructor it is common to follow it with a call to clear() on the container that holds the pointers.

Now that we have defined our data items (each represented by a Node), we are ready to create a model:

```
class RegExpModel : public QAbstractItemModel
{
public:
    RegExpModel(QObject *parent = 0);
    ~RegExpModel();

    void setRootNode(Node *node);

    QModelIndex index(int row, int column,
                      const QModelIndex &parent) const;
    QModelIndex parent(const QModelIndex &child) const;

    int rowCount(const QModelIndex &parent) const;
    int columnCount(const QModelIndex &parent) const;
    QVariant data(const QModelIndex &index, int role) const;
    QVariant headerData(int section, Qt::Orientation orientation,
                        int role) const;

private:
    Node *nodeFromIndex(const QModelIndex &index) const;

    Node *rootNode;
};
```

This time we have inherited from QAbstractItemModel rather than from its convenience subclass QAbstractTableModel, because we want to create a hierarchical model. The essential functions that we must reimplement remain the same, except that we must also implement index() and parent(). To set the model's data, we have a setRootNode() function that must be called with a parse tree's root node.

```
RegExpModel::RegExpModel(QObject *parent)
    : QAbstractItemModel(parent)
{
    rootNode = 0;
}
```

In the model's constructor, we just need to set the root node to a safe null value and pass on the parent to the base class.

```
RegExpModel::~RegExpModel()
{
    delete rootNode;
}
```

In the destructor we delete the root node. If the root node has children, each of these is deleted, and so on recursively, by the Node destructor.

```
void RegExpModel::setRootNode(Node *node)
{
    delete rootNode;
    rootNode = node;
    reset();
}
```

When a new root node is set, we begin by deleting any previous root node (and all of its children). Then we set the new root node and call reset() to notify any views that they must refetch the data for any visible items.

```
QModelIndex RegExpModel::index(int row, int column,
                               const QModelIndex &parent) const
{
    if (!rootNode)
        return QModelIndex();
    Node *parentNode = nodeFromIndex(parent);
    return createIndex(row, column, parentNode->children[row]);
}
```

The index() function is reimplemented from QAbstractItemModel. It is called whenever the model or the view needs to create a QModelIndex for a particular child item (or a top-level item if parent is an invalid QModelIndex). For table and list models, we don't need to reimplement this function, because QAbstractList-Model's and QAbstractTableModel's default implementations normally suffice.

In our index() implementation, if no parse tree is set, we return an invalid QModelIndex. Otherwise, we create a QModelIndex with the given row and column and with a Node * for the requested child. For hierarchical models, knowing the row and column of an item relative to its parent is not enough to uniquely identify it; we must also know *who* the parent is. To solve this, we can store a pointer to the internal node in the QModelIndex. QModelIndex gives us the option of storing a void * or an int in addition to the row and column numbers.

The Node * for the child is obtained through the parent node's children list. The parent node is extracted from the parent model index using the nodeFromIndex() private function:

```
Node *RegExpModel::nodeFromIndex(const QModelIndex &index) const
{
    if (index.isValid()) {
        return static_cast<Node *>(index.internalPointer());
    } else {
```

```
            return rootNode;
        }
    }
```

The nodeFromIndex() function casts the given index's void * to a Node *, or returns the root node if the index is invalid, since an invalid model index is used to represent the root in a model.

```
int RegExpModel::rowCount(const QModelIndex &parent) const
{
    Node *parentNode = nodeFromIndex(parent);
    if (!parentNode)
        return 0;
    return parentNode->children.count();
}
```

The number of rows for a given item is simply how many children it has.

```
int RegExpModel::columnCount(const QModelIndex & /* parent */) const
{
    return 2;
}
```

The number of columns is fixed at 2. The first column holds the node types; the second column holds the node values.

```
QModelIndex RegExpModel::parent(const QModelIndex &child) const
{
    Node *node = nodeFromIndex(child);
    if (!node)
        return QModelIndex();
    Node *parentNode = node->parent;
    if (!parentNode)
        return QModelIndex();
    Node *grandparentNode = parentNode->parent;
    if (!grandparentNode)
        return QModelIndex();

    int row = grandparentNode->children.indexOf(parentNode);
    return createIndex(row, child.column(), parentNode);
}
```

Retrieving the parent QModelIndex from a child is a bit more work than finding a parent's child. We can easily retrieve the parent node using nodeFromIndex() and going up using the Node's parent pointer, but to obtain the row number (the position of the parent among its siblings), we need to go back to the grandparent and find the parent's index position in its parent's (that is, the child's grandparent's) list of children.

```
QVariant RegExpModel::data(const QModelIndex &index, int role) const
{
    if (role != Qt::DisplayRole)
        return QVariant();

    Node *node = nodeFromIndex(index);
    if (!node)
```

```
            return QVariant();

    if (index.column() == 0) {
        switch (node->type) {
        case Node::RegExp:
            return tr("RegExp");
        case Node::Expression:
            return tr("Expression");
        case Node::Term:
            return tr("Term");
        case Node::Factor:
            return tr("Factor");
        case Node::Atom:
            return tr("Atom");
        case Node::Terminal:
            return tr("Terminal");
        default:
            return tr("Unknown");
        }
    } else if (index.column() == 1) {
        return node->str;
    }
    return QVariant();
}
```

In data(), we retrieve the Node * for the requested item and we use it to access the underlying data. If the caller wants a value for any role except Qt::DisplayRole or if we cannot retrieve a Node for the given model index, we return an invalid QVariant. If the column is 0, we return the name of the node's type; if the column is 1, we return the node's value (its string).

```
    QVariant RegExpModel::headerData(int section,
                                     Qt::Orientation orientation,
                                     int role) const
    {
        if (orientation == Qt::Horizontal && role == Qt::DisplayRole) {
            if (section == 0) {
                return tr("Node");
            } else if (section == 1) {
                return tr("Value");
            }
        }
        return QVariant();
    }
```

In our headerData() reimplementation, we return appropriate horizontal header labels. The QTreeView class, which is used to visualize hierarchical models, has no vertical header, so we ignore that possibility.

Now that we have covered the Node and RegExpModel classes, let's see how the root node is created when the user changes the text in the line edit:

```
    void RegExpWindow::regExpChanged(const QString &regExp)
    {
        RegExpParser parser;
```

```
        Node *rootNode = parser.parse(regExp);
        regExpModel->setRootNode(rootNode);
}
```

When the user changes the text in the application's line edit, the main window's regExpChanged() slot is called. In this slot, the user's text is parsed and the parser returns a pointer to the root node of the parse tree.

We have not shown the RegExpParser class because it is not relevant for GUI or model/view programming. The full source for this example is on the CD.

In this section, we have seen how to create three different custom models. Many models are much simpler than those shown here, with one-to-one correspondences between items and model indexes. Further model/view examples are provided with Qt itself, along with extensive documentation.

Implementing Custom Delegates

Individual items in views are rendered and edited using delegates. In most cases, the default delegate supplied by a view is sufficient. If we want to have finer control over the rendering of items, we can often achieve what we want simply by using a custom model: In our data() reimplementation we can handle the Qt::FontRole, Qt::TextAlignmentRole, Qt::TextColorRole, and Qt::BackgroundColorRole, and these are used by the default delegate. For example, in the Cities and Currencies examples shown earlier, we handled the Qt::TextAlignmentRole to get right-aligned numbers.

If we want even greater control, we can create our own delegate class and set it on the views that we want to make use of it. The Track Editor dialog shown below makes use of a custom delegate. It shows the titles of music tracks and their durations. The data held by the model will be simply QStrings (titles) and ints (seconds), but the durations will be separated into minutes and seconds and will be editable using a QTimeEdit.

Figure 10.15. The Track Editor dialog

The Track Editor dialog uses a QTableWidget, a convenience item view subclass that operates on QTableWidgetItems. The data is provided as a list of Tracks:

```cpp
class Track
{
public:
    Track(const QString &title = "", int duration = 0);

    QString title;
    int duration;
};
```

Here is an extract from the constructor that shows the creation and population of the table widget:

```cpp
TrackEditor::TrackEditor(QList<Track> *tracks, QWidget *parent)
    : QDialog(parent)
{
    this->tracks = tracks;

    tableWidget = new QTableWidget(tracks->count(), 2);
    tableWidget->setItemDelegate(new TrackDelegate(1));
    tableWidget->setHorizontalHeaderLabels(
            QStringList() << tr("Track") << tr("Duration"));

    for (int row = 0; row < tracks->count(); ++row) {
        Track track = tracks->at(row);

        QTableWidgetItem *item0 = new QTableWidgetItem(track.title);
        tableWidget->setItem(row, 0, item0);

        QTableWidgetItem *item1
            = new QTableWidgetItem(QString::number(track.duration));
        item1->setTextAlignment(Qt::AlignRight);
        tableWidget->setItem(row, 1, item1);
    }
    ...
}
```

The constructor creates a table widget, and instead of simply using the default delegate, we set our custom TrackDelegate, passing it the column that holds time data. We begin by setting the column headings, and then iterate through the data, populating the rows with the name and duration of each track.

The rest of the constructor and the rest of the TrackEditor dialog holds no surprises, so we will now look at the TrackDelegate that handles the rendering and editing of track data.

```cpp
class TrackDelegate : public QItemDelegate
{
    Q_OBJECT

public:
    TrackDelegate(int durationColumn, QObject *parent = 0);
```

```
        void paint(QPainter *painter, const QStyleOptionViewItem &option,
                const QModelIndex &index) const;
        QWidget *createEditor(QWidget *parent,
                          const QStyleOptionViewItem &option,
                          const QModelIndex &index) const;
        void setEditorData(QWidget *editor, const QModelIndex &index) const;
        void setModelData(QWidget *editor, QAbstractItemModel *model,
                      const QModelIndex &index) const;

    private slots:
        void commitAndCloseEditor();

    private:
        int durationColumn;
    };
```

We use `QItemDelegate` as our base class, so that we benefit from the default delegate implementation. We could also have used `QAbstractItemDelegate` if we had wanted to start from scratch. To provide a delegate that can edit data, we must implement `createEditor()`, `setEditorData()`, and `setModelData()`. We also implement `paint()` to change the rendering of the duration column.

```
    TrackDelegate::TrackDelegate(int durationColumn, QObject *parent)
        : QItemDelegate(parent)
    {
        this->durationColumn = durationColumn;
    }
```

The `durationColumn` parameter to the constructor tells the delegate which column holds the track duration.

```
    void TrackDelegate::paint(QPainter *painter,
                          const QStyleOptionViewItem &option,
                          const QModelIndex &index) const
    {
        if (index.column() == durationColumn) {
            int secs = index.model()->data(index, Qt::DisplayRole).toInt();
            QString text = QString("%1:%2")
                                .arg(secs / 60, 2, 10, QChar('0'))
                                .arg(secs % 60, 2, 10, QChar('0'));

            QStyleOptionViewItem myOption = option;
            myOption.displayAlignment = Qt::AlignRight | Qt::AlignVCenter;

            drawDisplay(painter, myOption, myOption.rect, text);
            drawFocus(painter, myOption, myOption.rect);
        } else{
            QItemDelegate::paint(painter, option, index);
        }
    }
```

Since we want to render the duration in the form "*minutes*:*seconds*", we have reimplemented the `paint()` function. The `arg()` calls take an integer to render as a string, how many characters the string should have, the base of the integer (10 for decimal), and the padding character.

To right-align the text, we copy the current style options and overwrite the default alignment. We then call QItemDelegate::drawDisplay() to draw the text, followed by QItemDelegate::drawFocus(), which will draw a focus rectangle if the item has focus and will do nothing otherwise. Using drawDisplay() is very convenient, especially when used with our own style options. We could also draw using the painter directly.

```
QWidget *TrackDelegate::createEditor(QWidget *parent,
        const QStyleOptionViewItem &option,
        const QModelIndex &index) const
{
    if (index.column() == durationColumn) {
        QTimeEdit *timeEdit = new QTimeEdit(parent);
        timeEdit->setDisplayFormat("mm:ss");
        connect(timeEdit, SIGNAL(editingFinished()),
                this, SLOT(commitAndCloseEditor()));
        return timeEdit;
    } else {
        return QItemDelegate::createEditor(parent, option, index);
    }
}
```

We only want to control the editing of track durations, leaving the editing of track names to the default delegate. We achieve this by checking which column the delegate has been asked to provide an editor for. If it's the duration column, we create a QTimeEdit, set the display format appropriately, and connect its editingFinished() signal to our commitAndCloseEditor() slot. For any other column, we pass on the edit handling to the default delegate.

```
void TrackDelegate::commitAndCloseEditor()
{
    QTimeEdit *editor = qobject_cast<QTimeEdit *>(sender());
    emit commitData(editor);
    emit closeEditor(editor);
}
```

If the user presses Enter or moves the focus out of the QTimeEdit (but not if they press Esc), the editingFinished() signal is emitted and the commitAndCloseEditor() slot is called. This slot emits the commitData() signal to inform the view that there is edited data to replace existing data. It also emits the closeEditor() signal to notify the view that this editor is no longer required, at which point the model will delete it. The editor is retrieved using QObject::sender(), which returns the object that emitted the signal that triggered the slot. If the user cancels (by pressing Esc), the view will simply delete the editor.

```
void TrackDelegate::setEditorData(QWidget *editor,
                                  const QModelIndex &index) const
{
    if (index.column() == durationColumn) {
        int secs = index.model()->data(index, Qt::DisplayRole).toInt();
        QTimeEdit *timeEdit = qobject_cast<QTimeEdit *>(editor);
        timeEdit->setTime(QTime(0, secs / 60, secs % 60));
    } else {
```

```
        QItemDelegate::setEditorData(editor, index);
    }
}
```

When the user initiates editing, the view calls createEditor() to create an editor, and then setEditorData() to initialize the editor with the item's current data. If the editor is for the duration column, we extract the track's duration in seconds and set the QTimeEdit's time to the corresponding number of minutes and seconds; otherwise, we let the default delegate handle the initialization.

```
void TrackDelegate::setModelData(QWidget *editor,
                                 QAbstractItemModel *model,
                                 const QModelIndex &index) const
{
    if (index.column() == durationColumn) {
        QTimeEdit *timeEdit = qobject_cast<QTimeEdit *>(editor);
        QTime time = timeEdit->time();
        int secs = (time.minute() * 60) + time.second();
        model->setData(index, secs);
    } else {
        QItemDelegate::setModelData(editor, model, index);
    }
}
```

If the user completes the edit (for example, by left-clicking outside the editor widget, or by pressing Enter or Tab) rather than canceling it, the model must be updated with the editor's data. If the duration was edited, we extract the minutes and seconds from the QTimeEdit, and set the data to the corresponding number of seconds.

Although not necessary in this case, it is entirely possible to create a custom delegate that finely controls the editing and rendering of any item in a model. We have chosen to take control of a particular column, but since the QModelIndex is passed to all the QItemDelegate functions that we reimplement, we can take control by column, row, rectangular region, parent, or any combination of these, right down to individual items if required.

In this chapter, we have presented a broad overview of Qt's model/view architecture. We have shown how to use the view convenience subclasses, how to use Qt's predefined models, and how to create custom models and custom delegates. But the model/view architecture is so rich that we have not had the space to cover all the things it makes possible. For example, we could create a custom view that does not render its items as a list, table, or tree. This is done by the Chart example located in Qt's examples/itemviews/chart directory, which shows a custom view that renders model data in the form of a pie chart.

It is also possible to use multiple views to view the same model without any formality. Any edits made through one view will be automatically and immediately reflected in the other views. This kind of functionality is particularly useful for viewing large data sets where the user may wish to see sections of data that are logically far apart. The architecture also supports selections: Where two or more views are using the same model, each view can be set to have its own independent selections, or the selections can be shared across the views.

Qt's online documentation provides comprehensive coverage of item view programming and the classes that implement it. See `http://doc.trolltech.com/4.1/model-view.html` for a list of all the relevant classes, and `http://doc.trolltech.com/4.1/model-view-programming.html` for additional information and links to the relevant examples included with Qt.

- *Sequential Containers*
- *Associative Containers*
- *Generic Algorithms*
- *Strings, Byte Arrays, and Variants*

11. Container Classes

Container classes are general-purpose template classes that store items of a given type in memory. C++ already offers many containers as part of the Standard Template Library (STL), which is included in the Standard C++ library.

Qt provides its own container classes, so for Qt programs we can use both the Qt and the STL containers. The main advantages of the Qt containers are that they behave the same on all platforms and that they are implicitly shared. Implicit sharing, or "copy on write", is an optimization that makes it possible to pass entire containers as values without any significant performance cost. The Qt containers also feature easy-to-use iterator classes inspired by Java, they can be streamed using QDataStream, and they usually result in less code in the executable than the corresponding STL containers. Finally, on some hardware platforms supported by Qtopia Core (the Qt version for mobile devices), the Qt containers are the only ones available.

Qt offers both sequential containers such as QVector<T>, QLinkedList<T>, and QList<T>, and associative containers such as QMap<K, T> and QHash<K, T>. Conceptually, the sequential containers store items one after another, whereas the associative containers store key–value pairs.

Qt also provides generic algorithms that perform operations on arbitrary containers. For example, the qSort() algorithm sorts a sequential container, and qBinaryFind() performs a binary search on a sorted sequential container. These algorithms are similar to those offered by the STL.

If you are already familiar with the STL containers and have STL available on your target platforms, you might want to use them instead of, or in addition to, the Qt containers. For more information about the STL classes and functions, a good place to start is SGI's STL web site: http://www.sgi.com/tech/stl/.

In this chapter, we will also look at QString, QByteArray, and QVariant, since they have a lot in common with containers. QString is a 16-bit Unicode string used throughout Qt's API. QByteArray is an array of 8-bit chars useful for storing raw binary data. QVariant is a type that can store most C++ and Qt value types.

Sequential Containers

A QVector<T> is an array-like data structure that stores its items at adjacent positions in memory. What distinguishes a vector from a plain C++ array is that a vector knows its own size and can be resized. Appending extra items to the end of a vector is fairly efficient, while inserting items at the front or in the middle of a vector can be expensive.

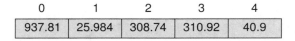

Figure 11.1. A vector of doubles

If we know in advance how many items we are going to need, we can give the vector an initial size when we define it and use the [] operator to assign a value to the items; otherwise, we must either resize the vector later on or append items. Here's an example where we specify the initial size:

```
QVector<double> vect(3);
vect[0] = 1.0;
vect[1] = 0.540302;
vect[2] = -0.416147;
```

Here's the same example, this time starting with an empty vector and using the append() function to append items at the end:

```
QVector<double> vect;
vect.append(1.0);
vect.append(0.540302);
vect.append(-0.416147);
```

We can also use the << operator instead of append():

```
vect << 1.0 << 0.540302 << -0.416147;
```

One way to iterate over the vector's items is to use [] and count():

```
double sum = 0.0;
for (int i = 0; i < vect.count(); ++i)
    sum += vect[i];
```

Vector entries that are created without being assigned an explicit value are initialized using the item class's default constructor. Basic types and pointer types are initialized to zero.

Inserting items at the beginning or in the middle of a QVector<T>, or removing items from these positions, can be inefficient for large vectors. For this reason, Qt also offers QLinkedList<T>, a data structure that stores its items at non-adjacent locations in memory. Unlike vectors, linked lists don't support random access, but they provide "constant time" insertions and removals.

Figure 11.2. A linked list of `doubles`

Linked lists do not provide the [] operator, so iterators must be used to traverse their items. Iterators are also used to specify the position of items. For example, the following code inserts the string "Tote Hosen" between "Clash" and "Ramones":

```
QLinkedList<QString> list;
list.append("Clash");
list.append("Ramones");

QLinkedList<QString>::iterator i = list.find("Ramones");
list.insert(i, "Tote Hosen");
```

We will take a more detailed look at iterators later in this section.

The `QList<T>` sequential container is an "array-list" that combines the most important benefits of `QVector<T>` and `QLinkedList<T>` in a single class. It supports random access, and its interface is index-based like `QVector`'s. Inserting or removing an item at either end of a `QList<T>` is very fast, and inserting in the middle is fast for lists with up to about one thousand items. Unless we want to perform insertions in the middle of huge lists or need the list's items to occupy consecutive addresses in memory, `QList<T>` is usually the most appropriate general-purpose container class to use.

The `QStringList` class is a subclass of `QList<QString>` that is widely used in Qt's API. In addition to the functions it inherits from its base class, it provides some extra functions that make the class more versatile for string handling. `QStringList` is discussed in the last section of this chapter (p. 268).

`QStack<T>` and `QQueue<T>` are two more examples of convenience subclasses. `QStack<T>` is a vector that provides `push()`, `pop()`, and `top()`. `QQueue<T>` is a list that provides `enqueue()`, `dequeue()`, and `head()`.

For all the container classes seen so far, the value type `T` can be a basic type like `int` or `double`, a pointer type, or a class that has a default constructor (a constructor that takes no arguments), a copy constructor, and an assignment operator. Classes that qualify include `QByteArray`, `QDateTime`, `QRegExp`, `QString`, and `QVariant`. Qt classes that inherit from `QObject` do not qualify, because they lack a copy constructor and an assignment operator. This is no problem in practice, since we can simply store pointers to `QObject` types rather than the objects themselves.

The value type `T` can also be a container, in which case we must remember to separate consecutive angle brackets with spaces; otherwise, the compiler will choke on what it thinks is a >> operator. For example:

```
QList<QVector<double> > list;
```

In addition to the types just mentioned, a container's value type can be any custom class that meets the criteria described earlier. Here is an example of such a class:

```
class Movie
{
public:
    Movie(const QString &title = "", int duration = 0);

    void setTitle(const QString &title) { myTitle = title; }
    QString title() const { return myTitle; }
    void setDuration(int duration) { myDuration = duration; }
    QString duration() const { return myDuration; }

private:
    QString myTitle;
    int myDuration;
};
```

The class has a constructor that requires no arguments (although it can take up to two). It also has a copy constructor and an assignment operator, both implicitly provided by C++. For this class, member-by-member copy is sufficient, so there's no need to implement our own copy constructor and assignment operator.

Qt provides two categories of iterators for traversing the items stored in a container: Java-style iterators and STL-style iterators. The Java-style iterators are easier to use, whereas the STL-style iterators can be combined with Qt's and STL's generic algorithms and are more powerful.

For each container class, there are two Java-style iterator types: a read-only iterator and a read-write iterator. The read-only iterator classes are QVectorIterator<T>, QLinkedListIterator<T>, and QListIterator<T>. The corresponding read-write iterators have Mutable in their name (for example, QMutableVectorIterator<T>). In this discussion, we will concentrate on QList's iterators; the iterators for linked lists and vectors have the same API.

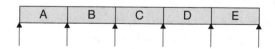

Figure 11.3. Valid positions for Java-style iterators

The first thing to keep in mind when using Java-style iterators is that they don't point directly at items. Instead, they can be located before the first item, after the last item, or between two items. A typical iteration loop looks like this:

```
QList<double> list;
...
QListIterator<double> i(list);
while (i.hasNext()) {
```

```
        do_something(i.next());
    }
```

The iterator is initialized with the container to traverse. At this point, the iterator is located just before the first item. The call to hasNext() returns true if there is an item to the right of the iterator. The next() function returns the item to the right of the iterator and advances the iterator to the next valid position.

Iterating backward is similar, except that we must first call toBack() to position the iterator after the last item:

```
    QListIterator<double> i(list);
    i.toBack();
    while (i.hasPrevious()) {
        do_something(i.previous());
    }
```

The hasPrevious() function returns true if there is an item to the left of the iterator; previous() returns the item to the left of the iterator and moves the iterator back by one position. Another way of thinking about the next() and previous() iterators is that they return the item that the iterator has just jumped over.

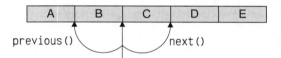

Figure 11.4. Effect of previous() and next() on a Java-style iterator

Mutable iterators provide functions to insert, modify, and remove items while iterating. The following loop removes all the negative numbers from a list:

```
    QMutableListIterator<double> i(list);
    while (i.hasNext()) {
        if (i.next() < 0.0)
            i.remove();
    }
```

The remove() function always operates on the last item that was jumped over. It also works when iterating backward:

```
    QMutableListIterator<double> i(list);
    i.toBack();
    while (i.hasPrevious()) {
        if (i.previous() < 0.0)
            i.remove();
    }
```

Similarly, the mutable Java-style iterators provide a setValue() function that modifies the last item that was jumped over. Here's how we would replace negative numbers with their absolute value:

```
QMutableListIterator<double> i(list);
while (i.hasNext()) {
    int val = i.next();
    if (val < 0.0)
        i.setValue(-val);
}
```

It is also possible to insert an item at the current iterator position by calling
insert(). The iterator is then advanced to point between the new item and the
following item.

In addition to the Java-style iterators, every sequential container class C<T>
has two STL-style iterator types: C<T>::iterator and C<T>::const_iterator.
The difference between the two is that const_iterator doesn't let us modify
the data.

A container's begin() function returns an STL-style iterator that refers to
the first item in the container (for example, list[0]), whereas end() returns
an iterator to the "one past the last" item (for example, list[5] for a list of
size 5). If a container is empty, begin() equals end(). This can be used to see
if the container has any items, although it is usually more convenient to call
isEmpty() for this purpose.

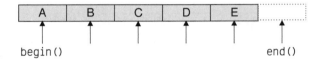

Figure 11.5. Valid positions for STL-style iterators

The STL-style iterator syntax is modeled after that of C++ pointers into an
array. We can use the ++ and -- operators to move to the next or previous item,
and the unary * operator to retrieve the current item. For QVector<T>, the iterator and const_iterator types are merely typedefs for T * and const T *. (This is
possible because QVector<T> stores its items in consecutive memory locations.)

The following example replaces each value in a QList<double> with its absolute
value:

```
QList<double>::iterator i = list.begin();
while (i != list.end()) {
    *i = qAbs(*i);
    ++i;
}
```

A few Qt functions return a container. If we want to iterate over the return
value of a function using an STL-style iterator, we must take a copy of the
container and iterate over the copy. For example, the following code is the
correct way to iterate over the QList<int> returned by QSplitter::sizes():

```
QList<int> list = splitter->sizes();
```

```
QList<int>::const_iterator i = list.begin();
while (i != list.end()) {
    do_something(*i);
    ++i;
}
```

The following code is wrong:

```
// WRONG
QList<int>::const_iterator i = splitter->sizes().begin();
while (i != splitter->sizes().end()) {
    do_something(*i);
    ++i;
}
```

This is because `QSplitter::sizes()` returns a new `QList<int>` by value every time it is called. If we don't store the return value, C++ automatically destroys it before we have even started iterating, leaving us with a dangling iterator. To make matters worse, each time the loop is run, `QSplitter::sizes()` must generate a new copy of the list because of the `splitter->sizes().end()` call. In summary: When using STL-style iterators, always iterate on a copy of a container returned by value.

With read-only Java-style iterators, we don't need to take a copy. The iterator takes a copy for us behind the scenes, ensuring that we always iterate over the data that the function first returned. For example:

```
QListIterator<int> i(splitter->sizes());
while (i.hasNext()) {
    do_something(i.next());
}
```

Copying a container like this sounds expensive, but it isn't, thanks to an optimization called *implicit sharing*. This means that copying a Qt container is about as fast as copying a single pointer. Only if one of the copies is changed is data actually copied—and this is all handled automatically behind the scenes. For this reason, implicit sharing is sometimes called "copy on write".

The beauty of implicit sharing is that it is an optimization that we don't need to think about; it simply works, without requiring any programmer intervention. At the same time, implicit sharing encourages a clean programming style where objects are returned by value. Consider the following function:

```
QVector<double> sineTable()
{
    QVector<double> vect(360);
    for (int i = 0; i < 360; ++i)
        vect[i] = sin(i / (2 * M_PI));
    return vect;
}
```

The call to the function looks like this:

```
QVector<double> table = sineTable();
```

STL, in comparison, encourages us to pass the vector as a non-const reference to avoid the copy that takes place when the function's return value is stored in a variable:

```
using namespace std;

void sineTable(vector<double> &vect)
{
    vect.resize(360);
    for (int i = 0; i < 360; ++i)
        vect[i] = sin(i / (2 * M_PI));
}
```

The call then becomes more tedious to write and less clear to read:

```
vector<double> table;
sineTable(table);
```

Qt uses implicit sharing for all of its containers and for many other classes, including QByteArray, QBrush, QFont, QImage, QPixmap, and QString. This makes these classes very efficient to pass by value, both as function parameters and as return values.

Implicit sharing is a guarantee from Qt that the data won't be copied if we don't modify it. To get the best out of implicit sharing, we can adopt a couple of new programming habits. One habit is to use the at() function rather than the [] operator for read-only access on a (non-const) vector or list. Since Qt's containers cannot tell whether [] appears on the left side of an assignment or not, it assumes the worst and forces a deep copy to occur—whereas at() isn't allowed on the left side of an assignment.

A similar issue arises when we iterate over a container with STL-style iterators. Whenever we call begin() or end() on a non-const container, Qt forces a deep copy to occur if the data is shared. To prevent this inefficiency, the solution is to use const_iterator, constBegin(), and constEnd() whenever possible.

Qt provides one last method for iterating over items in a sequential container: the foreach loop. It looks like this:

```
QLinkedList<Movie> list;
...
foreach (Movie movie, list) {
    if (movie.title() == "Citizen Kane") {
        cout << "Found Citizen Kane" << endl;
        break;
    }
}
```

The foreach pseudo-keyword is implemented in terms of the standard for loop. At each iteration of the loop, the iteration variable (movie) is set to a new item, starting at the first item in the container and progressing forward. The foreach loop automatically takes a copy of the container when the loop is entered, and for this reason the loop is not affected if the container is modified during iteration.

How Implicit Sharing Works

Implicit sharing works automatically behind the scenes, so we don't have to do anything in our code to make this optimization happen. But since it's nice to know how things work, we will study an example and see what happens under the hood. The example uses QString, one of Qt's many implicitly shared classes.

```
QString str1 = "Humpty";
QString str2 = str1;
```

We set str1 to "Humpty" and str2 to be equal to str1. At this point, both QString objects point to the same internal data structure in memory. Along with the character data, the data structure holds a reference count that indicates how many QStrings point to the same data structure. Since both str1 and str2 point to the same data, the reference count is 2.

```
str2[0] = 'D';
```

When we modify str2, it first makes a deep copy of the data, to ensure that str1 and str2 point to different data structures, and it then applies the change to its own copy of the data. The reference count of str1's data ("Humpty") becomes 1, and the reference count of str2's data ("Dumpty") is set to 1. A reference count of 1 means that the data isn't shared.

```
str2.truncate(4);
```

If we modify str2 again, no copying takes place because the reference count of str2's data is 1. The truncate() function operates directly on str2's data, resulting in the string "Dump". The reference count stays at 1.

```
str1 = str2;
```

When we assign str2 to str1, the reference count for str1's data goes down to 0, which means that no QString is using the "Humpty" data anymore. The data is then freed from memory. Both QStrings point to "Dump", which now has a reference count of 2.

Data sharing is often disregarded as an option in multithreaded programs, because of race conditions in the reference counting. With Qt, this is not an issue. Internally, the container classes use assembly language instructions to perform atomic reference counting. This technology is available to Qt users through the QSharedData and QSharedDataPointer classes.

The break and continue loop statements are supported. If the body consists of a single statement, the braces are unnecessary. Just like a for statement, the iteration variable can be defined outside the loop, like this:

```
QLinkedList<Movie> list;
Movie movie;
...
foreach (movie, list) {
```

```
        if (movie.title() == "Citizen Kane") {
            cout << "Found Citizen Kane" << endl;
            break;
        }
    }
```

Defining the iteration variable outside the loop is the only option for containers that hold data types that contain a comma (for example, QPair<QString, int>).

Associative Containers

An associative container holds an arbitrary number of items of the same type, indexed by a key. Qt provides two main associative container classes: QMap<K, T> and QHash<K, T>.

A QMap<K, T> is a data structure that stores key–value pairs in ascending key order. This arrangement makes it possible to provide good lookup and insertion performance, and in-order iteration. Internally, QMap<K, T> is implemented as a skip-list.

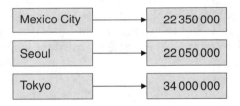

Figure 11.6. A map of QString to int

One simple way to insert items into a map is to call insert():

```
QMap<QString, int> map;
map.insert("eins", 1);
map.insert("sieben", 7);
map.insert("dreiundzwanzig", 23);
```

Alternatively, we can simply assign a value to a given key as follows:

```
map["eins"] = 1;
map["sieben"] = 7;
map["dreiundzwanzig"] = 23;
```

The [] operator can be used for both insertion and retrieval. If [] is used to retrieve a value for a non-existent key in a non-const map, a new item will be created with the given key and an empty value. To avoid accidentally creating empty values, we can use the value() function to retrieve items instead of []:

```
int val = map.value("dreiundzwanzig");
```

If the key doesn't exist, a default value is returned using the value type's default constructor, and no new item is created. For basic and pointer types, zero is returned. We can specify another default value as second argument to value(), for example:

```
int seconds = map.value("delay", 30);
```

This is equivalent to

```
int seconds = 30;
if (map.contains("delay"))
    seconds = map.value("delay");
```

The K and T data types of a QMap<K, T> can be basic data types like int and double, pointer types, or classes that have a default constructor, a copy constructor, and an assignment operator. In addition, the K type must provide an operator<() since QMap<K, T> uses this operator to store the items in ascending key order.

QMap<K, T> has a couple of convenience functions, keys() and values(), that are especially useful when dealing with small data sets. They return QLists of a map's keys and values.

Maps are normally single-valued: If a new value is assigned to an existing key, the old value is replaced by the new value, ensuring that no two items share the same key. It is possible to have multiple key–value pairs with the same key by using the insertMulti() function or the QMultiMap<K, T> convenience subclass. QMap<K, T> has a values(const K &) overload that returns a QList of all the values for a given key. For example:

```
QMultiMap<int, QString> multiMap;
multiMap.insert(1, "one");
multiMap.insert(1, "eins");
multiMap.insert(1, "uno");

QList<QString> vals = multiMap.values(1);
```

A QHash<K, T> is a data structure that stores key–value pairs in a hash table. Its interface is almost identical to that of QMap<K, T>, but it has different requirements for the K template type and usually provides much faster lookups than QMap<K, T> can achieve. Another difference is that QHash<K, T> is unordered.

In addition to the standard requirements on any value type stored in a container, the K type of a QHash<K, T> needs to provide an operator==() and be supported by a global qHash() function that returns a hash value for a key. Qt already provides qHash() functions for integer types, pointer types, QChar, QString, and QByteArray.

QHash<K, T> automatically allocates a prime number of buckets for its internal hash table and resizes this as items are inserted or removed. It is also possible to fine-tune performance by calling reserve() to specify the number of items expected to be stored in the hash and squeeze() to shrink the hash table based on the current number of items. A common idiom is to call reserve() with the maximum number of items we expect, then insert the data, and finally call squeeze() to minimize memory usage if there were fewer items than expected.

Hashes are normally single-valued, but multiple values can be assigned to the same key using the `insertMulti()` function or the `QMultiHash<K, T>` convenience subclass.

Besides `QHash<K, T>`, Qt also provides a `QCache<K, T>` class that can be used to cache objects associated with a key, and a `QSet<K>` container that only stores keys. Internally, both rely on `QHash<K, T>` and both have the same requirements for the K type as `QHash<K, T>`.

The easiest way to iterate through all the key–value pairs stored in an associative container is to use a Java-style iterator. Because the iterators must give access to both a key and a value, the Java-style iterators for associative containers work slightly differently from their sequential counterparts. The main difference is that the `next()` and `previous()` functions return an object that represents a key–value pair, rather than simply a value. The key and value components are accessible from this object as `key()` and `value()`. For example:

```
QMap<QString, int> map;
...
int sum = 0;
QMapIterator<QString, int> i(map);
while (i.hasNext())
    sum += i.next().value();
```

If we need to access both the key and the value, we can simply ignore the return value of `next()` or `previous()` and use the iterator's `key()` and `value()` functions, which operate on the last item that was jumped over:

```
QMapIterator<QString, int> i(map);
while (i.hasNext()) {
    i.next();
    if (i.value() > largestValue) {
        largestKey = i.key();
        largestValue = i.value();
    }
}
```

Mutable iterators have a `setValue()` function that modifies the value associated with the current item:

```
QMutableMapIterator<QString, int> i(map);
while (i.hasNext()) {
    i.next();
    if (i.value() < 0.0)
        i.setValue(-i.value());
}
```

STL-style iterators also provide `key()` and `value()` functions. With the non-const iterator types, `value()` returns a non-const reference, allowing us to change the value as we iterate. Note that although these iterators are called "STL-style", they deviate significantly from the STL's `map<K, T>` iterators, which are based on `pair<K, T>`.

The foreach loop also works on associative containers, but only on the value component of the key–value pairs. If we need both the key and the value components of the items, we can call the keys() and values(const K &) functions in nested foreach loops as follows:

```
QMultiMap<QString, int> map;
...
foreach (QString key, map.keys()) {
    foreach (int value, map.values(key)) {
        do_something(key, value);
    }
}
```

Generic Algorithms

The <QtAlgorithms> header declares a set of global template functions that implement basic algorithms on containers. Most of these functions operate on STL-style iterators.

The STL <algorithm> header provides a more complete set of generic algorithms. These algorithms can be used on Qt containers as well as STL containers. If STL implementations are available on all your platforms, there is probably no reason to avoid using the STL algorithms when Qt lacks an equivalent algorithm. Here, we will introduce the most important Qt algorithms.

The qFind() algorithm searches for a particular value in a container. It takes a "begin" and an "end" iterator and returns an iterator pointing to the first item that matches, or "end" if there is no match. In the following example, i is set to list.begin() + 1, whereas j is set to list.end().

```
QStringList list;
list << "Emma" << "Karl" << "James" << "Mariette";

QStringList::iterator i = qFind(list.begin(), list.end(), "Karl");
QStringList::iterator j = qFind(list.begin(), list.end(), "Petra");
```

The qBinaryFind() algorithm performs a search just like qFind(), except that it assumes that the items are sorted in ascending order and uses fast binary searching rather than qFind()'s linear searching.

The qFill() algorithm populates a container with a particular value:

```
QLinkedList<int> list(10);
qFill(list.begin(), list.end(), 1009);
```

Like the other iterator-based algorithms, we can also use qFill() on a portion of the container by varying the arguments. The following code snippet initializes the first five items of a vector to 1009 and the last five items to 2013:

```
QVector<int> vect(10);
qFill(vect.begin(), vect.begin() + 5, 1009);
qFill(vect.end() - 5, vect.end(), 2013);
```

The qCopy() algorithm copies values from one container to another:

```
QVector<int> vect(list.count());
qCopy(list.begin(), list.end(), vect.begin());
```

qCopy() can also be used to copy values within the same container, as long as the source range and the target range don't overlap. In the next code snippet, we use it to overwrite the last two items of a list with the first two items:

```
qCopy(list.begin(), list.begin() + 2, list.end() - 2);
```

The qSort() algorithm sorts the container's items into ascending order:

```
qSort(list.begin(), list.end());
```

By default, qSort() uses the < operator to compare the items. To sort items in descending order, pass qGreater<T>() as the third argument (where T is the container's value type), as follows:

```
qSort(list.begin(), list.end(), qGreater<int>());
```

We can use the third parameter to define custom sort criteria. For example, here's a "less than" comparison function that compares QStrings in a case-insensitive way:

```
bool insensitiveLessThan(const QString &str1, const QString &str2)
{
    return str1.toLower() < str2.toLower();
}
```

The call to qSort() then becomes

```
QStringList list;
...
qSort(list.begin(), list.end(), insensitiveLessThan);
```

The qStableSort() algorithm is similar to qSort(), except it guarantees that items that compare equal appear in the same order after the sort as before. This is useful if the sort criterion only takes into account parts of the value and the results are visible to the user. We used qStableSort() in Chapter 4 to implement sorting in the Spreadsheet application (p. 88).

The qDeleteAll() algorithm calls delete on every pointer stored in a container. It only makes sense on containers whose value type is a pointer type. After the call, the items are still present clear() on the container. For example:

```
qDeleteAll(list);
list.clear();
```

The qSwap() algorithm exchanges the value of two variables. For example:

```
int x1 = line.x1();
int x2 = line.x2();
if (x1 > x2)
    qSwap(x1, x2);
```

Finally, the `<QtGlobal>` header, which is included by every other Qt header, provides several useful definitions, including the `qAbs()` function, that returns the absolute value of its argument, and the `qMin()` and `qMax()` functions, that return the minimum or maximum of two values.

Strings, Byte Arrays, and Variants

`QString`, `QByteArray`, and `QVariant` are three classes that have many things in common with containers and that can be used as alternatives to containers in some contexts. Also, like the containers, these classes use implicit sharing as a memory and speed optimization.

We will start with `QString`. Strings are used by every GUI program, not only for the user interface but often also as data structures. C++ natively provides two kinds of strings: traditional C-style '\0'-terminated character arrays and the `std::string` class. Unlike these, `QString` holds 16-bit Unicode values. Unicode contains ASCII and Latin-1 as a subset, with their usual numeric values. But since `QString` is 16-bit, it can represent thousands of other characters for writing most of the world's languages. See Chapter 17 for more information about Unicode.

When using `QString`, we don't need to worry about such arcane details as allocating enough memory or ensuring that the data is '\0'-terminated. Conceptually, `QString`s can be thought of as a vector of `QChar`s. A `QString` can embed '\0' characters. The `length()` function returns the size of the entire string, including embedded '\0' characters.

`QString` provides a binary + operator to concatenate two strings and a += operator to append one string to another. Because `QString` automatically preallocates memory at the end of the string data, building up a string by repeatedly appending characters is very fast. Here's an example that combines + and +=:

```
QString str = "User: ";
str += userName + "\n";
```

There is also a `QString::append()` function that does the same thing as the += operator:

```
str = "User: ";
str.append(userName);
str.append("\n");
```

A completely different way of combining strings is to use `QString`'s `sprintf()` function:

```
str.sprintf("%s %.1f%%", "perfect competition", 100.0);
```

This function supports the same format specifiers as the C++ library's `sprintf()` function. In the example above, `str` is assigned "perfect competition 100.0%".

Yet another way of building a string from other strings or from numbers is to use `arg()`:

```
str = QString("%1 %2 (%3s-%4s)")
      .arg("permissive").arg("society").arg(1950).arg(1970);
```

In this example, "%1" is replaced by "permissive", "%2" is replaced by "society", "%3" is replaced by "1950", and "%4" is replaced by "1970". The result is "permissive society (1950s-1970s)". There are arg() overloads to handle various data types. Some overloads have extra parameters for controlling the field width, the numerical base, or the floating-point precision. In general, arg() is a much better solution than sprintf(), because it is type-safe, fully supports Unicode, and allows translators to reorder the "%n" parameters.

QString can convert numbers into strings using the QString::number() static function:

```
str = QString::number(59.6);
```

Or using the setNum() function:

```
str.setNum(59.6);
```

The reverse conversion, from a string to a number, is achieved using toInt(), toLongLong(), toDouble(), and so on. For example:

```
bool ok;
double d = str.toDouble(&ok);
```

These functions accept an optional pointer to a bool variable and set the variable to true or false depending on the success of the conversion. If the conversion fails, these functions return zero.

Once we have a string, we often want to extract parts of it. The mid() function returns the substring starting at a given position (the first argument) and of up to a given length (the second argument). For example, the following code prints "pays" to the console:*

```
QString str = "polluter pays principle";
qDebug() << str.mid(9, 4);
```

If we omit the second argument, mid() returns the substring starting at the given position and ending at the end of the string. For example, the following code prints "pays principle" to the console:

```
QString str = "polluter pays principle";
qDebug() << str.mid(9);
```

There are also left() and right() functions that perform a similar job. Both accept a number of characters, *n*, and return the first or last *n* characters of the string. For example, the following code prints "polluter principle" to the console:

```
QString str = "polluter pays principle";
```

---

*The convenient qDebug() << arg syntax used here requires the inclusion of the <QtDebug> header file, while the qDebug("...", arg) syntax is available in any file that includes at least one Qt header.

```
    qDebug() << str.left(8) << " " << str.right(9);
```

If we want to find out if a string contains a particular character, substring, or regular expression, we can use one of `QString`'s `indexOf()` functions:

```
    QString str = "the middle bit";
    int i = str.indexOf("middle");
```

This will set `i` to 4. The `indexOf()` function returns –1 on failure, and accepts an optional start position and case-sensitivity flag.

If we just want to check whether a string starts or ends with something, we can use the `startsWith()` and `endsWith()` functions:

```
    if (url.startsWith("http:") && url.endsWith(".png"))
        ...
```

This is both simpler and faster than this:

```
    if (url.left(5) == "http:" && url.right(4) == ".png")
        ...
```

String comparison with the `==` operator is case sensitive. If we are comparing user-visible strings, `localeAwareCompare()` is usually the right choice, and if we want to make the comparisons case-insensitive, we can use `toUpper()` or `toLower()`. For example:

```
    if (fileName.toLower() == "readme.txt")
        ...
```

If we want to replace a certain part of a string by another string, we can use `replace()`:

```
    QString str = "a cloudy day";
    str.replace(2, 6, "sunny");
```

The result is "a sunny day". The code can be rewritten to use `remove()` and `insert()`:

```
    str.remove(2, 6);
    str.insert(2, "sunny");
```

First, we remove six characters starting at position 2, resulting in the string "a day" (with two spaces), then we insert "sunny" at position 2.

There are overloaded versions of `replace()` that replace all occurrences of their first argument with their second argument. For example, here's how to replace all occurrences of "&" with "&" in a string:

```
    str.replace("&", "&amp;");
```

One very frequent need is to strip the whitespace (such as spaces, tabs, and newlines) from a string. `QString` has a function that eliminates whitespace from both ends of a string:

```
    QString str = "   BOB \t THE  \nDOG \n";
```

```
qDebug() << str.trimmed();
```

String `str` can be depicted as

| | | B|O|B | \t | | T|H|E | | \n|D|O|G | \n |

The string returned by `trimmed()` is

| B|O|B | \t | | T|H|E | | \n|D|O|G |

When handling user input, we often also want to replace every sequence of one or more internal whitespace characters with single spaces, in addition to stripping whitespace from both ends. This is what the `simplified()` function does:

```
QString str = "   BOB \t THE  \nDOG \n";
qDebug() << str.simplified();
```

The string returned by `simplified()` is

| B|O|B | | T|H|E | | D|O|G |

A string can be split into a `QStringList` of substrings using `QString::split()`:

```
QString str = "polluter pays principle";
QStringList words = str.split(" ");
```

In the example above, we split the string "polluter pays principle" into three substrings: "polluter", "pays", and "principle". The `split()` function has an optional third argument that specifies whether empty substrings should be kept (the default) or discarded.

The items in a `QStringList` can be joined to form a single string using `join()`. The argument to `join()` is inserted between each pair of joined strings. For example, here's how to create a single string that is composed of all the strings contained in a `QStringList` sorted into alphabetical order and separated by newlines:

```
words.sort();
str = words.join("\n");
```

When dealing with strings, we often need to determine whether a string is empty or not. This is done by calling `isEmpty()` or by checking whether `length()` is 0.

The conversion from `const char *` strings to `QString` is automatic in most cases, for example:

```
str += " (1870)";
```

Here we add a `const char *` to a `QString` without formality. To explicitly convert a `const char *` to a `QString`, simply use a `QString` cast, or call `fromAscii()` or `fromLatin1()`. (See Chapter 17 for an explanation of handling literal strings in other encodings.)

To convert a QString to a const char *, use toAscii() or toLatin1(). These functions return a QByteArray, which can be converted into a const char * using QByteArray::data() or QByteArray::constData(). For example:

```
printf("User: %s\n", str.toAscii().data());
```

For convenience, Qt provides the qPrintable() macro that performs the same as the sequence toAscii().constData():

```
printf("User: %s\n", qPrintable(str));
```

When we call data() or constData() on a QByteArray, the returned string is owned by the QByteArray object. This means that we don't need to worry about memory leaks; Qt will reclaim the memory for us. On the other hand, we must be careful not to use the pointer for too long. If the QByteArray is not stored in a variable, it will be automatically deleted at the end of the statement.

The QByteArray class has a very similar API to QString. Functions like left(), right(), mid(), toLower(), toUpper(), trimmed(), and simplified() exist in QByteArray with the same semantics as their QString counterparts. QByteArray is useful for storing raw binary data and 8-bit encoded text strings. In general, we recommend using QString for storing text rather than QByteArray because QString supports Unicode.

For convenience, QByteArray automatically ensures that the "one past the last" byte is always '\0', making it easy to pass a QByteArray to a function taking a const char *. QByteArray also supports embedded '\0' characters, allowing us to use it to store arbitrary binary data.

In some situations, we need to store data of different types in the same variable. One approach is to encode the data as a QByteArray or a QString. For example, a string could hold a textual value or a numeric value in string form. These approaches give complete flexibility, but do away with some of C++'s benefits, in particular type safety and efficiency. Qt provides a much cleaner way of handling variables that can hold different types: QVariant.

The QVariant class can hold values of many Qt types, including QBrush, QColor, QCursor, QDateTime, QFont, QKeySequence, QPalette, QPen, QPixmap, QPoint, QRect, QRegion, QSize, and QString, as well as basic C++ numeric types like double and int. The QVariant class can also hold containers: QMap<QString, QVariant>, QStringList, and QList<QVariant>.

Variants are used extensively by the item view classes, the database module, and QSettings, allowing us to read and write item data, database data, and user preferences for any QVariant-compatible type. We have already seen an example of this in Chapter 3, where we passed a QRect, a QStringList, and a couple of bools as variants to QSettings::setValue(), and retrieved them later as variants.

It is possible to create arbitrarily complex data structures using QVariant by nesting values of container types:

```
QMap<QString, QVariant> pearMap;
pearMap["Standard"] = 1.95;
pearMap["Organic"] = 2.25;

QMap<QString, QVariant> fruitMap;
fruitMap["Orange"] = 2.10;
fruitMap["Pineapple"] = 3.85;
fruitMap["Pear"] = pearMap;
```

Here we have created a map with string keys (product names) and values that are either floating-point numbers (prices) or maps. The top-level map contains three keys: "Orange", "Pear", and "Pineapple". The value associated with the "Pear" key is a map that contains two keys ("Standard" and "Organic"). When iterating over a map that holds variant values, we need to use type() to check the type that a variant holds so that we can respond appropriately.

Creating data structures like this can be very seductive since we can organize the data in any way we like. But the convenience of QVariant comes at the expense of efficiency and readability. As a rule, it is usually worth defining a proper C++ class to store our data whenever possible.

QVariant is used by Qt's meta-object system and is therefore part of the *QtCore* module. Nonetheless, when we link against the *QtGui* module, QVariant can store GUI-related types such as QColor, QFont, QIcon, QImage, and QPixmap:

```
QIcon icon("open.png");
QVariant variant = icon;
```

To retrieve the value of a GUI-related type from a QVariant, we can use the QVariant::value<T>() template member function as follows:

```
QIcon icon = variant.value<QIcon>();
```

The value<T>() function also works for converting between non-GUI data types and QVariant, but in practice we normally use the to...() conversion functions (for example, toString()) for non-GUI types.

QVariant can also be used to store custom data types, assuming they provide a default constructor and a copy constructor. For this to work, we must first register the type using the Q_DECLARE_METATYPE() macro, typically in a header file below the class definition:

```
Q_DECLARE_METATYPE(BusinessCard)
```

This enables us to write code like this:

```
BusinessCard businessCard;
QVariant variant = QVariant::fromValue(businessCard);
...
if (variant.canConvert<BusinessCard>()) {
    BusinessCard card = variant.value<BusinessCard>();
    ...
}
```

Because of a compiler limitation, these template member functions are not available for MSVC 6. If you need to use this compiler, use the `qVariantFromValue()`, `qVariantValue<T>()`, and `qVariantCanConvert<T>()` global functions instead.

If the custom data type has `<<` and `>>` operators for writing to and reading from a `QDataStream`, we can register them using `qRegisterMetaTypeStreamOperators<T>()`. This makes it possible to store preferences of custom data types using `QSettings`, among other things. For example:

```
qRegisterMetaTypeStreamOperators<BusinessCard>("BusinessCard");
```

This chapter has focused on the Qt containers, as well as on `QString`, `QByteArray`, and `QVariant`. In addition to these classes, Qt also provides a few other containers. One is `QPair<T1, T2>`, which simply stores two values and is similar to `std::pair<T1, T2>`. Another is `QBitArray`, which we will use in the first section of Chapter 19. Finally, there is `QVarLengthArray<T, Prealloc>`, a low-level alternative to `QVector<T>`. Because it preallocates memory on the stack and isn't implicitly shared, its overhead is less than that of `QVector<T>`, making it more appropriate for tight loops.

Qt's algorithms, including a few not covered here such as `qCopyBackward()` and `qEqual()`, are described in Qt's documentation at `http://doc.trolltech.com/4.1/algorithms.html`. And for more details of Qt's containers, including information on their time complexity and growth strategies, see `http://doc.trolltech.com/4.1/containers.html`.

12. Input/Output

The need to read from or write to files or other devices is common to almost every application. Qt provides excellent support for I/O through QIODevice, a powerful abstraction that encapsulates "devices" capable of reading and writing blocks of bytes. Qt includes the following QIODevice subclasses:

QFile	Accesses files in the local file system and in embedded resources
QTemporaryFile	Creates and accesses temporary files in the local file system
QBuffer	Reads data from or writes data to a QByteArray
QProcess	Runs external programs and handles inter-process communication
QTcpSocket	Transfers a stream of data over the network using TCP
QUdpSocket	Sends or receives UDP datagrams over the network

QProcess, QTcpSocket, and QUdpSocket are sequential devices, meaning that the data can only be accessed once, starting from the first byte and progressing serially to the last byte. QFile, QTemporaryFile, and QBuffer are random-access devices, so bytes can be read any number of times from any position; they provide the QIODevice::seek() function for repositioning the file pointer.

In addition to the device classes, Qt also provides two higher-level stream classes that we can use to read from and write to any I/O device: QDataStream for binary data and QTextStream for text. These classes take care of issues such as byte ordering and text encodings, ensuring that Qt applications running on different platforms or in different countries can read and write each other's files. This makes Qt's I/O classes much more convenient than the corresponding Standard C++ classes, which leave these issues to the application programmer.

QFile makes it easy to access individual files, whether they are in the file system or embedded in the application's executable as resources. For applications that need to identify whole sets of files to work on, Qt provides the QDir and

QFileInfo classes, which handle directories and provide information about the files inside them.

The QProcess class allows us to launch external programs and to communicate with them through their standard input, standard output, and standard error channels (cin, cout, and cerr). We can set the environment variables and working directory that the external application will use. By default, communication with the process is asynchronous (non-blocking), but it is also possible to block on certain operations.

Networking and reading and writing XML are such substantial topics that they are covered separately in their own dedicated chapters (Chapter 14 and Chapter 15).

Reading and Writing Binary Data

The simplest way to load and save binary data with Qt is to instantiate a QFile, to open the file, and to access it through a QDataStream object. QDataStream provides a platform-independent storage format that supports basic C++ types like int and double, and many Qt data types, including QByteArray, QFont, QImage, QPixmap, QString, and QVariant, as well as Qt container classes such as QList<T> and QMap<K, T>.

Here's how we would store an integer, a QImage, and a QMap<QString, QColor> in a file called facts.dat:

```
QImage image("philip.png");

QMap<QString, QColor> map;
map.insert("red", Qt::red);
map.insert("green", Qt::green);
map.insert("blue", Qt::blue);

QFile file("facts.dat");
if (!file.open(QIODevice::WriteOnly)) {
    cerr << "Cannot open file for writing: "
         << qPrintable(file.errorString()) << endl;
    return;
}

QDataStream out(&file);
out.setVersion(QDataStream::Qt_4_1);

out << quint32(0x12345678) << image << map;
```

If we cannot open the file, we inform the user and return. The qPrintable() macro returns a const char * for a QString. (Another approach would have been to use QString::toStdString(), which returns a std::string, for which <iostream> has a << overload.)

If the file is opened successfully, we create a QDataStream and set its version number. The version number is an integer that influences the way Qt data types are represented (basic C++ data types are always represented the same way). In Qt 4.1, the most comprehensive format is version 7. We can either hard-code the constant 7 or use the `QDataStream::Qt_4_1` symbolic name.

To ensure that the number `0x12345678` is written as an unsigned 32-bit integer on all platforms, we cast it to `quint32`, a data type that is guaranteed to be exactly 32 bits. To ensure interoperability, `QDataStream` standardizes on big-endian by default; this can be changed by calling `setByteOrder()`.

We don't need to explicitly close the file since this is done automatically when the `QFile` variable goes out of scope. If we want to verify that the data has actually been written, we can call `flush()` and check its return value (`true` on success).

The code to read back the data mirrors the code we used to write it:

```
quint32 n;
QImage image;
QMap<QString, QColor> map;

QFile file("facts.dat");
if (!file.open(QIODevice::ReadOnly)) {
    cerr << "Cannot open file for reading: "
         << qPrintable(file.errorString()) << endl;
    return;
}

QDataStream in(&file);
in.setVersion(QDataStream::Qt_4_1);

in >> n >> image >> map;
```

The `QDataStream` version we use for reading is the same as the one we used for writing. This must always be the case. By hard-coding the version number, we guarantee that the application can always read and write the data (assuming it is compiled with Qt 4.1 or any later Qt version).

`QDataStream` stores data in such a way that we can read it back seamlessly. For example, a `QByteArray` is represented as a 32-bit byte count followed by the bytes themselves. `QDataStream` can also be used to read and write raw bytes, without any byte count header, using `readRawBytes()` and `writeRawBytes()`.

Error handling when reading from a `QDataStream` is fairly easy. The stream has a `status()` value that can be `QDataStream::Ok`, `QDataStream::ReadPastEnd`, or `QDataStream::ReadCorruptData`. Once an error has occurred, the `>>` operator always reads zero or empty values. This means that we can often simply read an entire file without worrying about potential errors and check the `status()` value at the end to see if what we read was valid.

`QDataStream` handles a variety of C++ and Qt data types; the complete list is available at `http://doc.trolltech.com/4.1/datastreamformat.html`. We can also add support for our own custom types by overloading the `<<` and `>>` operators. Here's the definition of a custom data type that can be used with `QDataStream`:

```
class Painting
{
public:
    Painting() { myYear = 0; }
    Painting(const QString &title, const QString &artist, int year) {
        myTitle = title;
        myArtist = artist;
        myYear = year;
    }

    void setTitle(const QString &title) { myTitle = title; }
    QString title() const { return myTitle; }
    ...

private:
    QString myTitle;
    QString myArtist;
    int myYear;
};

QDataStream &operator<<(QDataStream &out, const Painting &painting);
QDataStream &operator>>(QDataStream &in, Painting &painting);
```

Here's how we would implement the << operator:

```
QDataStream &operator<<(QDataStream &out, const Painting &painting)
{
    out << painting.title() << painting.artist()
        << quint32(painting.year());
    return out;
}
```

To output a Painting, we simply output two QStrings and a quint32. At the end of the function, we return the stream. This is a common C++ idiom that allows us to use a chain of << operators with an output stream. For example:

```
out << painting1 << painting2 << painting3;
```

The implementation of operator>>() is similar to that of operator<<():

```
QDataStream &operator>>(QDataStream &in, Painting &painting)
{
    QString title;
    QString artist;
    quint32 year;

    in >> title >> artist >> year;
    painting = Painting(title, artist, year);
    return in;
}
```

There are several benefits to providing streaming operators for custom data types. One of them is that it allows us to stream containers that use the custom type. For example:

```
QList<Painting> paintings = ...;
```

```
out << paintings;
```

We can read in containers just as easily:

```
QList<Painting> paintings;
in >> paintings;
```

This would result in a compiler error if `Painting` didn't support `<<` or `>>`. Another benefit of providing streaming operators for custom types is that we can store values of these types as `QVariant`s, which makes them more widely usable, for example by `QSettings`. This works provided that we register the type using `qRegisterMetaTypeStreamOperators<T>()` beforehand, as explained in Chapter 11 (p. 270).

When we use `QDataStream`, Qt takes care of reading and writing each type, including containers with an arbitrary number of items. This relieves us from the need to structure what we write and from performing any kind of parsing on what we read. Our only obligation is to ensure that we read all the types in exactly the same order as we wrote them, leaving Qt to handle all the details.

`QDataStream` is useful both for our own custom application file formats and for standard binary formats. We can read and write standard binary formats using the streaming operators on basic types (like `quint16` or `float`) or using `readRawBytes()` and `writeRawBytes()`. If the `QDataStream` is being used purely to read and write basic C++ data types, we don't even need to call `setVersion()`.

So far, we loaded and saved data with the stream's version hard-coded as `QDataStream::Qt_4_1`. This approach is simple and safe, but it does have one small drawback: We cannot take advantage of new or updated formats. For example, if a later version of Qt added a new attribute to `QFont` (in addition to its point size, family, etc.) and we hard-coded the version number to `Qt_4_1`, that attribute wouldn't be saved or loaded. There are two solutions. The first approach is to embed the `QDataStream` version number in the file:

```
QDataStream out(&file);
out << quint32(MagicNumber) << quint16(out.version());
```

(`MagicNumber` is a constant that uniquely identifies the file type.) This approach ensures that we always write the data using the most recent version of `QDataStream`, whatever that happens to be. When we come to read the file, we read the stream version:

```
quint32 magic;
quint16 streamVersion;

QDataStream in(&file);
in >> magic >> streamVersion;

if (magic != MagicNumber) {
    cerr << "File is not recognized by this application" << endl;
} else if (streamVersion > in.version()) {
    cerr << "File is from a more recent version of the application"
        << endl;
```

```
        return false;
    }

    in.setVersion(streamVersion);
```

We can read the data as long as the stream version is less than or equal to the version used by the application; otherwise, we report an error.

If the file format contains a version number of its own, we can use it to deduce the stream version number instead of storing it explicitly. For example, let's suppose that the file format is for version 1.3 of our application. We might then write the data as follows:

```
    QDataStream out(&file);
    out.setVersion(QDataStream::Qt_4_1);
    out << quint32(MagicNumber) << quint16(0x0103);
```

When we read it back, we determine which QDataStream version to use based on the application's version number:

```
    QDataStream in(&file);
    in >> magic >> appVersion;

    if (magic != MagicNumber) {
        cerr << "File is not recognized by this application" << endl;
        return false;
    } else if (appVersion > 0x0103) {
        cerr << "File is from a more recent version of the application"
             << endl;
        return false;
    }

    if (appVersion < 0x0103) {
        in.setVersion(QDataStream::Qt_3_0);
    } else {
        in.setVersion(QDataStream::Qt_4_1);
    }
```

In this example, we specify that any file saved with versions prior to 1.3 of the application uses data stream version 4 (Qt_3_0), and that files saved with version 1.3 of the application use data stream version 7 (Qt_4_1).

In summary, there are three policies for handling QDataStream versions: hard-coding the version number, explicitly writing and reading the version number, and using different hard-coded version numbers depending on the application's version. Any of these policies can be used to ensure that data written by an old version of an application can be read by a new version, even if the new version links against a more recent version of Qt. Once we have chosen a policy for handling QDataStream versions, reading and writing binary data using Qt is both simple and reliable.

If we want to read or write a file in one go, we can avoid using QDataStream altogether and instead use QIODevice's write() and readAll() functions. For example:

```
bool copyFile(const QString &source, const QString &dest)
{
    QFile sourceFile(source);
    if (!sourceFile.open(QIODevice::ReadOnly))
        return false;

    QFile destFile(dest);
    if (!destFile.open(QIODevice::WriteOnly))
        return false;

    destFile.write(sourceFile.readAll());

    return sourceFile.error() == QFile::NoError
           && destFile.error() == QFile::NoError;
}
```

In the line where readAll() is called, the entire contents of the input file is read into a QByteArray, which is then passed to the write() function to be written to the output file. Having all the data in a QByteArray requires more memory than reading item by item, but it offers some advantages. For example, we can then use qCompress() and qUncompress() to compress and uncompress the data.

There are other scenarios where accessing QIODevice directly is more appropriate than using QDataStream. QIODevice provides a peek() function that returns the next data bytes without moving the device position as well as an unget-Char() function that "unreads" a byte. This works both for random-access devices (such as files) and for sequential devices (such as network sockets). There is also a seek() function that sets the device position, for devices that support random access.

Binary file formats provide the most versatile and most compact means of storing data, and QDataStream makes accessing binary data easy. In addition to the examples in this section, we have already seen the use of QDataStream in Chapter 4 to read and write Spreadsheet files, and we will see it again in Chapter 19, where we use it to read and write Windows cursor files.

Reading and Writing Text

While binary file formats are typically more compact than text-based formats, they are not human-readable or human-editable. In cases where this is an issue, we can use text formats instead. Qt provides the QTextStream class for reading and writing plain text files and for files using other text formats, such as HTML, XML, and source code. Handling XML files is covered separately in Chapter 15.

QTextStream takes care of converting between Unicode and the system's local encoding or any other encoding, and transparently handles the different line-ending conventions used by different operating systems ("\r\n" on Windows, "\n" on Unix and Mac OS X). QTextStream uses the 16-bit QChar type as its fundamental unit of data. In addition to characters and strings, QTextStream supports

C++'s basic numeric types, which it converts to and from strings. For example, the following code writes "Thomas M. Disch: 334\n" to the file sf-book.txt:

```
QFile file("sf-book.txt");
if (!file.open(QIODevice::WriteOnly)) {
    cerr << "Cannot open file for writing: "
        << qPrintable(file.errorString()) << endl;
    return;
}

QTextStream out(&file);
out << "Thomas M. Disch: " << 334 << endl;
```

Writing text is very easy, but reading text can be challenging, because textual data (unlike binary data written using QDataStream) is fundamentally ambiguous. Let's consider the following example:

```
out << "Norway" << "Sweden";
```

If out is a QTextStream, the data that actually gets written is the string "NorwaySweden". We can't really expect the following code to read back the data correctly:

```
in >> str1 >> str2;
```

In fact, what happens is that str1 gets the whole word "NorwaySweden", and str2 gets nothing. This problem doesn't occur with QDataStream because it stores the length of each string in front of the character data.

For complex file formats, a full-blown parser might be required. Such a parser might work by reading the data character-by-character using >> on a QChar, or line by line using QTextStream::readLine(). At the end of this section, we present two small examples, one that reads an input file line by line, and another that reads it character by character. For parsers that work on an entire text, we could read the complete file in one go using QTextStream::readAll() if we are not concerned about memory usage, or if we know the file will be small.

By default, QTextStream uses the system's local encoding (for example, ISO 8859-1 or ISO 8859-15 in America and much of Europe) for reading and writing. This can be changed using setCodec() as follows:

```
stream.setCodec("UTF-8");
```

The UTF-8 encoding used in the example is a popular ASCII-compatible encoding that can represent the entire Unicode character set. For more information about Unicode and QTextStream's support for encodings, see Chapter 17 (Internationalization).

QTextStream has various options modeled after those offered by <iostream>. These can be set by passing special objects, called *stream manipulators*, on the stream to alter its state. The following example sets the showbase, uppercasedigits, and hex options before it outputs the integer 12345678, producing the text "0xBC614E":

```
out << showbase << uppercasedigits << hex << 12345678;
```

Options can also be set using member functions:

```
out.setNumberFlags(QTextStream::ShowBase
                   | QTextStream::UppercaseDigits);
out.setIntegerBase(16);
out << 12345678;
```

`setIntegerBase(int)`	
0	Auto-detect based on prefix (when reading)
2	Binary
8	Octal
10	Decimal
16	Hexadecimal

`setNumberFlags(NumberFlags)`	
`ShowBase`	Show a prefix if the base is 2 ("0b"), 8 ("0"), or 16 ("0x")
`ForceSign`	Always show the sign in real numbers
`ForcePoint`	Always put the decimal separator in numbers
`UppercaseBase`	Use uppercase versions of base prefixes ("0X", "0B")
`UppercaseDigits`	Use uppercase letters in hexadecimal numbers

`setRealNumberNotation(RealNumberNotation)`	
`FixedNotation`	Fixed-point notation (e.g., "0.000123")
`ScientificNotation`	Scientific notation (e.g., "1.234568e-04")
`SmartNotation`	Fixed-point or scientific notation, whichever is most compact

`setRealNumberPrecision(int)`
Sets the maximum number of digits that should be generated (6 by default)

`setFieldWidth(int)`
Sets the minimum size of a field (0 by default)

`setFieldAlignment(FieldAlignment)`	
`AlignLeft`	Pad on the right side of the field
`AlignRight`	Pad on the left side of the field
`AlignCenter`	Pad on both sides of the field
`AlignAccountingStyle`	Pad between the sign and the number

`setPadChar(QChar)`
Sets the character used for padding fields (space by default)

Figure 12.1. Functions to set `QTextStream`'s options

Like QDataStream, QTextStream operates on a QIODevice subclass, which can be a QFile, a QTemporaryFile, a QBuffer, a QProcess, a QTcpSocket, or a QUdpSocket. In addition, it can be used directly on a QString. For example:

```
QString str;
QTextStream(&str) << oct << 31 << " " << dec << 25 << endl;
```

This makes the contents of str "37 25\n", since the decimal number 31 is expressed as 37 in octal. In this case, we don't need to set an encoding on the stream, since QString is always Unicode.

Let's look at a simple example of a text-based file format. In the Spreadsheet application described in Part I, we used a binary format for storing Spreadsheet data. The data consisted of a sequence of (*row, column, formula*) triples, one for every non-empty cell. Writing the data as text is straightforward; here is an extract from a revised version of Spreadsheet::writeFile():

```
QTextStream out(&file);
for (int row = 0; row < RowCount; ++row) {
    for (int column = 0; column < ColumnCount; ++column) {
        QString str = formula(row, column);
        if (!str.isEmpty())
            out << row << " " << column << " " << str << endl;
    }
}
```

We have used a simple format, with each line representing one cell and with spaces between the row and the column and between the column and the formula. The formula can contain spaces, but we can assume that it contains no '\n' (which we use to terminate lines). Now let's look at the corresponding reading code:

```
QTextStream in(&file);
while (!in.atEnd()) {
    QString line = in.readLine();
    QStringList fields = line.split(' ');
    if (fields.size() >= 3) {
        int row = fields.takeFirst().toInt();
        int column = fields.takeFirst().toInt();
        setFormula(row, column, fields.join(' '));
    }
}
```

We read in the Spreadsheet data one line at a time. The readLine() function removes the trailing '\n'. QString::split() returns a string list, having split its string wherever the separator it is given appears. For example, the line "5 19 Total value" results in the four-item list ["5", "19", "Total", "value"].

If we have at least three fields, we are ready to extract the data. The QString-List::takeFirst() function removes the first item in a list and returns the removed item. We use it to extract the row and column numbers. We don't perform any error checking; if we read a non-integer row or column value,

`QString::toInt()` will return 0. When we call `setFormula()`, we must concatenate the remaining fields back into a single string.

In our second `QTextStream` example, we will use a character by character approach to implement a program that reads in a text file and outputs the same text but with trailing spaces removed from lines and all tabs replaced by spaces. The program's work is done by the `tidyFile()` function:

```
void tidyFile(QIODevice *inDevice, QIODevice *outDevice)
{
    QTextStream in(inDevice);
    QTextStream out(outDevice);

    const int TabSize = 8;
    int endlCount = 0;
    int spaceCount = 0;
    int column = 0;
    QChar ch;

    while (!in.atEnd()) {
        in >> ch;

        if (ch == '\n') {
            ++endlCount;
            spaceCount = 0;
            column = 0;
        } else if (ch == '\t') {
            int size = TabSize - (column % TabSize);
            spaceCount += size;
            column += size;
        } else if (ch == ' ') {
            ++spaceCount;
            ++column;
        } else {
            while (endlCount > 0) {
                out << endl;
                --endlCount;
                column = 0;
            }
            while (spaceCount > 0) {
                out << ' ';
                --spaceCount;
                ++column;
            }
            out << ch;
            ++column;
        }
    }
    out << endl;
}
```

We create an input and an output `QTextStream` based on the `QIODevices` that are passed to the function. We maintain three elements of state: one counting newlines, one counting spaces, and one marking the current column position in the current line (for converting the tabs to the correct number of spaces).

The parsing is done in a while loop that iterates over every character in the input file, one at a time. The code is a bit subtle in places. For example, although we set TabSize to 8, we replace tabs with precisely enough spaces to pad to the next tab boundary, rather than crudely replacing each tab with eight spaces. If we get a newline, tab, or space, we simply update the state data. Only when we get another kind of character do we produce any output, and before writing the character we write any pending newlines and spaces (to respect blank lines and to preserve indentation) and update the state.

```
int main()
{
    QFile inFile;
    QFile outFile;

    inFile.open(stdin, QFile::ReadOnly);
    outFile.open(stdout, QFile::WriteOnly);

    tidyFile(&inFile, &outFile);

    return 0;
}
```

For this example, we don't need a QApplication object, because we are only using Qt's tool classes. See http://doc.trolltech.com/4.1/tools.html for the list of all tool classes. We have assumed that the program is used as a filter, for example:

```
tidy < cool.cpp > cooler.cpp
```

It would be easy to extend it to be able to handle file names given on the command line if they are given, and to filter cin to cout otherwise.

Since this is a console application, it has a slightly different .pro file from those we have seen for GUI applications:

```
TEMPLATE     = app
QT           = core
CONFIG      += console
CONFIG      -= app_bundle
SOURCES      = tidy.cpp
```

We only link against *QtCore* since we don't use any GUI functionality. Then we specify that we want to enable console output on Windows and that we don't want the application to live in a bundle on Mac OS X.

For reading and writing plain ASCII files or ISO 8859-1 (Latin-1) files, it is possible to use QIODevice's API directly instead of using a QTextStream. It is rarely wise to do this since most applications need support for other encodings at some point or other, and only QTextStream provides seamless support for these. If you still want to write text directly to a QIODevice, you must explicitly specify the QIODevice::Text flag to the open() function, for example:

```
file.open(QIODevice::WriteOnly | QIODevice::Text);
```

When writing, this flag tells `QIODevice` to convert '\n' characters into "\r\n" sequences on Windows. When reading, this flag tells the device to ignore '\r' characters on all platforms. We can then assume that the end of each line is signified with a '\n' newline character regardless of the line-ending convention used by the operating system.

Traversing Directories

The `QDir` class provides a platform-independent means of traversing directories and retrieving information about files. To see how `QDir` is used, we will write a small console application that calculates the space consumed by all the images in a particular directory and all its subdirectories to any depth.

The heart of the application is the `imageSpace()` function, which recursively computes the cumulative size of a given directory's images:

```
qlonglong imageSpace(const QString &path)
{
    QDir dir(path);
    qlonglong size = 0;

    QStringList filters;
    foreach (QByteArray format, QImageReader::supportedImageFormats())
        filters += "*." + format;

    foreach (QString file, dir.entryList(filters, QDir::Files))
        size += QFileInfo(dir, file).size();

    foreach (QString subDir, dir.entryList(QDir::Dirs
                                           | QDir::NoDotAndDotDot))
        size += imageSpace(path + QDir::separator() + subDir);

    return size;
}
```

We begin by creating a `QDir` object using the given path, which may be relative to the current directory or absolute. We pass the `entryList()` function two arguments. The first is a list of file name filters. These can contain '*' and '?' wildcard characters. In this example, we are filtering to include only file formats that `QImage` can read. The second argument specifies what kind of entries we want (normal files, directories, drives, etc.).

We iterate over the list of files, accumulating their sizes. The `QFileInfo` class allows us to access a file's attributes, such as the file's size, permissions, owner, and timestamps.

The second `entryList()` call retrieves all the subdirectories in this directory. We iterate over them (excluding . and ..) and recursively call `imageSpace()` to ascertain their accumulated image sizes.

To create each subdirectory's path, we combine the current directory's path with the subdirectory name, separating them with a slash. `QDir` treats '/' as a directory separator on all platforms, in addition to recognizing '\' on Windows. When presenting paths to the user, we can call the static function `QDir::convertSeparators()` to convert slashes to the correct platform-specific separator.

Let's add a `main()` function to our small program:

```
int main(int argc, char *argv[])
{
    QCoreApplication app(argc, argv);
    QStringList args = app.arguments();

    QString path = QDir::currentPath();
    if (args.count() > 1)
        path = args[1];

    cout << "Space used by images in " << qPrintable(path)
         << " and its subdirectories is " << (imageSpace(path) / 1024)
         << " KB" << endl;

    return 0;
}
```

We use `QDir::currentPath()` to initialize the path to the current directory. Alternatively, we could have used `QDir::homePath()` to initialize it to the user's home directory. If the user has specified a path on the command line, we use that instead. Finally, we call our `imageSpace()` function to calculate how much space is consumed by images.

The `QDir` class provides other file- and directory-related functions, including `entryInfoList()` (which returns a list of `QFileInfo` objects), `rename()`, `exists()`, `mkdir()`, and `rmdir()`. The `QFile` class provides some static convenience functions, including `remove()` and `exists()`.

Embedding Resources

So far in this chapter we have talked about accessing data in external devices, but with Qt it is also possible to embed binary data or text inside the application's executable. This is achieved using Qt's resource system. In other chapters, we used resource files to embed images in the executable, but it is possible to embed any kind of file. Embedded files can be read using `QFile` just like normal files in the file system.

Resources are converted into C++ code by `rcc`, Qt's resource compiler. We can tell `qmake` to include special rules to run `rcc` by adding this line to the `.pro` file:

```
RESOURCES     = myresourcefile.qrc
```

The `myresourcefile.qrc` file is an XML file that lists the files to embed in the executable.

Let's imagine that we are writing an application that keeps contact details. For the convenience of our users, we want to embed the international dialing codes in the executable. If the file is in the `datafiles` directory in the application's build directory, the resource file might look like this:

```
<!DOCTYPE RCC><RCC version="1.0">
<qresource>
    <file>datafiles/phone-codes.dat</file>
</qresource>
</RCC>
```

From the application, resources are identified by the `:/` path prefix. In this example, the dialing codes file has the path `:/datafiles/phone-codes.dat` and can be read just like any other file using `QFile`.

Embedding data in the executable has the advantage that it cannot get lost and makes it possible to create truly stand-alone executables (if static linking is also used). Two disadvantages are that if the embedded data needs changing the whole executable must be replaced, and the size of the executable will be larger because it must accommodate the embedded data.

Qt's resource system provides more features than we presented in this example, including support for file name aliases and for localization. These facilities are documented at `http://doc.trolltech.com/4.1/resources.html`.

Inter-Process Communication

The `QProcess` class allows us to run external programs and to interact with them. The class works asynchronously, doing its work in the background so that the user interface remains responsive. `QProcess` emits signals to notify us when the external process has data or has finished.

We will review the code of a small application that provides a user interface for an external image conversion program. For this example, we rely on the ImageMagick `convert` program, which is freely available for all major platforms.

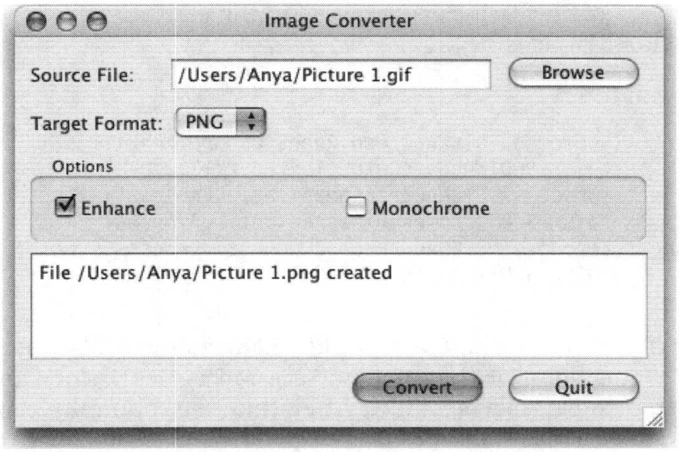

Figure 12.2. The Image Converter application

The user interface was created in *Qt Designer*. The .ui file is on the CD that accompanies this book. Here, we will focus on the subclass that inherits from the uic-generated Ui::ConvertDialog class, starting with the header:

```
#ifndef CONVERTDIALOG_H
#define CONVERTDIALOG_H

#include <QDialog>
#include <QProcess>

#include "ui_convertdialog.h"

class ConvertDialog : public QDialog, public Ui::ConvertDialog
{
    Q_OBJECT

public:
    ConvertDialog(QWidget *parent = 0);

private slots:
    void on_browseButton_clicked();
    void on_convertButton_clicked();
    void updateOutputTextEdit();
    void processFinished(int exitCode, QProcess::ExitStatus exitStatus);
    void processError(QProcess::ProcessError error);

private:
    QProcess process;
    QString targetFile;
};

#endif
```

The header follows the familiar pattern for subclasses of *Qt Designer* forms. Thanks to *Qt Designer*'s automatic connection mechanism (p. 28), the on_browseButton_clicked() and on_convertButton_clicked() slots are automatically connected to the Browse and Convert buttons' clicked() signals.

```
ConvertDialog::ConvertDialog(QWidget *parent)
    : QDialog(parent)
{
    setupUi(this);

    connect(&process, SIGNAL(readyReadStandardError()),
            this, SLOT(updateOutputTextEdit()));
    connect(&process, SIGNAL(finished(int, QProcess::ExitStatus)),
            this, SLOT(processFinished(int, QProcess::ExitStatus)));
    connect(&process, SIGNAL(error(QProcess::ProcessError)),
            this, SLOT(processError(QProcess::ProcessError)));
}
```

The setupUi() call creates and lays out all the form's widgets, establishes the signal–slot connections for the on_objectName_signalName() slots, and connects the Quit button to QDialog::accept(). After that, we manually connect three signals from the QProcess object to three private slots. Whenever the external process has data on its cerr, we will handle it in updateOutputTextEdit().

```
void ConvertDialog::on_browseButton_clicked()
{
    QString initialName = sourceFileEdit->text();
    if (initialName.isEmpty())
        initialName = QDir::homePath();
    QString fileName =
            QFileDialog::getOpenFileName(this, tr("Choose File"),
                                         initialName);
    fileName = QDir::convertSeparators(fileName);
    if (!fileName.isEmpty()) {
        sourceFileEdit->setText(fileName);
        convertButton->setEnabled(true);
    }
}
```

The Browse button's `clicked()` signal is automatically connected to the `on_browseButton_clicked()` slot by `setupUi()`. If the user has previously selected a file, we initialize the file dialog with that file's name; otherwise, we use the user's home directory.

```
void ConvertDialog::on_convertButton_clicked()
{
    QString sourceFile = sourceFileEdit->text();
    targetFile = QFileInfo(sourceFile).path() + QDir::separator()
                 + QFileInfo(sourceFile).baseName() + "."
                 + targetFormatComboBox->currentText().toLower();
    convertButton->setEnabled(false);
    outputTextEdit->clear();

    QStringList args;
    if (enhanceCheckBox->isChecked())
        args << "-enhance";
    if (monochromeCheckBox->isChecked())
        args << "-monochrome";
    args << sourceFile << targetFile;

    process.start("convert", args);
}
```

When the user clicks the Convert button, we copy the source file's name and change the extension to match the target file format. We use the platform-specific directory separator ('/' or '\', available as `QDir::separator()`) instead of hard-coding slashes because the file name will be visible to the user.

We then disable the Convert button to avoid the user accidentally launching multiple conversions, and we clear the text edit that we use to show status information.

To initiate the external process, we call `QProcess::start()` with the name of the program we want to run (convert) and any arguments it requires. In this case we pass the –enhance and –monochrome flags if the user checked the appropriate options, followed by the source and target file names. The convert program infers the required conversion from the file extensions.

```
void ConvertDialog::updateOutputTextEdit()
{
    QByteArray newData = process.readAllStandardError();
    QString text = outputTextEdit->toPlainText()
                    + QString::fromLocal8Bit(newData);
    outputTextEdit->setPlainText(text);
}
```

Whenever the external process writes to cerr, the updateOutputTextEdit() slot is called. We read the error text and add it to the QTextEdit's existing text.

```
void ConvertDialog::processFinished(int exitCode,
                                    QProcess::ExitStatus exitStatus)
{
    if (exitStatus == QProcess::CrashExit) {
        outputTextEdit->append(tr("Conversion program crashed"));
    } else if (exitCode != 0) {
        outputTextEdit->append(tr("Conversion failed"));
    } else {
        outputTextEdit->append(tr("File %1 created").arg(targetFile));
    }
    convertButton->setEnabled(true);
}
```

When the process has finished, we let the user know the outcome and enable the Convert button.

```
void ConvertDialog::processError(QProcess::ProcessError error)
{
    if (error == QProcess::FailedToStart) {
        outputTextEdit->append(tr("Conversion program not found"));
        convertButton->setEnabled(true);
    }
}
```

If the process cannot be started, QProcess emits error() instead of finished(). We report any error and enable the Click button.

In this example, we have performed the file conversions asynchronously—that is, we have told QProcess to run the convert program and to return control to the application immediately. This keeps the user interface responsive while the processing occurs in the background. But in some situations we need the external process to complete before we can go any further in our application, and in such cases we need QProcess to operate synchronously.

One common example where synchronous behavior is desirable is for applications that support plain text editing using the user's preferred text editor. This is straightforward to implement using QProcess. For example, let's assume that we have the plain text in a QTextEdit, and provide an Edit button that the user can click, connected to an edit() slot.

```
void ExternalEditor::edit()
{
    QTemporaryFile outFile;
```

```
        if (!outFile.open())
            return;

        QString fileName = outFile.fileName();
        QTextStream out(&outFile);
        out << textEdit->toPlainText();
        outFile.close();

        QProcess::execute(editor, QStringList() << options << fileName);

        QFile inFile(fileName);
        if (!inFile.open(QIODevice::ReadOnly))
            return;

        QTextStream in(&inFile);
        textEdit->setPlainText(in.readAll());
    }
```

We use QTemporaryFile to create an empty file with a unique name. We don't specify any arguments to QTemporaryFile::open() since it conveniently defaults to opening in read/write mode. We write the contents of the text edit to the temporary file, and then we close the file because some text editors cannot work on already open files.

The QProcess::execute() static function runs an external process and blocks until the process has finished. The editor argument is a QString holding the name of an editor executable (for example, "gvim"). The options argument is a QStringList (containing one item, "-f", if we are using gvim).

After the user has closed the text editor, the process finishes and the execute() call returns. We then open the temporary file and read its contents into the QTextEdit. QTemporaryFile automatically deletes the temporary file when the object goes out of scope.

Signal–slot connections are not needed when QProcess is used synchronously. If finer control is required than provided by the static execute() function, we can use an alternative approach. This involves creating a QProcess object and calling start() on it, and then forcing it to block by calling QProcess::waitForStarted(), and if that is successful, calling QProcess::waitForFinished(). See the QProcess reference documentation for an example that uses this approach.

In this section, we used QProcess to give us access to preexisting functionality. Using applications that already exist can save development time and can insulate us from the details of issues that are of marginal interest to our main application's purpose. Another way to access preexisting functionality is to link against a library that provides it. But where no suitable library exists, wrapping a console application using QProcess can work well.

Another use of QProcess is to launch other GUI applications, such as a web browser or an email client. However, if our aim is communication between applications rather than simply running one from another, we might be better off having them communicate directly, using Qt's networking classes or the ActiveQt extension on Windows.

◆ *Connecting and Querying*
◆ *Presenting Data in Tabular Form*
◆ *Implementing Master–Detail Forms*

13. Databases

The *QtSql* module provides a platform- and database-independent interface for accessing SQL databases. This interface is supported by a set of classes that use Qt's model/view architecture to provide database integration with the user interface. This chapter assumes familiarity with Qt's model/view classes, covered in Chapter 10.

A database connection is represented by a QSqlDatabase object. Qt uses drivers to communicate with the various database APIs. The Qt Desktop Edition includes the following drivers:

Driver	Database
QDB2	IBM DB2 version 7.1 and later
QIBASE	Borland InterBase
QMYSQL	MySQL
QOCI	Oracle (Oracle Call Interface)
QODBC	ODBC (includes Microsoft SQL Server)
QPSQL	PostgreSQL versions 6.x and 7.x
QSQLITE	SQLite version 3 and later
QSQLITE2	SQLite version 2
QTDS	Sybase Adaptive Server

Due to license restrictions, not all of the drivers are provided with the Qt Open Source Edition. When configuring Qt, we can choose between including the SQL drivers inside Qt itself and building them as plugins. Qt is supplied with the SQLite database, a public domain in-process database.

For users who are comfortable with SQL syntax, the QSqlQuery class provides a means of directly executing arbitrary SQL statements and handling their results. For users who prefer a higher-level database interface that avoids SQL syntax, QSqlTableModel and QSqlRelationalTableModel provide suitable abstractions. These classes represent an SQL table in the same way as Qt's other model classes (covered in Chapter 10). They can be used stand-alone to traverse and edit data in code, or they can be attached to views through which end-users can view and edit the data themselves.

Qt also makes it straightforward to program the common database idioms, such as master–detail and drill-down, as some of the examples in this chapter will demonstrate.

Connecting and Querying

To execute SQL queries, we must first establish a connection with a database. Typically, database connections are set up in a separate function that we call at application startup. For example:

```
bool createConnection()
{
    QSqlDatabase db = QSqlDatabase::addDatabase("QMYSQL");
    db.setHostName("mozart.konkordia.edu");
    db.setDatabaseName("musicdb");
    db.setUserName("gbatstone");
    db.setPassword("T17aV44");
    if (!db.open()) {
        QMessageBox::critical(0, QObject::tr("Database Error"),
                              db.lastError().text());
        return false;
    }
    return true;
}
```

First, we call `QSqlDatabase::addDatabase()` to create a `QSqlDatabase` object. The first argument to `addDatabase()` specifies which database driver Qt must use to access the database. In this case, we use MySQL.

Next, we set the database host name, the database name, the user name, and the password, and we open the connection. If `open()` fails, we show an error message.

Typically, we would call `createConnection()` in `main()`:

```
int main(int argc, char *argv[])
{
    QApplication app(argc, argv);
    if (!createConnection())
        return 1;
    ...
    return app.exec();
}
```

Once a connection is established, we can use `QSqlQuery` to execute any SQL statement that the underlying database supports. For example, here's how to execute a SELECT statement:

```
QSqlQuery query;
query.exec("SELECT title, year FROM cd WHERE year >= 1998");
```

After the exec() call, we can navigate through the query's result set:

```
while (query.next()) {
    QString title = query.value(0).toString();
    int year = query.value(1).toInt();
    cerr << qPrintable(title) << ": " << year << endl;
}
```

We call next() once to position the QSqlQuery on the *first* record of the result set. Subsequent calls to next() advance the record pointer by one record each time, until the end is reached, at which point next() returns false. If the result set is empty (or if the query failed), the first call to next() will return false.

The value() function returns the value of a field as a QVariant. The fields are numbered from 0 in the order given in the SELECT statement. The QVariant class can hold many C++ and Qt types, including int and QString. The different types of data that can be stored in a database are mapped into the corresponding C++ and Qt types and stored in QVariants. For example, a VARCHAR is represented as a QString and a DATETIME as a QDateTime.

QSqlQuery provides some other functions to navigate through the result set: first(), last(), previous(), and seek(). These functions are convenient, but for some databases they can be slower and more memory-hungry than next(). For an easy optimization when operating on large data sets, we can call QSqlQuery::setForwardOnly(true) before calling exec(), and then only use next() for navigating the result set.

Earlier we specified the SQL query as an argument to QSqlQuery::exec(), but we can also pass it directly to the constructor, which executes it immediately:

```
QSqlQuery query("SELECT title, year FROM cd WHERE year >= 1998");
```

We can check for an error by calling isActive() on the query:

```
if (!query.isActive())
    QMessageBox::warning(this, tr("Database Error"),
                         query.lastError().text());
```

If no error occurs, the query will become "active" and we can use next() to navigate through the result set.

Doing an INSERT is almost as easy as performing a SELECT:

```
QSqlQuery query("INSERT INTO cd (id, artistid, title, year) "
                "VALUES (203, 102, 'Living in America', 2002)");
```

After this, numRowsAffected() returns the number of rows that were affected by the SQL statement (or –1 on error).

If we need to insert a lot of records, or if we want to avoid converting values to strings (and escaping them correctly), we can use prepare() to specify a query that contains placeholders and then bind the values we want to insert. Qt supports both the Oracle-style and the ODBC-style syntax for placeholders for all databases, using native support where it is available and simulating it otherwise. Here's an example that uses the Oracle-style syntax with named place-holders:

```
QSqlQuery query;
query.prepare("INSERT INTO cd (id, artistid, title, year) "
              "VALUES (:id, :artistid, :title, :year)");
query.bindValue(":id", 203);
query.bindValue(":artistid", 102);
query.bindValue(":title", "Living in America");
query.bindValue(":year", 2002);
query.exec();
```

Here's the same example using ODBC-style positional placeholders:

```
QSqlQuery query;
query.prepare("INSERT INTO cd (id, artistid, title, year) "
              "VALUES (?, ?, ?, ?)");
query.addBindValue(203);
query.addBindValue(102);
query.addBindValue("Living in America");
query.addBindValue(2002);
query.exec();
```

After the call to exec(), we can call bindValue() or addBindValue() to bind new values, then call exec() again to execute the query with the new values.

Placeholders are often used to specify binary data or strings that contain non-ASCII or non-Latin-1 characters. Behind the scenes, Qt uses Unicode with those databases that support Unicode, and for those that don't, Qt transparently converts strings to the appropriate encoding.

Qt supports SQL transactions on databases where they are available. To start a transaction, we call transaction() on the QSqlDatabase object that represents the database connection. To finish the transaction, we call either commit() or rollback(). For example, here's how we would look up a foreign key and execute an INSERT statement inside a transaction:

```
QSqlDatabase::database().transaction();
QSqlQuery query;
query.exec("SELECT id FROM artist WHERE name = 'Gluecifer'");
if (query.next()) {
    int artistId = query.value(0).toInt();
    query.exec("INSERT INTO cd (id, artistid, title, year) "
               "VALUES (201, " + QString::number(artistId)
               + ", 'Riding the Tiger', 1997)");
}
QSqlDatabase::database().commit();
```

The QSqlDatabase::database() function returns a QSqlDatabase object representing the connection we created in createConnection(). If a transaction cannot be started, QSqlDatabase::transaction() returns false. Some databases don't support transactions. For those, the transaction(), commit(), and rollback() functions do nothing. We can test whether a database supports transactions using hasFeature() on the QSqlDriver associated with the database:

```
QSqlDriver *driver = QSqlDatabase::database().driver();
if (driver->hasFeature(QSqlDriver::Transactions))
    ...
```

Several other database features can be tested for, including whether the database supports BLOBs (Binary Large Objects), Unicode, and prepared queries.

In the examples so far, we have assumed that the application is using a single database connection. If we want to create multiple connections, we can pass a name as second argument to addDatabase(). For example:

```
QSqlDatabase db = QSqlDatabase::addDatabase("QPSQL", "OTHER");
db.setHostName("saturn.mcmanamy.edu");
db.setDatabaseName("starsdb");
db.setUserName("hilbert");
db.setPassword("ixtapa7");
```

We can then retrieve a pointer to the QSqlDatabase object by passing the name to QSqlDatabase::database():

```
QSqlDatabase db = QSqlDatabase::database("OTHER");
```

To execute queries using the other connection, we pass the QSqlDatabase object to the QSqlQuery constructor:

```
QSqlQuery query(db);
query.exec("SELECT id FROM artist WHERE name = 'Mando Diao'");
```

Multiple connections are useful if we want to perform more than one transaction at a time, since each connection can only handle a single active transaction. When we use multiple database connections, we can still have one unnamed connection, and QSqlQuery will use that connection if none is specified.

In addition to QSqlQuery, Qt provides the QSqlTableModel class as a higher-level interface, allowing us to avoid using raw SQL for performing the most common SQL operations (SELECT, INSERT, UPDATE, and DELETE). The class can be used stand-alone to manipulate a database without any GUI involvement, or it can be used as a data source for QListView or QTableView.

Here's an example that uses QSqlTableModel to perform a SELECT:

```
QSqlTableModel model;
model.setTable("cd");
model.setFilter("year >= 1998");
model.select();
```

This is equivalent to the query

```
SELECT * FROM cd WHERE year >= 1998
```

Navigating through the result set is done by retrieving a given record using QSqlTableModel::record() and by accessing individual fields using value():

```
for (int i = 0; i < model.rowCount(); ++i) {
    QSqlRecord record = model.record(i);
    QString title = record.value("title").toString();
    int year = record.value("year").toInt();
    cerr << qPrintable(title) << ": " << year << endl;
}
```

The `QSqlRecord::value()` function takes either a field name or a field index. When operating on large data sets, it is recommended that fields are specified by their indexes. For example:

```
int titleIndex = model.record().indexOf("title");
int yearIndex = model.record().indexOf("year");
for (int i = 0; i < model.rowCount(); ++i) {
    QSqlRecord record = model.record(i);
    QString title = record.value(titleIndex).toString();
    int year = record.value(yearIndex).toInt();
    cerr << qPrintable(title) << ": " << year << endl;
}
```

To insert a record into a database table, we use the same approach as we would inserting into any two-dimensional model: First, we call `insertRow()` to create a new empty row (record), and then we use `setData()` to set the values of each column (field).

```
QSqlTableModel model;
model.setTable("cd");
int row = 0;
model.insertRows(row, 1);
model.setData(model.index(row, 0), 113);
model.setData(model.index(row, 1), "Shanghai My Heart");
model.setData(model.index(row, 2), 224);
model.setData(model.index(row, 3), 2003);
. model.submitAll();
```

After the call to `submitAll()`, the record might be moved to a different row position, depending on how the table is ordered. The `submitAll()` call will return `false` if the insertion failed.

An important difference between an SQL model and a standard model is that for an SQL model we must call `submitAll()` to have any changes written to the database.

To update a record, we must first position the `QSqlTableModel` on the record we want to modify (for example, using `select()`). We then extract the record, update the fields we want to change, and write our changes back to the database:

```
QSqlTableModel model;
model.setTable("cd");
model.setFilter("id = 125");
model.select();
if (model.rowCount() == 1) {
    QSqlRecord record = model.record(0);
    record.setValue("title", "Melody A.M.");
```

```
        record.setValue("year", record.value("year").toInt() + 1);
        model.setRecord(0, record);
        model.submitAll();
    }
```

If there is a record that matches the specified filter, we retrieve it using `QSqlTableModel::record()`. We apply our changes and overwrite the original record with our modified record.

It is also possible to perform an update using `setData()`, just as we would do for a non-SQL model. The model indexes that we retrieve are for a given row and column:

```
    model.select();
    if (model.rowCount() == 1) {
        model.setData(model.index(0, 1), "Melody A.M.");
        model.setData(model.index(0, 3),
                      model.data(model.index(0, 3)).toInt() + 1);
        model.submitAll();
    }
```

Deleting a record is similar to updating:

```
    model.setTable("cd");
    model.setFilter("id = 125");
    model.select();
    if (model.rowCount() == 1) {
        model.removeRows(0, 1);
        model.submitAll();
    }
```

The `removeRows()` call takes the row number of the first record to delete and the number of records to delete. The next example deletes all the records that match the filter:

```
    model.setTable("cd");
    model.setFilter("year < 1990");
    model.select();
    if (model.rowCount() > 0) {
        model.removeRows(0, model.rowCount());
        model.submitAll();
    }
```

The `QSqlQuery` and `QSqlTableModel` classes provide an interface between Qt and an SQL database. Using these classes, we can create forms that present data to users and that let them insert, update, and delete records.

Presenting Data in Tabular Form

In many cases, it is simplest to present users with a tabular view of a data set. In this section and the following section, we present a simple CD Collection application that uses `QSqlTableModel` and its subclass `QSqlRelationalTableModel` to let users view and interact with data stored in a database.

The main form shows a master–detail view of CDs and the tracks on the currently selected CD, as shown in Figure 13.1.

Figure 13.1. The CD Collection application

The application uses three tables, defined as follows:

```
CREATE TABLE artist (
    id INTEGER PRIMARY KEY,
    name VARCHAR(40) NOT NULL,
    country VARCHAR(40));

CREATE TABLE cd (
    id INTEGER PRIMARY KEY,
    title VARCHAR(40) NOT NULL,
    artistid INTEGER NOT NULL,
    year INTEGER NOT NULL,
    FOREIGN KEY (artistid) REFERENCES artist);

CREATE TABLE track (
    id INTEGER PRIMARY KEY,
    title VARCHAR(40) NOT NULL,
    duration INTEGER NOT NULL,
    cdid INTEGER NOT NULL,
    FOREIGN KEY (cdid) REFERENCES cd);
```

Some databases don't support foreign keys. For those, we must remove the FOREIGN KEY clauses. The example will still work, but the database will not enforce referential integrity.

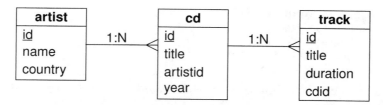

Figure 13.2. The CD Collection application's tables

In this section, we will write a dialog that allows the user to edit a list of artists using a simple tabular form. The user can insert or delete artists using the form's buttons. Updates can be applied directly, simply by editing cell text. Changes are applied to the database when the user presses Enter or navigates to another record.

Figure 13.3. The ArtistForm dialog

Here's the class definition for the ArtistForm dialog:

```
class ArtistForm : public QDialog
{
    Q_OBJECT

public:
    ArtistForm(const QString &name, QWidget *parent = 0);

private slots:
    void addArtist();
    void deleteArtist();
    void beforeInsertArtist(QSqlRecord &record);

private:
    enum {
        Artist_Id = 0,
        Artist_Name = 1,
        Artist_Country = 2
    };

    QSqlTableModel *model;
```

```
        QTableView *tableView;
        QPushButton *addButton;
        QPushButton *deleteButton;
        QPushButton *closeButton;
    };
```

The constructor is very similar to one that would be used to create a form based on a non-SQL model:

```
    ArtistForm::ArtistForm(const QString &name, QWidget *parent)
        : QDialog(parent)
    {
        model = new QSqlTableModel(this);
        model->setTable("artist");
        model->setSort(Artist_Name, Qt::AscendingOrder);
        model->setHeaderData(Artist_Name, Qt::Horizontal, tr("Name"));
        model->setHeaderData(Artist_Country, Qt::Horizontal, tr("Country"));
        model->select();
        connect(model, SIGNAL(beforeInsert(QSqlRecord &)),
                this, SLOT(beforeInsertArtist(QSqlRecord &)));

        tableView = new QTableView;
        tableView->setModel(model);
        tableView->setColumnHidden(Artist_Id, true);
        tableView->setSelectionBehavior(QAbstractItemView::SelectRows);
        tableView->resizeColumnsToContents();

        for (int row = 0; row < model->rowCount(); ++row) {
            QSqlRecord record = model->record(row);
            if (record.value(Artist_Name).toString() == name) {
                tableView->selectRow(row);
                break;
            }
        }
        ...
    }
```

We begin the constructor by creating a QSqlTableModel. We pass this as parent to give ownership to the form. We have chosen to sort by column 1 (specified by the constant Artist_Name), which corresponds to the name field. If we did not specify column headers, the field names would be used. We prefer to name them ourselves to ensure that they are properly capitalized and internationalized.

Next, we create a QTableView to visualize the model. We hide the id field and set the column widths to accommodate their text without needing to show ellipses.

The ArtistForm constructor takes the name of the artist that should be selected when the dialog pops up. We iterate through the artist table's records and select the specified artist. The rest of the constructor's code is used to create and connect the buttons and to lay out the child widgets.

```
    void ArtistForm::addArtist()
    {
```

```
        int row = model->rowCount();
        model->insertRow(row);
        QModelIndex index = model->index(row, Artist_Name);
        tableView->setCurrentIndex(index);
        tableView->edit(index);
    }
```

To add a new artist, we insert a single blank row at the bottom of the QTable-
View. Now the user can enter a new artist's name and country. If the user confirms the insertion by pressing Enter, the beforeInsert() signal is emitted and
then the new record is inserted into the database.

```
    void ArtistForm::beforeInsertArtist(QSqlRecord &record)
    {
        record.setValue("id", generateId("artist"));
    }
```

In the constructor, we connected the model's beforeInsert() signal to this slot.
We are passed a non-const reference to the record just before it is inserted into
the database. At this point, we populate its id field.

Since we will need generateId() a few times, we define it inline in a header
file and include it each time we need it. Here's a quick (and inefficient) way of
implementing it:

```
    inline int generateId(const QString &table)
    {
        QSqlQuery query;
        query.exec("SELECT MAX(id) FROM " + table);
        int id = 0;
        if (query.next())
            id = query.value(0).toInt() + 1;
        return id;
    }
```

The generateId() function can only be guaranteed to work correctly if it is
executed within the context of the same transaction as the corresponding
INSERT statement. Some databases support auto-generated fields, and it is
usually far better to use the database-specific support for this operation.

The last possibility the ArtistForm dialog offers is deletion. Rather than performing cascading deletions (covered shortly), we have chosen to only permit
deletions of artists who have no CDs in the collection.

```
    void ArtistForm::deleteArtist()
    {
        tableView->setFocus();
        QModelIndex index = tableView->currentIndex();
        if (!index.isValid())
            return;
        QSqlRecord record = model->record(index.row());

        QSqlTableModel cdModel;
        cdModel.setTable("cd");
        cdModel.setFilter("artistid = " + record.value("id").toString());
```

```
        cdModel.select();
        if (cdModel.rowCount() == 0) {
            model->removeRow(tableView->currentIndex().row());
        } else {
            QMessageBox::information(this,
                    tr("Delete Artist"),
                    tr("Cannot delete %1 because there are CDs associated "
                        "with this artist in the collection.")
                    .arg(record.value("name").toString()));
        }
    }
}
```

If there is a record selected, we check to see if the artist has any CDs, and if they don't, we delete them immediately. Otherwise, we pop up a message box explaining why the deletion was not performed. Strictly speaking, we should have used a transaction, because as the code stands, it is possible for a CD to have its artist set to the one we are deleting in-between the cdModel.select() and model->removeRow() calls. We will show a transaction in the next section.

Implementing Master–Detail Forms

We will now review the main form which takes a master–detail approach. The master view is a list of CDs. The detail view is a list of tracks for the current CD. This form is the main window of the CD Collection application as shown in Figure 13.1 (p. 300).

```
class MainForm : public QWidget
{
    Q_OBJECT

public:
    MainForm();

private slots:
    void addCd();
    void deleteCd();
    void addTrack();
    void deleteTrack();
    void editArtists();
    void currentCdChanged(const QModelIndex &index);
    void beforeInsertCd(QSqlRecord &record);
    void beforeInsertTrack(QSqlRecord &record);
    void refreshTrackViewHeader();

private:
    enum {
        Cd_Id = 0,
        Cd_Title = 1,
        Cd_ArtistId = 2,
        Cd_Year = 3
    };

    enum {
        Track_Id = 0,
```

```
                Track_Title = 1,
                Track_Duration = 2,
                Track_CdId = 3
        };

        QSqlRelationalTableModel *cdModel;
        QSqlTableModel *trackModel;
        QTableView *cdTableView;
        QTableView *trackTableView;
        QPushButton *addCdButton;
        QPushButton *deleteCdButton;
        QPushButton *addTrackButton;
        QPushButton *deleteTrackButton;
        QPushButton *editArtistsButton;
        QPushButton *quitButton;
};
```

We use a QSqlRelationalTableModel for the cd table rather than a plain QSqlTableModel because we need to handle foreign keys. We will now review each function in turn, beginning with the constructor, which we will look at in sections because it is quite long.

```
    MainForm::MainForm()
    {
        cdModel = new QSqlRelationalTableModel(this);
        cdModel->setTable("cd");
        cdModel->setRelation(Cd_ArtistId,
                             QSqlRelation("artist", "id", "name"));
        cdModel->setSort(Cd_Title, Qt::AscendingOrder);
        cdModel->setHeaderData(Cd_Title, Qt::Horizontal, tr("Title"));
        cdModel->setHeaderData(Cd_ArtistId, Qt::Horizontal, tr("Artist"));
        cdModel->setHeaderData(Cd_Year, Qt::Horizontal, tr("Year"));
        cdModel->select();
```

The constructor begins by setting up the QSqlRelationalTableModel that handles the cd table. The setRelation() call tells the model that its artistid field (whose field index is held by Cd_ArtistId) holds the id foreign key from the artist table, and that it should display the corresponding name field's contents instead of IDs. If the user chooses to edit this field (for example, by pressing F2), the model will automatically present a combobox with the names of all the artists, and if the user chooses a different artist, will update the cd table.

```
        cdTableView = new QTableView;
        cdTableView->setModel(cdModel);
        cdTableView->setItemDelegate(new QSqlRelationalDelegate(this));
        cdTableView->setSelectionMode(QAbstractItemView::SingleSelection);
        cdTableView->setSelectionBehavior(QAbstractItemView::SelectRows);
        cdTableView->setColumnHidden(Cd_Id, true);
        cdTableView->resizeColumnsToContents();
```

Setting up the view for the cd table is again similar to what we have already seen. The only significant difference is that instead of using the view's default delegate we use QSqlRelationalDelegate. It is this delegate that does the foreign key handling.

```
trackModel = new QSqlTableModel(this);
trackModel->setTable("track");
trackModel->setHeaderData(Track_Title, Qt::Horizontal, tr("Title"));
trackModel->setHeaderData(Track_Duration, Qt::Horizontal,
                          tr("Duration"));

trackTableView = new QTableView;
trackTableView->setModel(trackModel);
trackTableView->setItemDelegate(
        new TrackDelegate(Track_Duration, this));
trackTableView->setSelectionMode(
        QAbstractItemView::SingleSelection);
trackTableView->setSelectionBehavior(QAbstractItemView::SelectRows);
```

For tracks, we are only going to show their names and durations, so a QSql-TableModel is sufficient. (The id and cdid field's are hidden in the currentCd-Changed() slot shown later.) The only notable aspect of this part of the code is that we use the TrackDelegate developed in Chapter 10 to show track times as *"minutes:seconds"* and to allow them to be edited using a suitable QTimeEdit.

The creation, connecting, and laying out of the views and buttons holds no surprises, so the only other part of the constructor that we will show are a few non-obvious connections.

```
    ...
connect(cdTableView->selectionModel(),
        SIGNAL(currentRowChanged(const QModelIndex &,
                                 const QModelIndex &)),
        this, SLOT(currentCdChanged(const QModelIndex &)));
connect(cdModel, SIGNAL(beforeInsert(QSqlRecord &)),
        this, SLOT(beforeInsertCd(QSqlRecord &)));
connect(trackModel, SIGNAL(beforeInsert(QSqlRecord &)),
        this, SLOT(beforeInsertTrack(QSqlRecord &)));
connect(trackModel, SIGNAL(rowsInserted(const QModelIndex &, int,
                                        int)),
        this, SLOT(refreshTrackViewHeader()));
    ...
}
```

The first connection is unusual since instead of connecting a widget, we connect to a selection model. The QItemSelectionModel class is used to keep track of selections in views. By being connected to the table view's selection model, our currentCdChanged() slot will be called whenever the user navigates from one record to another.

```
void MainForm::currentCdChanged(const QModelIndex &index)
{
    if (index.isValid()) {
        QSqlRecord record = cdModel->record(index.row());
        int id = record.value("id").toInt();
        trackModel->setFilter(QString("cdid = %1").arg(id));
    } else {
        trackModel->setFilter("cdid = -1");
    }
```

```
    trackModel->select();
    refreshTrackViewHeader();
}
```

This slot is called whenever the current CD changes. This occurs when the user navigates to another CD (by clicking or by using the Up and Down keys). If the CD is invalid (for example, if there are no CDs or a new one is being inserted, or the current one has just been deleted), we set the track table's cdid to –1 (an invalid ID that we know will match no records).

Then, having set the filter, we select the matching track records. The refresh-TrackViewHeader() function will be explained in a moment.

```
void MainForm::addCd()
{
    int row = 0;
    if (cdTableView->currentIndex().isValid())
        row = cdTableView->currentIndex().row();

    cdModel->insertRow(row);
    cdModel->setData(cdModel->index(row, Cd_Year),
                     QDate::currentDate().year());

    QModelIndex index = cdModel->index(row, Cd_Title);
    cdTableView->setCurrentIndex(index);
    cdTableView->edit(index);
}
```

When the user clicks the Add CD button, a new blank row is inserted in the cdTableView and we enter edit mode. We also set a default value for the year field. At this point, the user can edit the record, filling in the blank fields and selecting an artist from the artist combobox that is automatically provided by the QSqlRelationalTableModel because of the setRelation() call, and edit the year if the default was not appropriate. If the user confirms the insertion by pressing Enter, the record is inserted. The user can cancel by pressing Esc.

```
void MainForm::beforeInsertCd(QSqlRecord &record)
{
    record.setValue("id", generateId("cd"));
}
```

This slot is called when the cdModel emits its beforeInsert() signal. We use it to populate the id field just as we did for inserting new artists, and the same caveat applies: It should be done within the scope of a transaction, and ideally the database-specific means of creating IDs (for example, auto-generated IDs) should be used instead.

```
void MainForm::deleteCd()
{
    QModelIndex index = cdTableView->currentIndex();
    if (!index.isValid())
        return;
    QSqlDatabase db = QSqlDatabase::database();
    db.transaction();
```

```
QSqlRecord record = cdModel->record(index.row());
int id = record.value(Cd_Id).toInt();
int tracks = 0;
QSqlQuery query;
query.exec(QString("SELECT COUNT(*) FROM track WHERE cdid = %1")
            .arg(id));
if (query.next())
    tracks = query.value(0).toInt();
if (tracks > 0) {
    int r = QMessageBox::question(this, tr("Delete CD"),
                    tr("Delete \"%1\" and all its tracks?")
                        .arg(record.value(Cd_ArtistId).toString()),
                    QMessageBox::Yes | QMessageBox::Default,
                    QMessageBox::No | QMessageBox::Escape);
    if (r == QMessageBox::No) {
        db.rollback();
        return;
    }
    query.exec(QString("DELETE FROM track WHERE cdid = %1")
                .arg(id));
}
cdModel->removeRow(index.row());
cdModel->submitAll();
db.commit();

currentCdChanged(QModelIndex());
}
```

If the user clicks the Delete CD button, this slot is called. If there is a current CD we find out how many tracks it has. If there are no tracks we simply delete the CD's record. If there is at least one track we ask the user to confirm the deletion, and if they click Yes, we delete all the track records, and then the CD's record. All this is done within the scope of a transaction, so the cascade deletion will either fail as a whole or succeed as a whole—assuming that the underlying database supports transactions.

Handling the track data is very similar to handling CD data. Updates can be performed simply by the user editing cells. In the case of track durations, our TrackDelegate ensures that times are shown in a nice format and are easily edited using a QTimeEdit.

```
void MainForm::addTrack()
{
    if (!cdTableView->currentIndex().isValid())
        return;

    int row = 0;
    if (trackTableView->currentIndex().isValid())
        row = trackTableView->currentIndex().row();

    trackModel->insertRow(row);
    QModelIndex index = trackModel->index(row, Track_Title);
    trackTableView->setCurrentIndex(index);
    trackTableView->edit(index);
}
```

This works in the same way as addCd(), with a new blank row being inserted into the view.

```
void MainForm::beforeInsertTrack(QSqlRecord &record)
{
    QSqlRecord cdRecord = cdModel->record(cdTableView->currentIndex()
                                                      .row());
    record.setValue("id", generateId("track"));
    record.setValue("cdid", cdRecord.value(Cd_Id).toInt());
}
```

If the user confirms the insertion initiated by addTrack(), this function is called to populate the id and cdid fields. The caveats mentioned earlier still apply of course.

```
void MainForm::deleteTrack()
{
    trackModel->removeRow(trackTableView->currentIndex().row());
    if (trackModel->rowCount() == 0)
        trackTableView->horizontalHeader()->setVisible(false);
}
```

If the user clicks the Delete Track button, we delete the track without formality. It would be easy to use a Yes/No message box if we preferred deletions to be confirmed.

```
void MainForm::refreshTrackViewHeader()
{
    trackTableView->horizontalHeader()->setVisible(
            trackModel->rowCount() > 0);
    trackTableView->setColumnHidden(Track_Id, true);
    trackTableView->setColumnHidden(Track_CdId, true);
    trackTableView->resizeColumnsToContents();
}
```

The refreshTrackViewHeader() slot is invoked from various places to ensure that the horizontal header of the track view is shown if and only if there are tracks to show. It also hides the id and cdid fields and resizes the visible table columns based on the current contents of the table.

```
void MainForm::editArtists()
{
    QSqlRecord record = cdModel->record(cdTableView->currentIndex()
                                                   .row());
    ArtistForm artistForm(record.value(Cd_ArtistId).toString(), this);
    artistForm.exec();
    cdModel->select();
}
```

This slot is called if the user clicks the Edit Artists button. It provides drill-down on the current CD's artist, invoking the ArtistForm covered in the previous section and selecting the appropriate artist. If there is no current record, a safe empty record is returned by record(), and this will harmlessly not match (and therefore not select) any artist in the artists form. What actually happens is that when we call record.value(Cd_ArtistId), because we are using a QSqlRelationalTableModel that maps artist IDs to artist names, the value that is returned is the artist's name (which will be an empty string if the record is empty). At the end, we get the cdModel to re-select its data, which causes the cdTableView to refresh its visible cells. This is done to ensure that the artist names are shown correctly since some could have been changed by the user in the ArtistForm dialog.

For projects that use the SQL classes, we must add the line

```
QT              += sql
```

to the .pro files; this will ensure that the application is linked against the *QtSql* library.

This chapter has shown that Qt's model/view classes make viewing and editing data in SQL databases as easy as possible. In cases where foreign keys refer to tables with lots of records (say, thousands or more), it is probably best to create our own delegate and use it to present a "list of values" form with a search capability rather than relying on QSqlRelationalTableModel's default comboboxes. And in situations where we want to present records using a form view, we must handle this ourselves: by using a QSqlQuery or QSqlTableModel to handle the database interaction, and mapping the contents of the user interface widgets we want to use for presenting and editing the data to the underlying database in our own code.

- ◆ *Writing FTP Clients*
- ◆ *Writing HTTP Clients*
- ◆ *Writing TCP Client–Server Applications*
- ◆ *Sending and Receiving UDP Datagrams*

14. Networking

Qt provides the QFtp and QHttp classes for working with FTP and HTTP. These protocols are easy to use for downloading and uploading files and, in the case of HTTP, for sending requests to web servers and retrieving the results.

Qt also provides the lower-level QTcpSocket and QUdpSocket classes, which implement the TCP and UDP transport protocols. TCP is a reliable connection-oriented protocol that operates in terms of data streams transmitted between network nodes, while UDP is an unreliable connectionless protocol based on discrete packets sent between network nodes. Both can be used to create network client and server applications. For servers, we also need the QTcpServer class to handle incoming TCP connections.

Writing FTP Clients

The QFtp class implements the client side of the FTP protocol in Qt. It offers various functions to perform the most common FTP operations and lets us execute arbitrary FTP commands.

The QFtp class works asynchronously. When we call a function like get() or put(), it returns immediately and the data transfer occurs when control passes back to Qt's event loop. This ensures that the user interface remains responsive while FTP commands are executed.

We will start with an example that shows how to retrieve a single file using get(). The example is a console application called ftpget that downloads the remote file specified on the command line. Let's begin with the main() function:

```
int main(int argc, char *argv[])
{
    QCoreApplication app(argc, argv);
    QStringList args = app.arguments();

    if (args.count() != 2) {
        cerr << "Usage: ftpget url" << endl
```

```
                << "Example:" << endl
                << "       ftpget ftp://ftp.trolltech.com/mirrors" << endl;
            return 1;
        }

        FtpGet getter;
        if (!getter.getFile(QUrl(args[1])))
            return 1;

        QObject::connect(&getter, SIGNAL(done()), &app, SLOT(quit()));

        return app.exec();
    }
```

We create a QCoreApplication rather than its subclass QApplication to avoid linking in the *QtGui* library. The QCoreApplication::arguments() function returns the command-line arguments as a QStringList, with the first item being the name the program was invoked as, and any Qt-specific arguments such as –style removed. The heart of the main() function is the construction of the FtpGet object and the getFile() call. If the call succeeds, we let the event loop run until the download finishes.

All the work is done by the FtpGet subclass, which is defined as follows:

```
    class FtpGet : public QObject
    {
        Q_OBJECT

    public:
        FtpGet(QObject *parent = 0);

        bool getFile(const QUrl &url);

    signals:
        void done();

    private slots:
        void ftpDone(bool error);

    private:
        QFtp ftp;
        QFile file;
    };
```

The class has a public function, getFile(), that retrieves the file specified by a URL. The QUrl class provides a high-level interface for extracting the different parts of a URL, such as the file name, path, protocol, and port.

FtpGet has a private slot, ftpDone(), that is called when the file transfer is completed, and a done() signal that it emits when the file has been downloaded. The class also has two private variables: The ftp variable, of type QFtp, encapsulates the connection to an FTP server, and the file variable that is used for writing the downloaded file to disk.

```
    FtpGet::FtpGet(QObject *parent)
        : QObject(parent)
```

```
    {
        connect(&ftp, SIGNAL(done(bool)), this, SLOT(ftpDone(bool)));
    }
```

In the constructor, we connect the QFtp::done(bool) signal to our ftpDone(bool) private slot. QFtp emits done(bool) when it has finished processing all requests. The bool parameter indicates whether an error occurred or not.

```
    bool FtpGet::getFile(const QUrl &url)
    {
        if (!url.isValid()) {
            cerr << "Error: Invalid URL" << endl;
            return false;
        }

        if (url.scheme() != "ftp") {
            cerr << "Error: URL must start with 'ftp:'" << endl;
            return false;
        }

        if (url.path().isEmpty()) {
            cerr << "Error: URL has no path" << endl;
            return false;
        }

        QString localFileName = QFileInfo(url.path()).fileName();
        if (localFileName.isEmpty())
            localFileName = "ftpget.out";

        file.setFileName(localFileName);
        if (!file.open(QIODevice::WriteOnly)) {
            cerr << "Error: Cannot open " << qPrintable(file.fileName())
                 << " for writing: " << qPrintable(file.errorString())
                 << endl;
            return false;
        }

        ftp.connectToHost(url.host(), url.port(21));
        ftp.login();
        ftp.get(url.path(), &file);
        ftp.close();
        return true;
    }
```

The getFile() function begins by checking the URL that was passed in. If a problem is encountered, the function prints an error message to cerr and returns false to indicate that the download failed.

Instead of forcing the user to make up a local file name, we try to create a sensible name using the URL itself, with a fallback of ftpget.out. If we fail to open the file, we print an error message and return false.

Next, we execute a sequence of four FTP commands using our QFtp object. The url.port(21) call returns the port number specified in the URL, or port 21 if none is specified in the URL itself. Since no user name or password are given to the login() function, an anonymous login is attempted. The second argument to get() specifies the output I/O device.

The FTP commands are queued and executed in Qt's event loop. The completion of all the commands is indicated by QFtp's done(bool) signal, which we connected to ftpDone(bool) in the constructor.

```
void FtpGet::ftpDone(bool error)
{
    if (error) {
        cerr << "Error: " << qPrintable(ftp.errorString()) << endl;
    } else {
        cerr << "File downloaded as " << qPrintable(file.fileName())
             << endl;
    }
    file.close();
    emit done();
}
```

Once the FTP commands have all been executed, we close the file and emit our own done() signal. It may appear strange that we close the file here, rather than after the ftp.close() call at the end of the getFile() function, but remember that the FTP commands are executed asynchronously and may well be in progress after the getFile() function has returned. Only when the QFtp object's done() signal is emitted do we know that the download is finished and that it is safe to close the file.

QFtp provides several FTP commands, including connectToHost(), login(), close(), list(), cd(), get(), put(), remove(), mkdir(), rmdir(), and rename(). All of these functions schedule an FTP command and return an ID number that identifies the command. It is also possible to control the transfer mode (the default is passive) and the transfer type (the default is binary).

Arbitrary FTP commands can be executed using rawCommand(). For example, here's how to execute a SITE CHMOD command:

```
ftp.rawCommand("SITE CHMOD 755 fortune");
```

QFtp emits the commandStarted(int) signal when it starts executing a command, and it emits the commandFinished(int, bool) signal when the command is finished. The int parameter is the ID number that identifies the command. If we are interested in the fate of individual commands, we can store the ID numbers when we schedule the commands. Keeping track of the ID numbers allows us to provide detailed feedback to the user. For example:

```
bool FtpGet::getFile(const QUrl &url)
{
    ...
    connectId = ftp.connectToHost(url.host(), url.port(21));
    loginId = ftp.login();
    getId = ftp.get(url.path(), &file);
    closeId = ftp.close();
```

```
        return true;
    }

    void FtpGet::ftpCommandStarted(int id)
    {
        if (id == connectId) {
            cerr << "Connecting..." << endl;
        } else if (id == loginId) {
            cerr << "Logging in..." << endl;
        ...
    }
```

Another way of providing feedback is to connect to QFtp's stateChanged() signal, which is emitted whenever the connection enters a new state (QFtp::Connecting, QFtp::Connected, QFtp::LoggedIn, etc.).

In most applications, we are only interested in the fate of the sequence of commands as a whole rather than in particular commands. In such cases, we can simply connect to the done(bool) signal, which is emitted whenever the command queue becomes empty.

When an error occurs, QFtp automatically clears the command queue. This means that if the connection or the login fails, the commands that follow in the queue are never executed. If we schedule new commands after the error has occurred using the same QFtp object, these commands will be queued and executed.

In the application's .pro file, we need the following line to link against the *QtNetwork* library:

```
    QT              += network
```

We will now review a more advanced example. The spider command-line program downloads all the files located in an FTP directory, recursively downloading from all the directory's subdirectories. The network logic is located in the Spider class:

```
    class Spider : public QObject
    {
        Q_OBJECT

    public:
        Spider(QObject *parent = 0);

        bool getDirectory(const QUrl &url);

    signals:
        void done();

    private slots:
        void ftpDone(bool error);
        void ftpListInfo(const QUrlInfo &urlInfo);

    private:
        void processNextDirectory();
```

```
    QFtp ftp;
    QList<QFile *> openedFiles;
    QString currentDir;
    QString currentLocalDir;
    QStringList pendingDirs;
};
```

The starting directory is specified as a QUrl and is set using the getDirectory() function.

```
Spider::Spider(QObject *parent)
    : QObject(parent)
{
    connect(&ftp, SIGNAL(done(bool)), this, SLOT(ftpDone(bool)));
    connect(&ftp, SIGNAL(listInfo(const QUrlInfo &)),
            this, SLOT(ftpListInfo(const QUrlInfo &)));
}
```

In the constructor, we establish two signal–slot connections. The listInfo(const QUrlInfo &) signal is emitted by QFtp when we request a directory listing (in getDirectory()) for each file that it retrieves. This signal is connected to a slot called ftpListInfo(), which downloads the file associated with the URL it is given.

```
bool Spider::getDirectory(const QUrl &url)
{
    if (!url.isValid()) {
        cerr << "Error: Invalid URL" << endl;
        return false;
    }

    if (url.scheme() != "ftp") {
        cerr << "Error: URL must start with 'ftp:'" << endl;
        return false;
    }

    ftp.connectToHost(url.host(), url.port(21));
    ftp.login();

    QString path = url.path();
    if (path.isEmpty())
        path = "/";

    pendingDirs.append(path);
    processNextDirectory();

    return true;
}
```

When the getDirectory() function is called, it begins by doing some sanity checks, and if all is well, attempts to establish an FTP connection. It keeps track of the paths that it must process and calls processNextDirectory() to start downloading the root directory.

```
void Spider::processNextDirectory()
{
```

```
            if (!pendingDirs.isEmpty()) {
                currentDir = pendingDirs.takeFirst();
                currentLocalDir = "downloads/" + currentDir;
                QDir(".").mkpath(currentLocalDir);

                ftp.cd(currentDir);
                ftp.list();
            } else {
                emit done();
            }
        }
```

The processNextDirectory() function takes the first remote directory out of the pendingDirs list and creates a corresponding directory in the local file system. It then tells the QFtp object to change directory into the taken directory and to list its files. For every file that list() processes, it emits a listInfo() signal that causes the ftpListInfo() slot to be called.

If there are no more directories to process, the function emits the done() signal to indicate that the downloading is complete.

```
        void Spider::ftpListInfo(const QUrlInfo &urlInfo)
        {
            if (urlInfo.isFile()) {
                if (urlInfo.isReadable()) {
                    QFile *file = new QFile(currentLocalDir + "/"
                                            + urlInfo.name());

                    if (!file->open(QIODevice::WriteOnly)) {
                        cerr << "Warning: Cannot open file "
                            << qPrintable(
                                    QDir::convertSeparators(file->fileName()))
                            << endl;
                        return;
                    }

                    ftp.get(urlInfo.name(), file);
                    openedFiles.append(file);
                }
            } else if (urlInfo.isDir() && !urlInfo.isSymLink()) {
                pendingDirs.append(currentDir + "/" + urlInfo.name());
            }
        }
```

The ftpListInfo() slot's urlInfo parameter provides detailed information about a remote file. If the file is a normal file (not a directory) and is readable, we call get() to download it. The QFile object used for downloading is allocated using new and a pointer to it is stored in the openedFiles list.

If the QUrlInfo holds the details of a remote directory that is not a symbolic link, we add this directory to the pendingDirs list. We skip symbolic links because they can easily lead to infinite recursion.

```
        void Spider::ftpDone(bool error)
        {
```

```
        if (error) {
            cerr << "Error: " << qPrintable(ftp.errorString()) << endl;
        } else {
            cout << "Downloaded " << qPrintable(currentDir) << " to "
                    << qPrintable(QDir::convertSeparators(
                                        QDir(currentLocalDir).canonicalPath())));
        }

        qDeleteAll(openedFiles);
        openedFiles.clear();

        processNextDirectory();
    }
```

The `ftpDone()` slot is called when all the FTP commands have finished or if
an error occurred. We delete the `QFile` objects to prevent memory leaks and
also to close each file. Finally, we call `processNextDirectory()`. If there are any
directories left, the whole process begins again with the next directory in the
list; otherwise, the downloading stops and `done()` is emitted.

If there are no errors, the sequence of FTP commands and signals is as
follows:

```
connectToHost(host, port)
login()

cd(directory_1)
list()
    emit listInfo(file_1_1)
        get(file_1_1)
    emit listInfo(file_1_2)
        get(file_1_2)
    ...
emit done()

...

cd(directory_N)
list()
    emit listInfo(file_N_1)
        get(file_N_1)
    emit listInfo(file_N_2)
        get(file_N_2)
    ...
emit done()
```

If a file is in fact a directory, it is added to the `pendingDirs` list, and when the last
file of the current `list()` command has been downloaded, a new `cd()` command
is issued, followed by a new `list()` command with the next pending directory,
and the whole process begins again with the new directory. This is repeated,
with new files being downloaded, and new directories added to the `pendingDirs`
list, until every file has been downloaded from every directory, at which point
the `pendingDirs` list will finally be empty.

If a network error occurs while downloading the fifth of, say, twenty files in a directory, the remaining files will not be downloaded. If we wanted to download as many files as possible, one solution would be to schedule the GET operations one at a time and to wait for the done(bool) signal before scheduling a new GET operation. In listInfo(), we would simply append the file name to a QStringList, instead of calling get() right away, and in done(bool) we would call get() on the next file to download in the QStringList. The sequence of execution would then look like this:

```
connectToHost(host, port)
login()

cd(directory_1)
list()
...
cd(directory_N)
list()
    emit listInfo(file_1_1)
    emit listInfo(file_1_2)
    ...
    emit listInfo(file_N_1)
    emit listInfo(file_N_2)
    ...
emit done()

get(file_1_1)
emit done()

get(file_1_2)
emit done()

...

get(file_N_1)
emit done()

get(file_N_2)
emit done()

...
```

Another solution would be to use one QFtp object per file. This would enable us to download the files in parallel, through separate FTP connections.

```
int main(int argc, char *argv[])
{
    QCoreApplication app(argc, argv);
    QStringList args = app.arguments();

    if (args.count() != 2) {
        cerr << "Usage: spider url" << endl
             << "Example:" << endl
             << "    spider ftp://ftp.trolltech.com/freebies/leafnode"
             << endl;
        return 1;
    }
```

```
    Spider spider;
    if (!spider.getDirectory(QUrl(args[1])))
        return 1;

    QObject::connect(&spider, SIGNAL(done()), &app, SLOT(quit()));

    return app.exec();
}
```

The main() function completes the program. If the user does not specify a URL on the command line, we give an error message and terminate the program.

In both FTP examples, the data retrieved using get() was written to a QFile. This need not be the case. If we wanted the data in memory, we could use a QBuffer, the QIODevice subclass that wraps a QByteArray. For example:

```
    QBuffer *buffer = new QBuffer;
    buffer->open(QIODevice::WriteOnly);
    ftp.get(urlInfo.name(), buffer);
```

We could also omit the I/O device argument to get() or pass a null pointer. The QFtp class then emits a readyRead() signal every time new data is available, and the data can be read using read() or readAll().

Writing HTTP Clients

The QHttp class implements the client side of the HTTP protocol in Qt. It provides various functions to perform the most common HTTP operations, including get() and post(), and provides a means of sending arbitrary HTTP requests. If you have read the previous section about QFtp, you will find that there are many similarities between QFtp and QHttp.

The QHttp class works asynchronously. When we call a function like get() or post(), the function returns immediately, and the data transfer occurs later, when control returns to Qt's event loop. This ensures that the application's user interface remains responsive while HTTP requests are being processed.

We will review a console application example called httpget that shows how to download a file using the HTTP protocol. It is very similar to the ftpget example from the previous section, both in functionality and implementation, so we will not show the header file.

```
    HttpGet::HttpGet(QObject *parent)
        : QObject(parent)
    {
        connect(&http, SIGNAL(done(bool)), this, SLOT(httpDone(bool)));
    }
```

In the constructor, we connect the QHttp object's done(bool) signal to the private httpDone(bool) slot.

```
    bool HttpGet::getFile(const QUrl &url)
    {
```

```
        if (!url.isValid()) {
            cerr << "Error: Invalid URL" << endl;
            return false;
        }

        if (url.scheme() != "http") {
            cerr << "Error: URL must start with 'http:'" << endl;
            return false;
        }

        if (url.path().isEmpty()) {
            cerr << "Error: URL has no path" << endl;
            return false;
        }

        QString localFileName = QFileInfo(url.path()).fileName();
        if (localFileName.isEmpty())
            localFileName = "httpget.out";

        file.setFileName(localFileName);
        if (!file.open(QIODevice::WriteOnly)) {
            cerr << "Error: Cannot open " << qPrintable(file.fileName())
                 << " for writing: " << qPrintable(file.errorString())
                 << endl;
            return false;
        }

        http.setHost(url.host(), url.port(80));
        http.get(url.path(), &file);
        http.close();
        return true;
    }
```

The `getFile()` function performs the same kind of error checks as the `FtpGet::getFile()` shown earlier and uses the same approach to giving the file a local name. When retrieving from web sites, no login is necessary, so we simply set the host and port (using the default HTTP port 80 if none is specified in the URL) and download the data into the file, since the second argument to `QHttp::get()` specifies the output I/O device.

The HTTP requests are queued and executed asynchronously in Qt's event loop. The completion of the requests is indicated by `QHttp`'s `done(bool)` signal, which we connected to `httpDone(bool)` in the constructor.

```
    void HttpGet::httpDone(bool error)
    {
        if (error) {
            cerr << "Error: " << qPrintable(http.errorString()) << endl;
        } else {
            cerr << "File downloaded as " << qPrintable(file.fileName())
                 << endl;
        }
        file.close();
        emit done();
    }
```

Once the HTTP requests are finished, we close the file, notifying the user if an error occurred.

The `main()` function is very similar to the one used by `ftpget`:

```
int main(int argc, char *argv[])
{
    QCoreApplication app(argc, argv);
    QStringList args = app.arguments();

    if (args.count() != 2) {
        cerr << "Usage: httpget url" << endl
             << "Example:" << endl
             << "    httpget http://doc.trolltech.com/qq/index.html"
             << endl;
        return 1;
    }

    HttpGet getter;
    if (!getter.getFile(QUrl(args[1])))
        return 1;

    QObject::connect(&getter, SIGNAL(done()), &app, SLOT(quit()));

    return app.exec();
}
```

The `QHttp` class provides many operations, including `setHost()`, `get()`, `post()`, and `head()`. If a site requires authentication, `setUser()` can be used to supply a user name and password. `QHttp` can use a socket supplied by the programmer rather than its own internal `QTcpSocket`. This makes it possible to use a secure `QtSslSocket`, provided as a Qt Solution from Trolltech, to achieve HTTP over SSL.

To send a list of "*name = value*" pairs to a CGI script, we can use `post()`:

```
http.setHost("www.example.com");
http.post("/cgi/somescript.py", "x=200&y=320", &file);
```

We can pass the data either as an 8-bit string or by passing an open `QIODevice`, such as a `QFile`. For more control, we can use the `request()` function, which accepts an arbitrary HTTP header and data. For example:

```
QHttpRequestHeader header("POST", "/search.html");
header.setValue("Host", "www.trolltech.com");
header.setContentType("application/x-www-form-urlencoded");
http.setHost("www.trolltech.com");
http.request(header, "qt-interest=on&search=opengl");
```

`QHttp` emits the `requestStarted(int)` signal when it starts executing a request, and it emits the `requestFinished(int, bool)` signal when the request has finished. The `int` parameter is an ID number that identifies a request. If we are interested in the fate of individual requests, we can store the ID numbers when we schedule the requests. Keeping track of the ID numbers allows us to provide detailed feedback to the user.

In most applications, we only want to know whether the entire sequence of requests completed successfully or not. This is easily achieved by connecting to the done(bool) signal, which is emitted when the request queue becomes empty.

When an error occurs, the request queue is automatically cleared. But if we schedule new requests after the error has occurred using the same QHttp object, these requests will be queued and sent as usual.

Like QFtp, QHttp provides a readyRead() signal as well as the read() and readAll() functions that we can use instead of specifying an I/O device.

Writing TCP Client–Server Applications

The QTcpSocket and QTcpServer classes can be used to implement TCP clients and servers. TCP is a transport protocol that forms the basis of most application-level Internet protocols, including FTP and HTTP, and that can also be used for custom protocols.

TCP is a stream-oriented protocol. For applications, the data appears to be a long stream, rather like a large flat file. The high-level protocols built on top of TCP are typically either line-oriented or block-oriented:

* Line-oriented protocols transfer data as lines of text, each terminated by a newline.
* Block-oriented protocols transfer data as binary data blocks. Each block consists of a size field followed by that much data.

QTcpSocket inherits from QIODevice through QAbstractSocket, so it can be read from and written to using a QDataStream or a QTextStream. One notable difference when reading data from a network compared with reading from a file is that we must make sure that we have received enough data from the peer before we use the >> operator. Failing to do so may result in undefined behavior.

In this section, we will review the code of a client and a server that use a custom block-oriented protocol. The client is called Trip Planner and allows users to plan their next train trip. The server is called Trip Server and provides the trip information to the client. We will start by writing the Trip Planner client.

The Trip Planner provides a From field, a To field, a Date field, an Approximate Time field, and two radio buttons to select whether the approximate time is that of departure or arrival. When the user clicks Search, the application sends a request to the server, which responds with a list of train trips that match the user's criteria. The list is shown in a QTableWidget in the Trip Planner window. The very bottom of the window is occupied by a QLabel that shows the status of the last operation and a QProgressBar.

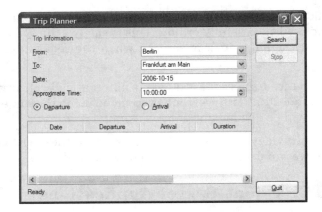

Figure 14.1. The Trip Planner application

The Trip Planner's user interface was created using *Qt Designer* in a file called
tripplanner.ui. Here, we will focus on the source code of the QDialog subclass
that implements the application's functionality:

```cpp
#include "ui_tripplanner.h"

class TripPlanner : public QDialog, public Ui::TripPlanner
{
    Q_OBJECT

public:
    TripPlanner(QWidget *parent = 0);

private slots:
    void connectToServer();
    void sendRequest();
    void updateTableWidget();
    void stopSearch();
    void connectionClosedByServer();
    void error();

private:
    void closeConnection();

    QTcpSocket tcpSocket;
    quint16 nextBlockSize;
};
```

The TripPlanner class inherits from Ui::TripPlanner (which is generated by uic
from tripplanner.ui) in addition to QDialog. The tcpSocket member variable
encapsulates the TCP connection. The nextBlockSize variable is used when
parsing the blocks received from the server.

```cpp
TripPlanner::TripPlanner(QWidget *parent)
    : QDialog(parent)
{
    setupUi(this);
```

```
    QDateTime dateTime = QDateTime::currentDateTime();
    dateEdit->setDate(dateTime.date());
    timeEdit->setTime(QTime(dateTime.time().hour(), 0));

    progressBar->hide();
    progressBar->setSizePolicy(QSizePolicy::Preferred,
                               QSizePolicy::Ignored);

    tableWidget->verticalHeader()->hide();
    tableWidget->setEditTriggers(QAbstractItemView::NoEditTriggers);

    connect(searchButton, SIGNAL(clicked()),
            this, SLOT(connectToServer()));
    connect(stopButton, SIGNAL(clicked()), this, SLOT(stopSearch()));

    connect(&tcpSocket, SIGNAL(connected()), this, SLOT(sendRequest()));
    connect(&tcpSocket, SIGNAL(disconnected()),
            this, SLOT(connectionClosedByServer()));
    connect(&tcpSocket, SIGNAL(readyRead()),
            this, SLOT(updateTableWidget()));
    connect(&tcpSocket, SIGNAL(error(QAbstractSocket::SocketError)),
            this, SLOT(error()));
}
```

In the constructor, we initialize the date and time editors based on the current date and time. We also hide the progress bar, because we only want to show it when a connection is active. In *Qt Designer*, the progress bar's minimum and maximum properties were both set to 0. This tells the QProgressBar to behave as a busy indicator instead of as a standard percentage-based progress bar.

Also in the constructor, we connect the QTcpSocket's connected(), disconnected(), readyRead(), and error(QAbstractSocket::SocketError) signals to private slots.

```
    void TripPlanner::connectToServer()
    {
        tcpSocket.connectToHost("tripserver.zugbahn.de", 6178);

        tableWidget->setRowCount(0);
        searchButton->setEnabled(false);
        stopButton->setEnabled(true);
        statusLabel->setText(tr("Connecting to server..."));
        progressBar->show();

        nextBlockSize = 0;
    }
```

The connectToServer() slot is executed when the user clicks Search to start a search. We call connectToHost() on the QTcpSocket object to connect to the server, which we assume is accessible at port 6178 on the fictitious host tripserver.zugbahn.de. (If you want to try the example on your own machine, replace the host name with QHostAddress::LocalHost.) The connectToHost() call is asynchronous; it always returns immediately. The connection is typically established later. The QTcpSocket object emits the connected() signal when the connection is up and running, or error(QAbstractSocket::SocketError) if the connection failed.

Next, we update the user interface, in particular making the progress bar visible.

Finally, we set the nextBlockSize variable to 0. This variable stores the length of the next block received from the server. We have chosen to use the value of 0 to mean that we don't yet know the size of the next block.

```cpp
void TripPlanner::sendRequest()
{
    QByteArray block;
    QDataStream out(&block, QIODevice::WriteOnly);
    out.setVersion(QDataStream::Qt_4_1);
    out << quint16(0) << quint8('S') << fromComboBox->currentText()
        << toComboBox->currentText() << dateEdit->date()
        << timeEdit->time();

    if (departureRadioButton->isChecked()) {
        out << quint8('D');
    } else {
        out << quint8('A');
    }
    out.device()->seek(0);
    out << quint16(block.size() - sizeof(quint16));
    tcpSocket.write(block);

    statusLabel->setText(tr("Sending request..."));
}
```

The sendRequest() slot is executed when the QTcpSocket object emits the connected() signal, indicating that a connection has been established. The slot's task is to generate a request to the server, with all the information entered by the user.

The request is a binary block with the following format:

quint16	Block size in bytes (excluding this field)
quint8	Request type (always 'S')
QString	Departure city
QString	Arrival city
QDate	Date of travel
QTime	Approximate time of travel
quint8	Time is for departure ('D') or arrival ('A')

We first write the data to a QByteArray called block. We can't write the data directly to the QTcpSocket because we don't know the size of the block, which must be sent first, until after we have put all the data into the block.

We initially write 0 as the block size, followed by the rest of the data. Then we call seek(0) on the I/O device (a QBuffer created by QDataStream behind the scenes) to move back to the beginning of the byte array, and overwrite the initial 0 with the size of the block's data. The size is calculated by taking the block's size and subtracting sizeof(quint16) (that is, 2) to exclude the size field from the byte count. After that, we call write() on the QTcpSocket to send the block to the server.

```
void TripPlanner::updateTableWidget()
{
    QDataStream in(&tcpSocket);
    in.setVersion(QDataStream::Qt_4_1);

    forever {
        int row = tableWidget->rowCount();

        if (nextBlockSize == 0) {
            if (tcpSocket.bytesAvailable() < sizeof(quint16))
                break;
            in >> nextBlockSize;
        }

        if (nextBlockSize == 0xFFFF) {
            closeConnection();
            statusLabel->setText(tr("Found %1 trip(s)").arg(row));
            break;
        }

        if (tcpSocket.bytesAvailable() < nextBlockSize)
            break;

        QDate date;
        QTime departureTime;
        QTime arrivalTime;
        quint16 duration;
        quint8 changes;
        QString trainType;

        in >> date >> departureTime >> duration >> changes >> trainType;
        arrivalTime = departureTime.addSecs(duration * 60);

        tableWidget->setRowCount(row + 1);

        QStringList fields;
        fields << date.toString(Qt::LocalDate)
               << departureTime.toString(tr("hh:mm"))
               << arrivalTime.toString(tr("hh:mm"))
               << tr("%1 hr %2 min").arg(duration / 60)
                                     .arg(duration % 60)
               << QString::number(changes)
               << trainType;
        for (int i = 0; i < fields.count(); ++i)
            tableWidget->setItem(row, i,
                                 new QTableWidgetItem(fields[i]));
        nextBlockSize = 0;
    }
}
```

The updateTableWidget() slot is connected to the QTcpSocket's readyRead() signal, which is emitted whenever the QTcpSocket has received new data from the server. The server sends us a list of possible train trips that match the user's criteria. Each matching trip is sent as a single block, and each block starts with a size. The forever loop is necessary because we don't necessarily get one block of data from the server at a time.* We might have received an entire block, or just part of a block, or one and a half blocks, or even all of the blocks at once.

Figure 14.2. The Trip Server's blocks

So how does the forever loop work? If the nextBlockSize variable is 0, this means that we have not read the size of the next block. We try to read it (assuming there are at least 2 bytes available for reading). The server uses a size value of 0xFFFF to signify that there is no more data to receive, so if we read this value, we know that we have reached the end.

If the block size is not 0xFFFF, we try to read in the next block. First, we check to see if there are block size bytes available to read. If there are not, we stop there for now. The readyRead() signal will be emitted again when more data is available, and we will try again then.

Once we are sure that an entire block has arrived, we can safely use the >> operator on the QDataStream to extract the information related to a trip, and we create QTableWidgetItems with that information. A block received from the server has the following format:

quint16	Block size in bytes (excluding this field)
QDate	Departure date
QTime	Departure time
quint16	Duration (in minutes)
quint8	Number of changes
QString	Train type

At the end, we reset the nextBlockSize variable to 0 to indicate that the next block's size is unknown and needs to be read.

```
void TripPlanner::closeConnection()
{
    tcpSocket.close();
    searchButton->setEnabled(true);
    stopButton->setEnabled(false);
    progressBar->hide();
}
```

---

*The forever keyword is provided by Qt. It simply expands to for (;;).

The `closeConnection()` private function closes the connection to the TCP server and updates the user interface. It is called from `updateTableWidget()` when the `0xFFFF` is read and from several other slots that we will cover shortly.

```
void TripPlanner::stopSearch()
{
    statusLabel->setText(tr("Search stopped"));
    closeConnection();
}
```

The `stopSearch()` slot is connected to the Stop button's `clicked()` signal. Essentially it just calls `closeConnection()`.

```
void TripPlanner::connectionClosedByServer()
{
    if (nextBlockSize != 0xFFFF)
        statusLabel->setText(tr("Error: Connection closed by server"));
    closeConnection();
}
```

The `connectionClosedByServer()` slot is connected to `QTcpSocket`'s `disconnected()` signal. If the server closes the connection and we have not yet received the `0xFFFF` end-of-data marker, we tell the user that an error occurred. We call `closeConnection()` as usual to update the user interface.

```
void TripPlanner::error()
{
    statusLabel->setText(tcpSocket.errorString());
    closeConnection();
}
```

The `error()` slot is connected to `QTcpSocket`'s `error(QAbstractSocket::SocketError)` signal. We ignore the error code and use `QTcpSocket::errorString()`, which returns a human-readable error message for the last error that occurred.

This is all for the `TripPlanner` class. The `main()` function for the Trip Planner application looks just as we would expect:

```
int main(int argc, char *argv[])
{
    QApplication app(argc, argv);
    TripPlanner tripPlanner;
    tripPlanner.show();
    return app.exec();
}
```

Now let's implement the server. The server consists of two classes: `TripServer` and `ClientSocket`. The `TripServer` class inherits `QTcpServer`, a class that allows us to accept incoming TCP connections. `ClientSocket` reimplements `QTcpSocket` and handles a single connection. At any one time, there are as many `ClientSocket` objects in memory as there are clients being served.

```
class TripServer : public QTcpServer
{
```

```
    Q_OBJECT
public:
    TripServer(QObject *parent = 0);

private:
    void incomingConnection(int socketId);
};
```

The `TripServer` class reimplements the `incomingConnection()` function from `QTcpServer`. This function is called whenever a client attempts to connect to the port the server is listening to.

```
TripServer::TripServer(QObject *parent)
    : QTcpServer(parent)
{
}
```

The `TripServer` constructor is trivial.

```
void TripServer::incomingConnection(int socketId)
{
    ClientSocket *socket = new ClientSocket(this);
    socket->setSocketDescriptor(socketId);
}
```

In `incomingConnection()`, we create a `ClientSocket` object as a child of the `TripServer` object, and we set its socket descriptor to the number provided to us. The `ClientSocket` object will delete itself automatically when the connection is terminated.

```
class ClientSocket : public QTcpSocket
{
    Q_OBJECT

public:
    ClientSocket(QObject *parent = 0);

private slots:
    void readClient();

private:
    void generateRandomTrip(const QString &from, const QString &to,
                            const QDate &date, const QTime &time);

    quint16 nextBlockSize;
};
```

The `ClientSocket` class inherits from `QTcpSocket` and encapsulates the state of a single client.

```
ClientSocket::ClientSocket(QObject *parent)
    : QTcpSocket(parent)
{
    connect(this, SIGNAL(readyRead()), this, SLOT(readClient()));
    connect(this, SIGNAL(disconnected()), this, SLOT(deleteLater()));
```

```
            nextBlockSize = 0;
    }
```

In the constructor, we establish the necessary signal–slot connections, and we set the `nextBlockSize` variable to 0, indicating that we do not yet know the size of the block sent by the client.

The `disconnected()` signal is connected to `deleteLater()`, a `QObject`-inherited function that deletes the object when control returns to Qt's event loop. This ensures that the `ClientSocket` object is deleted when the socket connection is closed.

```
    void ClientSocket::readClient()
    {
        QDataStream in(this);
        in.setVersion(QDataStream::Qt_4_1);

        if (nextBlockSize == 0) {
            if (bytesAvailable() < sizeof(quint16))
                return;
            in >> nextBlockSize;
        }
        if (bytesAvailable() < nextBlockSize)
            return;

        quint8 requestType;
        QString from;
        QString to;
        QDate date;
        QTime time;
        quint8 flag;

        in >> requestType;
        if (requestType == 'S') {
            in >> from >> to >> date >> time >> flag;

            srand(from.length() * 3600 + to.length() * 60 + time.hour());
            int numTrips = rand() % 8;
            for (int i = 0; i < numTrips; ++i)
                generateRandomTrip(from, to, date, time);

            QDataStream out(this);
            out << quint16(0xFFFF);
        }

        close();
    }
```

The `readClient()` slot is connected to `QTcpSocket`'s `readyRead()` signal. If `nextBlockSize` is 0, we start by reading the block size; otherwise, we have already read it, and instead we check to see if a whole block has arrived. Once an entire block is ready for reading, we read it in one go. We use the `QDataStream` directly on the `QTcpSocket` (the `this` object) and read the fields using the `>>` operator.

Once we have read the client's request, we are ready to generate a reply. If this were a real application, we would look up the information in a train schedule database and try to find matching train trips. But here we will be content with a function called generateRandomTrip() that will generate a random trip. We call the function a random number of times, and then we send 0xFFFF to signify the end of the data. At the end, we close the connection.

```
void ClientSocket::generateRandomTrip(const QString & /* from */,
        const QString & /* to */, const QDate &date, const QTime &time)
{
    QByteArray block;
    QDataStream out(&block, QIODevice::WriteOnly);
    out.setVersion(QDataStream::Qt_4_1);
    quint16 duration = rand() % 200;
    out << quint16(0) << date << time << duration << quint8(1)
        << QString("InterCity");
    out.device()->seek(0);
    out << quint16(block.size() - sizeof(quint16));

    write(block);
}
```

The generateRandomTrip() function shows how to send a block of data over a TCP connection. This is very similar to what we did in the client in the sendRequest() function (p. 326). Once again, we write the block to a QByteArray so that we can determine its size before we send it using write().

```
int main(int argc, char *argv[])
{
    QApplication app(argc, argv);
    TripServer server;
    if (!server.listen(QHostAddress::Any, 6178)) {
        cerr << "Failed to bind to port" << endl;
        return 1;
    }

    QPushButton quitButton(QObject::tr("&Quit"));
    quitButton.setWindowTitle(QObject::tr("Trip Server"));
    QObject::connect(&quitButton, SIGNAL(clicked()),
                     &app, SLOT(quit()));
    quitButton.show();
    return app.exec();
}
```

In main(), we create a TripServer object and a QPushButton that enables the user to stop the server. We start the server by calling QTcpSocket::listen(), which takes the IP address and port number on which we want to accept connections. The special address 0.0.0.0 (QHostAddress::Any) signifies any IP interface present on the local host.

This completes our client–server example. In this case, we used a block-oriented protocol that allows us to use QDataStream for reading and writing. If we wanted to use a line-oriented protocol, the simplest approach would be to use QTcpSocket's `canReadLine()` and `readLine()` functions in a slot connected to the `readyRead()` signal:

```
QStringList lines;
while (tcpSocket.canReadLine())
    lines.append(tcpSocket.readLine());
```

We would then process each line that has been read. As for sending data, that can be done using a `QTextStream` on the `QTcpSocket`.

The server implementation that we have used doesn't scale very well when there are lots of connections. The problem is that while we are processing a request, we don't handle the other connections. A more scalable approach would be to start a new thread for each connection. The Threaded Fortune Server example located in Qt's `examples/network/threadedfortuneserver` directory illustrates how to do this.

Sending and Receiving UDP Datagrams

The `QUdpSocket` class can be used to send and receive UDP datagrams. UDP is an unreliable, datagram-oriented protocol. Some application-level protocols use UDP because it is more lightweight than TCP. With UDP, data is sent as packets (datagrams) from one host to another. There is no concept of connection, and if a UDP packet doesn't get delivered successfully, no error is reported to the sender.

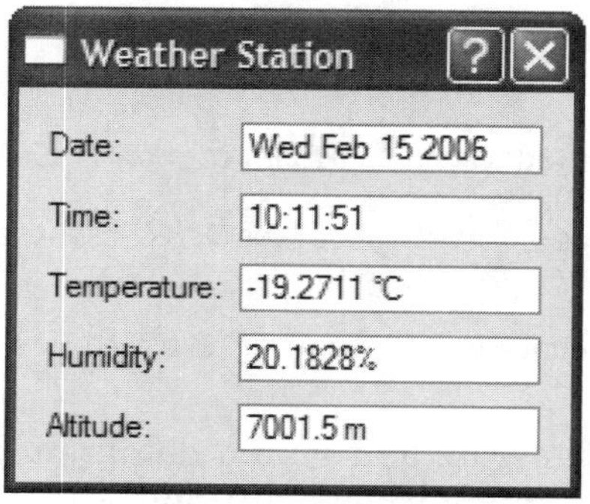

Figure 14.3. The Weather Station application

We will see how to use UDP from a Qt application through the Weather Balloon and Weather Station example. The Weather Balloon application mimics a weather balloon that sends a UDP datagram (presumably using a wireless connection) containing the current atmospheric conditions every 2 seconds. The Weather Station application receives these datagrams and displays them on screen. We will start by reviewing the code for the Weather Balloon.

```
class WeatherBalloon : public QPushButton
{
    Q_OBJECT
```

```
public:
    WeatherBalloon(QWidget *parent = 0);

    double temperature() const;
    double humidity() const;
    double altitude() const;

private slots:
    void sendDatagram();

private:
    QUdpSocket udpSocket;
    QTimer timer;
};
```

The WeatherBalloon class inherits from QPushButton. It uses its QUdpSocket private variable for communicating with the Weather Station.

```
WeatherBalloon::WeatherBalloon(QWidget *parent)
    : QPushButton(tr("Quit"), parent)
{
    connect(this, SIGNAL(clicked()), this, SLOT(close()));
    connect(&timer, SIGNAL(timeout()), this, SLOT(sendDatagram()));

    timer.start(2 * 1000);

    setWindowTitle(tr("Weather Balloon"));
}
```

In the constructor, we start a QTimer to invoke sendDatagram() every 2 seconds.

```
void WeatherBalloon::sendDatagram()
{
    QByteArray datagram;
    QDataStream out(&datagram, QIODevice::WriteOnly);
    out.setVersion(QDataStream::Qt_4_1);
    out << QDateTime::currentDateTime() << temperature() << humidity()
        << altitude();

    udpSocket.writeDatagram(datagram, QHostAddress::LocalHost, 5824);
}
```

In sendDatagram(), we generate and send a datagram containing the current date, time, temperature, humidity, and altitude:

QDateTime	Date and time of measurement
double	Temperature (in °C)
double	Humidity (in %)
double	Altitude (in meters)

The datagram is sent using QUdpSocket::writeDatagram(). The second and third arguments to writeDatagram() are the IP address and the port number of the peer (the Weather Station). For this example, we assume that the Weather Station is running on the same machine as the Weather Balloon, so we use an IP address of 127.0.0.1 (QHostAddress::LocalHost), a special address that designates the local host.

Unlike the QAbstractSocket subclasses, QUdpSocket does not accept host names, only host addresses. If we wanted to resolve a host name to its IP address here, we have two choices: If we are prepared to block while the lookup takes place, we can use the static QHostInfo::fromName() function. Otherwise, we can use the static QHostInfo::lookupHost() function, which returns immediately and calls the slot it is passed with a QHostInfo object containing the corresponding addresses when the lookup is complete.

```
int main(int argc, char *argv[])
{
    QApplication app(argc, argv);
    WeatherBalloon balloon;
    balloon.show();
    return app.exec();
}
```

The main() function simply creates a WeatherBalloon object, which serves both as a UDP peer and as a QPushButton on screen. By clicking the QPushButton, the user can quit the application.

Now let's review the source code for the Weather Station client.

```
class WeatherStation : public QDialog
{
    Q_OBJECT

public:
    WeatherStation(QWidget *parent = 0);

private slots:
    void processPendingDatagrams();

private:
    QUdpSocket udpSocket;

    QLabel *dateLabel;
    QLabel *timeLabel;
    ...
    QLineEdit *altitudeLineEdit;
};
```

The WeatherStation class inherits from QDialog. It listens to a particular UDP port, parses any incoming datagrams (from the Weather Balloon), and displays their contents in five read-only QLineEdits. The only private variable of interest here is udpSocket of type QUdpSocket, which we will use to receive datagrams.

```
WeatherStation::WeatherStation(QWidget *parent)
    : QDialog(parent)
{
    udpSocket.bind(5824);

    connect(&udpSocket, SIGNAL(readyRead()),
```

```
                           this, SLOT(processPendingDatagrams())));
        ...
    }
```

In the constructor, we start by binding the QUdpSocket to the port that the weather balloon is transmitting to. Since we have not specified a host address, the socket will accept datagrams sent to any IP address that belongs to the machine the Weather Station is running on. Then, we connect the socket's readyRead() signal to the private processPendingDatagrams() that extracts and displays the data.

```
    void WeatherStation::processPendingDatagrams()
    {
        QByteArray datagram;

        do {
            datagram.resize(udpSocket.pendingDatagramSize());
            udpSocket.readDatagram(datagram.data(), datagram.size());
        } while (udpSocket.hasPendingDatagrams());

        QDateTime dateTime;
        double temperature;
        double humidity;
        double altitude;

        QDataStream in(&datagram, QIODevice::ReadOnly);
        in.setVersion(QDataStream::Qt_4_1);
        in >> dateTime >> temperature >> humidity >> altitude;

        dateLineEdit->setText(dateTime.date().toString());
        timeLineEdit->setText(dateTime.time().toString());
        temperatureLineEdit->setText(tr("%1 °C").arg(temperature));
        humidityLineEdit->setText(tr("%1%").arg(humidity));
        altitudeLineEdit->setText(tr("%1 m").arg(altitude));
    }
```

The processPendingDatagrams() slot is called when a datagram has arrived. QUdpSocket queues the incoming datagrams and lets us access them one at a time. Normally, there should be only one datagram, but we can't exclude the possibility that the sender would send a few datagrams in a row before the readyRead() signal is emitted. In that case, we can ignore all the datagrams except the last one, since the earlier ones contain obsolete atmospheric conditions.

The pendingDatagramSize() function returns the size of the first pending datagram. From the application's point of view, datagrams are always sent and received as a single unit of data. This means that if any bytes are available, an entire datagram can be read. The readDatagram() call copies the contents of the first pending datagram into the specified char * buffer (truncating data if the buffer is too small) and advances to the next pending datagram. Once we have read all the datagrams, we decompose the last one (the one with the most recent atmospheric measurements) into its parts and populate the QLineEdits with the new data.

```
int main(int argc, char *argv[])
{
    QApplication app(argc, argv);
    WeatherStation station;
    station.show();
    return app.exec();
}
```

Finally, in main(), we create and show the WeatherStation.

We have now finished our UDP sender and receiver. The applications are as simple as possible, with the Weather Balloon sending datagrams and the Weather Station receiving them. In most real-world applications, both applications would need to both read and write on their socket. The QUdpSocket::writeDatagram() functions can be passed a host address and port number, so the QUdpSocket can read from the host and port it is bound to with bind(), and write to some other host and port.

15. XML

XML (Extensible Markup Language) is a general-purpose text file format that is popular for data interchange and data storage. Qt provides two distinct APIs for reading XML documents as part of the *QtXml* module:

- SAX (Simple API for XML) reports "parsing events" directly to the application through virtual functions.
- DOM (Document Object Model) converts an XML document into a tree structure, which the application can then navigate.

There are many factors to take into account when choosing between DOM and SAX for a particular application. SAX is more low level and usually faster, which makes it especially appropriate both for simple tasks (like finding all the occurrences of a given tag in an XML document) and for reading very large files that may not fit in memory. But for many applications, the convenience offered by DOM outweighs the potential speed and memory benefits of SAX.

For writing XML files, two options are available as well: We can generate the XML by hand, or we can represent the data as a DOM tree in memory and ask the tree to write itself to a file.

Reading XML with SAX

SAX is a public domain de facto standard API for reading XML documents. Qt's SAX classes are modeled after the SAX2 Java implementation, with some differences in naming to match the Qt conventions. For more information about SAX, see http://www.saxproject.org/.

Qt provides a SAX-based non-validating XML parser called QXmlSimpleReader. This parser recognizes well-formed XML and supports XML namespaces. When the parser goes through the document, it calls virtual functions in registered handler classes to indicate parsing events. (These "parsing events" are unrelated to Qt events, such as key and mouse events.) For example, let's assume the parser is analyzing the following XML document:

```
<doc>
    <quote>Ars longa vita brevis</quote>
</doc>
```

The parser would call the following parsing event handlers:

```
startDocument()
startElement("doc")
startElement("quote")
characters("Ars longa vita brevis")
endElement("quote")
endElement("doc")
endDocument()
```

The above functions are all declared in `QXmlContentHandler`. For simplicity, we omitted some of the arguments to `startElement()` and `endElement()`.

`QXmlContentHandler` is just one of many handler classes that can be used in conjunction with `QXmlSimpleReader`. The others are `QXmlEntityResolver`, `QXmlDTDHandler`, `QXmlErrorHandler`, `QXmlDeclHandler`, and `QXmlLexicalHandler`. These classes only declare pure virtual functions and give information about different kinds of parsing events. For most applications, `QXmlContentHandler` and `QXmlErrorHandler` are the only two that are needed.

For convenience, Qt also provides `QXmlDefaultHandler`, a class that inherits from all the handler classes and that provides trivial implementations for all the functions. This design, with many abstract handler classes and one trivial subclass, is unusual for Qt; it was adopted to closely follow the model Java implementation.

We will now review an example that shows how to use `QXmlSimpleReader` and `QXmlDefaultHandler` to parse an ad hoc XML file format and render its contents in a `QTreeWidget`. The `QXmlDefaultHandler` subclass is called `SaxHandler`, and the format it handles is that of a book index, with index entries and subentries.

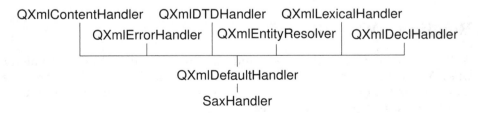

Figure 15.1. Inheritance tree for `SaxHandler`

Here's the book index file that is displayed in the `QTreeWidget` in Figure 15.2:

```
<?xml version="1.0"?>
<bookindex>
    <entry term="sidebearings">
        <page>10</page>
        <page>34-35</page>
```

```
            <page>307-308</page>
        </entry>
        <entry term="subtraction">
            <entry term="of pictures">
                <page>115</page>
                <page>244</page>
            </entry>
            <entry term="of vectors">
                <page>9</page>
            </entry>
        </entry>
    </bookindex>
```

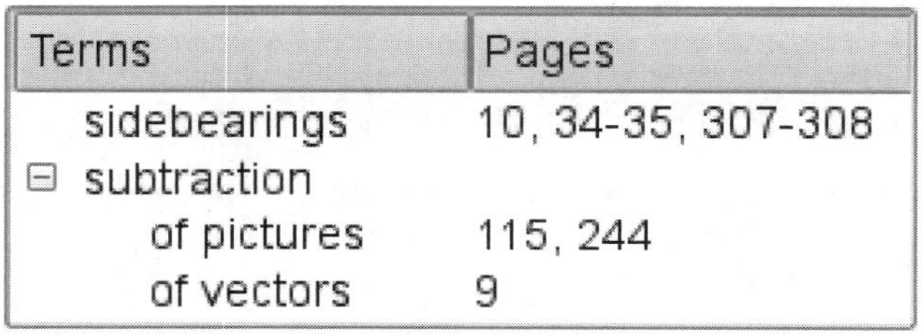

Terms	Pages
sidebearings	10, 34-35, 307-308
⊟ subtraction	
of pictures	115, 244
of vectors	9

Figure 15.2. A book index file displayed in a `QTreeWidget`

The first step to implement the parser is to subclass `QXmlDefaultHandler`:

```
class SaxHandler : public QXmlDefaultHandler
{
public:
    SaxHandler(QTreeWidget *tree);

    bool startElement(const QString &namespaceURI,
                      const QString &localName,
                      const QString &qName,
                      const QXmlAttributes &attributes);
    bool endElement(const QString &namespaceURI,
                    const QString &localName,
                    const QString &qName);
    bool characters(const QString &str);
    bool fatalError(const QXmlParseException &exception);

private:
    QTreeWidget *treeWidget;
    QTreeWidgetItem *currentItem;
    QString currentText;
};
```

The `SaxHandler` class inherits `QXmlDefaultHandler` and reimplements four functions: `startElement()`, `endElement()`, `characters()`, and `fatalError()`. The first three functions are declared in `QXmlContentHandler`; the last function is declared in `QXmlErrorHandler`.

```
SaxHandler::SaxHandler(QTreeWidget *tree)
{
```

```
        treeWidget = tree;
        currentItem = 0;
}
```

The `SaxHandler` constructor accepts the `QTreeWidget` we want to populate with the information stored in the XML file.

```
bool SaxHandler::startElement(const QString & /* namespaceURI */,
                             const QString & /* localName */,
                             const QString &qName,
                             const QXmlAttributes &attributes)
{
    if (qName == "entry") {
        if (currentItem) {
            currentItem = new QTreeWidgetItem(currentItem);
        } else {
            currentItem = new QTreeWidgetItem(treeWidget);
        }
        currentItem->setText(0, attributes.value("term"));
    } else if (qName == "page") {
        currentText.clear();
    }
    return true;
}
```

The `startElement()` function is called when the reader encounters a new opening tag. The third parameter is the tag's name (or more precisely, its "qualified name"). The fourth parameter is the list of attributes. In this example, we ignore the first and second parameters. They are useful for XML files that use XML's namespace mechanism, a subject that is discussed in detail in the reference documentation.

If the tag is ⟨entry⟩, we create a new `QTreeWidget` item. If the tag is nested within another ⟨entry⟩ tag, the new tag defines a subentry in the index, and the new `QTreeWidgetItem` is created as a child of the `QTreeWidgetItem` that represents the encompassing entry. Otherwise, we create the `QTreeWidgetItem` with `treeWidget` as its parent, making it a top-level item. We call `setText()` to set the text shown in column 0 to the value of the ⟨entry⟩ tag's `term` attribute.

If the tag is ⟨page⟩, we set the `currentText` to be an empty string. The currentText serves as an accumulator for the text located between the ⟨page⟩ and ⟨/page⟩ tags.

At the end, we return `true` to tell SAX to continue parsing the file. If we wanted to report unknown tags as errors, we would return `false` in those cases. We would then also reimplement `errorString()` from `QXmlDefaultHandler` to return an appropriate error message.

```
bool SaxHandler::characters(const QString &str)
{
    currentText += str;
    return true;
}
```

The `characters()` function is called to report character data in the XML document. We simply append the characters to the `currentText` variable.

```cpp
bool SaxHandler::endElement(const QString & /* namespaceURI */,
                            const QString & /* localName */,
                            const QString &qName)
{
    if (qName == "entry") {
        currentItem = currentItem->parent();
    } else if (qName == "page") {
        if (currentItem) {
            QString allPages = currentItem->text(1);
            if (!allPages.isEmpty())
                allPages += ", ";
            allPages += currentText;
            currentItem->setText(1, allPages);
        }
    }
    return true;
}
```

The `endElement()` function is called when the reader encounters a closing tag. Just as with `startElement()`, the third parameter is the name of the tag.

If the tag is `</entry>`, we update the `currentItem` private variable to point to the current `QTreeWidgetItem`'s parent. This ensures that the `currentItem` variable is restored to the value it held before the corresponding `<entry>` tag was read.

If the tag is `</page>`, we add the specified page number or page range to the comma-separated list in the current item's text in column 1.

```cpp
bool SaxHandler::fatalError(const QXmlParseException &exception)
{
    QMessageBox::warning(0, QObject::tr("SAX Handler"),
                         QObject::tr("Parse error at line %1, column "
                                     "%2:\n%3.")
                         .arg(exception.lineNumber())
                         .arg(exception.columnNumber())
                         .arg(exception.message()));
    return false;
}
```

The `fatalError()` function is called when the reader fails to parse the XML file. If this occurs, we simply display a message box, giving the line number, the column number, and the parser's error text.

This completes the implementation of the `SaxHandler` class. Now let's see how we can make use of it:

```cpp
bool parseFile(const QString &fileName)
{
    QStringList labels;
    labels << QObject::tr("Terms") << QObject::tr("Pages");

    QTreeWidget *treeWidget = new QTreeWidget;
```

```
        treeWidget->setHeaderLabels(labels);
        treeWidget->setWindowTitle(QObject::tr("SAX Handler"));
        treeWidget->show();

        QFile file(fileName);
        QXmlInputSource inputSource(&file);
        QXmlSimpleReader reader;
        SaxHandler handler(treeWidget);
        reader.setContentHandler(&handler);
        reader.setErrorHandler(&handler);
        return reader.parse(inputSource);
    }
```

We set up a QTreeWidget with two columns. Then we create a QFile object for the file that is to be read and a QXmlSimpleReader to parse the file. We don't need to open the QFile ourselves; QXmlInputSource does that automatically.

Finally, we create a SaxHandler object, we install it on the reader both as a content handler and as an error handler, and we call parse() on the reader to perform the parsing.

Instead of passing a simple file object to the parse() function, we pass a QXml-InputSource. This class opens the file it is given, reads it (taking into account any character encoding specified in the <?xml?> declaration), and provides an interface through which the parser reads the file.

In SaxHandler, we only reimplemented functions from the QXmlContentHandler and QXmlErrorHandler classes. If we had implemented functions from other handler classes, we would also have needed to call their corresponding setter functions on the reader.

To link the application against the *QtXml* library, we must add this line to the .pro file:

```
    QT              += xml
```

Reading XML with DOM

DOM is a standard API for parsing XML developed by the World Wide Web Consortium (W3C). Qt provides a non-validating DOM Level 2 implementation for reading, manipulating, and writing XML documents.

DOM represents an XML file as a tree in memory. We can navigate through the DOM tree as much as we want, and we can modify the tree and save it back to disk as an XML file.

Let's consider the following XML document:

```
    <doc>
        <quote>Ars longa vita brevis</quote>
        <translation>Art is long, life is short</translation>
    </doc>
```

It corresponds to the following DOM tree:

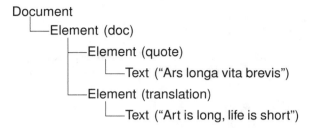

The DOM tree contains nodes of different types. For example, an `Element` node corresponds to an opening tag and its matching closing tag. The material that falls between the tags appears as child nodes of the `Element` node.

In Qt, the node types (like all other DOM-related classes) have a `QDom` prefix. Thus, `QDomElement` represents an `Element` node, and `QDomText` represents a `Text` node.

Different types of nodes can have different kinds of child nodes. For example, an `Element` node can contain other `Element` nodes, and also `EntityReference`, `Text`, `CDATASection`, `ProcessingInstruction`, and `Comment` nodes. Figure 15.3 shows which nodes can have which kinds of child nodes. The nodes shown in gray cannot have any child nodes of their own.

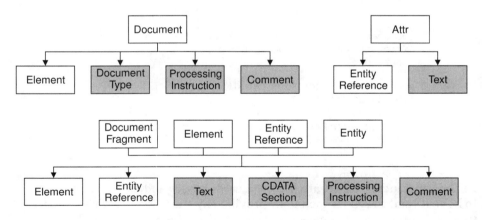

Figure 15.3. Parent–child relationships between DOM nodes

To illustrate how to use DOM for reading XML files, we will write a parser for the book index file format described in the previous section (p. 340).

```
class DomParser
{
public:
    DomParser(QIODevice *device, QTreeWidget *tree);

private:
```

```
        void parseEntry(const QDomElement &element,
                        QTreeWidgetItem *parent);

        QTreeWidget *treeWidget;
};
```

We define a class called DomParser that will parse a book index XML document and display the result in a QTreeWidget. This class does not inherit from any other class.

```
DomParser::DomParser(QIODevice *device, QTreeWidget *tree)
{
    treeWidget = tree;

    QString errorStr;
    int errorLine;
    int errorColumn;

    QDomDocument doc;
    if (!doc.setContent(device, true, &errorStr, &errorLine,
                        &errorColumn)) {
        QMessageBox::warning(0, QObject::tr("DOM Parser"),
                             QObject::tr("Parse error at line %1, "
                                         "column %2:\n%3")
                             .arg(errorLine)
                             .arg(errorColumn)
                             .arg(errorStr));
        return;
    }

    QDomElement root = doc.documentElement();
    if (root.tagName() != "bookindex")
        return;

    QDomNode node = root.firstChild();
    while (!node.isNull()) {
        if (node.toElement().tagName() == "entry")
            parseEntry(node.toElement(), 0);
        node = node.nextSibling();
    }
}
```

In the constructor, we create a QDomDocument object and call setContent() on it to have it read the XML document provided by the QIODevice. The setContent() function automatically opens the device if it isn't already open. Then we call documentElement() on the QDomDocument to obtain its single QDomElement child, and we check that it is a <bookindex> element. We iterate over all the child nodes, and if the node is an <entry> element, we call parseEntry() to parse it.

The QDomNode class can store any type of node. If we want to process a node further, we must first convert it to the right data type. In this example, we only care about Element nodes, so we call toElement() on the QDomNode to convert it to a QDomElement and then call tagName() to retrieve the element's tag name. If the node is *not* of type Element, the toElement() function returns a null QDomElement object, with an empty tag name.

```
    void DomParser::parseEntry(const QDomElement &element,
                               QTreeWidgetItem *parent)
{
    QTreeWidgetItem *item;
    if (parent) {
        item = new QTreeWidgetItem(parent);
    } else {
        item = new QTreeWidgetItem(treeWidget);
    }
    item->setText(0, element.attribute("term"));

    QDomNode node = element.firstChild();
    while (!node.isNull()) {
        if (node.toElement().tagName() == "entry") {
            parseEntry(node.toElement(), item);
        } else if (node.toElement().tagName() == "page") {
            QDomNode childNode = node.firstChild();
            while (!childNode.isNull()) {
                if (childNode.nodeType() == QDomNode::TextNode) {
                    QString page = childNode.toText().data();
                    QString allPages = item->text(1);
                    if (!allPages.isEmpty())
                        allPages += ", ";
                    allPages += page;
                    item->setText(1, allPages);
                    break;
                }
                childNode = childNode.nextSibling();
            }
        }
        node = node.nextSibling();
    }
}
```

In parseEntry(), we create a QTreeWidget item. If the tag is nested within another <entry> tag, the new tag defines a subentry in the index, and we create the QTreeWidgetItem as a child of the QTreeWidgetItem that represents the encompassing entry. Otherwise, we create the QTreeWidgetItem with treeWidget as its parent, making it a top-level item. We call setText() to set the text shown in column 0 to the value of the <entry> tag's term attribute.

Once we have initialized the QTreeWidgetItem, we iterate over the child nodes of the QDomElement node corresponding to the current <entry> tag.

If the element is <entry>, we call parseEntry() with the current item as the second argument. The new entry's QTreeWidgetItem will then be created with the encompassing entry's QTreeWidgetItem as its parent.

If the element is <page>, we navigate through the element's child list to find a Text node. Once we have found it, we call toText() to convert it to a QDomText object and data() to extract the text as a QString. Then we add the text to the comma-separated list of page numbers in column 1 of the QTreeWidgetItem.

Let's now see how we can use the DomParser class to parse a file:

```
void parseFile(const QString &fileName)
{
    QStringList labels;
    labels << QObject::tr("Terms") << QObject::tr("Pages");

    QTreeWidget *treeWidget = new QTreeWidget;
    treeWidget->setHeaderLabels(labels);
    treeWidget->setWindowTitle(QObject::tr("DOM Parser"));
    treeWidget->show();

    QFile file(fileName);
    DomParser(&file, treeWidget);
}
```

We start by setting up a QTreeWidget. Then we create a QFile and a DomParser. When the DomParser is constructed, it parses the file and populates the tree widget.

Like the previous example, we need the following line in the application's .pro file to link against the *QtXml* library:

```
QT            += xml
```

As the example illustrates, navigating through a DOM tree can be cumbersome. Simply extracting the text between <page> and </page> required us to iterate through a list of QDomNodes using firstChild() and nextSibling(). Programmers who use DOM a lot often write their own higher-level wrapper functions to simplify commonly needed operations, such as extracting the text between opening and closing tags.

Writing XML

There are basically two approaches for generating XML files from Qt applications:

- We can build a DOM tree and call save() on it.
- We can generate XML by hand.

The choice between these approaches is often independent of whether we use SAX or DOM for reading XML documents.

Here's a code snippet that illustrates how we can create a DOM tree and write it using a QTextStream:

```
const int Indent = 4;

QDomDocument doc;
QDomElement root = doc.createElement("doc");
QDomElement quote = doc.createElement("quote");
QDomElement translation = doc.createElement("translation");
QDomText latin = doc.createTextNode("Ars longa vita brevis");
QDomText english = doc.createTextNode("Art is long, life is short");
```

```
        doc.appendChild(root);
        root.appendChild(quote);
        root.appendChild(translation);
        quote.appendChild(latin);
        translation.appendChild(english);

        QTextStream out(&file);
        doc.save(out, Indent);
```

The second argument to save() is the indentation size to use. A non-zero value
makes the file easier for humans to read. Here's the XML file output:

```
<doc>
    <quote>Ars longa vita brevis</quote>
    <translation>Art is long, life is short</translation>
</doc>
```

Another scenario occurs in applications that use the DOM tree as their primary
data structure. These applications would normally read in XML documents
using DOM, then modify the DOM tree in memory, and finally call save() to
convert the tree back to XML.

By default, QDomDocument::save() uses UTF-8 as the encoding for the generated
file. We can use another encoding by prepending an XML declaration such as

```
<?xml version="1.0" encoding="ISO-8859-1"?>
```

to the DOM tree. The following code snippet shows how to do this:

```
QTextStream out(&file);
QDomNode xmlNode = doc.createProcessingInstruction("xml",
                        "version=\"1.0\" encoding=\"ISO-8859-1\"");
doc.insertBefore(xmlNode, doc.firstChild());
doc.save(out, Indent);
```

Generating XML files by hand isn't much harder than using DOM. We can use
QTextStream and write the strings as we would do with any other text file. The
most tricky part is to escape special characters in text and attribute values.
The Qt::escape() function escapes the characters '<', '>', and '&'. Here's some
code that makes use of it:

```
QTextStream out(&file);
out.setCodec("UTF-8");
out << "<doc>\n"
    << "    <quote>" << Qt::escape(quoteText) << "</quote>\n"
    << "    <translation>" << Qt::escape(translationText)
    << "</translation>\n"
    << "</doc>\n";
```

The *Qt Quarterly* article "Generating XML", available online at http://doc.
trolltech.com/qq/qq05-generating-xml.html, presents a very simple class that
makes it easy to generate XML files. The class takes care of the details such
as special characters, indentation, and encoding issues, leaving us free to
concentrate on the XML we want to generate. The class was designed to work
with Qt 3 but it is trivial to port to Qt 4.

- ◆ *Tooltips, Status Tips, and "What's This?" Help*
- ◆ *Using QTextBrowser as a Simple Help Engine*
- ◆ *Using Qt Assistant for Powerful Online Help*

16. Providing Online Help

Most applications provide their users with online help. Some help is short, such as tooltips, status tips, and "What's This?" help. Naturally, Qt supports all of these. Other help can be much more extensive, involving many pages of text. For this kind of help, you can use QTextBrowser as a simple online help browser, or you can invoke *Qt Assistant* or an HTML browser from your application.

Tooltips, Status Tips, and "What's This?" Help

A tooltip is a small piece of text that appears when the mouse hovers over a widget for a certain period of time. Tooltips are presented with black text on a yellow background. Their primary use is to provide textual descriptions of toolbar buttons.

We can add tooltips to arbitrary widgets in code using QWidget::setToolTip(). For example:

```
findButton->setToolTip(tr("Find next"));
```

To set the tooltip of a QAction that could be added to a menu or a toolbar, we can simply call setToolTip() on the action. For example:

```
newAction = new QAction(tr("&New"), this);
newAction->setToolTip(tr("New document"));
```

If we don't explicitly set a tooltip, QAction will automatically use the action text.

A status tip is also a short piece of descriptive text, usually a little longer than a tooltip. When the mouse hovers over a toolbar button or a menu option, a status tip appears in the status bar. Call setStatusTip() to add a status tip to an action or to a widget:

```
newAction->setStatusTip(tr("Create a new document"));
```

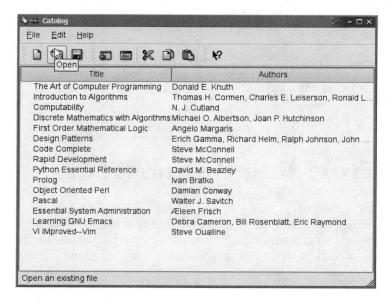

Figure 16.1. An application showing a tooltip and a status tip

In some situations, it is desirable to provide more information about a widget than can be given by tooltips or status tips. For example, we might want to provide a complex dialog with explanatory text about each field without forcing the user to invoke a separate help window. "What's This?" mode is an ideal solution for this. When a window is in "What's This?" mode, the cursor changes to ⟨?⟩ and the user can click on any user interface component to obtain its help text. To enter "What's This?" mode, the user can either click the ? button in the dialog's title bar (on Windows and KDE) or press Shift+F1.

Here is an example of a "What's This?" text set on a dialog:

```
dialog->setWhatsThis(tr("<img src=\":/images/icon.png\">"
                        " The meaning of the Source field depends "
                        "on the Type field:"
                        "<ul>"
                        "<li><b>Books</b> have a Publisher"
                        "<li><b>Articles</b> have a Journal name with "
                        "volume and issue number"
                        "<li><b>Theses</b> have an Institution name "
                        "and a Department name"
                        "</ul>"));
```

We can use HTML tags to format the text of a "What's This?" text. In the example, we include an image (which is listed in the application's resource file), a bulleted list, and some text in bold. The tags and attributes that Qt supports are specified at http://doc.trolltech.com/4.1/richtext-html-subset.html.

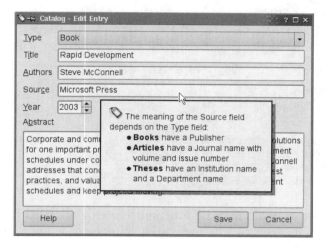

Figure 16.2. A dialog showing a "What's This?" help text

When we set a "What's This?" text on an action, the text will be shown when the user clicks the menu item or toolbar button or presses the shortcut key while in "What's This?" mode. When the user interface components of an application's main window provide "What's This?" text, it is customary to provide a What's This? option in the Help menu and a corresponding toolbar button. This can be done by creating a What's This? action with the static `QWhatsThis::createAction()` function and adding the action it returns to a Help menu and to a toolbar. The `QWhatsThis` class also provides static functions to programmatically enter and leave "What's This?" mode.

Using QTextBrowser as a Simple Help Engine

Large applications may require more online help than tooltips, status tips, and "What's This?" help can reasonably show. A simple solution to this is to provide a help browser. Applications that include a help browser typically have a Help entry in the main window's Help menu and a Help button in every dialog.

In this section, we present the simple help browser shown in Figure 16.3 and explain how it can be used within an application. The window uses a `QText-Browser` to display help pages that are marked up with an HTML-based syntax. `QTextBrowser` can handle a lot of HTML tags, so it is ideal for this purpose.

We begin with the header file:

```
#include <QWidget>

class QPushButton;
class QTextBrowser;

class HelpBrowser : public QWidget
{
    Q_OBJECT
```

```
public:
    HelpBrowser(const QString &path, const QString &page,
                QWidget *parent = 0);

    static void showPage(const QString &page);

private slots:
    void updateWindowTitle();

private:
    QTextBrowser *textBrowser;
    QPushButton *homeButton;
    QPushButton *backButton;
    QPushButton *closeButton;
};
```

The HelpBrowser provides a static function that can be called from anywhere
in the application. This function creates a HelpBrowser window and shows the
given page.

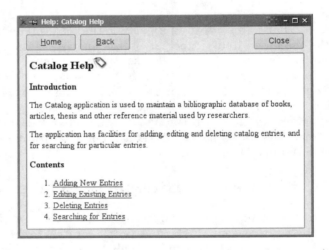

Figure 16.3. The HelpBrowser widget

Here's the beginning of the implementation:

```
#include <QtGui>

#include "helpbrowser.h"

HelpBrowser::HelpBrowser(const QString &path, const QString &page,
                        QWidget *parent)
    : QWidget(parent)
{
    setAttribute(Qt::WA_DeleteOnClose);
    setAttribute(Qt::WA_GroupLeader);

    textBrowser = new QTextBrowser;

    homeButton = new QPushButton(tr("&Home"));
```

```
    backButton = new QPushButton(tr("&Back"));
    closeButton = new QPushButton(tr("Close"));
    closeButton->setShortcut(tr("Esc"));

    QHBoxLayout *buttonLayout = new QHBoxLayout;
    buttonLayout->addWidget(homeButton);
    buttonLayout->addWidget(backButton);
    buttonLayout->addStretch();
    buttonLayout->addWidget(closeButton);

    QVBoxLayout *mainLayout = new QVBoxLayout;
    mainLayout->addLayout(buttonLayout);
    mainLayout->addWidget(textBrowser);
    setLayout(mainLayout);

    connect(homeButton, SIGNAL(clicked()), textBrowser, SLOT(home()));
    connect(backButton, SIGNAL(clicked()),
            textBrowser, SLOT(backward()));
    connect(closeButton, SIGNAL(clicked()), this, SLOT(close()));
    connect(textBrowser, SIGNAL(sourceChanged(const QUrl &)),
            this, SLOT(updateWindowTitle()));

    textBrowser->setSearchPaths(QStringList() << path << ":/images");
    textBrowser->setSource(page);
}
```

We set the `Qt::WA_GroupLeader` attribute because we want to pop up `HelpBrowser` windows from modal dialogs in addition to the main window. Modal dialogs normally prevent the user from interacting with any other window in the application. However, after requesting help, the user must obviously be allowed to interact with both the modal dialog and with the help browser. Setting the `Qt::WA_GroupLeader` attribute makes this interaction possible.

We provide two search paths, the first a path in the file system that contains the application's documentation, and the second the location of the image resources. The HTML can include references to images in the file system in the normal way and also references to image resources by using a path that begins with :/ (colon slash). The `page` parameter is the name of the documentation file, with an optional HTML anchor.

```
void HelpBrowser::updateWindowTitle()
{
    setWindowTitle(tr("Help: %1").arg(textBrowser->documentTitle()));
}
```

Whenever the source page changes, the `updateWindowTitle()` slot is called. The `documentTitle()` function returns the text specified in the page's `<title>` tag.

```
void HelpBrowser::showPage(const QString &page)
{
    QString path = QApplication::applicationDirPath() + "/doc";
    HelpBrowser *browser = new HelpBrowser(path, page);
    browser->resize(500, 400);
    browser->show();
}
```

In the `showPage()` static function, we create the `HelpBrowser` window and then show it. The window will be destroyed automatically when the user closes it, since we set the `Qt::WA_DeleteOnClose` attribute in the `HelpBrowser` constructor.

For this example, we assume that the documentation is located in the `doc` subdirectory of the directory containing the application's executable. All the pages passed to the `showPage()` function will be taken from this subdirectory.

Now we are ready to invoke the help browser from the application. In the application's main window, we would create a `Help` action and connect it to a `help()` slot that could look like this:

```
void MainWindow::help()
{
    HelpBrowser::showPage("index.html");
}
```

This assumes that the main help file is called `index.html`. For dialogs, we would connect the `Help` button to a `help()` slot that might look like this:

```
void EntryDialog::help()
{
    HelpBrowser::showPage("forms.html#editing");
}
```

Here we look in a different help file, `forms.html`, and scroll the `QTextBrowser` to the `editing` anchor.

Using Qt Assistant for Powerful Online Help

Qt Assistant is a redistributable online help application supplied by Trolltech. Its main virtues are that it supports indexing and full text search and that it can handle documentation sets for multiple applications.

To make use of *Qt Assistant*, we must incorporate the necessary code in our application, and we must make *Qt Assistant* aware of our documentation.

Communication between a Qt application and *Qt Assistant* is handled by the `QAssistantClient` class, which is located in a separate library. To link this library with an application, we must add the following line to the application's `.pro` file:

```
CONFIG      += assistant
```

We will now review the code of a new `HelpBrowser` class that uses *Qt Assistant*.

```
#ifndef HELPBROWSER_H
#define HELPBROWSER_H

class QAssistantClient;
class QString;

class HelpBrowser
{
```

```
public:
    static void showPage(const QString &page);

private:
    static QAssistantClient *assistant;
};

#endif
```

Here's the new `helpbrowser.cpp` file:

```
#include <QApplication>
#include <QAssistantClient>

#include "helpbrowser.h"

QAssistantClient *HelpBrowser::assistant = 0;

void HelpBrowser::showPage(const QString &page)
{
    QString path = QApplication::applicationDirPath() + "/doc/" + page;
    if (!assistant)
        assistant = new QAssistantClient("");
    assistant->showPage(path);
}
```

The `QAssistantClient` constructor accepts a path string as its first argument, which it uses to locate the *Qt Assistant* executable. By passing an empty path, we signify that `QAssistantClient` should look for the executable in the PATH environment variable. `QAssistantClient` has a `showPage()` function that accepts a page name with an optional HTML anchor.

The next step is to prepare a table of contents and an index for the documentation. This is done by creating a *Qt Assistant* profile and writing a `.dcf` file that provides information about the documentation. All this is explained in *Qt Assistant*'s online documentation, so we will not duplicate that information here.

An alternative to using `QTextBrowser` or *Qt Assistant* is to use platform-specific approaches to providing online help. For Windows applications, it might be desirable to create Windows HTML Help files and to provide access to them using Microsoft Internet Explorer. You could use Qt's `QProcess` class or the ActiveQt framework for this. For X11 applications, a suitable approach might be to provide HTML files and to launch a web browser using `QProcess`. On Mac OS X, Apple Help provides similar functionality to *Qt Assistant*.

We have now reached the end of Part II. The chapters that follow in Part III cover more advanced and specialized features of Qt. The C++ and Qt coding they present are no more difficult than that seen in Part II, but some of the concepts and ideas may be more challenging in those areas that are new to you.

Part III

Advanced Qt

17. Internationalization

In addition to the Latin alphabet used for English and for many European languages, Qt 4 also provides extensive support for the rest of the world's writing systems:

- Qt uses Unicode throughout the API and internally. No matter what language we use for the user interface, the application can support all users alike.

- Qt's text engine can handle all the major non-Latin writing systems, including Arabic, Chinese, Cyrillic, Hebrew, Japanese, Korean, Thai, and the Indic languages.

- Qt's layout engine supports right-to-left layouts for languages such as Arabic and Hebrew.

- Certain languages require special input methods for entering text. Editor widgets such as QLineEdit and QTextEdit work well with any input method installed on the user's system.

Often, it isn't enough to allow users to enter text in their native language; the entire user interface's must be translated as well. Qt makes this easy: Simply wrap all user-visible strings with the tr() function (as we have done in earlier chapters) and use Qt's supporting tools to prepare translation files in the required languages. Qt provides a GUI tool called *Qt Linguist* for use by translators. *Qt Linguist* is complemented by two command-line programs, lupdate and lrelease, which are typically run by the application's developers.

For most applications, a translation file is loaded at startup, based on the user's locale settings. But in a few cases, it is also necessary for users to be able to switch language at run-time. This is perfectly possible with Qt, although it does require a bit of extra work. And thanks to Qt's layout system, the various user interface components will automatically adjust to make room for the translated texts when they are longer than the original texts.

Working with Unicode

Unicode is a character encoding standard that supports most of the world's writing systems. The original idea behind Unicode is that by using 16 bits for storing characters instead of 8 bits, it would be possible to encode around 65,000 characters instead of only 256.* Unicode contains ASCII and ISO 8859-1 (Latin-1) as subsets at the same code positions. For example, the character 'A' has value 0x41 in ASCII, Latin-1, and Unicode, and the character 'Ñ' has value 0xD1 in both Latin-1 and Unicode.

Qt's QString class stores strings as Unicode. Each character in a QString is a 16-bit QChar rather than an 8-bit char. Here are two ways of setting the first character of a string to 'A':

```
str[0] = 'A';
str[0] = QChar(0x41);
```

If the source file is encoded in Latin-1, specifying Latin-1 characters is just as easy:

```
str[0] = 'Ñ';
```

And if the source file has another encoding, the numeric value works fine:

```
str[0] = QChar(0xD1);
```

We can specify any Unicode character by its numeric value. For example, here's how to specify the Greek capital letter sigma ('Σ') and the euro currency symbol ('€'):

```
str[0] = QChar(0x3A3);
str[0] = QChar(0x20AC);
```

The numeric values of all the characters supported by Unicode are listed at http://www.unicode.org/standard/. If you rarely need non-Latin-1 Unicode characters, looking up characters online is sufficient; but Qt provides more convenient ways of entering Unicode strings in a Qt program, as we will see later in this section.

Qt 4's text engine supports the following writing systems on all platforms: Arabic, Chinese, Cyrillic, Greek, Hebrew, Japanese, Korean, Lao, Latin, Thai, and Vietnamese. It also supports all the Unicode 4.1 scripts that don't require any special processing. In addition, the following writing systems are supported on X11 with Fontconfig and on recent versions of Windows: Bengali, Devanagari, Gujarati, Gurmukhi, Kannada, Khmer, Malayalam, Syriac, Tamil, Telugu, Thaana (Dhivehi), and Tibetan. Finally, Oriya is supported on X11, and Mongolian and Sinhala are supported on Windows XP. Assuming that the proper fonts are installed on the system, Qt can render text using any of these writing

---

*Recent versions of the Unicode standard assign character values above 65,535. These characters can be represented using sequences of two 16-bit values called "surrogate pairs".

systems. And assuming that the proper input methods are installed, users will be able to enter text that uses these writing systems in their Qt applications.

Programming with QChar is slightly different from programming with char. To obtain the numeric value of a QChar, call unicode() on it. To obtain the ASCII or Latin-1 value of a QChar (as a char), call toLatin1(). For non-Latin-1 characters, toLatin1() returns '\0'.

If we know that all the strings in a program are ASCII, we can use standard <cctype> functions like isalpha(), isdigit(), and isspace() on the return value of toLatin1(). However, it is generally better to use QChar's member functions for performing these operations, since they will work for any Unicode character. The functions QChar provides include isPrint(), isPunct(), isSpace(), isMark(), isLetter(), isNumber(), isLetterOrNumber(), isDigit(), isSymbol(), isLower(), and isUpper(). For example, here's one way to test that a character is a digit or an uppercase letter:

```
if (ch.isDigit() || ch.isUpper())
    ...
```

The code snippet works for any alphabet that distinguishes between uppercase and lowercase, including Latin, Greek, and Cyrillic.

Once we have a Unicode string, we can use it anywhere in Qt's API where a QString is expected. It is then Qt's responsibility to display it properly and to convert it to the relevant encodings when talking to the operating system.

Special care is needed when we read and write text files. Text files can use a variety of encodings, and it is often impossible to guess a text file's encoding from its contents. By default, QTextStream uses the system's local 8-bit encoding (available as QTextCodec::codecForLocale()) for both reading and writing. For American and West European locales, this usually means Latin-1.

If we design our own file format and want to be able to read and write arbitrary Unicode characters, we can save the data as Unicode by calling

```
stream.setCodec("UTF-16");
stream.setGenerateByteOrderMark(true);
```

before we start writing to the QTextStream. The data will then be saved in UTF-16, a format that requires two bytes per character, and will be prefixed with a special 16-bit value (the Unicode byte order mark, 0xFFFE) identifying that the file is in Unicode and whether the bytes are in little-endian or big-endian order. The UTF-16 format is identical to the memory representation of a QString, so reading and writing Unicode strings in UTF-16 can be very fast. However, there is an inherent overhead when saving pure ASCII data in UTF-16 format, since it stores two bytes for every character instead of just one.

Other encodings can be specified by calling setCodec() with an appropriate QTextCodec. A QTextCodec is an object that converts between Unicode and a given encoding. QTextCodecs are used in a variety of contexts by Qt. Internally, they are used to support fonts, input methods, the clipboard, drag and drop, and file names. But they are also available to us when we write Qt applications.

When reading a text file, `QTextStream` detects Unicode automatically if the file starts with the byte order mark. This behavior can be turned off by calling `setAutoDetectUnicode(false)`. If the data can't be assumed to start with the byte order mark, it is best to call `setCodec()` with "UTF-16" before reading.

Another encoding that supports the whole of Unicode is UTF-8. Its main advantage over UTF-16 is that it is a superset of ASCII. Any character in the range `0x00` to `0x7F` is represented as a single byte. Other characters, including Latin-1 characters above `0x7F`, are represented by multi-byte sequences. For text that is mostly ASCII, UTF-8 takes up about half the space consumed by UTF-16. To use UTF-8 with `QTextStream`, call `setCodec()` with "UTF-8" as the codec name before reading and writing.

If we always want to read and write Latin-1 regardless of the user's locale, we can set the "ISO 8859-1" codec on the `QTextStream`. For example:

```
QTextStream in(&file);
in.setCodec("ISO 8859-1");
```

Some file formats specify their encoding in their header. The header is typically plain ASCII to ensure that it is read correctly no matter what encoding is used (assuming that it is a superset of ASCII). The XML file format is an interesting example of this. XML files are normally encoded as UTF-8 or UTF-16. The proper way to read them in is to call `setCodec()` with "UTF-8". If the format is UTF-16, `QTextStream` will automatically detect this and adjust itself. The `<?xml?>` header of an XML file sometimes contains an `encoding` argument, for example:

```
<?xml version="1.0" encoding="EUC-KR"?>
```

Since `QTextStream` doesn't allow us to change the encoding once it has started reading, the right way to respect an explicit encoding is to start reading the file afresh, using the correct codec (obtained from `QTextCodec::codecForName()`). In the case of XML, we can avoid having to handle the encoding ourselves by using Qt's XML classes, described in Chapter 15.

Another use of `QTextCodec`s is to specify the encoding of strings that occur in the source code. Let's consider for example a team of Japanese programmers who are writing an application targeted primarily at Japan's home market. These programmers are likely to write their source code in a text editor that uses an encoding such as EUC-JP or Shift-JIS. Such an editor allows them to type in Japanese characters seamlessly, so that they can write code like this:

```
QPushButton *button = new QPushButton(tr("日諾"));
```

By default, Qt interprets arguments to `tr()` as Latin-1. To change this, call the `QTextCodec::setCodecForTr()` static function. For example:

```
QTextCodec::setCodecForTr(QTextCodec::codecForName("EUC-JP"));
```

This must be done before the first call to tr(). Typically, we would do this in main(), immediately after the QApplication object is created.

Other strings specified in the program will still be interpreted as Latin-1 strings. If the programmers want to enter Japanese characters in those as well, they can explicitly convert them to Unicode using a QTextCodec:

```
QString text = japaneseCodec->toUnicode("海鮮料理");
```

Alternatively, they can tell Qt to use a specific codec when converting between const char * and QString by calling QTextCodec::setCodecForCStrings():

```
QTextCodec::setCodecForCStrings(QTextCodec::codecForName("EUC-JP"));
```

The techniques described above can be applied to any non-Latin-1 language, including Chinese, Greek, Korean, and Russian.

Here's a list of the encodings supported by Qt 4:

- Apple Roman
- Big5
- Big5-HKSCS
- EUC-JP
- EUC-KR
- GB18030-0
- IBM 850
- IBM 866
- IBM 874
- ISO 2022-JP
- ISO 8859-1
- ISO 8859-2
- ISO 8859-3
- ISO 8859-4

- ISO 8859-5
- ISO 8859-6
- ISO 8859-7
- ISO 8859-8
- ISO 8859-9
- ISO 8859-10
- ISO 8859-13
- ISO 8859-14
- ISO 8859-15
- ISO 8859-16
- Iscii-Bng
- Iscii-Dev
- Iscii-Gjr
- Iscii-Knd

- Iscii-Mlm
- Iscii-Ori
- Iscii-Pnj
- Iscii-Tlg
- Iscii-Tml
- JIS X 0201
- JIS X 0208
- KOI8-R
- KOI8-U
- MuleLao-1
- ROMAN8
- Shift-JIS
- TIS-620
- TSCII

- UTF-8
- UTF-16
- UTF-16BE
- UTF-16LE
- Windows-1250
- Windows-1251
- Windows-1252
- Windows-1253
- Windows-1254
- Windows-1255
- Windows-1256
- Windows-1257
- Windows-1258
- WINSAMI2

For all of these, QTextCodec::codecForName() will always return a valid pointer. Other encodings can be supported by subclassing QTextCodec.

Making Applications Translation-Aware

If we want to make our applications available in multiple languages, we must do two things:

- Make sure that every user-visible string goes through tr().
- Load a translation (.qm) file at startup.

Neither of these is necessary for applications that will never be translated. However, using tr() requires almost no effort and leaves the door open for doing translations at a later date.

The tr() function is a static function defined in QObject and overridden in every subclass defined with the Q_OBJECT macro. When writing code inside a QObject subclass, we can call tr() without formality. A call to tr() returns a translation if one is available; otherwise, the original text is returned.

To prepare translation files, we must run Qt's lupdate tool. This tool extracts all the string literals that appear in tr() calls and produces translation files that contain all of these strings ready to be translated. The files can then be sent to a translator to have the translations added. This process is explained in the "Translating Applications" section later in this chapter.

A tr() call has the following general syntax:

```
Context::tr(sourceText, comment)
```

The Context part is the name of a QObject subclass defined with the Q_OBJECT macro. We don't need to specify it if we call tr() from a member function of the class in question. The sourceText part is the string literal that needs to be translated. The comment part is optional; it can be used to provide additional information to the translator.

Here are a few examples:

```
RockyWidget::RockyWidget(QWidget *parent)
    : QWidget(parent)
{
    QString str1 = tr("Letter");
    QString str2 = RockyWidget::tr("Letter");
    QString str3 = SnazzyDialog::tr("Letter");
    QString str4 = SnazzyDialog::tr("Letter", "US paper size");
}
```

The first two calls to tr() have "RockyWidget" as context, and the last two calls have "SnazzyDialog". All four have "Letter" as source text. The last call also has a comment to help the translator understand the meaning of the source text.

Strings in different contexts (classes) are translated independently of each other. Translators typically work on one context at a time, often with the application running and showing the widget or dialog being translated.

When we call tr() from a global function, we must specify the context explicitly. Any QObject subclass in the application can be used as the context. If none is appropriate, we can always use QObject itself. For example:

```
int main(int argc, char *argv[])
{
    QApplication app(argc, argv);
    ...
    QPushButton button(QObject::tr("Hello Qt!"));
    button.show();
    return app.exec();
}
```

In every example so far, the context has been a class name. This is convenient, because we can almost always omit it, but this doesn't have to be the case. The most general way of translating a string in Qt is to use the `QApplication::translate()` function, which accepts up to three arguments: the context, the source text, and the optional comment. For example, here's another way to translate "Hello Qt!":

```
QApplication::translate("Global Stuff", "Hello Qt!")
```

This time, we put the text in the "Global Stuff" context.

The `tr()` and `translate()` functions serve a dual purpose: They are markers that lupdate uses to find user-visible strings, and at the same time they are C++ functions that translate text. This has an impact on how we write code. For example, the following will not work:

```
// WRONG
const char *appName = "OpenDrawer 2D";
QString translated = tr(appName);
```

The problem here is that lupdate will not be able to extract the "OpenDrawer 2D" string literal, as it doesn't appear inside a `tr()` call. This means that the translator will not have the opportunity to translate the string. This issue often arises in conjunction with dynamic strings:

```
// WRONG
statusBar()->showMessage(tr("Host " + hostName + " found"));
```

Here, the string we pass to `tr()` varies depending on the value of `hostName`, so we can't reasonably expect `tr()` to translate it correctly.

The solution is to use `QString::arg()`:

```
statusBar()->showMessage(tr("Host %1 found").arg(hostName));
```

Notice how it works: The string literal "Host %1 found" is passed to `tr()`. Assuming that a French translation file is loaded, `tr()` would return something like "Hôte %1 trouvé". Then the "%1" parameter is replaced with the contents of the `hostName` variable.

Although it is generally inadvisable to call `tr()` on a variable, it can be made to work. We must use the `QT_TR_NOOP()` macro to mark the string literals for translation before we assign them to a variable. This is mostly useful for static arrays of strings. For example:

```
void OrderForm::init()
{
    static const char * const flowers[] = {
        QT_TR_NOOP("Medium Stem Pink Roses"),
        QT_TR_NOOP("One Dozen Boxed Roses"),
        QT_TR_NOOP("Calypso Orchid"),
        QT_TR_NOOP("Dried Red Rose Bouquet"),
        QT_TR_NOOP("Mixed Peonies Bouquet"),
        0
```

```
    };

    for (int i = 0; flowers[i]; ++i)
        comboBox->addItem(tr(flowers[i]));
}
```

The QT_TR_NOOP() macro simply returns its argument. But lupdate will extract all the strings wrapped in QT_TR_NOOP() so that they can be translated. When using the variable later on, we call tr() to perform the translation as usual. Even though we have passed tr() a variable, the translation will still work.

There is also a QT_TRANSLATE_NOOP() macro that works like QT_TR_NOOP() but also takes a context. This macro is useful when initializing variables outside of a class:

```
    static const char * const flowers[] = {
        QT_TRANSLATE_NOOP("OrderForm", "Medium Stem Pink Roses"),
        QT_TRANSLATE_NOOP("OrderForm", "One Dozen Boxed Roses"),
        QT_TRANSLATE_NOOP("OrderForm", "Calypso Orchid"),
        QT_TRANSLATE_NOOP("OrderForm", "Dried Red Rose Bouquet"),
        QT_TRANSLATE_NOOP("OrderForm", "Mixed Peonies Bouquet"),
        0
    };
```

The context argument must be the same as the context given to tr() or translate() later on.

When we start using tr() in an application, it's easy to forget to surround some user-visible strings with a tr() call, especially when we are just beginning to use it. These missing tr() calls are eventually discovered by the translator or, worse, by users of the translated application, when some strings appear in the original language. To avoid this problem, we can tell Qt to forbid implicit conversions from const char * to QString. We do this by defining the QT_NO_CAST_FROM_ASCII preprocessor symbol before including any Qt header. The easiest way to ensure this symbol is set is to add the following line to the application's .pro file:

```
    DEFINES      += QT_NO_CAST_FROM_ASCII
```

This will force every string literal to require wrapping by tr() or by QLatin1String(), depending on whether it should be translated or not. Strings that are not suitably wrapped will produce a compile-time error, thereby compelling us to add the missing tr() or QLatin1String() call.

Once we have wrapped every user-visible string by a tr() call, the only thing left to do to enable translation is to load a translation file. Typically, we would do this in the application's main() function. For example, here's how we would try to load a translation file depending on the user's locale:

```
    int main(int argc, char *argv[])
    {
        QApplication app(argc, argv);
        QTranslator appTranslator;
```

```
        appTranslator.load("myapp_" + QLocale::system().name(),
                           qApp->applicationDirPath());
        app.installTranslator(&appTranslator);
        ...
        return app.exec();
}
```

The `QLocale::system()` function returns a `QLocale` object that provides information about the user's locale. Conventionally, we use the locale's name as part of the `.qm` file name. Locale names can be more or less precise; for example, `fr` specifies a French-language locale, `fr_CA` specifies a French Canadian locale, and `fr_CA.ISO8859-15` specifies a French Canadian locale with ISO 8859-15 encoding (an encoding that supports '€', 'Œ', 'œ', and 'Ÿ').

Assuming that the locale is `fr_CA.ISO8859-15`, the `QTranslator::load()` function first tries to load the file `myapp_fr_CA.ISO8859-15.qm`. If this file does not exist, `load()` next tries `myapp_fr_CA.qm`, then `myapp_fr.qm`, and finally `myapp.qm`, before giving up. Normally, we would only provide `myapp_fr.qm`, containing a standard French translation, but if we need a different file for French-speaking Canada, we can also provide `myapp_fr_CA.qm` and it will be used for `fr_CA` locales.

The second argument to `QTranslator::load()` is the directory where we want `load()` to look for the translation file. In this case, we assume that the translation files are located in the same directory as the executable.

The Qt libraries contain a few strings that need to be translated. Trolltech provides French, German, and Simplified Chinese translations in Qt's translations directory. A few other languages are provided as well, but these are contributed by Qt users and are not officially supported. The Qt libraries' translation file should also be loaded:

```
QTranslator qtTranslator;
qtTranslator.load("qt_" + QLocale::system().name(),
                  qApp->applicationDirPath());
app.installTranslator(&qtTranslator);
```

A `QTranslator` object can only hold one translation file at a time, so we use a separate `QTranslator` for Qt's translation. Having just one file per translator is not a problem since we can install as many translators as we need. `QApplication` will use all of them when searching for a translation.

Some languages, such as Arabic and Hebrew, are written right-to-left instead of left-to-right. In those languages, the whole layout of the application must be reversed, and this is done by calling `QApplication::setLayoutDirection(Qt::RightToLeft)`. The translation files for Qt contain a special marker called "LTR" that tells Qt whether the language is left-to-right or right-to-left, so we normally don't need to call `setLayoutDirection()` ourselves.

It may prove more convenient for our users if we supply our applications with the translation files embedded in the executable, using Qt's resource system. Not only does this reduce the number of files distributed as part of the product, it also avoids the risk of translation files getting lost or deleted by accident.

Assuming that the .qm files are located in a translations subdirectory in the source tree, we would then have a myapp.qrc file with the following contents:

```
<!DOCTYPE RCC><RCC version="1.0">
<qresource>
    <file>translations/myapp_de.qm</file>
    <file>translations/myapp_fr.qm</file>
    <file>translations/myapp_zh.qm</file>
    <file>translations/qt_de.qm</file>
    <file>translations/qt_fr.qm</file>
    <file>translations/qt_zh.qm</file>
</qresource>
</RCC>
```

The .pro file would contain the following entry:

```
RESOURCES     = myapp.qrc
```

Finally, in main(), we must specify :/translations as the path for the translation files. The leading colon indicates that the path refers to a resource as opposed to a file in the file system.

We have now covered all that is required to make an application able to operate using translations into other languages. But language and the direction of the writing system are not the only things that vary between countries and cultures. An internationalized program must also take into account the local date and time formats, monetary formats, numeric formats, and string collation order. Qt includes a QLocale class that provides localized numeric and date/time formats. To query other locale-specific information, we can use the standard C++ setlocale() and localeconv() functions.

Some Qt classes and functions adapt their behavior to the locale:

• QString::localeAwareCompare() compares two strings in a locale-dependent manner. It is useful for sorting user-visible items.

• The toString() function provided by QDate, QTime, and QDateTime returns a string in a local format when called with Qt::LocalDate as argument.

• By default, the QDateEdit and QDateTimeEdit widgets present dates in the local format.

Finally, a translated application may need to use different icons in certain situations rather than the original icons. For example, the left and right arrows on a web browser's Back and Forward buttons should be swapped when dealing with a right-to-left language. We can do this as follows:

```
if (QApplication::isRightToLeft()) {
    backAction->setIcon(forwardIcon);
    forwardAction->setIcon(backIcon);
} else {
    backAction->setIcon(backIcon);
    forwardAction->setIcon(forwardIcon);
}
```

Icons that contain alphabetic characters very commonly need to be translated. For example, the letter 'I' on a toolbar button associated with a word processor's Italic option should be replaced by a 'C' in Spanish (Cursivo) and by a 'K' in Danish, Dutch, German, Norwegian, and Swedish (Kursiv). Here's a simple way to do it:

```
if (tr("Italic")[0] == 'C') {
    italicAction->setIcon(iconC);
} else if (tr("Italic")[0] == 'K') {
    italicAction->setIcon(iconK);
} else {
    italicAction->setIcon(iconI);
}
```

An alternative is to use the resource system's support for multiple locales. In the .qrc file, we can specify a locale for a resource using the lang attribute. For example:

```
<qresource>
    <file>italic.png</file>
</qresource>
<qresource lang="es">
    <file alias="italic.png">cursivo.png</file>
</qresource>
<qresource lang="sv">
    <file alias="italic.png">kursiv.png</file>
</qresource>
```

If the user's locale is es (Español), :/italic.png becomes a reference to the cursivo.png image. If the locale is sv (Svenska), the kursiv.png image is used. For other locales, italic.png is used.

Dynamic Language Switching

For most applications, detecting the user's preferred language in main() and loading the appropriate .qm files there is perfectly satisfactory. But there are some situations where users might need the ability to switch language dynamically. An application that is used continuously by different people in shifts may need to change language without having to be restarted. For example, applications used by call center operators, by simultaneous translators, and by computerized cash register operators often require this capability.

Making an application able to switch language dynamically requires a little more work than loading a single translation at startup, but it is not difficult. Here's what must be done:

- Provide a means by which the user can switch language.

- For every widget or dialog, set all of its translatable strings in a separate function (often called retranslateUi()) and call this function when the language changes.

Let's review the relevant parts of a "call center" application's source code. The application provides a Language menu to allow the user to set the language at run-time. The default language is English.

Figure 17.1. A dynamic Language menu

Since we don't know which language the user will want to use when the application is started, we no longer load translations in the main() function. Instead, we will load them dynamically when they are needed, so all the code that we need to handle translations must go in the main window and dialog classes.

Let's have a look at the application's QMainWindow subclass.

```
MainWindow::MainWindow()
{
    journalView = new JournalView;
    setCentralWidget(journalView);

    qApp->installTranslator(&appTranslator);
    qApp->installTranslator(&qtTranslator);
    qmPath = qApp->applicationDirPath() + "/translations";

    createActions();
    createMenus();

    retranslateUi();
}
```

In the constructor, we set the central widget to be a JournalView, a QTableWidget subclass. Then we set up a few private member variables related to translation:

- The appTranslator variable is a QTranslator object used for storing the current application's translation.

- The qtTranslator variable is a QTranslator object used for storing Qt's translation.

- The qmPath variable is a QString that specifies the path of the directory that contains the application's translation files.

At the end, we call the createActions() and createMenus() private functions to create the menu system, and we call retranslateUi(), also a private function, to set the user-visible strings for the first time.

```
void MainWindow::createActions()
{
    newAction = new QAction(this);
    connect(newAction, SIGNAL(triggered()), this, SLOT(newFile()));
    ...
    aboutQtAction = new QAction(this);
    connect(aboutQtAction, SIGNAL(triggered()), qApp, SLOT(aboutQt()));
}
```

The createActions() function creates the QAction objects as usual, but without setting any of the texts or shortcut keys. These will be done in retranslate-Ui().

```
void MainWindow::createMenus()
{
    fileMenu = new QMenu(this);
    fileMenu->addAction(newAction);
    fileMenu->addAction(openAction);
    fileMenu->addAction(saveAction);
    fileMenu->addAction(exitAction);
    ...
    createLanguageMenu();

    helpMenu = new QMenu(this);
    helpMenu->addAction(aboutAction);
    helpMenu->addAction(aboutQtAction);

    menuBar()->addMenu(fileMenu);
    menuBar()->addMenu(editMenu);
    menuBar()->addMenu(reportsMenu);
    menuBar()->addMenu(languageMenu);
    menuBar()->addMenu(helpMenu);
}
```

The createMenus() function creates menus, but does not give them any titles. Again, this will be done in retranslateUi().

In the middle of the function, we call createLanguageMenu() to fill the Language menu with the list of supported languages. We will review its source code in a moment. First, let's look at retranslateUi():

```
void MainWindow::retranslateUi()
{
    newAction->setText(tr("&New"));
    newAction->setShortcut(tr("Ctrl+N"));
    newAction->setStatusTip(tr("Create a new journal"));
    ...
    aboutQtAction->setText(tr("About &Qt"));
    aboutQtAction->setStatusTip(tr("Show the Qt library's About box"));

    fileMenu->setTitle(tr("&File"));
    editMenu->setTitle(tr("&Edit"));
    reportsMenu->setTitle(tr("&Reports"));
    languageMenu->setTitle(tr("&Language"));
    helpMenu->setTitle(tr("&Help"));
```

```
        setWindowTitle(tr("Call Center"));
    }
```

The `retranslateUi()` function is where all the `tr()` calls for the `MainWindow` class occur. It is called at the end of the `MainWindow` constructor and also every time a user changes the application's language using the Language menu.

We set each `QAction`'s text, shortcut key, and status tip. We also set each `QMenu`'s title, as well as the window title.

The `createMenus()` function presented earlier called `createLanguageMenu()` to populate the Language menu with a list of languages:

```
    void MainWindow::createLanguageMenu()
    {
        languageMenu = new QMenu(this);

        languageActionGroup = new QActionGroup(this);
        connect(languageActionGroup, SIGNAL(triggered(QAction *)),
                this, SLOT(switchLanguage(QAction *)));

        QDir dir(qmPath);
        QStringList fileNames =
                dir.entryList(QStringList("callcenter_*.qm"));

        for (int i = 0; i < fileNames.size(); ++i) {
            QString locale = fileNames[i];
            locale.remove(0, locale.indexOf('_') + 1);
            locale.truncate(locale.lastIndexOf('.'));

            QTranslator translator;
            translator.load(fileNames[i], qmPath);
            QString language = translator.translate("MainWindow",
                                                    "English");

            QAction *action = new QAction(tr("&%1 %2")
                                          .arg(i + 1).arg(language), this);
            action->setCheckable(true);
            action->setData(locale);

            languageMenu->addAction(action);
            languageActionGroup->addAction(action);

            if (language == "English")
                action->setChecked(true);
        }
    }
```

Instead of hard-coding the languages supported by the application, we create one menu entry for each `.qm` file located in the application's `translations` directory. For simplicity, we assume that English also has a `.qm` file. An alternative would have been to call `clear()` on the `QTranslator` objects when the user chooses English.

One particular difficulty is to present a nice name for the language provided by each `.qm` file. Just showing "en" for "English" or "de" for "Deutsch", based on the name of the `.qm` file, looks crude and will confuse some users. The solution used in `createLanguageMenu()` is to check the translation of the string "English" in the "MainWindow" context. That string should be translated to "Deutsch" in a German translation, to "Français" in a French translation, and to "日本語" in a Japanese translation.

We create one checkable `QAction` for each language and store the locale name in the action's "data" item. We add them to a `QActionGroup` object to ensure that only one Language menu item is checked at a time. When an action from the group is chosen by the user, the `QActionGroup` emits the `triggered(QAction *)` signal, which is connected to `switchLanguage()`.

```
void MainWindow::switchLanguage(QAction *action)
{
    QString locale = action->data().toString();
    appTranslator.load("callcenter_" + locale, qmPath);
    qtTranslator.load("qt_" + locale, qmPath);
    retranslateUi();
}
```

The `switchLanguage()` slot is called when the user chooses a language from the Language menu. We load the translation files for the application and for Qt, and we call `retranslateUi()` to retranslate all the strings for the main window.

On Windows, an alternative to providing a Language menu is to respond to `LocaleChange` events, a type of event emitted by Qt when it detects a change in the environment's locale. The event type exists on all platforms supported by Qt, but is only actually generated on Windows, when the user changes the system's locale settings (in the Control Panel's Regional and Language Options). To handle `LocaleChange` events, we can reimplement `QWidget::changeEvent()` as follows:

```
void MainWindow::changeEvent(QEvent *event)
{
    if (event->type() == QEvent::LocaleChange) {
        appTranslator.load("callcenter_"
                           + QLocale::system().name(), qmPath);
        qtTranslator.load("qt_" + QLocale::system().name(), qmPath);
        retranslateUi();
    }
    QMainWindow::changeEvent(event);
}
```

If the user switches locale while the application is being run, we attempt to load the correct translation files for the new locale and call `retranslateUi()` to update the user interface. In all cases, we pass the event on to the base class's `changeEvent()` function, since the base class may also be interested in `LocaleChange` or other change events.

We have now finished our review of the `MainWindow` code. Next we will look at the code for one of the application's widget classes, the `JournalView` class, to see what changes are needed to make it support dynamic translation.

```
JournalView::JournalView(QWidget *parent)
    : QTableWidget(parent)
{
    ...
    retranslateUi();
}
```

The `JournalView` class is a `QTableWidget` subclass. At the end of the constructor, we call the private function `retranslateUi()` to set the widget's strings. This is similar to what we did for `MainWindow`.

```
void JournalView::changeEvent(QEvent *event)
{
    if (event->type() == QEvent::LanguageChange)
        retranslateUi();
    QTableWidget::changeEvent(event);
}
```

We also reimplement the `changeEvent()` function to call `retranslateUi()` on LanguageChange events. Qt generates a `LanguageChange` event when the contents of a `QTranslator` currently installed on `QApplication` changes. In our application, this occurs when we call `load()` on `appTranslator` or `qtTranslator`, either from `MainWindow::switchLanguage()` or from `MainWindow::changeEvent()`.

`LanguageChange` events should not be confused with `LocaleChange` events. LocaleChange events are generated by the system and tell the application, "Maybe you should load a new translation." `LanguageChange` events are generated by Qt and tell the application's widgets, "Maybe you should retranslate all your strings."

When we implemented `MainWindow`, we didn't need to respond to `LanguageChange`. Instead, we simply called `retranslateUi()` whenever we called `load()` on a `QTranslator`.

```
void JournalView::retranslateUi()
{
    QStringList labels;
    labels << tr("Time") << tr("Priority") << tr("Phone Number")
           << tr("Subject");
    setHorizontalHeaderLabels(labels);
}
```

The `retranslateUi()` function updates the column headers with newly translated texts, completing the translation-related code of a hand written widget. For widgets and dialogs developed with *Qt Designer*, the `uic` tool automatically generates a function similar to our `retranslateUi()` function that is automatically called in response to `LanguageChange` events.

Translating Applications

Translating a Qt application that contains `tr()` calls is a three-step process:

1. Run `lupdate` to extract all the user-visible strings from the application's source code.

2. Translate the application using *Qt Linguist*.

3. Run `lrelease` to generate binary `.qm` files that the application can load using `QTranslator`.

Steps 1 and 3 are performed by application developers. Step 2 is handled by translators. This cycle can be repeated as often as necessary during the application's development and lifetime.

As an example, we will show how to translate the Spreadsheet application of Chapter 3. The application already contains `tr()` calls around every user-visible string.

First, we must modify the application's `.pro` file slightly to specify which languages we want to support. For example, if we want to support German and French in addition to English, we would add the following TRANSLATIONS entry to `spreadsheet.pro`:

```
TRANSLATIONS = spreadsheet_de.ts \
               spreadsheet_fr.ts
```

Here, we specify two translation files: one for German and one for French. These files will be created the first time we run `lupdate` and are updated every time we subsequently run `lupdate`.

These files normally have a `.ts` extension. They are in a straightforward XML format and are not as compact as the binary `.qm` files understood by `QTranslator`. It is `lrelease`'s job to convert human-readable `.ts` files into machine-efficient `.qm` files. For the curious, `.ts` stands for "translation source" and `.qm` for "Qt message" file.

Assuming that we are located in the directory that contains the Spreadsheet application's source code, we can run `lupdate` on `spreadsheet.pro` from the command line as follows:

```
lupdate -verbose spreadsheet.pro
```

The `-verbose` option tells `lupdate` to provide more feedback than usual. Here's the expected output:

```
Updating 'spreadsheet_de.ts'...
    Found 98 source texts (98 new and 0 already existing)
Updating 'spreadsheet_fr.ts'...
    Found 98 source texts (98 new and 0 already existing)
```

Every string that appears within a `tr()` call in the application's source code is stored in the `.ts` files, along with an empty translation. Strings that appear in the application's `.ui` files are also included.

The `lupdate` tool assumes by default that the arguments to `tr()` are Latin-1 strings. If this isn't the case, we must add a CODECFORTR entry to the `.pro` file. For example:

```
CODECFORTR = EUC-JP
```

This must be done in addition to calling `QTextCodec::setCodecForTr()` from the application's `main()` function.

Translations then need to be added to the `spreadsheet_de.ts` and `spreadsheet_fr.ts` files using *Qt Linguist*.

To run *Qt Linguist*, click Qt by Trolltech v4.x.y|Linguist in the Start menu on Windows, type `linguist` on the command line on Unix, or double-click Linguist in the Mac OS X Finder. To start adding translations to a `.ts` file, click File|Open and choose the file to translate.

The left-hand side of *Qt Linguist*'s main window shows the list of contexts for the application being translated. For the Spreadsheet application, the contexts are "FindDialog", "GoToCellDialog", "MainWindow", "SortDialog", and "Spreadsheet". The top-right area is the list of source texts for the current context. Each source text is shown along with a translation and a Done flag. The middle-right area is where we can enter a translation for the current source item. The bottom-right area is a list of suggestions automatically provided by *Qt Linguist*.

Once we have a translated `.ts` file, we need to convert it to a binary `.qm` file for it to be usable by `QTranslator`. To do this from within *Qt Linguist*, click File|Release. Typically, we would start by translating only a few strings and run the application with the `.qm` file to make sure that everything works properly.

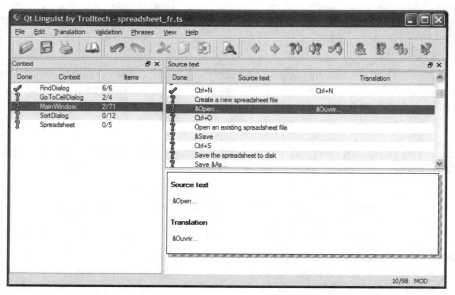

Figure 17.2. *Qt Linguist* in action

If we want to regenerate the `.qm` files for all `.ts` files, we can use the `lrelease` tool as follows:

```
lrelease -verbose spreadsheet.pro
```

Assuming that we translated 19 strings to French and clicked the Done flag for 17 of them, lrelease produces the following output:

```
Updating 'spreadsheet_de.qm'...
    Generated 0 translations (0 finished and 0 unfinished)
    Ignored 98 untranslated source texts
Updating 'spreadsheet_fr.qm'...
    Generated 19 translations (17 finished and 2 unfinished)
    Ignored 79 untranslated source texts
```

Untranslated strings are shown in the original languages when running the application. The Done flag is ignored by lrelease; it can be used by translators to identify which translations are finished and which ones must be revisited.

When we modify the source code of the application, the translation files may become out of date. The solution is to run lupdate again, provide translations for the new strings, and regenerate the .qm files. Some development teams find it useful to run lupdate frequently, while others prefer to wait until the application is almost ready to release.

The lupdate and *Qt Linguist* tools are quite smart. Translations that are no longer used are kept in the .ts files in case they are needed in later releases. When updating .ts files, lupdate uses an intelligent merging algorithm that can save translators considerable time with text that is the same or similar in different contexts.

For more information about *Qt Linguist*, lupdate, and lrelease, refer to the *Qt Linguist* manual at http://doc.trolltech.com/4.1/linguist-manual.html. The manual contains a full explanation of *Qt Linguist*'s user interface and a step-by-step tutorial for programmers.

- ◆ *Creating Threads*
- ◆ *Synchronizing Threads*
- ◆ *Communicating with the Main Thread*
- ◆ *Using Qt's Classes in Secondary Threads*

18. Multithreading

Conventional GUI applications have one thread of execution and perform one operation at a time. If the user invokes a time-consuming operation from the user interface, the interface typically freezes while the operation is in progress. Chapter 7 (Event Processing) presents some solutions to this problem. Multithreading is another solution.

In a multithreaded application, the GUI runs in its own thread and the processing takes place in one or more other threads. This results in applications that have responsive GUIs even during intensive processing. Another benefit of multithreading is that multiprocessor systems can execute several threads simultaneously on different processors, resulting in better performance.

In this chapter, we will start by showing how to subclass QThread and how to use QMutex, QSemaphore, and QWaitCondition to synchronize threads. Then we will see how to communicate with the main thread from secondary threads while the event loop is running. Finally, we round off with a review of which Qt classes can be used in secondary threads and which cannot.

Multithreading is a large topic with many books devoted exclusively to the subject. Here it is assumed that you already understand the fundamentals of multithreaded programming, so the focus is on explaining how to develop multithreaded Qt applications rather than on the subject of threading itself.

Creating Threads

Providing multiple threads in a Qt application is straightforward: We just subclass QThread and reimplement its run() function. To show how this works, we will start by reviewing the code for a very simple QThread subclass that repeatedly prints a given string on a console.

```
class Thread : public QThread
{
    Q_OBJECT
```

```
public:
    Thread();

    void setMessage(const QString &message);
    void stop();
protected:
    void run();

private:
    QString messageStr;
    volatile bool stopped;
};
```

The Thread class inherits from QThread and reimplements the run() function. It provides two additional functions: setMessage() and stop().

The stopped variable is declared volatile because it is accessed from different threads and we want to be sure that it is freshly read every time it is needed. If we omitted the volatile keyword, the compiler might optimize access to the variable, possibly leading to incorrect results.

```
Thread::Thread()
{
    stopped = false;
}
```

We set stopped to false in the constructor.

```
void Thread::run()
{
    while (!stopped)
        cerr << qPrintable(messageStr);
    stopped = false;
    cerr << endl;
}
```

The run() function is called to start executing the thread. As long as the stopped variable is false, the function keeps printing the given message to the console. The thread terminates when control leaves the run() function.

```
void Thread::stop()
{
    stopped = true;
}
```

The stop() function sets the stopped variable to true, thereby telling run() to stop printing text to the console. This function can be called from any thread at any time. For the purposes of this example, we assume that assignment to a bool is an atomic operation. This is a reasonable assumption, considering that a bool can only have two states. We will see later in this section how to use QMutex to guarantee that assigning to a variable is an atomic operation.

QThread provides a terminate() function that terminates the execution of a thread while it is still running. Using terminate() is not recommended, since it can stop the thread at any point and does not give the thread any chance to clean up after itself. It is always safer to use a stopped variable and a stop() function as we did here.

Figure 18.1. The Threads application

We will now see how to use the Thread class in a small **Qt** application that uses two threads, A and B, in addition to the main thread.

```cpp
class ThreadDialog : public QDialog
{
    Q_OBJECT

public:
    ThreadDialog(QWidget *parent = 0);

protected:
    void closeEvent(QCloseEvent *event);

private slots:
    void startOrStopThreadA();
    void startOrStopThreadB();

private:
    Thread threadA;
    Thread threadB;
    QPushButton *threadAButton;
    QPushButton *threadBButton;
    QPushButton *quitButton;
};
```

The ThreadDialog class declares two variables of type Thread and some buttons to provide a basic user interface.

```cpp
ThreadDialog::ThreadDialog(QWidget *parent)
    : QDialog(parent)
{
    threadA.setMessage("A");
    threadB.setMessage("B");

    threadAButton = new QPushButton(tr("Start A"));
    threadBButton = new QPushButton(tr("Start B"));
    quitButton = new QPushButton(tr("Quit"));
    quitButton->setDefault(true);

    connect(threadAButton, SIGNAL(clicked()),
            this, SLOT(startOrStopThreadA()));
```

```
        connect(threadBButton, SIGNAL(clicked()),
                this, SLOT(startOrStopThreadB()));
    ...
}
```

In the constructor, we call `setMessage()` to make the first thread repeatedly print 'A's and the second thread 'B's.

```
void ThreadDialog::startOrStopThreadA()
{
    if (threadA.isRunning()) {
        threadA.stop();
        threadAButton->setText(tr("Start A"));
    } else {
        threadA.start();
        threadAButton->setText(tr("Stop A"));
    }
}
```

When the user clicks the button for thread A, `startOrStopThreadA()` stops the thread if it was running and starts it otherwise. It also updates the button's text.

```
void ThreadDialog::startOrStopThreadB()
{
    if (threadB.isRunning()) {
        threadB.stop();
        threadBButton->setText(tr("Start B"));
    } else {
        threadB.start();
        threadBButton->setText(tr("Stop B"));
    }
}
```

The code for `startOrStopThreadB()` is very similar.

```
void ThreadDialog::closeEvent(QCloseEvent *event)
{
    threadA.stop();
    threadB.stop();
    threadA.wait();
    threadB.wait();
    event->accept();
}
```

If the user clicks Quit or closes the window, we stop any running threads and wait for them to finish (using `QThread::wait()`) before we call `QCloseEvent::accept()`. This ensures that the application exits in a clean state, although it doesn't really matter in this example.

If you run the application and click Start A, the console will be filled with 'A's. If you click Start B, it will now fill with alternating sequences of 'A's and 'B's. Click Stop A, and now it will only print 'B's.

Synchronizing Threads

A common requirement for multithreaded applications is that of synchronizing several threads. Qt provides the following synchronization classes: QMutex, QReadWriteLock, QSemaphore, and QWaitCondition.

The QMutex class provides a means of protecting a variable or a piece of code so that only one thread can access it at a time. The class provides a lock() function that locks the mutex. If the mutex is unlocked, the current thread seizes it immediately and locks it; otherwise, the current thread is blocked until the thread that holds the mutex unlocks it. Either way, when the call to lock() returns, the current thread holds the mutex until it calls unlock(). The QMutex class also provides a tryLock() function that returns immediately if the mutex is already locked.

For example, let's suppose that we wanted to protect the stopped variable of the Thread class from the previous section with a QMutex. We would then add the following data member to Thread:

```
private:
    ...
    QMutex mutex;
};
```

The run() function would change to this:

```
void Thread::run()
{
    forever {
        mutex.lock();
        if (stopped) {
            stopped = false;
            mutex.unlock();
            break;
        }
        mutex.unlock();

        cerr << qPrintable(messageStr);
    }
    cerr << endl;
}
```

The stop() function would become this:

```
void Thread::stop()
{
    mutex.lock();
    stopped = true;
    mutex.unlock();
}
```

Locking and unlocking a mutex in complex functions, or functions that use C++ exceptions, can be error-prone. Qt offers the QMutexLocker convenience class to simplify mutex handling. QMutexLocker's constructor accepts a QMutex as argument and locks it. QMutexLocker's destructor unlocks the mutex. For example, we could rewrite the previous run() and stop() functions as follows:

```
void Thread::run()
{
    forever {
        {
            QMutexLocker locker(&mutex);
            if (stopped) {
                stopped = false;
                break;
            }
        }

        cerr << qPrintable(messageStr);
    }
    cerr << endl;
}

void Thread::stop()
{
    QMutexLocker locker(&mutex);
    stopped = true;
}
```

One issue with using mutexes is that only one thread can access the same variable at a time. In programs with lots of threads trying to read the same variable simultaneously (without modify it), the mutex can be a serious performance bottleneck. In these cases, we can use QReadWriteLock, a synchronization class that allows simultaneous read-only access without compromising performance.

In the Thread class, it would make no sense to replace QMutex with QReadWriteLock to protect the stopped variable, because at most one thread might try to read the variable at any given time. A more appropriate example would involve one or many reader threads accessing some shared data and one or many writer threads modifying the data. For example:

```
MyData data;
QReadWriteLock lock;

void ReaderThread::run()
{
    ...
    lock.lockForRead();
    access_data_without_modifying_it(&data);
    lock.unlock();
    ...
}

void WriterThread::run()
{
    ...
    lock.lockForWrite();
    modify_data(&data);
```

```
        lock.unlock();
        ...
    }
```

For convenience, we can use the QReadLocker and QWriteLocker classes to lock and unlock a QReadWriteLock.

QSemaphore is another generalization of mutexes, but unlike read/write locks, semaphores can be used to guard a certain number of identical resources. The following two code snippets show the correspondence between QSemaphore and QMutex:

```
QSemaphore semaphore(1);          QMutex mutex;
semaphore.acquire();              mutex.lock();
semaphore.release();              mutex.unlock();
```

By passing 1 to the constructor, we tell the semaphore that it controls a single resource. The advantage of using a semaphore is that we can pass numbers other than 1 to the constructor and then call acquire() multiple times to acquire many resources.

A typical application of semaphores is when transferring a certain amount of data (DataSize) between two threads using a shared circular buffer of a certain size (BufferSize):

```
const int DataSize = 100000;
const int BufferSize = 4096;
char buffer[BufferSize];
```

The producer thread writes data to the buffer until it reaches the end and then restarts from the beginning, overwriting existing data. The consumer thread reads the data as it is generated. Figure 18.2 illustrates this, assuming a tiny 16-byte buffer.

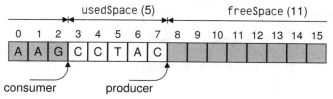

Figure 18.2. The producer–consumer model

The need for synchronization in the producer–consumer example is twofold: If the producer generates the data too fast, it will overwrite data that the consumer hasn't yet read; if the consumer reads the data too fast, it will pass the producer and read garbage.

A crude way to solve this problem is to have the producer fill the buffer, then wait until the consumer has read the entire buffer, and so on. However, on multiprocessor machines, this isn't as fast as letting the producer and consumer threads operate on different parts of the buffer at the same time.

One way to efficiently solve the problem involves two semaphores:

```
QSemaphore freeSpace(BufferSize);
QSemaphore usedSpace(0);
```

The freeSpace semaphore governs the part of the buffer that the producer can fill with data. The usedSpace semaphore governs the area that the consumer can read. These two areas are complementary. The freeSpace semaphore is initialized with BufferSize (4096), meaning that it has that many resources that can be acquired. When the application starts, the reader thread will start acquiring "free" bytes and convert them into "used" bytes. The usedSpace semaphore is initialized with 0 to ensure that the consumer won't read garbage at startup.

For this example, each byte counts as one resource. In a real-world application, we would probably operate on larger units (for example, 64 or 256 bytes at a time) to reduce the overhead associated with using semaphores.

```
void Producer::run()
{
    for (int i = 0; i < DataSize; ++i) {
        freeSpace.acquire();
        buffer[i % BufferSize] = "ACGT"[uint(rand()) % 4];
        usedSpace.release();
    }
}
```

In the producer, every iteration starts by acquiring one "free" byte. If the buffer is full of data that the consumer hasn't read yet, the call to acquire() will block until the consumer has started to consume the data. Once we have acquired the byte, we fill it with some random data ('A', 'C', 'G', or 'T') and release the byte as "used", so that it can be read by the consumer thread.

```
void Consumer::run()
{
    for (int i = 0; i < DataSize; ++i) {
        usedSpace.acquire();
        cerr << buffer[i % BufferSize];
        freeSpace.release();
    }
    cerr << endl;
}
```

In the consumer, we start by acquiring one "used" byte. If the buffer contains no data to read, the call to acquire() will block until the producer has produced some. Once we have acquired the byte, we print it and release the byte as "free", making it possible for the producer to fill it with data again.

```
int main()
{
    Producer producer;
    Consumer consumer;
    producer.start();
```

```
        consumer.start();
        producer.wait();
        consumer.wait();
        return 0;
}
```

Finally, in `main()`, we start the producer and consumer threads. What happens then is that the producer converts some "free" space into "used" space, and the consumer can then convert it back to "free" space.

When we run the program, it writes a random sequence of 100,000 'A's, 'C's, 'G's, and 'T's to the console and terminates. To really understand what is going on, we can disable writing the output and instead write 'P' each time the producer generates a byte and 'c' each time the consumer reads a byte. And to make things as simple to follow as possible, we can use smaller values for `DataSize` and `BufferSize`.

For example, here's a possible run with a `DataSize` of 10 and a `BufferSize` of 4: "PcPcPcPcPcPcPcPcPcPc". In this case, the consumer reads the bytes as soon as they are generated by the producer; the two threads are executing at the same speed. Another possibility is that the producer fills the whole buffer before the consumer even starts reading it: "PPPPccccPPPPccccPPcc". There are many other possibilities. Semaphores give a lot of latitude to the system-specific thread scheduler, which can study the threads' behavior and choose an appropriate scheduling policy.

A different approach to the problem of synchronizing a producer and a consumer is to use `QWaitCondition` and `QMutex`. A `QWaitCondition` allows a thread to wake up other threads when some condition has been met. This allows for more precise control than is possible with mutexes alone. To show how it works, we will redo the producer–consumer example using wait conditions.

```
const int DataSize = 100000;
const int BufferSize = 4096;
char buffer[BufferSize];

QWaitCondition bufferIsNotFull;
QWaitCondition bufferIsNotEmpty;
QMutex mutex;
int usedSpace = 0;
```

In addition to the buffer, we declare two `QWaitConditions`, one `QMutex`, and one variable that stores how many bytes in the buffer are "used" bytes.

```
void Producer::run()
{
    for (int i = 0; i < DataSize; ++i) {
        mutex.lock();
        while (usedSpace == BufferSize)
            bufferIsNotFull.wait(&mutex);
        buffer[i % BufferSize] = "ACGT"[uint(rand()) % 4];
        ++usedSpace;
        bufferIsNotEmpty.wakeAll();
```

```
            mutex.unlock();
        }
    }
```

In the producer, we start by checking whether the buffer is full. If it is, we wait on the "buffer is not full" condition. When that condition is met, we write one byte to the buffer, increment usedSpace, and wake any thread waiting for the "buffer is not empty" condition to turn true.

We use a mutex to protect all accesses to the usedSpace variable. The QWaitCondition::wait() function can take a locked mutex as its first argument, which it unlocks before blocking the current thread and then locks before returning.

For this example, we could have replaced the while loop

```
    while (usedSpace == BufferSize)
        bufferIsNotFull.wait(&mutex);
```

with this if statement:

```
    if (usedSpace == BufferSize) {
        mutex.unlock();
        bufferIsNotFull.wait();
        mutex.lock();
    }
```

However, this would break as soon as we allow more than one producer thread, since another producer could seize the mutex immediately after the wait() call and make the "buffer is not full" condition false again.

```
    void Consumer::run()
    {
        for (int i = 0; i < DataSize; ++i) {
            mutex.lock();
            while (usedSpace == 0)
                bufferIsNotEmpty.wait(&mutex);
            cerr << buffer[i % BufferSize];
            --usedSpace;
            bufferIsNotFull.wakeAll();
            mutex.unlock();
        }
        cerr << endl;
    }
```

The consumer does the exact opposite of the producer: It waits for the "buffer is not empty" condition and wakes up any thread waiting for the "buffer is not full" condition.

In all the examples so far, our threads have accessed the same global variables. But some threaded applications need to have a global variable hold different values in different threads. This is often called thread-local storage or thread-specific data. We can fake it using a map keyed on thread IDs (returned by QThread::currentThread()), but a nicer approach is to use the QThreadStorage<T> class.

A common use of `QThreadStorage<T>` is for caches. By having a separate cache in different threads, we avoid the overhead of locking, unlocking, and possibly waiting for a mutex. For example:

```
QThreadStorage<QHash<int, double> *> cache;

void insertIntoCache(int id, double value)
{
    if (!cache.hasLocalData())
        cache.setLocalData(new QHash<int, double>);
    cache.localData()->insert(id, value);
}

void removeFromCache(int id)
{
    if (cache.hasLocalData())
        cache.localData()->remove(id);
}
```

The `cache` variable holds one pointer to a `QMap<int, double>` per thread. (Because of problems with some compilers, the template type in `QThreadStorage<T>` must be a pointer type.) The first time we use the cache in a particular thread, `has-LocalData()` returns `false` and we create the `QHash<int, double>` object.

In addition to caching, `QThreadStorage<T>` can be used for global error-state variables (similar to `errno`) to ensure that modifications in one thread don't affect other threads.

Communicating with the Main Thread

When a Qt application starts, only one thread is running—the main thread. This is the only thread that is allowed to create the `QApplication` or `QCoreApplication` object and call `exec()` on it. After the call to `exec()`, this thread is either waiting for an event or processing an event.

The main thread can start new threads by creating objects of a `QThread` subclass, as we did in the previous section. If these new threads need to communicate among themselves, they can use shared variables together with mutexes, read/write locks, semaphores, or wait conditions. But none of these techniques can be used to communicate with the main thread, since they would lock the event loop and freeze the user interface.

The solution for communicating from a secondary thread to the main thread is to use signal–slot connections across threads. Normally, the signals and slots mechanism operates synchronously, meaning that the slots connected to a signal are invoked immediately when the signal is emitted, using a direct function call.

However, when we connect objects that "live" in different threads, the mechanism becomes asynchronous. (This behavior can be changed through an optional fifth parameter to `QObject::connect()`.) Behind the scenes, these connections are implemented by posting an event. The slot is then called by the event loop of the thread in which the receiver object exists. By default, a `QObject` exists in the thread in which it was created; this can be changed at any time by calling `QObject::moveToThread()`.

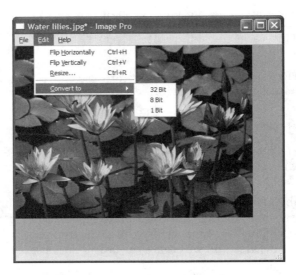

Figure 18.3. The Image Pro application

To illustrate how signal–slot connections across threads work, we will review the code of the Image Pro application, a basic image processing application that allows the user to rotate, resize, and change the color depth of an image. The application uses one secondary thread to perform operations on images without locking the event loop. This makes a significant difference when processing very large images. The secondary thread has a list of tasks, or "transactions", to accomplish and sends events to the main window to report progress.

```
ImageWindow::ImageWindow()
{
    imageLabel = new QLabel;
    imageLabel->setBackgroundRole(QPalette::Dark);
    imageLabel->setAutoFillBackground(true);
    imageLabel->setAlignment(Qt::AlignLeft | Qt::AlignTop);
    setCentralWidget(imageLabel);

    createActions();
    createMenus();

    statusBar()->showMessage(tr("Ready"), 2000);

    connect(&thread, SIGNAL(transactionStarted(const QString &)),
            statusBar(), SLOT(showMessage(const QString &)));
    connect(&thread, SIGNAL(finished()),
            this, SLOT(allTransactionsDone()));

    setCurrentFile("");
}
```

The interesting part of the ImageWindow constructor is the two signal–slot connections. Both of them involve signals emitted by the TransactionThread object, which we will cover in a moment.

```
void ImageWindow::flipHorizontally()
{
    addTransaction(new FlipTransaction(Qt::Horizontal));
}
```

The flipHorizontally() slot creates a "flip" transaction and registers it using the private function addTransaction(). The flipVertically(), resizeImage(), convertTo32Bit(), convertTo8Bit(), and convertTo1Bit() functions are similar.

```
void ImageWindow::addTransaction(Transaction *transact)
{
    thread.addTransaction(transact);
    openAction->setEnabled(false);
    saveAction->setEnabled(false);
    saveAsAction->setEnabled(false);
}
```

The addTransaction() function adds a transaction to the secondary thread's transaction queue and disables the Open, Save, and Save As actions while transactions are being processed.

```
void ImageWindow::allTransactionsDone()
{
    openAction->setEnabled(true);
    saveAction->setEnabled(true);
    saveAsAction->setEnabled(true);
    imageLabel->setPixmap(QPixmap::fromImage(thread.image()));
    setWindowModified(true);
    statusBar()->showMessage(tr("Ready"), 2000);
}
```

The allTransactionsDone() slot is called when the TransactionThread's transaction queue becomes empty.

Now, let's turn to the TransactionThread class:

```
class TransactionThread : public QThread
{
    Q_OBJECT

public:
    void addTransaction(Transaction *transact);
    void setImage(const QImage &image);
    QImage image();

signals:
    void transactionStarted(const QString &message);

protected:
    void run();

private:
```

```
    QMutex mutex;
    QImage currentImage;
    QQueue<Transaction *> transactions;
};
```

The `TransactionThread` class maintains a list of transactions to process and executes them one after the other in the background.

```
void TransactionThread::addTransaction(Transaction *transact)
{
    QMutexLocker locker(&mutex);
    transactions.enqueue(transact);
    if (!isRunning())
        start();
}
```

The `addTransaction()` function adds a transaction to the transaction queue and starts the transaction thread if it isn't already running. All accesses to the `transactions` member variable are protected by a mutex, because the main thread might modify them through `addTransaction()` at the same time as the secondary thread is iterating over `transactions`.

```
void TransactionThread::setImage(const QImage &image)
{
    QMutexLocker locker(&mutex);
    currentImage = image;
}

QImage TransactionThread::image()
{
    QMutexLocker locker(&mutex);
    return currentImage;
}
```

The `setImage()` and `image()` functions let the main thread set the image on which to perform the transactions and retrieve the resulting image once all transactions are done. Again, we protect accesses to a member variable using a mutex.

```
void TransactionThread::run()
{
    Transaction *transact;

    forever {
        mutex.lock();
        if (transactions.isEmpty()) {
            mutex.unlock();
            break;
        }
        QImage oldImage = currentImage;
        transact = transactions.dequeue();
        mutex.unlock();

        emit transactionStarted(transact->message());

        QImage newImage = transact->apply(oldImage);
```

```
            delete transact;

            mutex.lock();
            currentImage = newImage;
            mutex.unlock();
        }
    }
```

The `run()` function goes through the transaction queue and executes each transaction in turn by calling `apply()` on them.

When a transaction is started, we emit the `transactionStarted()` signal with a message to display in the application's status bar. When all the transactions have finished processing, the `run()` function returns and `QThread` emits the `finished()` signal.

```
class Transaction
{
public:
    virtual ~Transaction() { }

    virtual QImage apply(const QImage &image) = 0;
    virtual QString message() = 0;
};
```

The `Transaction` class is an abstract base class for operations that the user can perform on an image. The virtual destructor is necessary because we need to delete instances of `Transaction` subclasses through a `Transaction` pointer. (Also, if we omit it, some compilers emit a warning.) `Transaction` has three concrete subclasses: `FlipTransaction`, `ResizeTransaction`, and `ConvertDepthTransaction`. We will only review `FlipTransaction`; the other two classes are similar.

```
class FlipTransaction : public Transaction
{
public:
    FlipTransaction(Qt::Orientation orientation);

    QImage apply(const QImage &image);
    QString message();

private:
    Qt::Orientation orientation;
};
```

The `FlipTransaction` constructor takes one parameter that specifies the orientation of the flip (horizontal or vertical).

```
QImage FlipTransaction::apply(const QImage &image)
{
    return image.mirrored(orientation == Qt::Horizontal,
                          orientation == Qt::Vertical);
}
```

The `apply()` function calls `QImage::mirrored()` on the `QImage` it receives as parameter and returns the resulting `QImage`.

```
QString FlipTransaction::message()
{
    if (orientation == Qt::Horizontal) {
        return QObject::tr("Flipping image horizontally...");
    } else {
        return QObject::tr("Flipping image vertically...");
    }
}
```

The message() function returns the message to display in the status bar while the operation is in progress. This function is called in TransactionThread::run() when emitting the transactionStarted() signal.

Using Qt's Classes in Secondary Threads

A function is said to be *thread-safe* when it can safely be called from different threads simultaneously. If two thread-safe functions are called from different threads on the same shared data, the result is always defined. By extension, a class is said to be thread-safe when all of its functions can be called from different threads simultaneously without interfering with each other, even when operating on the same object.

Qt's thread-safe classes are QMutex, QMutexLocker, QReadWriteLock, QReadLocker, QWriteLocker, QSemaphore, QThreadStorage<T>, QWaitCondition, and parts of the QThread API. In addition, several functions are thread-safe, including QObject:: connect(), QObject::disconnect(), QCoreApplication::postEvent(), QCoreApplication::removePostedEvent(), and QCoreApplication::removePostedEvents().

Most of Qt's non-GUI classes meet a less stringent requirement: They are *reentrant*. A class is reentrant if different instances of the class can be used simultaneously in different threads. However, accessing the same reentrant object in multiple threads simultaneously is not safe, and such accesses should be protected with a mutex. Reentrant classes are marked as such in the Qt reference documentation. Typically, any C++ class that doesn't reference global or otherwise shared data is reentrant.

QObject is reentrant, but there are three constraints to keep in mind:

- **Child QObjects must be created in their parent's thread.**

  In particular, this means that the objects created in a secondary thread must never be created with the QThread object as their parent, because that object was created in another thread (either the main thread or a different secondary thread).

- **We must delete all QObjects created in a secondary thread before deleting the corresponding QThread object.**

  This can be done by creating the objects on the stack in QThread::run().

- **QObjects must be deleted in the thread that created them.**

  If we need to delete a QObject that exists in a different thread, we must call the thread-safe QObject::deleteLater() function instead, which posts a "deferred delete" event.

Non-GUI QObject subclasses such as QTimer, QProcess, and the network classes are reentrant. We can use them in any thread, as long as the thread has an event loop. For secondary threads, the event loop is started by calling QThread::exec() or by convenience functions such as QProcess::waitForFinished() and QAbstractSocket::waitForDisconnected().

Because of limitations inherited from the low-level libraries on which Qt's GUI support is built, QWidget and its subclasses are not reentrant. One consequence of this is that we cannot directly call functions on a widget from a secondary thread. If we want to, say, change the text of a QLabel from a secondary thread, we can emit a signal connected to QLabel::setText() or call QMetaObject::invokeMethod() from that thread. For example:

```
void MyThread::run()
{
    ...
    QMetaObject::invokeMethod(label, SLOT(setText(const QString &)),
                              Q_ARG(QString, "Hello"));
    ...
}
```

Many of Qt's non-GUI classes, including QImage, QString, and the container classes, use implicit sharing as an optimization technique. While this optimization usually makes a class non-reentrant, in Qt this is not an issue because Qt uses atomic assembly language instructions to implement thread-safe reference counting, making Qt's implicitly shared classes reentrant.

Qt's *QtSql* module can also be used in multithreaded applications, but it has its own restrictions, which vary from database to database. For details, see http://doc.trolltech.com/4.1/sql-driver.html. For a complete list of multi-threading caveats, see http://doc.trolltech.com/4.1/threads.html.

- ◆ *Extending Qt with Plugins*
- ◆ *Making Applications Plugin-Aware*
- ◆ *Writing Application Plugins*

19. Creating Plugins

Dynamic libraries (also called shared libraries or DLLs) are independent modules that are stored in a separate file on disk and can be accessed by multiple applications. Programs usually specify which dynamic libraries they need at link time, in which case the libraries are automatically loaded when the application starts. This approach usually involves adding the library and possibly its include path to the application's .pro file and including the relevant headers in the source files. For example:

```
LIBS        += -ldb_cxx
INCLUDEPATH += /usr/local/BerkeleyDB.4.2/include
```

The alternative is to dynamically load the library when it is required, and then resolve the symbols that we want to use from it. Qt provides the QLibrary class to achieve this in a platform-independent manner. Given the stem of a library's name, QLibrary searches the platform's standard locations for the library looking for an appropriate file. For example, given the name mimetype, it will look for mimetype.dll on Windows, mimetype.so on Linux, and mimetype. dylib on Mac OS X.

Modern GUI applications can often be extended by the use of plugins. A plugin is a dynamic library that implements a particular interface to provide optional extra functionality. For example, in Chapter 5, we created a plugin to integrate a custom widget with *Qt Designer* (p. 113).

Qt recognizes its own set of plugin interfaces for various domains, including image formats, database drivers, widget styles, text encodings, and accessibility. This chapter's first section explains how to extend Qt with a Qt plugin.

It is also possible to create application-specific plugins for particular Qt applications. Qt makes writing such plugins easy through its plugin framework, which adds crash safety and convenience to QLibrary. In the last two sections of this chapter, we show how to make an application support plugins and how to create a custom plugin for an application.

Extending Qt with Plugins

Qt can be extended with a variety of plugin types, the most common being database drivers, image formats, styles, and text codecs. For each type of plugin, we normally need at least two classes: a plugin wrapper class that implements the generic plugin API functions, and one or more handler classes that each implement the API for a particular type of plugin. The handlers are accessed through the wrapper class.

Plugin Class	Handler Base Class
QAccessibleBridgePlugin	QAccessibleBridge
QAccessiblePlugin	QAccessibleInterface
QIconEnginePlugin	QIconEngine
QImageIOPlugin	QImageIOHandler
QInputContextPlugin	QInputContext
QPictureFormatPlugin	N/A
QSqlDriverPlugin	QSqlDriver
QStylePlugin	QStyle
QTextCodecPlugin	QTextCodec

Figure 19.1. Qt plugin and handler classes (excluding Qtopia Core)

To demonstrate this, we will implement a plugin that can read monochrome Windows cursor files (.cur files). These files can hold several images of the same cursor at different sizes. Once the cursor plugin is built and installed, Qt will be able to read .cur files and access individual cursors (for example, through QImage, QImageReader, or QMovie), and will be able to write the cursors out in any of Qt's other image file formats, such as BMP, JPEG, and PNG. The plugin could also be deployed with Qt applications since they automatically check the standard locations for Qt plugins and load any that they find.

New image format plugin wrappers must subclass QImageIOPlugin and reimplement a few virtual functions:

```
class CursorPlugin : public QImageIOPlugin
{
public:
    QStringList keys() const;
    Capabilities capabilities(QIODevice *device,
                      const QByteArray &format) const;
    QImageIOHandler *create(QIODevice *device,
                      const QByteArray &format) const;
};
```

The keys() function returns a list of the image formats the plugin supports. The format parameter of the capabilities() and create() functions can be assumed to have a value from that list.

```
QStringList CursorPlugin::keys() const
{
    return QStringList() << "cur";
}
```

Our plugin only supports one image format, so it returns a list with just one name. Ideally the name should be the file extension used by the format. When dealing with formats with several extensions (such as .jpg and .jpeg for JPEG), we can return a list with several entries for the same format, one for each extension.

```
QImageIOPlugin::Capabilities
CursorPlugin::capabilities(QIODevice *device,
                           const QByteArray &format) const
{
    if (format == "cur")
        return CanRead;

    if (format.isEmpty()) {
        CursorHandler handler;
        handler.setDevice(device);
        if (handler.canRead())
            return CanRead;
    }

    return 0;
}
```

The capabilities() function returns what the image handler is capable of doing with the given image format. There are three capabilities (CanRead, CanWrite, and CanReadIncremental), and the return value is a bitwise OR of those that apply.

If the format is "cur", our implementation returns CanRead. If no format is given, we create a cursor handler and check whether it is capable of reading the data from the given device. The canRead() function only peeks at the data, seeing if it recognizes the file, without changing the file pointer. A capability of 0 means that the file cannot be read or written by this handler.

```
QImageIOHandler *CursorPlugin::create(QIODevice *device,
                                      const QByteArray &format) const
{
    CursorHandler *handler = new CursorHandler;
    handler->setDevice(device);
    handler->setFormat(format);
    return handler;
}
```

When a cursor file is opened (for example, by QImageReader), the plugin wrapper's create() function will be called with the device pointer and with "cur" as the format. We create a CursorHandler instance and set it up with the specified device and format. The caller takes ownership of the handler and will delete it when it is no longer required. If multiple files are to be read, a fresh handler will be created for each one.

```
Q_EXPORT_PLUGIN2(cursorplugin, CursorPlugin)
```

At the end of the .cpp file, we use the `Q_EXPORT_PLUGIN2()` macro to ensure that the plugin is recognized by Qt. The first parameter is an arbitrary name that we want to give to the plugin. The second parameter is the plugin class name.

Subclassing `QImageIOPlugin` is straightforward. The real work of the plugin is done in the handler. Image format handlers must subclass `QImageIOHandler` and reimplement some or all of its public functions. Let's start with the header:

```
class CursorHandler : public QImageIOHandler
{
public:
    CursorHandler();

    bool canRead() const;
    bool read(QImage *image);
    bool jumpToNextImage();
    int currentImageNumber() const;
    int imageCount() const;

private:
    enum State { BeforeHeader, BeforeImage, AfterLastImage, Error };

    void readHeaderIfNecessary() const;
    QBitArray readBitmap(int width, int height, QDataStream &in) const;
    void enterErrorState() const;

    mutable State state;
    mutable int currentImageNo;
    mutable int numImages;
};
```

The signatures of all the public functions are fixed. We have omitted several functions that we don't need to reimplement for a read-only handler, in particular `write()`. The member variables are declared with the `mutable` keyword because they are modified inside const functions.

```
CursorHandler::CursorHandler()
{
    state = BeforeHeader;
    currentImageNo = 0;
    numImages = 0;
}
```

When the handler is constructed, we begin by setting its state. We set the current cursor image number to the first cursor, but since we set `numImages` to 0 it is clear that we have no images yet.

```
bool CursorHandler::canRead() const
{
    if (state == BeforeHeader) {
        return device()->peek(4) == QByteArray("\0\0\2\0", 4);
    } else {
```

```
            return state != Error;
        }
    }
```

The `canRead()` function can be called at any time to determine whether the image handler can read more data from the device. If the function is called before we have read any data, while we are still in the `BeforeHeader` state, we check for the particular signature that identifies Windows cursor files. The `QIODevice::peek()` call reads the first four bytes *without* changing the device's file pointer. If `canRead()` is called later on, we return `true` unless an error has occurred.

```
    int CursorHandler::currentImageNumber() const
    {
        return currentImageNo;
    }
```

This trivial function returns the number of the cursor at which the device file pointer is positioned.

Once the handler is constructed, it is possible for the user to call any of its public functions, in any order. This is a potential problem since we must assume that we can only read serially, so we need to read the file header once before doing anything else. We solve the problem by calling the `readHeaderIfNecessary()` function in those functions that depend on the header having been read.

```
    int CursorHandler::imageCount() const
    {
        readHeaderIfNecessary();
        return numImages;
    }
```

This function returns the number of images in the file. For a valid file where no reading errors have occurred, it will return a count of at least 1.

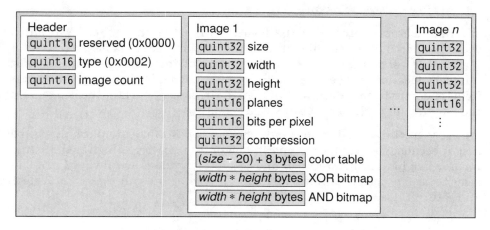

Figure 19.2. The `.cur` file format

The next function is quite involved, so we will review it in pieces:

```
bool CursorHandler::read(QImage *image)
{
    readHeaderIfNecessary();

    if (state != BeforeImage)
        return false;
```

The `read()` function reads the data for whichever image begins at the current device pointer position. If the file's header is read successfully, or after an image has been read and the device pointer is at the start of another image, we can read the next image.

```
    quint32 size;
    quint32 width;
    quint32 height;
    quint16 numPlanes;
    quint16 bitsPerPixel;
    quint32 compression;

    QDataStream in(device());
    in.setByteOrder(QDataStream::LittleEndian);
    in >> size;
    if (size != 40) {
        enterErrorState();
        return false;
    }
    in >> width >> height >> numPlanes >> bitsPerPixel >> compression;
    height /= 2;

    if (numPlanes != 1 || bitsPerPixel != 1 || compression != 0) {
        enterErrorState();
        return false;
    }

    in.skipRawData((size - 20) + 8);
```

We create a `QDataStream` to read the device. We must set the byte order to match that specified by the `.cur` file format specification. There is no need to set a `QDataStream` version number since the format of integers and floating-point numbers does not vary between data stream versions. Next, we read in various items of cursor header data, and we skip the irrelevant parts of the header and the 8-byte color table using `QDataStream::skipRawData()`.

We must account for all the format's idiosyncrasies—for example, halving the height because the `.cur` format gives a height that is twice as high as the actual image's height. The `bitsPerPixel` and `compression` values are always 1 and 0 in a monochrome `.cur` file. If we have any problems, we call `enterErrorState()` and return `false`.

```
    QBitArray xorBitmap = readBitmap(width, height, in);
    QBitArray andBitmap = readBitmap(width, height, in);
```

```
        if (in.status() != QDataStream::Ok) {
            enterErrorState();
            return false;
        }
```

The next items in the file are two bitmaps, one an XOR mask and the other an AND mask. We read these into `QBitArray`s rather than into `QBitmap`s. A `QBitmap` is a class designed to be drawn on and painted on-screen, but what we need here is a plain array of bits.

When we are done with reading the file, we check the `QDataStream`'s status. This works because if a `QDataStream` enters an error state, it stays in that state and can only return zeros. For example, if reading fails on the first bit array, the attempt to read the second will result in an empty `QBitArray`.

```
    *image = QImage(width, height, QImage::Format_ARGB32);

    for (int i = 0; i < int(height); ++i) {
        for (int j = 0; j < int(width); ++j) {
            QRgb color;
            int bit = (i * width) + j;

            if (andBitmap.testBit(bit)) {
                if (xorBitmap.testBit(bit)) {
                    color = 0x7F7F7F7F;
                } else {
                    color = 0x00FFFFFF;
                }
            } else {
                if (xorBitmap.testBit(bit)) {
                    color = 0xFFFFFFFF;
                } else {
                    color = 0xFF000000;
                }
            }
            image->setPixel(j, i, color);
        }
    }
```

We construct a new `QImage` of the correct size and set `image` to point to it. Then we iterate over every pixel in the XOR and AND bit arrays and convert them into 32-bit ARGB color specifications. The AND and XOR bit arrays are used as shown in the following table to obtain the color of each cursor pixel:

AND	XOR	Result
1	1	Inverted background pixel
1	0	Transparent pixel
0	1	White pixel
0	0	Black pixel

Black, white, and transparent pixels are no problem, but there's no way of obtaining an inverted background pixel using an ARGB color specification without knowing the color of the original background pixel. As a substitute, we use a semi-transparent gray color (0x7F7F7F7F).

```
++currentImageNo;
if (currentImageNo == numImages)
    state = AfterLastImage;
return true;
}
```

Once we have finished reading the image, we update the current image number and update the state if we have reached the last image. At the end of the function, the device will be positioned at the next image or at the end of the file.

```
bool CursorHandler::jumpToNextImage()
{
    QImage image;
    return read(&image);
}
```

The jumpToNextImage() function is used to skip an image. For simplicity, we simply call read() and ignore the resulting QImage. A more efficient implementation would use the information stored in the .cur file header to skip directly to the appropriate offset in the file.

```
void CursorHandler::readHeaderIfNecessary() const
{
    if (state != BeforeHeader)
        return;

    quint16 reserved;
    quint16 type;
    quint16 count;

    QDataStream in(device());
    in.setByteOrder(QDataStream::LittleEndian);

    in >> reserved >> type >> count;
    in.skipRawData(16 * count);

    if (in.status() != QDataStream::Ok || reserved != 0
            || type != 2 || count == 0) {
        enterErrorState();
        return;
    }

    state = BeforeImage;
    currentImageNo = 0;
    numImages = int(count);
}
```

The readHeaderIfNecessary() private function is called from imageCount() and read(). If the file's header has already been read, the state is not BeforeHeader and we return immediately. Otherwise, we open a data stream on the device, read in some generic data (including the number of cursors in the file), and set the state to `BeforeImage`. At the end, the device's file pointer is positioned before the first image.

```
void CursorHandler::enterErrorState() const
{
    state = Error;
    currentImageNo = 0;
    numImages = 0;
}
```

If an error occurs, we assume that there are no valid images and set the state to `Error`. Once in the `Error` state, the handler's state cannot change.

```
QBitArray CursorHandler::readBitmap(int width, int height,
                                    QDataStream &in) const
{
    QBitArray bitmap(width * height);
    quint8 byte;
    quint32 word;

    for (int i = 0; i < height; ++i) {
        for (int j = 0; j < width; ++j) {
            if ((j % 32) == 0) {
                word = 0;
                for (int k = 0; k < 4; ++k) {
                    in >> byte;
                    word = (word << 8) | byte;
                }
            }

            bitmap.setBit(((height - i - 1) * width) + j,
                          word & 0x80000000);
            word <<= 1;
        }
    }
    return bitmap;
}
```

The `readBitmap()` function is used to read a cursor's AND and XOR masks. These masks have two unusual features. First, they store the rows from bottom to top, instead of the more common top-to-bottom approach. Second, the endianness of the data appears to be reversed from that used everywhere else in .cur files. In view of this, we must invert the *y* coordinate in the `setBit()` call, and we read in the mask values one byte at a time, bit-shifting and masking to extract their correct values.

This completes the implementation of the `CursorHandler` image format plugin. Plugins for other image formats would follow the same pattern, although some might implement more of the `QImageIOHandler` API, in particular the functions used for writing images. Plugins of other kinds, for example, text codecs or database drivers, follow the same pattern of having a plugin wrapper to provide a generic API that applications can use, and a handler to provide the underlying functionality.

The .pro file is different for plugins than for applications, so we will end with that:

```
TEMPLATE      = lib
CONFIG       += plugin
HEADERS       = cursorhandler.h \
                cursorplugin.h
SOURCES       = cursorhandler.cpp \
                cursorplugin.cpp
DESTDIR       = $(QTDIR)/plugins/imageformats
```

By default, .pro files use the app template, but here we must specify the lib template because a plugin is a library, not a stand-alone application. The CON-FIG line is used to tell Qt that the library is not just a plain library, but a plugin library. The DESTDIR specifies the directory where the plugin should go. All Qt plugins must go in the appropriate plugins subdirectory where Qt was installed, and since our plugin provides a new image format we put it in plugins/imageformats. The list of directory names and plugin types is given at http://doc.trolltech.com/4.1/plugins-howto.html. For this example, we assume that the QTDIR environment variable is set to the directory where Qt is installed.

Plugins built for Qt in release mode and debug mode are different, so if both versions of Qt are installed, it is wise to specify which one to use in the .pro file—for example, by adding the line

```
CONFIG       += release
```

Applications that use Qt plugins must be deployed with the plugins they are intended to use. Qt plugins must be placed in specific subdirectories (for example, imageformats for image formats). Qt applications search for plugins in the plugins directory in the directory where the application's executable resides, so for image plugins they search application_dir/plugins/imageformats. If we want to deploy Qt plugins in a different directory, the plugins search path can be augmented by using QCoreApplication::addLibraryPath().

Making Applications Plugin-Aware

An application plugin is a dynamic library that implements one or more *interfaces*. An interface is a class that consists exclusively of pure virtual functions. The communication between the application and the plugins is done through the interface's virtual table. In this section, we will focus on how to use a plugin in a Qt application through its interfaces, and in the next section we will show how to implement a plugin.

To provide a concrete example, we will create the simple Text Art application shown in Figure 19.3. The text effects are provided by plugins; the application retrieves the list of text effects provided by each plugin and iterates over them to show each one as an item in a QListWidget.

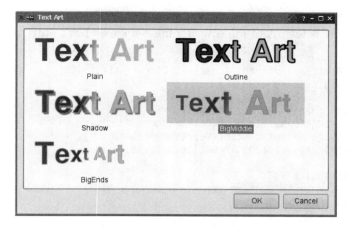

Figure 19.3. The Text Art application

The Text Art application defines one interface:

```
class TextArtInterface
{
public:
    virtual ~TextArtInterface() { }

    virtual QStringList effects() const = 0;
    virtual QPixmap applyEffect(const QString &effect,
                               const QString &text,
                               const QFont &font, const QSize &size,
                               const QPen &pen,
                               const QBrush &brush) = 0;
};

Q_DECLARE_INTERFACE(TextArtInterface,
                   "com.software-inc.TextArt.TextArtInterface/1.0")
```

An interface class normally declares a virtual destructor, a virtual function that returns a `QStringList`, and one or more other virtual functions. The destructor is there primarily to silence the compiler, which might otherwise complain about the lack of a virtual destructor in a class that has virtual functions. In this example, the `effects()` function returns a list of the text effects the plugin can provide. We can think of this list as a list of keys. Every time we call one of the other functions, we pass one of these keys as first argument, making it possible to implement multiple effects in one plugin.

At the end, we use the `Q_DECLARE_INTERFACE()` macro to associate an identifier to the interface. The identifier normally has four components: an inverted domain name specifying the creator of the interface, the name of the application, the name of the interface, and a version number. Whenever we alter the interface (for example, by adding a virtual function or changing the signature of an existing function), we must remember to increase the version number; otherwise, the application might crash trying to access an outdated plugin.

The application is implemented in a class called `TextArtDialog`. We will only show the code relevant to making it plugin-aware. Let's start with the constructor:

```
TextArtDialog::TextArtDialog(const QString &text, QWidget *parent)
    : QDialog(parent)
{
    listWidget = new QListWidget;
    listWidget->setViewMode(QListWidget::IconMode);
    listWidget->setMovement(QListWidget::Static);
    listWidget->setIconSize(QSize(260, 80));
    ...
    loadPlugins();
    populateListWidget(text);
    ...
}
```

The constructor creates a `QListWidget` to list the available effects. It calls the private function `loadPlugins()` to find and load any plugins that implement the `TextArtInterface` and populates the list widget accordingly by calling another private function, `populateListWidget()`.

```
void TextArtDialog::loadPlugins()
{
    QDir pluginDir(QApplication::applicationDirPath());

#if defined(Q_OS_WIN)
    if (pluginDir.dirName().toLower() == "debug"
            || pluginDir.dirName().toLower() == "release")
        pluginDir.cdUp();
#elif defined(Q_OS_MAC)
    if (pluginDir.dirName() == "MacOS") {
        pluginDir.cdUp();
        pluginDir.cdUp();
        pluginDir.cdUp();
    }
#endif
    if (!pluginDir.cd("plugins"))
        return;

    foreach (QString fileName, pluginDir.entryList(QDir::Files)) {
        QPluginLoader loader(pluginDir.absoluteFilePath(fileName));
        if (TextArtInterface *interface =
                    qobject_cast<TextArtInterface *>(loader.instance()))
            interfaces.append(interface);
    }
}
```

In `loadPlugins()`, we attempt to load all the files in the application's `plugins` directory. (On Windows, the application's executable usually lives in a `debug` or `release` subdirectory, so we move one directory up. On Mac OS X, we take the bundle directory structure into account.)

If the file we try to load is a Qt plugin that uses the same version of Qt as the application, `QPluginLoader::instance()` will return a `QObject *` that points to a

Qt plugin. We use `qobject_cast<T>()` to check whether the plugin implements the `TextArtInterface`. Each time the cast is successful, we add the interface to the `TextArtDialog`'s list of interfaces (of type `QList<TextArtInterface *>`).

Some applications may want to load two or more different interfaces, in which case the code for obtaining the interfaces would look more like that shown below:

```
QObject *plugin = loader.instance();
if (TextArtInterface *i = qobject_cast<TextArtInterface *>(plugin))
    textArtInterfaces.append(i);
if (BorderArtInterface *i = qobject_cast<BorderArtInterface *>(plugin))
    borderArtInterfaces.append(i);


if (TextureInterface *i = qobject_cast<TextureInterface *>(plugin))
    textureInterfaces.append(i);
```

The same plugin may successfully cast to more than one interface pointer, since it is possible for plugins to provide multiple interfaces by using multiple inheritance.

```
void TextArtDialog::populateListWidget(const QString &text)
{
    QSize iconSize = listWidget->iconSize();
    QPen pen(QColor("darkseagreen"));

    QLinearGradient gradient(0, 0, iconSize.width() / 2,
                                   iconSize.height() / 2);
    gradient.setColorAt(0.0, QColor("darkolivegreen"));
    gradient.setColorAt(0.8, QColor("darkgreen"));
    gradient.setColorAt(1.0, QColor("lightgreen"));

    QFont font("Helvetica", iconSize.height(), QFont::Bold);

    foreach (TextArtInterface *interface, interfaces) {
        foreach (QString effect, interface->effects()) {
            QListWidgetItem *item = new QListWidgetItem(effect,
                                                        listWidget);
            QPixmap pixmap = interface->applyEffect(effect, text, font,
                                                    iconSize, pen,
                                                    gradient);
            item->setData(Qt::DecorationRole, pixmap);
        }
    }
    listWidget->setCurrentRow(0);
}
```

The `populateListWidget()` function begins by creating some variables to pass to the `applyEffect()` function, in particular a pen, a linear gradient, and a font. It then iterates over every `TextArtInterface` that was found by `loadPlugins()`. For each effect provided by each interface, a new `QListWidgetItem` is created with its text set to the name of the effect it represents, and a `QPixmap` is created using `applyEffect()`.

In this section we have seen how to load plugins by calling loadPlugins() in the constructor, and how to make use of them in populateListWidget(). The code copes gracefully whether there are no plugins providing TextArtInterfaces, just one, or more than one. Furthermore, additional plugins could be added later: Every time the application starts up it loads whatever plugins it finds that provide the interfaces it wants. This makes it easy to extend the application's functionality without changing the application itself.

Writing Application Plugins

An application plugin is a subclass of QObject and of the interfaces it wants to provide. The CD that accompanies this book includes two plugins for the Text Art application presented in the previous section, to show that the application correctly handles multiple plugins.

Here, we will only review the code for one of them, the Basic Effects Plugin. We will assume that the plugin's source code is located in a directory called basiceffectsplugin and that the Text Art application is located in a parallel directory called textart. Here's the declaration of the plugin class:

```
class BasicEffectsPlugin : public QObject, public TextArtInterface
{
    Q_OBJECT
    Q_INTERFACES(TextArtInterface)

public:
    QStringList effects() const;
    QPixmap applyEffect(const QString &effect, const QString &text,
                        const QFont &font, const QSize &size,
                        const QPen &pen, const QBrush &brush);
};
```

The plugin implements only one interface, TextArtInterface. In addition to Q_OBJECT, we must use the Q_INTERFACES() macro for each of the interfaces that are subclassed to ensure smooth cooperation between moc and qobject_cast<T>().

```
QStringList BasicEffectsPlugin::effects() const
{
    return QStringList() << "Plain" << "Outline" << "Shadow";
}
```

The effects() function returns a list of text effects supported by the plugin. This plugin supports three effects, so we just return a list containing the name of each one.

The applyEffect() function provides the plugin's functionality and is slightly involved, so we will review it in pieces.

```
QPixmap BasicEffectsPlugin::applyEffect(const QString &effect,
        const QString &text, const QFont &font, const QSize &size,
        const QPen &pen, const QBrush &brush)
{
```

```
QFont myFont = font;
QFontMetrics metrics(myFont);
while ((metrics.width(text) > size.width()
        || metrics.height() > size.height())
       && myFont.pointSize() > 9) {
    myFont.setPointSize(myFont.pointSize() - 1);
    metrics = QFontMetrics(myFont);
}
```

We want to ensure that the given text will fit in the specified size if possible. For this reason, we use the font's metrics to see if the text is too large to fit, and if it is we enter a loop where we reduce the point size until we find a size that will fit, or until we reach 9 points, our fixed minimum size.

```
QPixmap pixmap(size);

QPainter painter(&pixmap);
painter.setFont(myFont);
painter.setPen(pen);
painter.setBrush(brush);
painter.setRenderHint(QPainter::Antialiasing, true);
painter.setRenderHint(QPainter::TextAntialiasing, true);
painter.setRenderHint(QPainter::SmoothPixmapTransform, true);
painter.eraseRect(pixmap.rect());
```

We create a pixmap of the required size and a painter to paint onto the pixmap. We also set some render hints to ensure the smoothest possible results. The call to eraseRect() clears the pixmap with the background color.

```
if (effect == "Plain") {
    painter.setPen(Qt::NoPen);
} else if (effect == "Outline") {
    QPen pen(Qt::black);
    pen.setWidthF(2.5);
    painter.setPen(pen);
} else if (effect == "Shadow") {
    QPainterPath path;
    painter.setBrush(Qt::darkGray);
    path.addText(((size.width() - metrics.width(text)) / 2) + 3,
                 (size.height() - metrics.descent()) + 3, myFont,
                 text);
    painter.drawPath(path);
    painter.setBrush(brush);
}
```

For the "Plain" effect, no outline is required. For the "Outline" effect, we ignore the original pen and create our own black pen with a 2.5-pixel width. For the "Shadow" effect, we need to draw the shadow first, so that the text can be painted on top of it.

```
QPainterPath path;
path.addText((size.width() - metrics.width(text)) / 2,
             size.height() - metrics.descent(), myFont, text);
```

```
        painter.drawPath(path);

        return pixmap;
    }
```

We now have the pen and brushes set appropriately for each text effect, and in the "Shadow" effect case have drawn the shadow. We are now ready to render the text. The text is horizontally centered and drawn far enough above the bottom of the pixmap to allow room for descenders.

```
    Q_EXPORT_PLUGIN2(basiceffectsplugin, BasicEffectsPlugin)
```

At the end of the .cpp file, we use the Q_EXPORT_PLUGIN2() macro to make the plugin available to Qt.

The .pro file is similar to the one we used for the Windows cursor plugin earlier in this chapter (p. 408):

```
    TEMPLATE        = lib
    CONFIG         += plugin
    HEADERS         = ../textart/textartinterface.h \
                      basiceffectsplugin.h
    SOURCES         = basiceffectsplugin.cpp
    DESTDIR         = ../textart/plugins
```

If this chapter has whet your appetite for application plugins, you might like to study the more advanced Plug & Paint example provided with Qt. The application supports three different interfaces and includes a useful Plugin Information dialog that lists the plugins and interfaces that are available to the application.

20. Platform-Specific Features

In this chapter, we will review some of the platform-specific options available to Qt programmers. We begin by looking at how to access native APIs such as the Win32 API on Windows, Carbon on Mac OS X, and Xlib on X11. We then move on to explore the ActiveQt extension, showing how to use ActiveX controls within Qt/Windows applications and how to create applications that act as ActiveX servers. In the last section, we explain how to make Qt applications cooperate with the session manager under X11.

In addition to the features presented here, Trolltech offers several platform-specific Qt Solutions, including the Qt/Motif and Qt/MFC migration frameworks to ease the migration of Motif/Xt and MFC applications to Qt. A similar extension for Tcl/Tk applications is provided by *froglogic*, and a Microsoft Windows resource converter is available from Klarälvdalens Datakonsult. See the following web pages for details:

- http://www.trolltech.com/products/solutions/catalog/
- http://www.froglogic.com/tq/
- http://www.kdab.net/knut/

For embedded development, Trolltech offers the Qtopia application platform. This is covered in Chapter 21.

Interfacing with Native APIs

Qt's comprehensive API caters for most needs on all platforms, but in some circumstances, we may want to use the underlying platform-specific APIs. In this section, we will show how to use the native APIs for the different platforms supported by Qt to accomplish particular tasks.

On every platform, QWidget provides a winId() function that returns the window ID or handle. QWidget also provides a static function called find() that returns the QWidget with a particular window ID. We can pass this ID to native API functions to achieve platform-specific effects. For example, the following code uses `winId()` to move the title bar of a tool window to the left using native Mac OS X functions:

```
#ifdef Q_WS_MAC
    ChangeWindowAttributes(HIViewGetWindow(HIViewRef(toolWin.winId()))),
                           kWindowSideTitlebarAttribute,
                           kWindowNoAttributes);
#endif
```

Figure 20.1. A Mac OS X tool window with the title bar on the side

On X11, here's how we would modify a window property:

```
#ifdef Q_WS_X11
    Atom atom = XInternAtom(QX11Info::display(), "MY_PROPERTY", False);
    long data = 1;
    XChangeProperty(QX11Info::display(), window->winId(), atom, atom,
                    32, PropModeReplace,
                    reinterpret_cast<uchar *>(&data), 1);
#endif
```

The `#ifdef` and `#endif` directives around the platform-specific code ensure that the application will still compile on other platforms.

For a Windows-only application, here's an example of how we can use GDI calls to draw on a Qt widget:

```
void GdiControl::paintEvent(QPaintEvent * /* event */)
{
    RECT rect;
    GetClientRect(winId(), &rect);
    HDC hdc = GetDC(winId());

    FillRect(hdc, &rect, HBRUSH(COLOR_WINDOW + 1));
    SetTextAlign(hdc, TA_CENTER | TA_BASELINE);
    TextOutW(hdc, width() / 2, height() / 2, text.utf16(), text.size());

    ReleaseDC(winId(), hdc);
}
```

For this to work, we must also reimplement QPaintDevice::paintEngine() to return a null pointer and set the Qt::WA_PaintOnScreen attribute in the widget's constructor.

The next example shows how to combine QPainter and GDI calls in a paint event handler using QPaintEngine's getDC() and releaseDC() functions:

```
void MyWidget::paintEvent(QPaintEvent * /* event */)
{
    QPainter painter(this);
    painter.fillRect(rect().adjusted(20, 20, -20, -20), Qt::red);
#ifdef Q_WS_WIN
    HDC hdc = painter.paintEngine()->getDC();
    Rectangle(hdc, 40, 40, width() - 40, height() - 40);
    painter.paintEngine()->releaseDC();
#endif
}
```

Mixing QPainter and GDI calls like this can sometimes lead to strange results, especially when QPainter calls occur after GDI calls, because QPainter makes some assumptions about the state of the underlying drawing layer.

Qt defines one of the following four window system symbols: Q_WS_WIN, Q_WS_X11, Q_WS_MAC, and Q_WS_QWS (Qtopia). We must include at least one Qt header before we can use them in applications. Qt also provides preprocessor symbols to identify the operating system:

- Q_OS_AIX
- Q_OS_BSD4
- Q_OS_BSDI
- Q_OS_CYGWIN
- Q_OS_DGUX
- Q_OS_DYNIX
- Q_OS_FREEBSD
- Q_OS_HPUX
- Q_OS_HURD
- Q_OS_IRIX
- Q_OS_LINUX
- Q_OS_LYNX
- Q_OS_MAC
- Q_OS_NETBSD
- Q_OS_OPENBSD
- Q_OS_OS2EMX
- Q_OS_OSF
- Q_OS_QNX6
- Q_OS_QNX
- Q_OS_RELIANT
- Q_OS_SCO
- Q_OS_SOLARIS
- Q_OS_ULTRIX
- Q_OS_UNIXWARE
- Q_OS_WIN32
- Q_OS_WIN64

We can assume that at most one of these will be defined. For convenience, Qt also defines Q_OS_WIN when either Win32 or Win64 is detected, and Q_OS_UNIX when any Unix-based operating system (including Linux and Mac OS X) is detected. At run-time, we can check QSysInfo::WindowsVersion or QSysInfo::MacintoshVersion to distinguish between different versions of Windows (2000, ME, etc.) or Mac OS X (10.2, 10.3, etc.).

In addition to the operating system and window system macros, there is also a set of compiler macros. For example, Q_CC_MSVC is defined if the compiler is Microsoft Visual C++. These can be useful for working around compiler bugs.

Several of Qt's GUI-related classes provide platform-specific functions that return low-level handles to the underlying object. These are listed in Figure 20.2.

Mac OS X	
ATSFontFormatRef	QFont::handle()
CGImageRef	QPixmap::macCGHandle()
GWorldPtr	QPixmap::macQDAlphaHandle()
GWorldPtr	QPixmap::macQDHandle()
RgnHandle	QRegion::handle()
HIViewRef	QWidget::winId()
Windows	
HCURSOR	QCursor::handle()
HDC	QPaintEngine::getDC()
HDC	QPrintEngine::getPrinterDC()
HFONT	QFont::handle()
HPALETTE	QColormap::hPal()
HRGN	QRegion::handle()
HWND	QWidget::winId()
X11	
Cursor	QCursor::handle()
Font	QFont::handle()
Picture	QPixmap::x11PictureHandle()
Picture	QWidget::x11PictureHandle()
Pixmap	QPixmap::handle()
QX11Info	QPixmap::x11Info()
QX11Info	QWidget::x11Info()
Region	QRegion::handle()
Screen	QCursor::x11Screen()
SmcConn	QSessionManager::handle()
Window	QWidget::handle()
Window	QWidget::winId()

Figure 20.2. Platform-specific functions to access low-level handles

On X11, QPixmap::x11Info() and QWidget::x11Info() return a QX11Info object that provides various pointers or handles, such as display(), screen(), colormap(), and visual(). We can use these to set up an X11 graphics context on a QPixmap or QWidget, for example.

Qt applications that need to interface with other toolkits or libraries frequently need to access the low-level events (XEvents on X11, MSGs on Windows, EventRef on Mac OS X, QWSEvents on Qtopia) before they are converted into

`QEvents`. We can do this by subclassing `QApplication` and reimplementing the relevant platform-specific event filter, one of `x11EventFilter()`, `winEventFilter()`, `macEventFilter()`, and `qwsEventFilter()`. Alternatively, we can access the platform-specific events that are sent to a given `QWidget` by reimplementing one of `x11Event()`, `winEvent()`, `macEvent()`, and `qwsEvent()`. This can be useful for handling certain types of events that Qt normally ignores, such as joystick events.

For more information about platform-specific issues, including how to deploy Qt applications on different platforms, see `http://doc.trolltech.com/4.1/win-system.html`.

Using ActiveX on Windows

Microsoft's ActiveX technology allows applications to incorporate user interface components provided by other applications or libraries. It is built on Microsoft COM and defines one set of interfaces for applications that use components and another set of interfaces for applications and libraries that provide components.

The Qt/Windows Desktop Edition provides the ActiveQt framework to seamlessly combine ActiveX and Qt. ActiveQt consists of two modules:

- The *QAxContainer* module allows us to use COM objects and to embed ActiveX controls in Qt applications.

- The *QAxServer* module allows us to export custom COM objects and ActiveX controls written using Qt.

Our first example will embed the Windows Media Player in a Qt application using the *QAxContainer* module. The Qt application adds an Open button, a Play/Pause button, a Stop button, and a slider to the Windows Media Player ActiveX control.

Figure 20.3. The Media Player application

The application's main window is of type PlayerWindow:

```
class PlayerWindow : public QWidget
{
    Q_OBJECT
    Q_ENUMS(ReadyStateConstants)

public:
    enum PlayStateConstants { Stopped = 0, Paused = 1, Playing = 2 };
    enum ReadyStateConstants { Uninitialized = 0, Loading = 1,
                               Interactive = 3, Complete = 4 };

    PlayerWindow();

protected:
    void timerEvent(QTimerEvent *event);

private slots:
    void onPlayStateChange(int oldState, int newState);
    void onReadyStateChange(ReadyStateConstants readyState);
    void onPositionChange(double oldPos, double newPos);
    void sliderValueChanged(int newValue);
    void openFile();

private:
    QAxWidget *wmp;
    QToolButton *openButton;
    QToolButton *playPauseButton;
    QToolButton *stopButton;
    QSlider *seekSlider;
    QString fileFilters;
    int updateTimer;
};
```

The PlayerWindow class inherits from QWidget. The Q_ENUMS() macro (just below Q_OBJECT) is necessary to tell moc that the ReadyStateConstants type used in the onReadyStateChange() slot is an enum type. In the private section, we declare a QAxWidget * data member.

```
PlayerWindow::PlayerWindow()
{
    wmp = new QAxWidget;
    wmp->setControl("{22D6F312-B0F6-11D0-94AB-0080C74C7E95}");
```

In the constructor, we start by creating a QAxWidget object to encapsulate the Windows Media Player ActiveX control. The *QAxContainer* module consists of three classes: QAxObject encapsulates a COM object, QAxWidget encapsulates an ActiveX control, and QAxBase implements the core COM functionality for QAxObject and QAxWidget.

We call setControl() on the QAxWidget with the class ID of the Windows Media Player 6.4 control. This will create an instance of the required component. From then on, all the properties, events, and methods of the ActiveX control are available as Qt properties, signals, and slots through the QAxWidget object.

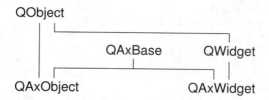

Figure 20.4. Inheritance tree for the *QAxContainer* module

The COM data types are automatically converted into the corresponding Qt types, as summarized in Figure 20.5. For example, an in-parameter of type VARIANT_BOOL becomes a bool, and an out-parameter of type VARIANT_BOOL becomes a bool &. If the resulting type is a Qt class (QString, QDateTime, etc.), the in-parameter is a const reference (for example, const QString &).

COM types	Qt types
VARIANT_BOOL	bool
char, short, int, long	int
unsigned char, unsigned short, unsigned int, unsigned long	uint
float, double	double
CY	qlonglong, qulonglong
BSTR	QString
DATE	QDateTime, QDate, QTime
OLE_COLOR	QColor
SAFEARRAY(VARIANT)	QList<QVariant>
SAFEARRAY(BSTR)	QStringList
SAFEARRAY(BYTE)	QByteArray
VARIANT	QVariant
IFontDisp *	QFont
IPictureDisp *	QPixmap
User defined type	QRect, QSize, QPoint

Figure 20.5. Relationship between COM types and Qt types

To obtain the list of all the properties, signals, and slots available in a QAxObject or QAxWidget with their Qt data types, call QAxBase::generateDocumentation() or use Qt's dumpdoc command-line tool, located in Qt's tools\activeqt\dumpdoc directory.

Let's continue with the PlayerWindow constructor:

```
wmp->setProperty("ShowControls", false);
wmp->setSizePolicy(QSizePolicy::Expanding, QSizePolicy::Expanding);
```

```
connect(wmp, SIGNAL(PlayStateChange(int, int)),
        this, SLOT(onPlayStateChange(int, int)));
connect(wmp, SIGNAL(ReadyStateChange(ReadyStateConstants)),
        this, SLOT(onReadyStateChange(ReadyStateConstants)));
connect(wmp, SIGNAL(PositionChange(double, double)),
        this, SLOT(onPositionChange(double, double)));
```

After calling `QAxWidget::setControl()`, we call `QObject::setProperty()` to set the `ShowControls` property of the Windows Media Player to `false`, since we provide our own buttons to manipulate the component. `QObject::setProperty()` can be used both for COM properties and for normal Qt properties. Its second parameter is of type `QVariant`.

Next, we call `setSizePolicy()` to make the ActiveX control take all the available space in the layout, and we connect three ActiveX events from the COM component to three slots.

```
    ...
stopButton = new QToolButton;
stopButton->setText(tr("&Stop"));
stopButton->setEnabled(false);
connect(stopButton, SIGNAL(clicked()), wmp, SLOT(Stop()));
    ...
}
```

The rest of the `PlayerWindow` constructor follows the usual pattern, except that we connect some Qt signals to slots provided by the COM object (`Play()`, `Pause()`, and `Stop()`). Since the buttons are similar, we have only shown the Stop button's implementation here.

Let's leave the constructor and look at the `timerEvent()` function:

```
void PlayerWindow::timerEvent(QTimerEvent *event)
{
    if (event->timerId() == updateTimer) {
        double curPos = wmp->property("CurrentPosition").toDouble();
        onPositionChange(-1, curPos);
    } else {
        QWidget::timerEvent(event);
    }
}
```

The `timerEvent()` function is called at regular intervals while a media clip is playing. We use it to advance the slider. This is done by calling `property()` on the ActiveX control to obtain the value of the `CurrentPosition` property as a `QVariant` and calling `toDouble()` to convert it to a `double`. We then call `onPositionChange()` to perform the update.

We will not review the rest of the code because most of it isn't directly relevant to ActiveX and doesn't show anything that we haven't covered already. The code is included on the CD.

In the `.pro` file, we need this entry to link with the *QAxContainer* module:

```
CONFIG       += qaxcontainer
```

One frequent need when dealing with COM objects is to be able to call a COM method directly (as opposed to connecting it to a Qt signal). The easiest way to do this is to invoke QAxBase::dynamicCall() with the name and signature of the method as first parameter and the arguments to the method as additional parameters. For example:

```
wmp->dynamicCall("TitlePlay(uint)", 6);
```

The dynamicCall() function takes up to eight parameters of type QVariant and returns a QVariant. If we need to pass an IDispatch * or an IUnknown * this way, we can encapsulate the component in a QAxObject and call asVariant() on it to convert it to a QVariant. If we need to call a COM method that returns an IDispatch * or an IUnknown *, or if we need to access a COM property of one of those types, we can use querySubObject() instead:

```
QAxObject *session = outlook.querySubObject("Session");
QAxObject *defaultContacts =
        session->querySubObject("GetDefaultFolder(OlDefaultFolders)",
                                "olFolderContacts");
```

If we want to call methods that have unsupported data types in their parameter list, we can use QAxBase::queryInterface() to retrieve the COM interface and call the method directly. As usual with COM, we must call Release() when we have finished using the interface. If we often need to call such methods, we can subclass QAxObject or QAxWidget and provide member functions that encapsulate the COM interface calls. Be aware that QAxObject and QAxWidget subclasses cannot define their own properties, signals, or slots.

We will now review the *QAxServer* module. This module enables us to turn a standard Qt program into an ActiveX server. The server can either be a shared library or a stand-alone application. Servers built as shared libraries are often called in-process servers; stand-alone applications are called out-of-process servers.

Our first *QAxServer* example is an in-process server that provides a widget that shows a ball bouncing left and right. We will also see how to embed the widget in Internet Explorer.

Here's the beginning of the class definition of the AxBouncer widget:

```
class AxBouncer : public QWidget, public QAxBindable
{
    Q_OBJECT
    Q_ENUMS(SpeedValue)
    Q_PROPERTY(QColor color READ color WRITE setColor)
    Q_PROPERTY(SpeedValue speed READ speed WRITE setSpeed)
    Q_PROPERTY(int radius READ radius WRITE setRadius)
    Q_PROPERTY(bool running READ isRunning)
```

AxBouncer inherits from both QWidget and QAxBindable. The QAxBindable class provides an interface between the widget and an ActiveX client. Any QWidget can be exported as an ActiveX control, but by subclassing QAxBindable we can notify the client when a property's value changes, and we can implement COM interfaces to supplement those already implemented by *QAxServer*.

Figure 20.6. The AxBouncer widget in Internet Explorer

When doing multiple inheritance involving a QObject-derived class, we must always put the QObject-derived class first so that moc can pick it up.

We declare three read-write properties and one read-only property. The Q_ ENUMS() macro is necessary to tell moc that the SpeedValue type is an enum type. The enum is declared in the public section of the class:

```
public:
    enum SpeedValue { Slow, Normal, Fast };

    AxBouncer(QWidget *parent = 0);

    void setSpeed(SpeedValue newSpeed);
    SpeedValue speed() const { return ballSpeed; }
    void setRadius(int newRadius);
    int radius() const { return ballRadius; }
    void setColor(const QColor &newColor);
    QColor color() const { return ballColor; }
    bool isRunning() const { return myTimerId != 0; }
    QSize sizeHint() const;
    QAxAggregated *createAggregate();
```

```
public slots:
    void start();
    void stop();

signals:
    void bouncing();
```

The AxBouncer constructor is a standard constructor for a widget, with a parent parameter. The QAXFACTORY_DEFAULT() macro, which we will use to export the component, expects a constructor with this signature.

The createAggregate() function is reimplemented from QAxBindable. We will explain it in a moment.

```
protected:
    void paintEvent(QPaintEvent *event);
    void timerEvent(QTimerEvent *event);

private:
    int intervalInMilliseconds() const;

    QColor ballColor;
    SpeedValue ballSpeed;
    int ballRadius;
    int myTimerId;
    int x;
    int delta;
};
```

The protected and private sections of the class are the same as those we would have if this was a standard Qt widget.

```
AxBouncer::AxBouncer(QWidget *parent)
    : QWidget(parent)
{
    ballColor = Qt::blue;
    ballSpeed = Normal;
    ballRadius = 15;
    myTimerId = 0;
    x = 20;
    delta = 2;
}
```

The AxBouncer constructor initializes the class's private variables.

```
void AxBouncer::setColor(const QColor &newColor)
{
    if (newColor != ballColor && requestPropertyChange("color")) {
        ballColor = newColor;
        update();
        propertyChanged("color");
    }
}
```

The setColor() function sets the value of the color property. It calls update() to repaint the widget.

The unusual part is the requestPropertyChange() and propertyChanged() calls. These functions are inherited from QAxBindable and should ideally be called whenever we change a property. The requestPropertyChange() asks the client's permission to change a property, and returns true if the client allows the change. The propertyChanged() function notifies the client that the property has been changed.

The setSpeed() and setRadius() property setters also follow this pattern, and so do the start() and stop() slots, since they change the value of the running property.

There is one interesting AxBouncer member function left:

```
QAxAggregated *AxBouncer::createAggregate()
{
    return new ObjectSafetyImpl;
}
```

The createAggregate() function is reimplemented from QAxBindable. It allows us to implement COM interfaces that the *QAxServer* module doesn't already implement or to bypass *QAxServer*'s default COM interfaces. Here, we do it to provide the IObjectSafety interface, which is used by Internet Explorer to access a component's safety options. This is the standard trick to get rid of Internet Explorer's infamous "Object not safe for scripting" error message.

Here's the definition of the class that implements the IObjectSafety interface:

```
class ObjectSafetyImpl : public QAxAggregated, public IObjectSafety
{
public:
    long queryInterface(const QUuid &iid, void **iface);

    QAXAGG_IUNKNOWN

    HRESULT WINAPI GetInterfaceSafetyOptions(REFIID riid,
            DWORD *pdwSupportedOptions, DWORD *pdwEnabledOptions);
    HRESULT WINAPI SetInterfaceSafetyOptions(REFIID riid,
            DWORD pdwSupportedOptions, DWORD pdwEnabledOptions);
};
```

The ObjectSafetyImpl class inherits both QAxAggregated and IObjectSafety. The QAxAggregated class is an abstract base class for implementations of additional COM interfaces. The COM object that the QAxAggregated extends is accessible through controllingUnknown(). This COM object is created behind the scenes by the *QAxServer* module.

The QAXAGG_IUNKNOWN macro provides standard implementations of QueryInterface(), AddRef(), and Release(). These implementations simply call the same functions on the controlling COM object.

```
long ObjectSafetyImpl::queryInterface(const QUuid &iid, void **iface)
{
    *iface = 0;
    if (iid == IID_IObjectSafety) {
```

```
            *iface = static_cast<IObjectSafety *>(this);
        } else {
            return E_NOINTERFACE;
        }
        AddRef();
        return S_OK;
    }
```

The `queryInterface()` function is a pure virtual function of `QAxAggregated`. It is called by the controlling COM object to give access to the interfaces provided by the `QAxAggregated` subclass. We must return `E_NOINTERFACE` for interfaces that we don't implement and for `IUnknown`.

```
HRESULT WINAPI ObjectSafetyImpl::GetInterfaceSafetyOptions(
        REFIID /* riid */, DWORD *pdwSupportedOptions,
        DWORD *pdwEnabledOptions)
{
    *pdwSupportedOptions = INTERFACESAFE_FOR_UNTRUSTED_DATA
                            | INTERFACESAFE_FOR_UNTRUSTED_CALLER;
    *pdwEnabledOptions = *pdwSupportedOptions;
    return S_OK;
}

HRESULT WINAPI ObjectSafetyImpl::SetInterfaceSafetyOptions(
        REFIID /* riid */, DWORD /* pdwSupportedOptions */,
        DWORD /* pdwEnabledOptions */)
{
    return S_OK;
}
```

The `GetInterfaceSafetyOptions()` and `SetInterfaceSafetyOptions()` functions are declared in `IObjectSafety`. We implement them to tell the world that our object is safe for scripting.

Let's now review `main.cpp`:

```
#include <QAxFactory>

#include "axbouncer.h"

QAXFACTORY_DEFAULT(AxBouncer,
                    "{5e2461aa-a3e8-4f7a-8b04-307459a4c08c}",
                    "{533af11f-4899-43de-8b7f-2ddf588d1015}",
                    "{772c14a5-a840-4023-b79d-19549ece0cd9}",
                    "{dbce1e56-70dd-4f74-85e0-95c65d86254d}",
                    "{3f3db5e0-78ff-4e35-8a5d-3d3b96c83e09}")
```

The `QAXFACTORY_DEFAULT()` macro exports an ActiveX control. We can use it for ActiveX servers that export only one control. The next example in this section will show how to export many ActiveX controls.

The first argument to `QAXFACTORY_DEFAULT()` is the name of the Qt class to export. This is also the name under which the control is exported. The other five arguments are the class ID, the interface ID, the event interface ID, the type library ID, and the application ID. We can use standard tools like guidgen or uuidgen to generate these identifiers. Because the server is a library, we don't need a main() function.

Here's the .pro file for our in-process ActiveX server:

```
TEMPLATE      = lib
CONFIG       += dll qaxserver
HEADERS       = axbouncer.h \
                objectsafetyimpl.h
SOURCES       = axbouncer.cpp \
                main.cpp \
                objectsafetyimpl.cpp
RC_FILE       = qaxserver.rc
DEF_FILE      = qaxserver.def
```

The qaxserver.rc and qaxserver.def files referred to in the .pro file are standard files that can be copied from Qt's src\activeqt\control directory.

The makefile or Visual C++ project file generated by qmake contains rules to register the server in the Windows registry. To register the server on end-user machines, we can use the regsvr32 tool available on all Windows systems.

We can then include the Bouncer component in an HTML page using the <object> tag:

```
<object id="AxBouncer"
        classid="clsid:5e2461aa-a3e8-4f7a-8b04-307459a4c08c">
<b>The ActiveX control is not available. Make sure you have built and
registered the component server.</b>
</object>
```

We can create buttons that invoke slots:

```
<input type="button" value="Start" onClick="AxBouncer.start()">
<input type="button" value="Stop" onClick="AxBouncer.stop()">
```

We can manipulate the widget using JavaScript or VBScript just like any other ActiveX control. See the demo.html file on the CD for a rudimentary page that uses the ActiveX server.

Our last example is a scriptable Address Book application. The application can serve as a standard Qt/Windows application or an out-of-process ActiveX server. The latter possibility allows us to script the application using, say, Visual Basic.

```
class AddressBook : public QMainWindow
{
    Q_OBJECT
    Q_PROPERTY(int count READ count)
    Q_CLASSINFO("ClassID", "{588141ef-110d-4beb-95ab-ee6a478b576d}")
    Q_CLASSINFO("InterfaceID", "{718780ec-b30c-4d88-83b3-79b3d9e78502}")
    Q_CLASSINFO("ToSuperClass", "AddressBook")

public:
    AddressBook(QWidget *parent = 0);
    ~AddressBook();
```

```
        int count() const;

    public slots:
        ABItem *createEntry(const QString &contact);
        ABItem *findEntry(const QString &contact) const;
        ABItem *entryAt(int index) const;

    private slots:
        void addEntry();
        void editEntry();
        void deleteEntry();

    private:
        void createActions();
        void createMenus();

        QTreeWidget *treeWidget;
        QMenu *fileMenu;
        QMenu *editMenu;
        QAction *exitAction;
        QAction *addEntryAction;
        QAction *editEntryAction;
        QAction *deleteEntryAction;
    };
```

The AddressBook widget is the application's main window. The property and the slots it provides will be available for scripting. The Q_CLASSINFO() macro is used to specify the class and interface IDs associated with the class. These were generated using a tool such as guid or uuid.

In the previous example, we specified the class and interface IDs when we exported the QAxBouncer class using the QAXFACTORY_DEFAULT() macro. In this example, we want to export several classes, so we cannot use QAXFACTORY_DEFAULT(). There are two options available to us:

- We can subclass QAxFactory, reimplement its virtual functions to provide information about the types we want to export, and use the QAXFACTORY_EXPORT() macro to register the factory.

- We can use the QAXFACTORY_BEGIN(), QAXFACTORY_END(), QAXCLASS(), and QAX-TYPE() macros to declare and register the factory. This approach requires us to specify the class and interface IDs using Q_CLASSINFO().

Back to the AddressBook class definition: The third occurrence of Q_CLASSINFO() may seem a bit mysterious. By default, ActiveX controls expose not only their own properties, signals, and slots to clients, but also those of their superclasses up to QWidget. The ToSuperClass attribute lets us specify the highest superclass (in the inheritance tree) that we want to expose. Here, we specify the class name of the component (AddressBook) as the highest superclass to export, meaning that properties, signals, and slots defined in AddressBook's superclasses will not be exported.

```
class ABItem : public QObject, public QTreeWidgetItem
{
    Q_OBJECT
    Q_PROPERTY(QString contact READ contact WRITE setContact)
    Q_PROPERTY(QString address READ address WRITE setAddress)
    Q_PROPERTY(QString phoneNumber READ phoneNumber WRITE setPhoneNumber)
    Q_CLASSINFO("ClassID", "{bc82730e-5f39-4e5c-96be-461c2cd0d282}")
    Q_CLASSINFO("InterfaceID", "{c8bc1656-870e-48a9-9937-fbe1ceff8b2e}")
    Q_CLASSINFO("ToSuperClass", "ABItem")

public:
    ABItem(QTreeWidget *treeWidget);

    void setContact(const QString &contact);
    QString contact() const { return text(0); }
    void setAddress(const QString &address);
    QString address() const { return text(1); }
    void setPhoneNumber(const QString &number);
    QString phoneNumber() const { return text(2); }

public slots:
    void remove();
};
```

The ABItem class represents one entry in the address book. It inherits from QTreeWidgetItem so that it can be shown in a QTreeWidget and from QObject so that it can be exported as a COM object.

```
int main(int argc, char *argv[])
{
    QApplication app(argc, argv);
    if (!QAxFactory::isServer()) {
        AddressBook addressBook;
        addressBook.show();
        return app.exec();
    }
    return app.exec();
}
```

In main(), we check whether the application is being run stand-alone or as a server. The -activex command-line option is recognized by QApplication and makes the application run as a server. If the application isn't run as a server, we create the main widget and show it as we would normally do in any stand-alone Qt application.

In addition to -activex, ActiveX servers understand the following command-line options:

- -regserver registers the server in the system registry.

- -unregserver unregisters the server from the system registry.

- -dumpidl file writes the server's IDL to the specified file.

When the application is run as a server, we must export the AddressBook and ABItem classes as COM components:

```
QAXFACTORY_BEGIN("{2b2b6f3e-86cf-4c49-9df5-80483b47f17b}",
                 "{8e827b25-148b-4307-ba7d-23f275244818}")
QAXCLASS(AddressBook)
QAXTYPE(ABItem)
QAXFACTORY_END()
```

The above macros export a factory for creating COM objects. Since we want to export two types of COM objects, we cannot simply use QAXFACTORY_DEFAULT() as we did in the previous example.

The first argument to QAXFACTORY_BEGIN() is the type library ID; the second argument is the application ID. Between QAXFACTORY_BEGIN() and QAXFACTORY_END(), we specify all the classes that can be instantiated and all the data types that we want to make accessible as COM objects.

This is the .pro file for our out-of-process ActiveX server:

```
TEMPLATE    = app
CONFIG     += qaxserver
HEADERS     = abitem.h \
              addressbook.h \
              editdialog.h
SOURCES     = abitem.cpp \
              addressbook.cpp \
              editdialog.cpp \
              main.cpp
FORMS       = editdialog.ui
RC_FILE     = qaxserver.rc
```

The qaxserver.rc file referred to in the .pro file is a standard file that can be copied from Qt's src\activeqt\control directory.

Look in the example's vb directory for a Visual Basic project that uses the Address Book server.

This completes our overview of the ActiveQt framework. The Qt distribution includes additional examples, and the documentation contains information about how to build the *QAxContainer* and *QAxServer* modules and how to solve common interoperability issues.

Handling X11 Session Management

When we log out on X11, some window managers ask us whether we want to save the session. If we say yes, the applications that were running are automatically restarted the next time we log in, with the same screen positions and, ideally, with the same state as they had when we logged out.

The X11-specific component that takes care of saving and restoring the session is called the *session manager*. To make a Qt/X11 application aware of the session manager, we must reimplement QApplication::saveState() and save the application's state there.

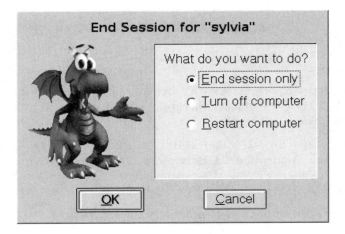

Figure 20.7. Logging out on KDE

Windows 2000 and XP, and some Unix systems, offer a different mechanism called hibernation. When the user puts the computer into hibernation, the operating system simply dumps the computer's memory onto disk and reloads it when it wakes up. Applications do not need to do anything or even be aware that this happens.

When the user initiates a shutdown, we can take control just before the shutdown occurs by reimplementing QApplication::commitData(). This allows us to save any unsaved data and to interact with the user if required. This part of session management is supported on both X11 and Windows.

We will explore session management by going through the code of a session-aware Tic-Tac-Toe application. First, let's look at the main() function:

```
int main(int argc, char *argv[])
{
    Application app(argc, argv);
    TicTacToe toe;
    toe.setObjectName("toe");
    app.setTicTacToe(&toe);
    toe.show();
    return app.exec();
}
```

We create an Application object. The Application class inherits from QApplication and reimplements both commitData() and saveState() to support session management.

Next, we create a TicTacToe widget, make the Application object aware of it, and show it. We have called the TicTacToe widget "toe". We must give unique object names to top-level widgets if we want the session manager to restore the windows' sizes and positions.

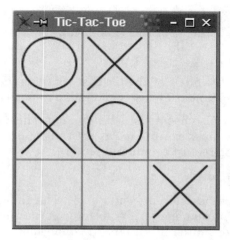

Figure 20.8. The Tic-Tac-Toe application

Here's the definition of the Application class:

```
class Application : public QApplication
{
    Q_OBJECT

public:
    Application(int &argc, char *argv[]);

    void setTicTacToe(TicTacToe *tic);
    void saveState(QSessionManager &sessionManager);
    void commitData(QSessionManager &sessionManager);

private:
    TicTacToe *ticTacToe;
};
```

The Application class keeps a pointer to the TicTacToe widget as a private variable.

```
void Application::saveState(QSessionManager &sessionManager)
{
    QString fileName = ticTacToe->saveState();

    QStringList discardCommand;
    discardCommand << "rm" << fileName;
    sessionManager.setDiscardCommand(discardCommand);
}
```

On X11, the saveState() function is called when the session manager wants the application to save its state. The function is available on other platforms as well, but it is never called. The QSessionManager parameter allows us to communicate with the session manager.

We start by asking the TicTacToe widget to save its state to a file. Then we set the session manager's discard command. A *discard command* is a command that the session manager must execute to delete any stored information regarding the current state. For this example, we set it to

```
rm sessionfile
```

where `sessionfile` is the name of the file that contains the saved state for the session, and `rm` is the standard Unix command to remove files.

The session manager also has a *restart command*. This is the command that the session manager must execute to restart the application. By default, Qt provides the following restart command:

```
appname -session id_key
```

The first part, `appname`, is derived from `argv[0]`. The `id` part is the session ID provided by the session manager; it is guaranteed to be unique among different applications and among different runs of the same application. The `key` part is added to uniquely identify the time at which the state was saved. For various reasons, the session manager can call `saveState()` multiple times during the same session, and the different states must be distinguished.

Because of limitations in existing session managers, we must ensure that the application's directory is in the PATH environment variable if we want the application to restart correctly. In particular, if you want to try out the Tic-Tac-Toe example for yourself, you must install it in, say, /usr/bin and invoke it as `tictactoe`.

For simple applications, including Tic-Tac-Toe, we could save the state as an additional command-line argument to the restart command. For example:

```
tictactoe -state OX-XO-X-O
```

This would save us from storing the data in a file and providing a discard command to remove the file.

```
void Application::commitData(QSessionManager &sessionManager)
{
    if (ticTacToe->gameInProgress()
            && sessionManager.allowsInteraction()) {
        int r = QMessageBox::warning(ticTacToe, tr("Tic-Tac-Toe"),
                        tr("The game hasn't finished.\n"
                           "Do you really want to quit?"),
                        QMessageBox::Yes | QMessageBox::Default,
                        QMessageBox::No | QMessageBox::Escape);
        if (r == QMessageBox::Yes) {
            sessionManager.release();
        } else {
            sessionManager.cancel();
        }
    }
}
```

The `commitData()` function is called when the user logs out. We can reimplement it to pop up a message box warning the user about potential data loss. The default implementation closes all top-level widgets, which results in the same behavior as when the user closes the windows one after another by clicking the close button in their title bars. In Chapter 3, we saw how to reimplement closeEvent() to catch this and pop up a message box.

For the purposes of this example, we reimplement commitData() and pop up a message box asking the user to confirm the log out if a game is in progress and if the session manager allows us to interact with the user. If the user clicks Yes, we call release() to tell the session manager to continue logging out; if the user clicks No, we call cancel() to cancel the log out.

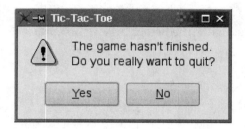

Figure 20.9. "Do you really want to quit?"

Now let's look at the TicTacToe class:

```
class TicTacToe : public QWidget
{
    Q_OBJECT

public:
    TicTacToe(QWidget *parent = 0);

    bool gameInProgress() const;
    QString saveState() const;
    QSize sizeHint() const;

protected:
    void paintEvent(QPaintEvent *event);
    void mousePressEvent(QMouseEvent *event);

private:
    enum { Empty = '-', Cross = 'X', Nought = 'O' };

    void clearBoard();
    void restoreState();
    QString sessionFileName() const;
    QRect cellRect(int row, int column) const;
    int cellWidth() const { return width() / 3; }
    int cellHeight() const { return height() / 3; }
    bool threeInARow(int row1, int col1, int row3, int col3) const;

    char board[3][3];
    int turnNumber;
};
```

The TicTacToe class inherits QWidget and reimplements sizeHint(), paintEvent(), and mousePressEvent(). It also provides the gameInProgress() and saveState() functions that we used in our Application class.

```
TicTacToe::TicTacToe(QWidget *parent)
    : QWidget(parent)
{
    clearBoard();
    if (qApp->isSessionRestored())
        restoreState();

    setWindowTitle(tr("Tic-Tac-Toe"));
}
```

In the constructor, we clear the board, and if the application was invoked with the –session option, we call the private function restoreState() to reload the old session.

```
void TicTacToe::clearBoard()
{
    for (int row = 0; row < 3; ++row) {
        for (int column = 0; column < 3; ++column) {
            board[row][column] = Empty;
        }
    }
    turnNumber = 0;
}
```

In clearBoard(), we clear all the cells and set turnNumber to 0.

```
QString TicTacToe::saveState() const
{
    QFile file(sessionFileName());
    if (file.open(QIODevice::WriteOnly)) {
        QTextStream out(&file);
        for (int row = 0; row < 3; ++row) {
            for (int column = 0; column < 3; ++column)
                out << board[row][column];
        }
    }
    return file.fileName();
}
```

In saveState(), we write the state of the board to disk. The format is straightforward, with 'X' for crosses, 'O' for noughts, and '–' for empty cells.

```
QString TicTacToe::sessionFileName() const
{
    return QDir::homePath() + "/.tictactoe_" + qApp->sessionId() + "_"
           + qApp->sessionKey();
}
```

The sessionFileName() private function returns the file name for the current session ID and session key. This function is used for both saveState() and restoreState(). The file name is derived from the session ID and session key.

```
void TicTacToe::restoreState()
{
    QFile file(sessionFileName());
    if (file.open(QIODevice::ReadOnly)) {
        QTextStream in(&file);
        for (int row = 0; row < 3; ++row) {
            for (int column = 0; column < 3; ++column) {
                in >> board[row][column];
                if (board[row][column] != Empty)
                    ++turnNumber;
            }
        }
    }
    update();
}
```

In restoreState(), we load the file that corresponds to the restored session and fill the board with that information. We deduce the value of turnNumber from the number of X's and O's on the board.

In the TicTacToe constructor, we called restoreState() if QApplication::isSessionRestored() returned true. In that case, sessionId() and sessionKey() return the same values as when the application's state was saved, and so sessionFileName() returns the file name for that session.

Testing and debugging session management can be frustrating, because we need to log in and out all the time. One way to avoid this is to use the standard xsm utility provided with X11. The first time we invoke xsm, it pops up a session manager window and a terminal. The applications we start from that terminal will all use xsm as their session manager instead of the usual, system-wide session manager. We can then use xsm's window to end, restart, or discard a session, and see if our application behaves as it should. For details about how to do this, see http://doc.trolltech.com/4.1/session.html.

21. Embedded Programming

Developing software to run on mobile devices such as PDAs and mobile phones can be very challenging because embedded systems generally have slower processors, less permanent storage (flash memory or hard disk), less memory, and smaller displays than desktop computers.

Qtopia Core (previously called Qt/Embedded) is a version of Qt optimized for embedded Linux. Qtopia Core provides the same API and tools as the desktop versions of Qt (Qt/Windows, Qt/X11, and Qt/Mac), and adds the classes and tools necessary for embedded programming. Through dual licensing, it is available for both open source and commercial development.

Qtopia Core can run on any hardware that runs Linux (including Intel x86, MIPS, ARM, StrongARM, Motorola 68000, and PowerPC architectures). It has a memory-mapped frame buffer and supports a C++ compiler. Unlike Qt/X11, it does not need the X Window System; instead, it implements its own window system (QWS), enabling significant storage and memory savings. To reduce its memory footprint even more, Qtopia Core can be recompiled to exclude unused features. If the applications and components used on a device are known in advance, they can be compiled together into one executable that links statically against the Qtopia Core libraries.

Qtopia Core also benefits from various features that are also part of the desktop versions of Qt, including the extensive use of implicit data sharing ("copy on write") as a memory-saving technique, support for custom widget styles through QStyle, and a layout system that adapts to make the best use of the available screen space.

Qtopia Core forms the basis of Trolltech's embedded offering, which also includes Qtopia Platform, Qtopia PDA, and Qtopia Phone. These provide classes and applications designed specifically for portable devices and can be integrated with several third-party Java virtual machines.

Getting Started with Qtopia

Qtopia Core applications can be developed on any platform equipped with a multi-platform tool chain. The most common option is to build a GNU C++ cross-compiler on a Unix system. This process is simplified by a script and a set of patches provided by Dan Kegel at http://kegel.com/crosstool/. Since Qtopia Core contains the Qt API, it is usually possible to use a desktop version of Qt, such as Qt/X11 or Qt/Windows, for most of the development.

Qtopia Core's configuration system supports cross-compilers, through the configure script's –embedded option. For example, to build for the ARM architecture we would type

```
./configure -embedded arm
```

We can create custom configurations by adding new files to Qt's mkspecs/ qws directory.

Qtopia Core draws directly to the Linux frame buffer (the memory area associated with the video display). To access the frame buffer, you might need to grant write permissions to the /dev/fb0 device.

To run Qtopia Core applications, we must first start one process to act as a server. The server is responsible for allocating screen regions to clients and for generating mouse and keyboard events. Any Qtopia Core application can become a server by specifying –qws on its command line or by passing QApplication:: GuiServer as the third parameter to the QApplication constructor.

Client applications communicate with the Qtopia Core server using shared memory. Behind the scenes, the clients draw themselves into shared memory and are responsible for painting their own window decorations. This keeps communication between the clients and the server to a minimum, resulting in a snappy user interface. Qtopia Core applications normally use QPainter to draw themselves, but they can also access the video hardware directly using QDirectPainter.

Clients can communicate with each other using the QCOP procotol. A client can listen on a named channel by creating a QCopChannel object and connecting to its received() signal. For example:

```
QCopChannel *channel = new QCopChannel("System", this);
connect(channel, SIGNAL(received(const QString &, const QByteArray &)),
        this, SLOT(received(const QString &, const QByteArray &)));
```

A QCOP message consists of a name and an optional QByteArray. The static QCopChannel::send() broadcasts a message on a channel. For example:

```
QByteArray data;
QDataStream out(&data, QIODevice::WriteOnly);
out << QDateTime::currentDateTime();

QCopChannel::send("System", "clockSkew(QDateTime)", data);
```

The previous example illustrates a common idiom: We use QDataStream to encode the data, and to ensure that the QByteArray is interpreted correctly by the receiver, we mangle the data format in the message name as if it were a C++ function.

Various environment variables affect Qtopia Core applications. The most important ones are QWS_MOUSE_PROTO and QWS_KEYBOARD, which specify the mouse device and the keyboard type. See http://doc.trolltech.com/4.1/emb-envvars. html for a complete list of environment variables.

If we use Unix as our development platform, we can test the application using the Qtopia virtual frame buffer (qvfb), an X11 application that simulates, pixel for pixel, the actual frame buffer. This accelerates the development cycle considerably. To enable virtual buffer support in Qtopia Core, pass the -qvfb option to the configure script. Be aware that this option is not intended for production use. The virtual frame buffer application is located in tools/qvfb and can be invoked as follows:

```
qvfb -width 320 -height 480 -depth 32
```

Another option that works on most platforms is to use VNC (Virtual Network Computing) to run the applications remotely. To enable VNC support in Qtopia Core, pass the -qt-gfx-vnc option to configure. Then launch your Qtopia Core applications with the -display VNC:0 command-line option and run a VNC client pointing at the host on which your applications are running. The display size and bit depth can be specified by setting the QWS_SIZE and QWS_DEPTH environment variables on the host that runs the Qtopia Core applications (for example, QWS_SIZE=320x480 and QWS_DEPTH=32).

Customizing Qtopia Core

When installing Qtopia Core, we can specify features we want to leave out to reduce its memory footprint. Qtopia Core includes over a hundred configurable features, each of which is associated to a preprocessor symbol. For example, QT_NO_FILEDIALOG excludes QFileDialog from the *QtGui* library, and QT_NO_I18N leaves out all support for internationalization. The features are listed src/ corelib/qfeatures.txt.

Qtopia Core provides five example configurations (minimum, small, medium, large, and dist) that are stored in src/corelib/qconfig_xxx.h files. These configurations can be specified using the configure script's -qconfig xxx option, for example:

```
./configure -qconfig small
```

To create custom configurations, we can manually provide a qconfig-xxx.h file and use it as if it were a standard configuration. Alternatively, we can use the qconfig graphical tool, located in Qt's tools subdirectory.

Qtopia Core provides the following classes for interfacing with input and output devices and for customizing the look and feel of the window system:

Class	Base class for
QScreen	screen drivers
QScreenDriverPlugin	screen driver plugins
QWSMouseHandler	mouse drivers
QMouseDriverPlugin	mouse driver plugins
QWSKeyboardHandler	keyboard drivers
QKbdDriverPlugin	keyboard driver plugins
QWSInputMethod	input methods
QDecoration	window decoration styles
QDecorationPlugin	plugins providing window decoration styles

To obtain the list of predefined drivers, input methods, and window decoration styles, run the configure script with the -help option.

The screen driver can be specified using the -display command-line option when starting the Qtopia Core server, as seen in the previous section, or by setting the QWS_DISPLAY environment variable. The mouse driver and the associated device can be specified using the QWS_MOUSE_PROTO environment variable, whose value must have the syntax *type*:*device*, where *type* is one of the supported drivers and device the path to the device (for example, QWS_MOUSE_PROTO=IntelliMouse:/dev/mouse). Keyboards are handled similarly through the QWS_KEYBOARD environment variable. Input methods and window decorations are set programmatically in the server using QWSServer::setCurrentInputMethod() and QApplication::qwsSetDecoration().

Window decoration styles can be set independently of the widget style, which inherits from QStyle. For example, it is entirely possible to set Windows as the window decoration style and Plastique as the widget style. If desired, decorations can be set on a per-window basis.

The QWSServer class provides various functions for customizing the window system. Applications that run as Qtopia Core servers can access the unique QWSServer instance through the qwsServer global variable, which is initialized by the QApplication constructor.

Qtopia Core supports the following font formats: TrueType (TTF), Post-Script Type 1, Bitmap Distribution Format (BDF), and Qt Pre-rendered Fonts (QPF).

Because QPF is a raster format, it is faster and usually more compact than vector formats such as TTF and Type 1 if we need it only at one or two different sizes. The makeqpf tool lets us pre-render a TTF or a Type 1 file and save the result in QPF format. An alternative is to run our applications with the -savefonts command-line option.

At the time of writing, Trolltech is developing an additional layer on top of Qtopia Core to make embedded application development even faster and more convenient. It is hoped that a later edition of this book will include more information on this topic.

Appendices

Installing Qt

This appendix explains how to install Qt from the CD that accompanies this book onto your system. The CD has editions of Qt 4.1.1 for Windows, Mac OS X, and X11 (for Linux and most versions of Unix). They all include SQLite, a public domain in-process database, together with a SQLite driver. The editions of Qt on the CD are provided for your convenience. For serious software development, it is best to download the latest version of Qt from `http://www.trolltech.com/download/` or to buy a commercial version.

Trolltech also provides Qtopia Core for building applications for Linux-based embedded devices such as PDAs and mobile phones. If you are interested in creating embedded applications, you can obtain Qtopia Core from Trolltech's download web page.

The example applications used in the book are on the CD in the `examples` directory. In addition, Qt provides many small example applications located in the `examples` subdirectory.

A Note on Licensing

Qt is produced in two forms: open source and commercial. The open source editions are available free of charge; the commercial editions must be paid for.

The software on the CD is suitable for creating applications for your own educational and personal use.

If you want to distribute the applications that you create with an open source edition of Qt, you must comply with the specific terms and conditions laid down in the licenses for the software you use to create the applications. For open source editions, the terms and conditions include the requirement to use the GNU General Public License (GPL). Open licenses like the GPL give the applications' users certain rights, including the right to view and modify the source and to distribute the applications (on the same terms). If you want to distribute your applications without source code (to keep your code private) or if you want

447

to apply your own commercial license conditions to your applications, you must buy commercial editions of the software you use to create the applications. The commercial editions of the software allow you to sell and distribute your applications on your own terms.

The CD contains GPL versions of Qt for Windows, Mac OS X, and X11. The full legal texts of the licenses are included with the packages on the CD, along with information on how to obtain commercial versions.

Installing Qt/Windows

When you insert the CD on a Windows machine, the installation program should start automatically. If this does not occur, use File Explorer to navigate to the CD's root folder and double-click `install.exe`. (This program may appear as `install` depending on how your system is configured.)

If you already have the MinGW C++ compiler you must specify the directory where it is located; otherwise, set the check box and have the installer install MinGW for you. The GPL version of Qt supplied on the CD will not work with Visual C++, so if you do not have MinGW already installed you will need to install it. The installer also gives you the option to install the examples that accompany the book. Qt's standard examples are automatically installed, along with the documentation.

If you choose to install the MinGW compiler, there may be a small delay between the completion of the MinGW installation and the start of the Qt installation.

After installation you will have a new folder in the Start menu called "Qt by Trolltech v4.1.1 (opensource)". This folder has shortcuts to *Qt Assistant* and *Qt Designer*, and also one called "Qt 4.1.1 Command Prompt" that starts a console window. When you start this window it will set the environment variables for compiling Qt programs with MinGW. It is in this window that you can run `qmake` and `make` to build Qt applications.

Installing Qt/Mac

Before Qt can be installed on Mac OS X, Apple's Xcode Tools must already be installed. The CD (or DVD) containing these tools is usually supplied with Mac OS X; they can also be downloaded from the Apple Developer Connection, `http://developer.apple.com`.

If you have Mac OS X 10.4 (Tiger) and Xcode Tools 2.x (with GCC 4.0.x), you can use the installer described below. If you have an earlier version of Mac OS X, or an older version of GCC, you will need to install the source package manually. This package is called `qt-mac-opensource-4.1.1.tar.gz` and is located in the `mac` folder on the CD. If you install this package, follow the instructions in the next section for installing Qt on X11.

To use the installer, insert the CD and double-click the package called Qt.mpkg. This will launch the installer, Installer.app, and Qt will be installed with the standard examples, documentation, and the examples that accompany this book. Qt will be installed in /Developer, with the book's examples in /Developer/Examples/Qt4Book.

To run commands like qmake and make, you will need to use a terminal window, for example, Terminal.app in /Applications/Utilities. It is also possible to generate Xcode projects using qmake. For example, to generate an Xcode project for the hello example, start a console such as Terminal.app, change directory to /Developer/Examples/Qt4Book/chap01/hello, and enter the following command:

```
qmake -spec macx-xcode hello.pro
```

Installing Qt/X11

To install Qt in its default location on X11, you will need to be root. If you do not have root access, use configure's -prefix argument to specify a directory to which you have permission to write.

1. Change directory to a temporary directory. For example:

   ```
   cd /tmp
   ```

2. Unpack the archive file from the CD:

   ```
   cp /cdrom/x11/qt-x11-opensource-src-4.1.1.tgz .
   gunzip qt-x11-opensource-src-4.1.1.tgz
   tar xvf qt-x11-opensource-src-4.1.1.tar
   ```

   This will create the directory /tmp/qt-x11-opensource-src-4.1.1, assuming that your CD-ROM is mounted at /cdrom. Qt requires GNU tar; on some systems it is called gtar.

3. Execute the configure tool with your preferred options to build the Qt library and the tools supplied with it:

   ```
   cd /tmp/qt-x11-opensource-src-4.1.1
   ./configure
   ```

   You can run ./configure -help to get a list of configuration options.

4. To build Qt, type

   ```
   make
   ```

   This will create the library and compile all the demos, examples, and tools. On some systems make is called gmake.

5. To install Qt, type

   ```
   su -c "make install"
   ```

and enter the root password. This will install Qt into /usr/local/Troll-tech/Qt-4.1.1. You can change the destination by using the -prefix option with configure, and if you have write access to the destination you can simply type:

```
make install
```

6. Set up certain environment variables for Qt.

   If your shell is bash, ksh, zsh, or sh, add the following lines to your .profile file:

   ```
   PATH=/usr/local/Trolltech/Qt-4.1.1/bin:$PATH
   export PATH
   ```

   If your shell is csh or tcsh, add the following line to your .login file:

   ```
   setenv PATH /usr/local/Trolltech/Qt-4.1.1/bin:$PATH
   ```

   If you used -prefix with configure, use the path you specified instead of the default path shown above.

   If you are using a compiler that does not support rpath you must also extend the LD_LIBRARY_PATH environment variable to include /usr/local/Trolltech/Qt-4.1.1/lib. This is not necessary on Linux with GCC.

Qt comes with a demo application, qtdemo, that shows off many of the library's features. It serves as a nice starting point to see what Qt can do. To see Qt's documentation, either visit http://doc.trolltech.com, or run *Qt Assistant*, Qt's help application, invoked by typing assistant in a console window.

◆ *Getting Started with C++*

◆ *Main Language Differences*

◆ *The Standard C++ Library*

Introduction to C++
for Java and C# Programmers

This appendix provides a short introduction to C++ for developers who already know Java or C#. It assumes that you are familiar with object-oriented concepts such as inheritance and polymorphism and want to learn C++. To avoid making this book an unwieldy 1,500 page doorstop by including a complete C++ primer, this appendix confines itself to essentials. It presents the basic knowledge and techniques necessary to understand the programs presented in the rest of the book, with enough information to start developing cross-platform C++ GUI applications using Qt.

At the time of writing, C++ is the only realistic option for writing cross-platform, high-performance object-oriented GUI applications. Its detractors usually point out that Java or C#, which dropped C compatibility, are nicer to use; in fact, Bjarne Stroustrup, the inventor of C++, noted in *The Design and Evolution of C++* that "within C++, there is a much smaller and cleaner language struggling to get out".

Fortunately, when we program with Qt, we usually stick to a subset of C++ that is very close to the utopian language envisioned by Stroustrup, leaving us free to concentrate on the problem at hand. Furthermore, Qt extends C++ in several respects, through its innovative "signals and slots" mechanism, its Unicode support, and its `foreach` keyword.

In the first section of this appendix, we will see how to combine C++ source files to obtain an executable program. This will lead us to explore core C++ concepts such as compilation units, header files, object files, libraries—and to get familiar with the C++ preprocessor, compiler, and linker.

Then we will turn to the most important language differences between C++, Java and C#: how to define classes, how to use pointers and references, how to overload operators, how to use the preprocessor, and so on. Although the C++ syntax is superficially similar to that of Java or C#, the underlying concepts differ in subtle ways. At the same time, as an inspirational source for Java and

C#, the C++ language has a lot in common with these two languages, including similar data types, the same arithmetic operators, and the same basic control flow statements.

The last section is dedicated to the Standard C++ library, which provides ready-made functionality that can be used in any C++ program. The library is the result of over 30 years of evolution, and as such provides a wide range of approaches including procedural, object-oriented, and functional programming styles, and both macros and templates. Compared with the libraries provided with Java and C#, the Standard C++ library has a rather limited scope; for example, it has no support for GUI programming, multithreading, databases, internationalization, networking, XML, or Unicode. To broaden C++'s scope into these areas, C++ developers are expected to use various (often platform-specific) libraries.

This is where Qt saves the day. Qt began as a cross-platform GUI toolkit (a set of classes that makes it possible to write portable graphical user interface applications) but rapidly evolved into a full-blown framework that partly extends and partly replaces the Standard C++ library. Although this book uses Qt, it is useful to know what the Standard C++ library has to offer, since you may have to work with code that uses it.

Getting Started with C++

A C++ program consists of one or more *compilation units*. Each compilation unit is a separate source code file, typically with a `.cpp` extension (other common extensions are `.cc` and `.cxx`) that the compiler processes in one run. For each compilation unit, the compiler generates an *object file*, with the extension `.obj` (on Windows) or `.o` (on Unix and Mac OS X). The object file is a binary file that contains machine code for the architecture on which the program will run.

Once all the `.cpp` files have been compiled, we can combine the object files together to create an executable using a special program called the *linker*. The linker concatenates the object files and resolves the memory addresses of functions and other symbols referenced in the compilation units.

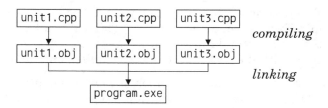

Figure B.1. The C++ compilation process (on Windows)

When building a program, exactly one compilation unit must contain a `main()` function that serves as the program's entry point. This function doesn't belong to any class; it is a *global function*.

Unlike Java, where each source file must contain exactly one class, C++ lets us organize the compilation units as we want. We can implement several classes in the same .cpp file, or spread the implementation of a class across several .cpp files, and we can give the source files any names we like. When we make a change in one particular .cpp file, we only need to recompile that file and then relink the application to create a new executable.

Before we go further, let's quickly review the source code of a trivial C++ program that computes the square of an integer. The program consists of two compilation units: main.cpp and square.cpp.

Here's square.cpp:

```
1  double square(double n)
2  {
3      return n * n;
4  }
```

This file simply contains a global function called square() that returns the square of its parameter.

Here's main.cpp:

```
1  #include <cstdlib>
2  #include <iostream>

3  using namespace std;

4  double square(double);

5  int main(int argc, char *argv[])
6  {
7      if (argc != 2) {
8          cerr << "Usage: square <number>" << endl;
9          return 1;
10     }

11     double n = strtod(argv[1], 0);
12     cout << "The square of " << argv[1] << " is " << square(n) << endl;
13     return 0;
14 }
```

The main.cpp source file contains the main() function's definition. In C++, this function takes an int and a char * array (an array of character strings) as parameters. The program's name is available as argv[0] and the command-line arguments as argv[1], argv[2], ..., argv[argc - 1]. The parameter names argc ("argument count") and argv ("argument values") are conventional. If the program doesn't access the command-line arguments, we can define main() with no parameters.

The `main()` function uses `strtod()` ("string to double"), `cout` (C++'s standard output stream), and `cerr` (C++'s standard error stream) from the Standard C++ library to convert the command-line argument to a `double` and to print text to the console. Strings, numbers, and end-of-line markers (`endl`) are output using the `<<` operator, which is also used for bit-shifting. To access this standard functionality, we need the `#include` directives on lines 1 and 2.

The `using namespace` directive on line 3 tells the compiler that we want to import all identifiers declared in the `std` namespace into the global namespace. This enables us to write `strtod()`, `cout`, `cerr`, and `endl` instead of the fully-qualified `std::strtod()`, `std::cout`, `std::cerr`, and `std::endl`. In C++, the `::` operator separates the components of a complex name.

The declaration on line 4 is a *function prototype*. It tells the compiler that a function exists with the given parameters and return value. The actual function can be located in the same compilation unit or in another compilation unit. Without the function prototype, the compiler wouldn't let us call the function on line 12. Parameter names in function prototypes are optional.

The procedure to compile the program varies from platform to platform. For example, to compile on Solaris with the Sun C++ compiler, we would type the following commands:

```
CC -c main.cpp
CC -c square.cpp
ld main.o square.o -o square
```

The first two lines invoke the compiler to generate `.o` files for the `.cpp` files. The third line invokes the linker and generates an executable called `square`, which we can invoke as follows:

```
./square 64
```

The program outputs the following message to the console:

```
The square of 64 is 4096
```

To compile the program, you probably want to get help from your local C++ guru. Failing this, you can still read the rest of this appendix without compiling anything and follow the instructions in Chapter 1 to compile your first C++/Qt application. Qt provides tools that make it easy to build applications on all platforms.

Back to our program: In a real-world application, we would normally put the `square()` function prototype in a separate file and include that file in all the compilation units where we need to call the function. Such a file is called a *header file* and usually has a `.h` extension (`.hh`, `.hpp`, and `.hxx` are also common). If we redo our example using the header file approach, we would create a file called `square.h` with the following contents:

```
1  #ifndef SQUARE_H
2  #define SQUARE_H
```

```
3  double square(double);

4  #endif
```

The header file is bracketed by three preprocessor directives (#ifndef, #define, and #endif). These directives ensure that the header file is processed only once, even if the header file is included several times in the same compilation unit (a situation that can arise when header files include other header files). By convention, the preprocessor symbol used to accomplish this is derived from the file name (in our example, SQUARE_H). We will come back to the preprocessor later in this appendix.

The new main.cpp file looks like this:

```
1  #include <cstdlib>
2  #include <iostream>

3  #include "square.h"

4  using namespace std;

5  int main(int argc, char *argv[])
6  {
7      if (argc != 2) {
8          cerr << "Usage: square <number>" << endl;
9          return 1;
10     }

11     double n = strtod(argv[1], 0);
12     cout << "The square of " << argv[1] << " is " << square(n) << endl;
13     return 0;
14 }
```

The #include directive on line 3 expands to the contents of the file square.h. Directives that start with a # are picked up by the C++ preprocessor before the compilation proper takes place. In the old days, the preprocessor was a separate program that the programmer invoked manually before running the compiler. Modern compilers handle the preprocessor step implicitly.

The #include directives on lines 1 and 2 expand to the contents of the cstdlib and iostream header files, which are part of the Standard C++ library. Standard header files have no .h suffix. The angle brackets around the file names indicate that the header files are located in a standard location on the system, while double quotes tell the compiler to look in the current directory. Includes are normally gathered at the top of a .cpp file.

Unlike .cpp files, header files are not compilation units in their own right and do not result in any object files. They may only contain declarations that enable different compilation units to communicate with each other. Consequently, it would be inappropriate to put the square() function's implementation in a header file. If we did so in our example, nothing bad would happen, because we include square.h only once, but if we included square.h from several .cpp files, we would get multiple implementations of the square() function (one per .cpp file that includes it). The linker would then complain about multiple (identical) definitions of square() and refuse to generate an executable. Inversely, if we declare a function but never implement it, the linker complains about an "unresolved symbol".

So far, we have assumed that an executable only consists of object files. In practice, they often also link against libraries that implement ready-made functionality. There are two main types of library:

- *Static libraries* are put directly into the executable, as if they were object files. This ensures that the library cannot get lost but increases the size of the executable.
- *Dynamic libraries* (also called shared libraries or DLLs) are located at a standard location on the user's machine and are automatically loaded at application startup.

For the square program, we link against the Standard C++ library, which is implemented as a dynamic library on most platforms. Qt itself is a collection of libraries that can be built either as static or as dynamic libraries (the default is dynamic).

Main Language Differences

We will now take a more structured look at the areas where C++ differs from Java and C#. Many of the language differences are due to C++'s compiled nature and commitment to performance. Thus, C++ does not check array bounds at run-time, and there is no garbage collector to reclaim unused dynamically allocated memory.

For the sake of brevity, C++ constructs that are nearly identical to their Java and C# counterparts are not reviewed. In addition, some C++ topics are not covered here because they are not necessary when programming using Qt. Among these are defining template classes and functions, defining union types, and using exceptions. For the whole story, refer to a book such as *The C++ Programming Language* by Bjarne Stroustrup or *C++ for Java Programmers* by Mark Allen Weiss.

Primitive Data Types

The primitive data types offered by the C++ language are similar to those found in Java or C#. Figure B.2 lists C++'s primitive types and their definition on the platforms supported by Qt 4.

By default, the short, int, long, and long long data types are signed, meaning that they can hold negative values as well as positive values. If we only need to store nonnegative integers, we can put the unsigned keyword in front of the type. While a short can hold any value between −32,768 and +32,767, an unsigned short goes from 0 to 65,535. The right-shift operator >> has unsigned ("fill with 0s") semantics if one of the operands is unsigned.

C++ type	Description
bool	Boolean value
char	8-bit integer
short	16-bit integer
int	32-bit integer
long	32-bit or 64-bit integer
long long*	64-bit integer
float	32-bit floating-point value (IEEE 754)
double	64-bit floating-point value (IEEE 754)

Figure B.2. Primitive C++ types

The bool type can take the values true and false. In addition, numeric types can be used where a bool is expected, with the rule that 0 means false and any non-zero value means true.

The char type is used both for storing ASCII characters and 8-bit integers (bytes). When used as an integer, it can be signed or unsigned, depending on the platform. The types signed char and unsigned char are available as unambiguous alternatives to char. Qt provides a QChar type that stores 16-bit Unicode characters.

Instances of built-in types are not initialized by default. When we create an int variable, its value could conceivably be 0, but could just as likely be −209,486,515. Fortunately, most compilers warn us when we attempt to read the contents of an uninitialized variable, and we can use tools like Rational PurifyPlus and Valgrind to detect unitialized memory accesses and other memory-related problems at run-time.

In memory, the numeric types (except long) have identical sizes on the different platforms supported by Qt, but their representation varies depending on the system's byte order. On big-endian architectures (such as PowerPC and SPARC), the 32-bit value 0x12345678 is stored as the four bytes 0x12 0x34 0x56 0x78, whereas on little-endian architectures (such as Intel x86), the byte sequence is reversed. This makes a difference in programs that copy memory areas onto disk or that send binary data over the network. Qt's QDataStream class, presented in Chapter 12 (Input/Output), can be used to store binary data in a platform-independent way.

---

*Microsoft calls the long long type __int64. In Qt programs, qlonglong is available as an alternative that works on all Qt platforms.

Class Definitions

Class definitions in C++ are similar to those in Java and C#, but there are several differences to be aware of. We will study these differences using a series of examples. Let's start with a class that represent an (x, y) coordinate pair:

```
#ifndef POINT2D_H
#define POINT2D_H

class Point2D
{
public:
    Point2D() {
        xVal = 0;
        yVal = 0;
    }
    Point2D(double x, double y) {
        xVal = x;
        yVal = y;
    }

    void setX(double x) { xVal = x; }
    void setY(double y) { yVal = y; }
    double x() const { return xVal; }
    double y() const { return yVal; }

private:
    double xVal;
    double yVal;
};

#endif
```

The above class definition would appear in a header file, typically called `point2d.h`. The example exhibits the following C++ idiosyncrasies:

- A class definition is divided in public, protected, and private sections, and ends with a semicolon. If no section is specified, the default is private. (For compatibility with C, C++ provides a `struct` keyword that is identical to `class` except that the default is public if no section is specified.)

- The class has two constructors (one that has no parameters and one that has two). If we declared no constructor, C++ would automatically supply one with no parameters and an empty body.

- The getter functions `x()` and `y()` are declared to be const. This means that they don't (and can't) modify the member variables or call non-const member functions (such as `setX()` and `setY()`).

The functions above were implemented inline, as part of the class definition. An alternative is to provide only function prototypes in the header file and to implement the functions in a `.cpp` file. Using this approach, the header file would look like this:

```
#ifndef POINT2D_H
```

```
    #define POINT2D_H

    class Point2D
    {
    public:
        Point2D();
        Point2D(double x, double y);

        void setX(double x);
        void setY(double y);
        double x() const;
        double y() const;

    private:
        double xVal;
        double yVal;
    };

    #endif
```

The functions would then be implemented in `point2d.cpp`:

```
    #include "point2d.h"

    Point2D::Point2D()
    {
        xVal = 0.0;
        yVal = 0.0;
    }

    Point2D::Point2D(double x, double y)
    {
        xVal = x;
        yVal = y;
    }

    void Point2D::setX(double x)
    {
        xVal = x;
    }

    void Point2D::setY(double y)
    {
        yVal = y;
    }

    double Point2D::x() const
    {
        return xVal;
    }

    double Point2D::y() const
    {
        return yVal;
    }
```

We start by including `point2d.h` because the compiler needs the class definition before it can parse member function implementations. Then we implement

the functions, prefixing the function name with the class name using the
:: operator.

We have seen how to implement a function inline and now how to implement
it in a .cpp file. The two approaches are semantically equivalent, but when we
call a function that is declared inline, most compilers simply expand the function's body instead of generating an actual function call. This normally leads
to faster code, but might increase the size of your application. For this reason, only very short functions should be implemented inline; longer functions
should always be implemented in a .cpp file. In addition, if we forget to implement a function and try to call it, the linker will complain about an unresolved
symbol.

Now, let's try to use the class.

```cpp
#include "point2d.h"

int main()
{
    Point2D alpha;
    Point2D beta(0.666, 0.875);

    alpha.setX(beta.y());
    beta.setY(alpha.x());

    return 0;
}
```

In C++, variables of any types can be declared directly without using new.
The first variable is initialized using the default Point2D constructor (the
constructor that has no parameters). The second variable is initialized using
the second constructor. Access to an object's member is performed using the
. (dot) operator.

Variables declared this way behave like Java/C# primitive types such as int
and double. For example, when we use the assignment operator, the contents
of the variable is copied—not just a reference to an object. And if we modify a variable later on, any other variables that were assigned from it are left
unchanged.

As an object-oriented language, C++ supports inheritance and polymorphism.
To illustrate how it works, we will review the example of a Shape abstract base
class and a subclass called Circle. Let's start with the base class:

```cpp
#ifndef SHAPE_H
#define SHAPE_H

#include "point2d.h"

class Shape
{
public:
    Shape(Point2D center) { myCenter = center; }
```

```
        virtual void draw() = 0;
    protected:
        Point2D myCenter;
    };

    #endif
```

The definition appears in a header file called shape.h. Since the class definition refers to the Point2D class, we include point2d.h.

The Shape class has no base class. Unlike Java and C#, C++ doesn't provide a generic Object class from which all classes inherit. Qt provides QObject as a natural base class for all kinds of objects.

The draw() function declaration has two interesting features: It contains the virtual keyword, and it ends with = 0. The virtual keyword indicates that the function may be reimplemented in subclasses. Like in C#, C++ member functions aren't reimplementable by default. The bizarre = 0 syntax indicates that the function is a *pure virtual function*—a function that has no default implementation and that must be implemented in subclasses. The concept of an "interface" in Java and C# maps to a class with only pure virtual functions in C++.

Here's the definition of the Circle subclass:

```
    #ifndef CIRCLE_H
    #define CIRCLE_H

    #include "shape.h"

    class Circle : public Shape
    {
    public:
        Circle(Point2D center, double radius = 0.5)
            : Shape(center) {
            myRadius = radius;
        }

        void draw() {
            // do something here
        }

    private:
        double myRadius;
    };

    #endif
```

The Circle class inherits publicly from Shape, meaning that all public members of Shape remain public in Circle. C++ also supports protected and private inheritance, which restrict the access of the base class's public and protected members.

The constructor takes two parameters. The second parameter is optional and takes the value 0.5 if not specified. The constructor passes the center parameter to the base class's constructor using a special syntax between the function signature and the function body. In the body, we initialize the `myRadius` member variable. We could also have initialized the variable on the same line as the base class constructor initialization:

```
Circle(Point2D center, double radius = 0.5)
    : Shape(center), myRadius(radius) { }
```

On the other hand, C++ doesn't allow us to initialize a member variable in the class definition, so the following code is wrong:

```
// WON'T COMPILE
private:
    double myRadius = 0.5;
};
```

The `draw()` function has the same signature as the virtual `draw()` function declared in `Shape`. It is a reimplementation and it will be invoked polymorphically when `draw()` is called on a `Circle` instance through a `Shape` reference or pointer. C++ has no `override` keyword like in C#. Nor does C++ have a `super` or `base` keyword that refers to the base class. If we need to call the base implementation of a function, we can prefix the function name with the base class name and the `::` operator. For example:

```
class LabeledCircle : public Circle
{
public:
    void draw() {
        Circle::draw();
        drawLabel();
    }
    ...
};
```

C++ supports multiple inheritance, meaning that a class can derive from several classes at the same time. The syntax is as follows:

```
class DerivedClass : public BaseClass1, public BaseClass2, ...,
                     public BaseClassN
{
    ...
};
```

By default, functions and variables declared in a class are associated with instances of that class. We can also declare static member functions and static member variables, which can be used without an instance. For example:

```
#ifndef TRUCK_H
#define TRUCK_H

class Truck
{
public:
    Truck() { ++counter; }
```

```
    ~Truck() { --counter; }
    static int instanceCount() { return counter; }
private:
    static int counter;
};

#endif
```

The static member variable `counter` keeps track of how many `Truck` instances exist at any time. The `Truck` constructor increments it. The destructor, recognizable by the ~ prefix, decrements it. In C++, the destructor is automatically invoked when a statically allocated variable goes out of scope or when a variable allocated using `new` is deleted. This is similar to the `finalize()` method in Java, except that we can rely on it being called at a specific point in time.

A static member variable has a single existence in a class: Such variables are "class variables" rather than "instance variables". Each static member variable must be defined in a `.cpp` file (but without repeating the `static` keyword). For example:

```
#include "truck.h"

int Truck::counter = 0;
```

Failing to do this would result in an "unresolved symbol" error at link time. The `instanceCount()` static function can be accessed from outside the class, prefixed by the class name. For example:

```
#include <iostream>

#include "truck.h"

using namespace std;

int main()
{
    Truck truck1;
    Truck truck2;

    cout << Truck::instanceCount() << " equals 2" << endl;

    return 0;
}
```

Pointers

A *pointer* in C++ is a variable that stores the memory address of an object (instead of storing the object directly). Java and C# have a similar concept, that of a "reference", but the syntax is different. We will start by studying a contrived example that illustrates pointers in action:

```
1  #include "point2d.h"

2  int main()
```

```
 3  {
 4      Point2D alpha;
 5      Point2D beta;

 6      Point2D *ptr;

 7      ptr = &alpha;
 8      ptr->setX(1.0);
 9      ptr->setY(2.5);

10      ptr = &beta;
11      ptr->setX(4.0);
12      ptr->setY(4.5);

13      ptr = 0;

14      return 0;
15  }
```

The example relies on the Point2D class from the previous subsection. Lines 4 and 5 define two objects of type Point2D. These objects are initialized to (0, 0) by the default Point2D constructor.

Line 6 defines a pointer to a Point2D object. The syntax for pointers uses an asterisk in front of the variable name. Since we did not initialize the pointer, it contains a random memory address. This is solved on line 7 by assigning alpha's address to the pointer. The unary & operator returns the memory address of an object. An address is typically a 32-bit or a 64-bit integer value specifying the offset of an object in memory.

On lines 8 and 9, we access the alpha object through the ptr pointer. Because ptr is a pointer and not an object, we must use the -> (arrow) operator instead of the . (dot) operator.

On line 10, we assign beta's address to the pointer. From then on, any operation we perform through the pointer will affect the beta object.

Line 13 sets the pointer to be a null pointer. C++ has no keyword for representing a pointer that does not point to an object; instead, we use the value 0 (or the symbolic constant NULL, which expands to 0). Trying to use a null pointer results in a crash with an error message such as "Segmentation fault", "General protection fault", or "Bus error". Using a debugger, we can find out which line of code caused the crash.

At the end of the function, the alpha object holds the coordinate pair (1.0, 2.5), whereas beta holds (4.0, 4.5).

Pointers are often used to store objects allocated dynamically using new. In C++ jargon, we say that these objects are allocated on the "heap", whereas local variables (variables defined inside a function) are stored on the "stack".

Here's a code snippet that illustrates dynamic memory allocation using new:

```
#include "point2d.h"
```

```
int main()
{
    Point2D *point = new Point2D;
    point->setX(1.0);
    point->setY(2.5);
    delete point;

    return 0;
}
```

The `new` operator returns the memory address of a newly allocated object. We store the address in a pointer variable and access the object through that pointer. When we are done with the object, we release its memory using the `delete` operator. Unlike Java and C#, C++ has no garbage collector; dynamically allocated objects must be explicitly released using `delete` when we don't need them anymore. Chapter 2 describes Qt's parent–child mechanism, which greatly simplifies memory management in C++ programs.

If we forget to call `delete`, the memory is kept around until the program finishes. This would not be an issue in the example above, because we only allocate one object, but in a program that allocates new objects all the time, this could cause the program to keep allocating memory until the machine's memory is exhausted. Once an object is deleted, the pointer variable still holds the address of the object. Such a pointer is a "dangling pointer" and should not be used to access the object. Qt provides a "smart" pointer, `QPointer<T>`, that automatically sets itself to 0 if the `QObject` it points to is deleted.

In the example above, we invoked the default constructor and called `setX()` and `setY()` to initialize the object. We could have used the two-parameter constructor instead:

```
Point2D *point = new Point2D(1.0, 2.5);
```

The example didn't require the use of `new` and `delete`. We could just as well have allocated the object on the stack as follows:

```
Point2D point;
point.setX(1.0);
point.setY(2.5);
```

Objects allocated like this are automatically freed at the end of the block in which they appear.

If we don't intend to modify the object through the pointer, we can declare the pointer const. For example:

```
const Point2D *ptr = new Point2D(1.0, 2.5);
double x = ptr->x();
double y = ptr->y();

// WON'T COMPILE
ptr->setX(4.0);
*ptr = Point2D(4.0, 4.5);
```

The ptr const pointer can only be used to call const member functions such as x() and y(). It is good style to declare pointers const when we don't intend to modify the object using them. Furthermore, if the object itself is const, we have no choice but to use a const pointer to store its address. The use of const provides information to the compiler that can lead to early bug detection and performance gains. C# has a const keyword that is very similar to that of C++. The closest Java equivalent is final, but it only protects variables from assignment, not from calling "non-const" member functions on it.

Pointers can be used with built-in types as well as with classes. In an expression, the unary * operator returns the value of the object associated with the pointer. For example:

```
int i = 10;
int j = 20;

int *p = &i;
int *q = &j;

cout << *p << " equals 10" << endl;
cout << *q << " equals 20" << endl;

*p = 40;

cout << i << " equals 40" << endl;

p = q;
*p = 100;

cout << i << " equals 40" << endl;
cout << j << " equals 100" << endl;
```

The -> operator, which can be used to access an object's members through a pointer, is pure syntactic sugar. Instead of ptr->member, we can also write (*ptr).member. The parentheses are necessary because the . (dot) operator has precedence over the unary * operator.

Pointers had a poor reputation in C and C++, to the extent that Java is often advertised as having no pointers. In reality, C++ pointers are conceptually similar to Java and C# references except that we can use pointers to iterate through memory, as we will see later in this section. Furthermore, the inclusion of "copy on write" container classes in Qt, along with C++'s ability to instantiate any class on the stack, means that we can often avoid pointers.

References

In addition to pointers, C++ also supports the concept of a "reference". Like a pointer, a C++ reference stores the address of an object. The main differences are these:

- References are declared using & instead of *.

- The reference must be initialized and can't be reassigned later.

- The object associated with a reference is directly accessible; there is no special syntax such as * or ->.
- A reference cannot be null.

References are mostly used when declaring parameters. By default, C++ uses call-by-value as its parameter-passing mechanism, meaning that when an argument is passed to a function, the function receives a brand new copy of the object. Here's the definition of a function that receives its parameters through call-by-value:

```
#include <cstdlib>

using namespace std;

double manhattanDistance(Point2D a, Point2D b)
{
    return abs(b.x() - a.x()) + abs(b.y() - a.y());
}
```

We would then invoke the function as follows:

```
Point2D broadway(12.5, 40.0);
Point2D harlem(77.5, 50.0);
double distance = manhattanDistance(broadway, harlem);
```

Reformed C programmers avoid needless copy operations by declaring their parameters as pointers instead of as values:

```
double manhattanDistance(const Point2D *ap, const Point2D *bp)
{
    return abs(bp->x() - ap->x()) + abs(bp->y() - ap->y());
}
```

They must then pass addresses instead of values when calling the function:

```
Point2D broadway(12.5, 40.0);
Point2D harlem(77.5, 50.0);
double distance = manhattanDistance(&broadway, &harlem);
```

C++ introduced references to make the syntax less cumbersome and to prevent the caller from passing a null pointer. If we use references instead of pointers, the function looks like this:

```
double manhattanDistance(const Point2D &a, const Point2D &b)
{
    return abs(b.x() - a.x()) + abs(b.y() - a.y());
}
```

The declaration of a reference is similar to that of a pointer, with & instead of *. But when we actually use the reference, we can forget that it is a memory address and treat it like an ordinary variable. In addition, calling a function that takes references as arguments doesn't require any special care (no & operator).

All in all, by replacing `Point2D` with `const Point2D &` in the parameter list, we reduced the overhead of the function call: Instead of copying 256 bits (the size of four `double`s), we copy only 64 or 128 bits, depending on the target platform's pointer size.

The previous example used const references, preventing the function from modifying the objects associated with the references. When this kind of side effect is desired, we can pass a non-const reference or pointer. For example:

```
void transpose(Point2D &point)
{
    double oldX = point.x();
    point.setX(point.y());
    point.setY(oldX);
}
```

In some cases, we have a reference and we need to call a function that takes a pointer, or vice versa. To convert a reference to a pointer, we can simply use the unary & operator:

```
Point2D point;
Point2D &ref = point;
Point2D *ptr = &ref;
```

To convert a pointer to a reference, there's the unary * operator:

```
Point2D point;
Point2D *ptr = &point;
Point2D &ref = *ptr;
```

References and pointers are represented the same way in memory, and they can often be used interchangeably, which begs the question of when to use which. On the one hand, references have a more convenient syntax; on the other hand, pointers can be reassigned at any time to point to another object, they can hold a null value, and their more explicit syntax is often a blessing in disguise. For these reasons, pointers tend to prevail, with references almost exclusively used for declaring function parameters, in conjunction with const.

Arrays

Arrays in C++ are declared by specifying the number of items in the array within brackets in the variable declaration *after* the variable name. Two-dimensional arrays are possible using an array of arrays. Here's the definition of a one-dimensional array containing 10 items of type `int`:

```
int fibonacci[10];
```

The items are accessible as `fibonacci[0]`, `fibonacci[1]`, ..., `fibonacci[9]`. Often we want to initialize the array as we define it:

```
int fibonacci[10] = { 0, 1, 1, 2, 3, 5, 8, 13, 21, 34 };
```

In such cases, we can then omit the array size, since the compiler can deduce it from the number of initializers:

```
int fibonacci[] = { 0, 1, 1, 2, 3, 5, 8, 13, 21, 34 };
```

Static initialization also works for complex types, such as `Point2D`:

```
Point2D triangle[] = {
    Point2D(0.0, 0.0), Point2D(1.0, 0.0), Point2D(0.5, 0.866)
};
```

If we have no intention of altering the array later on, we can make it const:

```
const int fibonacci[] = { 0, 1, 1, 2, 3, 5, 8, 13, 21, 34 };
```

To find out how many items an array contains, we can use the `sizeof()` operator as follows:

```
int n = sizeof(fibonacci) / sizeof(fibonacci[0]);
```

The `sizeof()` operator returns the size of its argument in bytes. The number of items in an array is its size in bytes divided by the size of one of its items. Because this is cumbersome to type, a common alternative is to declare a constant and to use it for defining the array:

```
enum { NFibonacci = 10 };
```

```
const int fibonacci[NFibonacci] = { 0, 1, 1, 2, 3, 5, 8, 13, 21, 34 };
```

It would have been tempting to declare the constant as a `const int` variable. Unfortunately, some compilers have issues with const variables as array size specifiers. The `enum` keyword will be explained later in this appendix.

Iterating through an array is normally done using an integer. For example:

```
for (int i = 0; i < NFibonacci; ++i)
    cout << fibonacci[i] << endl;
```

It is also possible to traverse the array using a pointer:

```
const int *ptr = &fibonacci[0];
while (ptr != &fibonacci[10]) {
    cout << *ptr << endl;
    ++ptr;
}
```

We initialize the pointer with the address of the first item and loop until we reach the "one past the last" item (the "eleventh" item, `fibonacci[10]`). At each iteration, the `++` operator advances the pointer to the next item.

Instead of `&fibonacci[0]`, we could also have written `fibonacci`. This is because the name of an array used alone is automatically converted into a pointer to the first item in the array. Similarly, we could substitute `fibonacci + 10` for `&fibonacci[10]`. This works the other way around as well: We can retrieve the contents of the current item using either `*ptr` or `ptr[0]` and could access the next item using `*(ptr + 1)` or `ptr[1]`. This principle is sometimes called "equivalence of pointers and arrays".

To prevent what it considers to be a gratuitous inefficiency, C++ does not let us pass arrays to functions by value. Instead, they must be passed by address. For example:

```
#include <iostream>

using namespace std;

void printIntegerTable(const int *table, int size)
{
    for (int i = 0; i < size; ++i)
        cout << table[i] << endl;
}

int main()
{
    const int fibonacci[10] = { 0, 1, 1, 2, 3, 5, 8, 13, 21, 34 };
    printIntegerTable(fibonacci, 10);
    return 0;
}
```

Ironically, although C++ doesn't give us any choice about whether we want to pass an array by address or by value, it gives us some freedom in the *syntax* used to declare the parameter type. Instead of `const int *table`, we could also have written `const int table[]` to declare a pointer-to-constant-int parameter. Similarly, the `argv` parameter to `main()` can be declared as either `char *argv[]` or `char **argv`.

To copy an array into another array, one approach is to loop through the array:

```
const int fibonacci[NFibonacci] = { 0, 1, 1, 2, 3, 5, 8, 13, 21, 34 };
int temp[NFibonacci];

for (int i = 0; i < NFibonacci; ++i)
    temp[i] = fibonacci[i];
```

For basic data types such as `int`, we can also use `std::memcpy()`, which copies a block of memory. For example:

```
memcpy(temp, fibonacci, sizeof(fibonacci));
```

When we declare a C++ array, the size must be a constant.[*] If we want to create an array of a variable size, we have several options.

- **We can dynamically allocate the array:**

```
int *fibonacci = new int[n];
```

---

[*] Some compilers allow variables in that context, but this feature should not be relied upon in portable programs.

The new [] operator allocates a certain number of items at consecutive memory locations and returns a pointer to the first item. Thanks to the "equivalence of pointers and arrays" principle, the items can be accessed through the pointer as fibonacci[0], fibonacci[1], ..., fibonacci[n - 1]. When we have finished using the array, we should release the memory it consumes using the delete [] operator:

```
delete [] fibonacci;
```

- **We can use the standard std::vector<T> class:**

```
#include <vector>

using namespace std;

vector<int> fibonacci(n);
```

Items are accessible using the [] operator, just like with a plain C++ array. With std::vector<T> (where T is the type of the items stored in the vector), we can resize the array at any time using resize() and we can copy it using the assignment operator. Classes that contain angle brackets (<>) in their name are called template classes.

- **We can use Qt's QVector<T> class:**

```
#include <QVector>

QVector<int> fibonacci(n);
```

QVector<T>'s API is very similar to that of std::vector<T>, but it also supports iteration using Qt's foreach keyword and uses implicit data sharing ("copy on write") as a memory and speed optimization. Chapter 11 presents Qt's container classes and explains how they relate to the Standard C++ containers.

You might be tempted to avoid built-in arrays whenever possible and use std:: vector<T> or QVector<T> instead. It is nonetheless worthwhile understanding how the built-in arrays work because sooner or later you might want to use them in highly optimized code, or need them to interface with existing C libraries.

Character Strings

The most basic way of representing character strings in C++ is to use an array of chars terminated by a null byte ('\0'). The following four functions demonstrate how these kinds of strings work:

```
void hello1()
{
    const char str[] = {
        'H', 'e', 'l', 'l', 'o', ' ', 'w', 'o', 'r', 'l', 'd', '\0'
    };
    cout << str << endl;
```

```
}

void hello2()
{
    const char str[] = "Hello world!";
    cout << str << endl;
}

void hello3()
{
    cout << "Hello world!" << endl;
}

void hello4()
{
    const char *str = "Hello world!";
    cout << str << endl;
}
```

In the first function, we declare the string as an array and initialize it the hard way. Notice the '\0' terminator at the end, which indicates the end of the string. The second function has a similar array definition, but this time we use a string literal to initialize the array. In C++, string literals are simply const char arrays with an implicit '\0' terminator. The third function uses a string literal directly, without giving it a name. Once translated into machine language instructions, it is identical to the previous two functions.

The fourth function is a bit different in that it creates not only an (anonymous) array but also a pointer variable called str that stores the address of the array's first item. In spite of this, the semantics of the function are identical to the previous three functions, and an optimizing compiler would eliminate the superfluous str variable.

Functions that take C++ strings as arguments usually take either a char * or a const char *. Here's a short program that illustrates the use of both:

```
#include <cctype>
#include <iostream>

using namespace std;

void makeUppercase(char *str)
{
    for (int i = 0; str[i] != '\0'; ++i)
        str[i] = toupper(str[i]);
}

void writeLine(const char *str)
{
    cout << str << endl;
}

int main(int argc, char *argv[])
{
    for (int i = 1; i < argc; ++i) {
```

```
        makeUppercase(argv[i]);
        writeLine(argv[i]);
    }
    return 0;
}
```

In C++, the char type normally holds an 8-bit value. This means that we can easily store ASCII, ISO 8859-1 (Latin-1), and other 8-bit-encoded strings in a char array, but that we can't store arbitrary Unicode characters without resorting to multibyte sequences. Qt provides the powerful QString class, which stores Unicode strings as sequences of 16-bit QChars and internally uses the implicit data sharing ("copy on write") optimization. Chapter 11 (Container Classes) and Chapter 17 (Internationalization) explain QString in more detail.

Enumerations

C++ has an enumeration feature for declaring a set of named constants similar to that provided by C#. Let's suppose that we want to store days of the week in a program:

```
enum DayOfWeek {
    Sunday, Monday, Tuesday, Wednesday, Thursday, Friday, Saturday
};
```

Normally, we would put this declaration in a header file, or even inside a class. The above declaration is superficially equivalent to the following constant definitions:

```
const int Sunday    = 0;
const int Monday    = 1;
const int Tuesday   = 2;
const int Wednesday = 3;
const int Thursday  = 4;
const int Friday    = 5;
const int Saturday  = 6;
```

By using the enumeration construct, we can later declare variables or parameters of type DayOfWeek and the compiler will ensure that only values from the DayOfWeek enumeration are assigned to it. For example:

```
DayOfWeek day = Sunday;
```

If we don't care about type safety, we can also write

```
int day = Sunday;
```

Notice that to refer to the Sunday constant from the DayOfWeek enum, we simply write Sunday, not DayOfWeek::Sunday.

By default, the compiler assigns consecutive integer values to the constants of an enum, starting at 0. We can specify other values if we want:

```
enum DayOfWeek {
    Sunday    = 628,
```

```
    Monday    = 616,
    Tuesday   = 735,
    Wednesday = 932,
    Thursday  = 852,
    Friday    = 607,
    Saturday  = 845
};
```

If we don't specify the value of an enum item, the item takes the value of the previous item, plus 1. Enums are sometimes used to declare integer constants, in which case we normally omit the name of the enum:

```
enum {
    FirstPort = 1024,
    MaxPorts  = 32767
};
```

Another frequent use of enums is to represent sets of options. Let's consider the example of a Find dialog, with four checkboxes controlling the search algorithm (Wildcard syntax, Case sensitive, Search backward, and Wrap around). We can represent this by an enum where the constants are powers of 2:

```
enum FindOption {
    NoOptions      = 0x00000000,
    WildcardSyntax = 0x00000001,
    CaseSensitive  = 0x00000002,
    SearchBackward = 0x00000004,
    WrapAround     = 0x00000008
};
```

Each option is often called a "flag". We can combine flags using the bitwise | or |= operators:

```
int options = NoOptions;
if (wilcardSyntaxCheckBox->isChecked())
    options |= WildcardSyntax;
if (caseSensitiveCheckBox->isChecked())
    options |= CaseSensitive;
if (searchBackwardCheckBox->isChecked())
    options |= SearchBackwardSyntax;
if (wrapAroundCheckBox->isChecked())
    options |= WrapAround;
```

We can test whether a flag is set or not using the bitwise & operator:

```
if (options & CaseSensitive) {
    // case-sensitive search
}
```

A variable of type FindOption can only contain one flag at a time. The result of combining several flags using | is a plain integer. Unfortunately, this is not type-safe: The compiler won't complain if a function expecting a combination of FindOptions through an int parameter receives Saturday instead. Qt uses QFlags<T> to provide type safety for its own flag types. The class is also available when we define custom flag types. See the QFlags<T> online documentation for details.

Typedefs

C++ lets us give an alias to a data type using the typedef keyword. For example, if we use QVector<Point2D> a lot and want to save a few keystrokes (or are unfortunate enough to be stuck with a Norwegian keyboard and have trouble locating the angle brackets), we can put this typedef declaration in one of our header files:

```
typedef QVector<Point2D> PointVector;
```

From then on, we can use PointVector as a shorthand for QVector<Point2D>. Notice that the new name for the type appears after the old name. The typedef syntax deliberately mimics that of variable declarations.

In Qt, typedefs are used mainly for three reasons:

- *Convenience*: Qt declares uint and QWidgetList as typedefs for unsigned int and QList<QWidget *> to save a few keystrokes.

- *Platform differences*: Certain types need different definitions on different platforms. For example, qlonglong is defined as __int64 on Windows and as long long on other platforms.

- *Compatibility*: The QIconSet class from Qt 3 was renamed QIcon in Qt 4. To help Qt 3 users port their applications to Qt 4, QIconSet is provided as a typedef for QIcon when Qt 3 compatibility is enabled.

Type Conversions

C++ provides several syntaxes for casting values from one type to another. The traditional syntax, inherited from C, involves putting the resulting type in parentheses before the value to convert:

```
const double Pi = 3.14159265359;
int x = (int)(Pi * 100);
cout << x << " equals 314" << endl;
```

This syntax is very powerful. It can be used to change the type of pointers, to remove const, and much more. For example:

```
short j = 0x1234;
if (*(char *)&j == 0x12)
    cout << "The byte order is big-endian" << endl;
```

In the example above, we cast a short * to a char * and we use the unary * operator to access the byte at the given memory location. On big-endian systems, that byte is 0x12; on little-endian systems, that byte is 0x34. Since pointers and references are represented the same way, it should come as no surprise that the code above can be rewritten using a reference cast:

```
short j = 0x1234;
if ((char &)j == 0x12)
    cout << "The byte order is big-endian" << endl;
```

If the data type is a class name, a typedef, or a primitive type that can be expressed as a single alphanumeric token, we can use the constructor syntax as a cast:

```
int x = int(Pi * 100);
```

Casting pointers and references using the traditional C-style casts is a kind of extreme sport, on par with paragliding and elevator surfing, because the compiler lets us cast any pointer (or reference) type into any other pointer (or reference) type. For that reason, C++ introduced four new-style casts with more precise semantics. For pointers and references, the new-style casts are preferable to the risky C-style casts and are used in this book.

- `static_cast<T>()` can be used to cast a pointer-to-A to a pointer-to-B, with the constraint that class B must inherit from class A. For example:

  ```
  A *obj = new B;
  B *b = static_cast<B *>(obj);
  b->someFunctionDeclaredInB();
  ```

  If the object isn't an instance of B (but still inherits from A), using the resulting pointer can lead to obscure crashes.

- `dynamic_cast<T>()` is similar to `static_cast<T>()`, except that it uses runtime type information (RTTI) to check that the object associated with the pointer is an instance of class B. If this is not the case, the cast returns a null pointer. For example:

  ```
  A *obj = new B;
  B *b = dynamic_cast<B *>(obj);
  if (b)
      b->someFunctionDeclaredInB();
  ```

  On some compilers, `dynamic_cast<T>()` doesn't work across dynamic library boundaries. It also relies on the compiler supporting RTTI, a feature that programmers can turn off to reduce the size of their executables. Qt solves these problems by providing `qobject_cast<T>()` for QObject subclasses.

- `const_cast<T>()` adds or removes a const qualifier to a pointer or reference. For example:

  ```
  int MyClass::someConstFunction() const
  {
      if (isDirty()) {
          MyClass *that = const_cast<MyClass *>(this);
          that->recomputeInternalData();
      }
      ...
  }
  ```

In the previous example, we cast away the const qualifier of the this pointer to call the non-const member function recomputeInternalData(). Doing so is not recommended and can normally be avoided by using the mutable keyword, as explained in Chapter 4 (Implementing Application Functionality).

- reinterpret_cast<T>() converts any pointer or reference type to any other such type. For example:

```
short j = 0x1234;
if (reinterpret_cast<char &>(j) == 0x12)
    cout << "The byte order is big-endian" << endl;
```

In Java and C#, any reference can be stored as an Object reference if needed. C++ doesn't have any universal base class, but it provides a special data type, void *, that stores the address of an instance of any type. A void * must be cast back to another type (using static_cast<T>()) before it can be used.

C++ provides many ways of casting types, but most of the time we don't even need a cast. When using container classes such as std::vector<T> or QVector<T>, we can specify the T type and extract items without casts. In addition, for primitive types, certain conversions occur implicitly (for example, from char to int), and for custom types we can define implicit conversions by providing a one-parameter constructor. For example:

```
class MyInteger
{
public:
    MyInteger();
    MyInteger(int i);
    ...
};

int main()
{
    MyInteger n;
    n = 5;
    ...
}
```

For some one-parameter constructors, the automatic conversion makes little sense. We can disable it by declaring the constructor with the explicit keyword:

```
class MyVector
{
public:
    explicit MyVector(int size);
    ...
};
```

Operator Overloading

C++ allows us to overload functions, meaning that we can declare several functions with the same name in the same scope, as long as they have different parameter lists. In addition, C++ supports *operator overloading*—the possibility of assigning special semantics to built-in operators (such as +, <<, and []) when they are used with custom types.

We have already seen a few examples of overloaded operators. When we used << to output text to cout or cerr, we didn't trigger C++'s left-shift operator, but rather a special version of the operator that takes an ostream object (such as cout and cerr) on the left and a string (alternatively, a number or a stream manipulator such as endl) on the right side and that returns the ostream object, allowing multiple calls in a row.

The beauty of operator overloading is that we can make custom types behave just like built-in types. To show how operator overloading works, we will overload +=, -=, +, and - to work on Point2D objects:

```cpp
#ifndef POINT2D_H
#define POINT2D_H

class Point2D
{
public:
    Point2D();
    Point2D(double x, double y);

    void setX(double x);
    void setY(double y);
    double x() const;
    double y() const;

    Point2D &operator+=(const Point2D &other) {
        xVal += other.xVal;
        yVal += other.yVal;
        return *this;
    }
    Point2D &operator-=(const Point2D &other) {
        xVal -= other.xVal;
        yVal -= other.yVal;
        return *this;
    }

private:
    double xVal;
    double yVal;
};

inline Point2D operator+(const Point2D &a, const Point2D &b)
{
    return Point2D(a.x() + b.x(), a.y() + b.y());
}
```

```
inline Point2D operator-(const Point2D &a, const Point2D &b)
{
    return Point2D(a.x() - b.x(), a.y() - b.y());
}
```

```
#endif
```

Operators can be implemented either as member functions or as global functions. In our example, we implemented += and -= as member functions, + and – as global functions.

The += and -= operators take a reference to another Point2D object and increment or decrement the x and y coordinates of the current object based on the other object. They return *this, which denotes a reference to the current object (this is of type Point2D *). Returning a reference allows us to write exotic code like

```
a += b += c;
```

The + and – operators take two parameters and return a Point2D object by value (not a reference to an existing object). The inline keyword allows us to put these function definitions in the header file. If the function's body had been longer, we would put a function prototype in the header file and the function definition (without the inline keyword) in a .cpp file.

The following code snippets shows all four overloaded operators in action:

```
Point2D alpha(12.5, 40.0);
Point2D beta(77.5, 50.0);

alpha += beta;
beta -= alpha;

Point2D gamma = alpha + beta;
Point2D delta = beta - alpha;
```

We can also invoke the operator functions just like any other functions:

```
Point2D alpha(12.5, 40.0);
Point2D beta(77.5, 50.0);

alpha.operator+=(beta);
beta.operator-=(alpha);

Point2D gamma = operator+(alpha, beta);
Point2D delta = operator-(beta, alpha);
```

Operator overloading in C++ is a complex topic, but we can go a long way without knowing all the details. It is still important to understand the fundamentals of operator overloading because several Qt classes (including QString and QVector<T>) use this feature to provide a simple and more natural syntax for such operations as concatenation and append.

Value Types

Java and C# distinguish between value types and reference types.

- *Value types*: These are primitive types such as `char`, `int`, and `float`, as well as C# structs. What characterizes them is that they aren't created using `new` and the assignment operator performs a copy of the value held by the variable. For example:

  ```
  int i = 5;
  int j = 10;
  i = j;
  ```

- *Reference types*: These are classes such as `Integer` (in Java), `String`, and `MyVeryOwnClass`. Instances are created using `new`. The assignment operator copies only a reference to the object; to obtain a deep copy, we must call `clone()` (in Java) or `Clone()` (in C#). For example:

  ```
  Integer i = new Integer(5);
  Integer j = new Integer(10);
  i = j.clone();
  ```

In C++, all types can be used as "reference types", and those that are copyable can be used as "value types" as well. For example, C++ doesn't need any `Integer` class, because we can use pointers and `new` as follows:

```
int *i = new int(5);
int *j = new int(10);
*i = *j;
```

Unlike Java and C#, C++ treats user-defined classes the same as built-in types:

```
Point2D *i = new Point2D(5, 5);
Point2D *j = new Point2D(10, 10);
*i = *j;
```

If we want to make a C++ class copyable, we must ensure that our class has a copy constructor and an assignment operator. The copy constructor is invoked when we initialize an object with another object of the same type. C++ provides two equivalent syntaxes for this:

```
Point2D i(20, 20);

Point2D j(i);          // first syntax
Point2D k = i;         // second syntax
```

The assignment operator is invoked when we use the assignment operator on an existing variable:

```
Point2D i(5, 5);
Point2D j(10, 10);
j = i;
```

When we define a class, the C++ compiler automatically provides a copy constructor and an assignment operator that perform member-by-member copy. For the Point2D class, this is as if we had written the following code in the class definition:

```
class Point2D
{
public:
    ...
    Point2D(const Point2D &other)
        : xVal(other.xVal), yVal(other.yVal) { }

    Point2D &operator=(const Point2D &other) {
        xVal = other.xVal;
        yVal = other.yVal;
        return *this;
    }
    ...

private:
    double xVal;
    double yVal;
};
```

For some classes, the default copy constructor and assignment operator are unsuitable. This typically occurs if the class uses dynamic memory. To make the class copyable, we must then implement the copy constructor and the assignment operator ourselves.

For classes that don't need to be copyable, we can disable the copy constructor and assignment operator by making them private. If we accidentally attempt to copy instances of such a class, the compiler reports an error. For example:

```
class BankAccount
{
public:
    ...

private:
    BankAccount(const BankAccount &other);
    BankAccount &operator=(const BankAccount &other);
};
```

In Qt, many classes are designed to be used as value classes. These have a copy constructor and an assignment operator, and are normally instantiated on the stack without new. This is the case for QDateTime, QImage, QString, and container classes such as QList<T>, QVector<T>, and QMap<K, T>.

Other classes fall in the "reference type" category, notably QObject and its subclasses (QWidget, QTimer, QTcpSocket, etc.). These have virtual functions and cannot be copied. For example, a QWidget represents a specific window or control on screen. If there are 75 QWidget instances in memory, there are also 75 windows or controls on screen. These classes are typically instantiated using the new operator.

Global Variables and Functions

C++ lets us declare functions and variables that don't belong to any classes and that are accessible from any other function. We have seen several examples of global functions, including `main()`, the program's entry point. Global variables are rarer, because they compromise modularity and thread reentrancy. It is still important to understand them because you might encounter them in code written by reformed C programmers and other C++ users.

To illustrate how global functions and variables work, we will study a small program that prints a list of 128 pseudo-random numbers using a quick-and-dirty algorithm. The program's source code is spread over two `.cpp` files.

The first source file is `random.cpp`:

```cpp
int randomNumbers[128];

static int seed = 42;

static int nextRandomNumber()
{
    seed = 1009 + (seed * 2011);
    return seed;
}

void populateRandomArray()
{
    for (int i = 0; i < 128; ++i)
        randomNumbers[i] = nextRandomNumber();
}
```

The file declares two global variables (`randomNumbers` and `seed`) and two global functions (`nextRandomNumber()` and `populateRandomArray()`). Two of the declarations contain the `static` keyword; these are visible only within the current compilation unit (`random.cpp`) and are said to have *static linkage*. The two others can be accessed from any compilation unit in the program; these have *external linkage*.

Static linkage is ideal for helper functions and internal variables that should not be used in other compilation units. It reduces the risks of having colliding identifiers (global variables with the same name or global functions with the same signature in different compilation units) and prevents malicious or otherwise ill-advised users from accessing the internals of a compilation unit.

Let's now look at the second file, `main.cpp`, which uses the two global variables declared with external linkage in `random.cpp`:

```cpp
#include <iostream>

using namespace std;

extern int randomNumbers[128];

void populateRandomArray();
```

```
int main()
{
    populateRandomArray();
    for (int i = 0; i < 128; ++i)
        cout << randomNumbers[i] << endl;
    return 0;
}
```

We declare the external variables and functions before we call them. The external variable declaration (which makes an external variable visible in the current compilation unit) for randomNumbers starts with the extern keyword. Without extern, the compiler would think it has to deal with a variable *definition*, and the linker would complain because the same variable is defined in two compilation units (random.cpp and main.cpp). Variables can be declared as many times as we want, but they may only be defined once. The definition is what causes the compiler to reserve space for the variable.

The populateRandomArray() function is declared using a function prototype. The extern keyword is optional for functions.

Typically we would put the external variable and function declarations in a header file and include it in all the files that need them:

```
#ifndef RANDOM_H
#define RANDOM_H

extern int randomNumbers[128];

void populateRandomArray();

#endif
```

We have already seen how static can be used to declare member variables and functions that are not attached to a specific instance of the class, and now we have seen how to use it to declare functions and variables with static linkage. There is one more use of the static keyword that should be noted in passing. In C++, we can declare a local variable static. Such variables are initialized the first time the function is called and hold their value between function invocations. For example:

```
void nextPrime()
{
    static int n = 1;

    do {
        ++n;
    } while (!isPrime(n));

    return n;
}
```

Static local variables are similar to global variables, except that they are only visible inside the function where they are defined.

Namespaces

Namespaces are a mechanism for reducing the risks of name clashes in C++ programs. Name clashes are often an issue in large programs that use several third-party libraries. In your own programs, you can choose whether you want to use namespaces or not.

Typically, we put a namespace around all the declarations in a header file to ensure that the identifiers declared in that header file don't leak into the global namespace. For example:

```
#ifndef SOFTWAREINC_RANDOM_H
#define SOFTWAREINC_RANDOM_H

namespace SoftwareInc
{
    extern int randomNumbers[128];

    void populateRandomArray();
}

#endif
```

(Notice that we have also renamed the preprocessor macro used to avoid multiple inclusions, reducing the risk of a name clash with a header file of the same name but located in a different directory.)

The namespace syntax is similar to that of a class, but it doesn't end with a semicolon. Here's the new random.cpp file:

```
#include "random.h"

int SoftwareInc::randomNumbers[128];

static int seed = 42;

static int nextRandomNumber()
{
    seed = 1009 + (seed * 2011);
    return seed;
}
void SoftwareInc::populateRandomArray()
{
    for (int i = 0; i < 128; ++i)
        randomNumbers[i] = nextRandomNumber();
}
```

Unlike classes, namespaces can be "reopened" at any time. For example:

```
namespace Alpha
{
    void alpha1();
    void alpha2();
}
```

```
namespace Beta
{
    void beta1();
}

namespace Alpha
{
    void alpha3();
}
```

This makes it possible to define hundreds of classes, located in as many header files, as part of a single namespace. Using this trick, the Standard C++ library puts all its identifiers in the `std` namespace. In Qt, namespaces are used for global-like identifiers such as `Qt::AlignBottom` and `Qt::yellow`. For historical reasons, Qt classes do not belong to any namespace but are prefixed with the letter 'Q'.

To refer to an identifier declared in a namespace from outside the namespace, we prefix it with the name of the namespace (and `::`). Alternatively, we can use one of the following three mechanisms, which are aimed at reducing the number of keystrokes we must type.

- **We can define a namespace alias:**

```
namespace ElPuebloDeLaReinaDeLosAngeles
{
    void beverlyHills();
    void culverCity();
    void malibu();
    void santaMonica();
}

namespace LA = ElPuebloDeLaReinaDeLosAngeles;
```

After the alias definition, the alias can be used instead of the original name.

- **We can import a single identifier from a namespace:**

```
int main()
{
    using ElPuebloDeLaReinaDeLosAngeles::beverlyHills;

    beverlyHills();
    ...
}
```

The `using` declaration allows us to access a given identifier from a namespace without having to prefix it with the name of the namespace.

- **We can import an entire namespace with a single directive:**

```
int main()
{
    using namespace ElPuebloDeLaReinaDeLosAngeles;
```

```
        santaMonica();
        malibu();
        ...
    }
```

With this approach, name clashes are more likely to occur. If the compiler complains about an ambiguous name (for example, two classes with the same name defined in two different namespaces), we can always qualify the identifier with the name of the namespace when referring to it.

The Preprocessor

The C++ preprocessor is a program that converts a .cpp source file containing #-directives (such as #include, #ifndef, and #endif) into a source file that contains no such directives. These directives perform simple textual operations on the source file, such as conditional compilation, file inclusion, and macro expansion. Normally, the preprocessor is invoked automatically by the compiler, but most systems still offer a way of invoking it alone (often through a -E or /E compiler option).

- The #include directive expands to the contents of the file specified within angle brackets (<>) or double quotes (""), depending on whether the header file is installed at a standard location or is part of the current project. The file name may contain .. and / (which Windows compilers correctly interpret as a directory separator). For example:

```
    #include "../shared/globaldefs.h"
```

- The #define directive defines a macro. Occurrences of the macro appearing after the #define directive are replaced with the macro's definition. For example, the directive

```
    #define PI 3.14159265359
```

tells the preprocessor to replace all future occurrences of the token PI in the current compilation unit with the token 3.14159265359. To avoid clashes with variable and class names, it is common practice to give macros all-uppercase names. It is possible to define macros that take arguments:

```
    #define SQUARE(x) ((x) * (x))
```

In the macro body, it is good style to surround all occurrences of the parameters with parentheses, as well as the entire body, to avoid problems with operator precedence. After all, we want 7 * SQUARE(2 + 3) to expand to 7 * ((2 + 3) * (2 + 3)), not to 7 * 2 + 3 * 2 + 3.

C++ compilers normally allow us to define macros on the command line, using the -D or /D option. For example:

```
    CC -DPI=3.14159265359 -c main.cpp
```

Macros were very popular in the old days, before typedefs, enums, constants, inline functions, and templates were introduced. Nowadays, their most important role is to protect header files against multiple inclusions.

- Macros can be undefined at any point using #undef:

    ```
    #undef PI
    ```

    This is useful if we want to redefine a macro, since the preprocessor doesn't let us define the same macro twice. It is also useful to control conditional compilation.

- Portions of code can be processed or skipped using #if, #elif, #else, and #endif, based on the numeric value of macros. For example:

    ```
    #define NO_OPTIM          0
    #define OPTIM_FOR_SPEED   1
    #define OPTIM_FOR_MEMORY  2

    #define OPTIMIZATION       OPTIM_FOR_MEMORY

    ...

    #if OPTIMIZATION == OPTIM_FOR_SPEED
    typedef int MyInt;
    #elif OPTIMIZATION == OPTIM_FOR_MEMORY
    typedef short MyInt;
    #else
    typedef long long MyInt;
    #endif
    ```

In the example above, only the second typedef declaration would be processed by the compiler, resulting in MyInt being defined as a synonym for short. By changing the definition of the OPTIMIZATION macro, we get different programs. If a macro isn't defined, its value is taken to be 0.

Another approach to conditional compilation is to test whether a macro is defined or not. This can be done using the using the defined() operator as follows:

```
#define OPTIM_FOR_MEMORY

...

#if defined(OPTIM_FOR_SPEED)
typedef int MyInt;
#elif defined(OPTIM_FOR_MEMORY)
typedef short MyInt;
#else
typedef long long MyInt;
#endif
```

- For convenience, the preprocessor recognizes #ifdef X and #ifndef X as synonyms for #if defined(X) and #if !defined(X). To protect a header file against multiple inclusions, we wrap its contents with the following idiom:

```
#ifndef MYHEADERFILE_H
#define MYHEADERFILE_H

...

#endif
```

The first time the header file is included, the symbol MYHEADERFILE_H is not defined, so the compiler processes the code between #ifndef and #endif. The second and any subsequent times the header file is included, MYHEADERFILE_H is defined, so the entire #ifndef ... #endif block is skipped.

- The #error directive emits a user-defined error message at compile time. This is often used in conjunction with conditional compilation to report an impossible case. For example:

```
class UniChar
{
public:
#if BYTE_ORDER == BIG_ENDIAN
    uchar row;
    uchar cell;
#elif BYTE_ORDER == LITTLE_ENDIAN
    uchar cell;
    uchar row;
#else
#error "BYTE_ORDER must be BIG_ENDIAN or LITTLE_ENDIAN"
#endif
};
```

Unlike most other C++ constructs, where whitespace is irrelevant, preprocessor directives stand alone on a line and require no semicolon. Very long directives can be split across multiple lines by ending every line except the last with a backslash.

The Standard C++ Library

In this section, we will briefly review the Standard C++ library. Figure B.3 lists the core C++ header files. The <exception>, <limits>, <new>, and <typeinfo> headers support the C++ language; for example, <limits> allows us to test properties of the compiler's integer and floating-point arithmetic support, and <typeinfo> offers basic introspection. The other headers provide generally useful classes, including a string class and a complex numeric type. The functionality offered by <bitset>, <locale>, <string>, and <typeinfo> loosely overlaps with the QBitArray, QLocale, QString, and QMetaObject classes in Qt.

Standard C++ also includes a set of header files that deal with I/O, listed in Figure B.4. The standard I/O classes' design harks back to the 1980s and is needlessly complex, making them very hard to extend—so difficult, in fact, that entire books have been written on the subject. It also leaves the programmer with a Pandora's box of unresolved issues related to character encodings and platform-dependent binary representations of primitive data types.

Header file	Description
`<bitset>`	Template class for representing fixed-length bit sequences
`<complex>`	Template class for representing complex numbers
`<exception>`	Types and functions related to exception handling
`<limits>`	Template class that specifies properties of numeric types
`<locale>`	Classes and functions related to localization
`<new>`	Functions that manage dynamic memory allocation
`<stdexcept>`	Predefined types of exceptions for reporting errors
`<string>`	Template string container and character traits
`<typeinfo>`	Class that provides basic meta-information about a type
`<valarray>`	Template classes for representing value arrays

Figure B.3. Core C++ library header files

Chapter 12 (Input/Output) presents the corresponding Qt classes, which feature Unicode I/O as well as a large set of national character encodings and a platform-independent abstraction for storing binary data. Qt's I/O classes form the basis of Qt's inter-process communication, networking, and XML support. Qt's binary and text stream classes are very easy to extend to handle custom data types.

Header file	Description
`<fstream>`	Template classes that manipulate external files
`<iomanip>`	I/O stream manipulators that take an argument
`<ios>`	Template base class for I/O streams
`<iosfwd>`	Forward declarations for several I/O stream template classes
`<iostream>`	Standard I/O streams (`cin`, `cout`, `cerr`, `clog`)
`<istream>`	Template class that controls input from a stream buffer
`<ostream>`	Template class that controls output to a stream buffer
`<sstream>`	Template classes that associate stream buffers with strings
`<streambuf>`	Template classes that buffer I/O operations
`<strstream>`	Classes for performing I/O stream operations on character arrays

Figure B.4. C++ I/O library header files

The early 1990s saw the introduction of the Standard Template Library (STL), a set of template-based container classes, iterators, and algorithms that slipped into the ISO C++ standard at the eleventh hour. Figure B.5 lists the header files that form the STL. The STL has a very clean, almost mathematical design that provides generic type-safe functionality. Qt provides its own container classes, whose design is partly inspired by STL. These are described in Chapter 11.

Header file	Description
`<algorithm>`	General-purpose template functions
`<deque>`	Double-ended queue template container
`<functional>`	Templates that help construct and manipulate functors
`<iterator>`	Templates that help construct and manipulate iterators
`<list>`	Doubly-linked list template container
`<map>`	Single-valued and multi-valued map template containers
`<memory>`	Utilities for simplifying memory management
`<numeric>`	Template numeric operations
`<queue>`	Queue template container
`<set>`	Single-valued and multi-valued set template containers
`<stack>`	Stack template container
`<utility>`	Basic template functions
`<vector>`	Vector template container

Figure B.5. STL header files

Since C++ is essentially a superset of the C programming language, C++ programmers also have the entire C library at their disposal. The C header files are available either with their traditional names (for example, `<stdio.h>`) or with new-style names with a `c-` prefix and no `.h` (for example, `<cstdio>`). When we use the new-style version, the functions and data types are declared in the `std` namespace. (This doesn't apply to macros such as `ASSERT()`, because the preprocessor is unaware of namespaces.) The new-style syntax is recommended if your compiler supports it.

Figure B.6 lists the C library header files. Most of these offer functionality that overlaps with more recent C++ headers or with Qt. One notable exception is `<cmath>`, which declares mathematical functions such as `sin()`, `sqrt()`, and `pow()`.

This completes our quick overview of the Standard C++ library. On the Internet, Dinkumware offers complete reference documentation for the Standard C++ library at `http://www.dinkumware.com/refxcpp.html`, and SGI has a comprehensive STL programmer's guide at `http://www.sgi.com/tech/stl/`. The official definition of the Standard C++ library is found in the C and C++ standards, available as PDF files or paper copies from the International Organization for Standardization (ISO).

Header file	Description
<cassert>	The ASSERT() macro
<cctype>	Functions for classifying and mapping characters
<cerrno>	Macros related to error condition reporting
<cfloat>	Macros that specify properties of primitive floating-point types
<ciso646>	Alternative spellings for ISO 646 charset users
<climits>	Macros that specify properties of primitive integer types
<clocale>	Functions and types related to localization
<cmath>	Mathematical functions and constants
<csetjmp>	Functions for performing non-local jumps
<csignal>	Functions for handling system signals
<cstdarg>	Macros for implementing variable argument list functions
<cstddef>	Common definitions for several standard headers
<cstdio>	Functions for performing I/O
<cstdlib>	General utility functions
<cstring>	Functions for manipulating char arrays
<ctime>	Types and functions for manipulating time
<cwchar>	Extended multibyte and wide character utilities
<cwctype>	Functions for classifying and mapping wide characters

Figure B.6. C++ header files for C library facilities

In this appendix, we have covered a lot of ground at a fast pace. When you start learning Qt from Chapter 1, you should find that the syntax is a lot simpler and clearer than this appendix might have suggested. Good Qt programming only requires the use of a subset of C++ and usually avoids the need for the more complex and obscure syntax that C++ makes possible. Once you start typing in code and building and running executables, the clarity and simplicity of the Qt approach will become apparent. And as soon as you start writing more ambitious programs, especially those that need fast and fancy graphics, the C++/Qt combination will continue to keep pace with your needs.

Index

B

S

About the Authors

Jasmin Blanchette

Jasmin graduated in computer science in 2001 from the University of Sherbrooke, Quebec. He did a work term at Trolltech in the summer of 2000 as a software engineer and has been working there continuously since early 2001. In 2003, Jasmin co-wrote *C++ GUI Programming with Qt 3*. He now combines the roles of Trolltech's documentation manager and senior software engineer. He was the driving force behind the *Qt Linguist* translation tool and is still a key player in Qt 4's container classes. He is also co-editor of *Qt Quarterly*, Trolltech's technical newsletter.

Mark Summerfield

Mark graduated in computer science in 1993 from the University of Wales Swansea. He followed this with a year's postgraduate research before going into industry. He spent many years working as a software engineer for a variety of firms before joining Trolltech. He spent almost three years as Trolltech's documentation manager, during which he founded *Qt Quarterly* and co-wrote *C++ GUI Programming with Qt 3*. Mark owns Qtraining.eu and works as an independent trainer and consultant specializing in C++, Qt, and Python.

Production

The authors wrote the text using NEdit and Vim. They typeset and indexed the text themselves, marking it up with a modified Lout syntax that they converted to pure Lout using a custom preprocessor written in Python. They produced all the diagrams in Lout and used ImageMagick and KView to convert screenshots to PostScript. The monospaced font used for code is derived from an early version of Crystal and was modified using FontForge. The cover was provided by the publisher. The marked-up text was converted to PostScript by Lout, then to PDF by Ghostscript. The authors did all the editing and processing on Debian GNU/Linux and Fedora Core systems under KDE. The example programs were tested on Windows, Linux, and Mac OS X.

THIS BOOK IS SAFARI ENABLED

INCLUDES FREE 45-DAY ACCESS TO THE ONLINE EDITION

The Safari® Enabled icon on the cover of your favorite technology book means the book is available through Safari Bookshelf. When you buy this book, you get free access to the online edition for 45 days.

Safari Bookshelf is an electronic reference library that lets you easily search thousands of technical books, find code samples, download chapters, and access technical information whenever and wherever you need it.

TO GAIN 45-DAY SAFARI ENABLED ACCESS TO THIS BOOK:

● Go to **http://www.prenhallprofessional.com/safarienabled**

● Complete the brief registration form

● Enter the coupon code found in the front of this book on the "Copyright" page

If you have difficulty registering on Safari Bookshelf or accessing the online edition, please e-mail customer-service@safaribooksonline.com.

PRENTICE
HALL

Also of Interest from Prentice Hall

ISBN: 0-13-187905-7

An Introduction to Design Patterns in C++ *with Qt 4*

Alan Ezust and Paul Ezust

If you enjoyed *C++ GUI Programming with Qt 4*, you'll also want to read *An Introduction to Design Patterns in C++ with Qt 4*.

With the help of this tutorial, you can master C++ and design patterns using the world's number one open source framework for cross-platform development: Qt 4. By the time you're done, you'll be creating multithreaded GUI applications that access databases and manipulate XML files— applications that run on platforms including Windows, Linux, UNIX, and Mac OS X. Best of all, you'll be writing code that's efficient, reusable, and elegant.

- Learn objects fast: classes, inheritance, polymorphism, and more
- Master powerful design patterns, from Iterator and Visitor to Abstract Factory and Facade
- Discover efficient high-level programming techniques utilizing libraries, generics, and containers
- Build graphical applications using Qt widgets, models, and views
- Learn advanced techniques ranging from multithreading to reflective programming
- Use Qt's built-in classes for accessing MySQL data
- Includes a complete C++ language reference

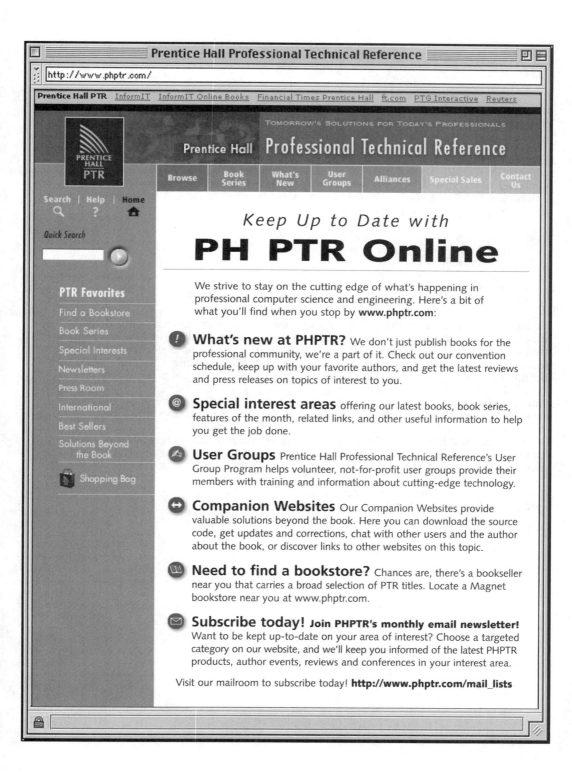